Hollywood's Road to Riches

Hollywood's Road to Riches

David Waterman

HARVARD UNIVERSITY PRESS
Cambridge, Massachusetts
London, England
2005

Library of Congress Cataloging-in-Publication Data

Waterman, David, 1947–
    Hollywood's road to riches / David Waterman.
      p. cm.
    Includes bibliographical references and index.
    ISBN 0-674-01945-8 (alk. paper)
    1. Motion picture industry—United States. 2. Motion pictures—
Economic aspects—United States. 1. Title.

PN1993.5.U6W39 2005
384'.83'0973—dc22   2005046300

To Sharon, Chloe, Jason, and Matthew

Contents

Figures and Tables

Tables

Preface

"Hollywood," America's movie business, is an industry that seems to succeed in spite of itself. Studios are routinely taken to task for disastrous box office performances of films that never should have been made. Costs go out of control, pushed upward by what seem outrageous demands of major stars. Stars and directors whose last efforts have flopped are hired yet again, while talented individuals without personal connections to industry insiders languish on the sidelines. Studio executives are said to favor the safety of sequels at the expense of innovation, while many critics contend that Hollywood's movies are getting worse.

The theatrical film business is nevertheless among America's most thriving industries. Hollywood's revenues, and thus its production resources, have grown spectacularly in the past thirty years. During this period, U.S.-produced movies have overwhelmed international competition and, by the 1990s, achieved a level of world dominance matched by few, if any, American products.

My purpose in this book is to explain Hollywood's economic success.

In doing so, I look back to the middle of the twentieth century to show how a rather predictable industry with little other than movie theaters to market its wares has been transformed into a volatile and complex multimedia enterprise.

My intended readership for this book is broad. The economic principles employed often have arcane academic origins, but I hope I have succeeded in making them reader friendly, through the use of simple numerical models or examples, or just words. Where the reader may find the going too slow, my advice is just to continue reading; the general idea will likely emerge.

There are quite a lot of statistics in this book—necessary to make the work a useful empirical study. The quality of economic data on the U.S. movie industry has for many years had a well-deserved poor reputation. At least since the 1980s, the availability and value of both industry-level and individual movie data have greatly improved. But in extending the economic analysis back to the late 1940s, constructing or selecting usable data has required considerable effort. Especially when examining the industry in the pre-1980s years, we are often limited to the identification of general trends or turning points.

In the text to follow, the collective "we" is used, to reflect the fact that this book is the result of a collaborative effort involving a number of research assistants. Their contributions have gone well beyond the mundane aspects of collecting and manipulating data. I owe a great debt to Sunitha Chitrapu, Jae Eun Chung, Aimee Hall, Matt Jackson, Krishna P. Jayakar, Jun-Seok Kang, Jeeyoun Lee, Sang-Woo Lee, Sung-Choon Lee, Weiting Lu, Xiaofei Wang, Michael Zhaoxu Yan, Susan Yang, and Jianqiang Tony Ye. In addition to other valuable contributions they made to the work, Sang-Woo Lee, Sung-Choon Lee, and Weiting Lu are coauthors of several of the statistical appendices.

This book could not have been written without the generous support of Indiana University's Department of Telecommunications, made possible by chairpersons Walter Gantz and Mike McGregor, and of the College of Arts and Sciences. The librarians at IU's Journalism Library have been a tremendous help; Linda Butler and Frances Wilhoit provided unfailing assistance in the best tradition of their profession. I am grateful as well to the Margaret Herrick Library of the Motion Picture Academy of Arts and Sciences and to the University of Southern California libraries.

I am indebted to several organizations that provided free or steeply discounted data to support this research: Nielsen EDI, the European Audiovisual Observatory (special thanks to André Lange), Kagan Research, Nielsen Media Research, Screen Digest, Home Media Retailing (special thanks to Judith McCourt), and ZenithOptimedia.

Many other people helped me understand the industry and how it works, often providing generous amounts of their time. I set out the following list with the caveat that they bear no responsibility for the results: Tom Aust, Ron Berger, Roger Burlage, Lavinia Carey, Robert Chapek, David Davis, Trevor Drinkwater, Lars Dwe, Robert Franklin, David Garber, Peter Guber, Keith Kleinberg, Craig Kornblau, William Krepick, Carol Lombardini, John Matulis, Bill Mechanic, Tom Paine, Catherine Paura, Bob Rehme, Steve Roberts, Leonard Shapiro, William Shields, Craig Smith, and John Wilkinson.

Many of my academic colleagues have commented on or otherwise contributed to the research undertaken for this book. I especially thank two anonymous reviewers of the manuscript, as well as Thom Gillespie, Matt Jackson, Neil Netanel, Harmeet Sawhney, Steven Wildman, seminar participants at Indiana University and Northwestern University, and participants at conferences held by the American Economic Association, the Columbia Institute for Tele-Information, the International Communications Association, the International Telecommunications Society, the National Bureau of Economic Research, and TPRC, Inc. (formerly the Telecommunications Policy Research Conference).

Donna Bouvier of Harvard University Press contributed expert copy-editing. I am especially grateful to Michael Aronson, my editor at the Press, for the guidance that came from his natural understanding of economics and of books, and for his patience.

Hollywood's Road to Riches

Introduction: American Success

When pay television and videocassettes emerged in the mid-1970s, some had marvelous visions of the riches these technologies might bring to the Hollywood studios. Others were more cautious. Still, most assumed that if these new technologies did prosper, it would surely be at the expense of the existing movie distribution channels: theaters and broadcast television. After all, as David Chasman, an MGM/UA production executive remarked, "What did the automobile mean to the average horse-and-buggy driver?"[1]

Chasman probably was thinking about the devastating blow that broadcast television had dealt to movie theaters years before. From the late 1940s until the early 1960s, as the percentage of U.S. households owning a TV quickly grew from near zero to over 90 percent, theater attendance dropped precipitously, until by the early 1970s it was at less than a quarter of its 1946 level. By then, the Hollywood studios (in addition to providing series and other new shows to the television networks) had made a business of selling films to the broadcast networks and independent TV stations after the films' theater runs. Those sales, though, fell far short of making up for the shortfall in income from theaters.

The early 1970s, before pay TV and videocassettes, were probably Hollywood's darkest days. The industry had made repeated attempts to recover its "lost audience" with exhibition technology by introducing wide-screen formats such as Cinerama, Cinemascope, 3-D, and 70 mm— and by presenting spectacular productions such as *Ben-Hur* (1959), *Cleopatra* (1963), and *Tora! Tora! Tora!* (1970). The downward trend in theater admissions showed no evident response. Although television's effect on theater admissions had mostly happened by 1960, the 1970s brought a realization that TV was here to stay and that this newer medium had a profound competitive edge. Retrenchment followed. Hollywood's extravagant "roadshow" productions declined, from a total of twelve in 1968 to only one in 1971.[2] In spite of income from series and other programs made for television, three of the major studios—Fox, United Artists, and MGM/Loews—reported their largest losses in history in 1970. Two others, Paramount and Columbia, followed with record losses in 1971.[3]

As we all know now, pay TV, videocassettes, and most dramatically DVDs, have proven vastly more effective than spectaculars were in finding the movies' lost audience. These media have prospered magnificently since the 1980s, and income of the movie studios has massively shifted toward these media. Together, pay television and home video now account for about two thirds of all studio income from distribution of theatrical films in the United States.

For the most part, though, there has been no horse and buggy effect among movie media. U.S. movie theater admissions have actually increased since the 1970s. Even broadcast television remains a robust presenter of old movies. The end result has been remarkable. Pay and basic cable television, video, theaters, and free TV have all fared well as exhibitors of theatrical films in the United States.

The American industry that earns its revenues from these media has prospered, perhaps beyond even the imagination of Hollywood script-writers—but at least beyond that of securities analysts. A *Wall Street Journal* article reported in 1995 that "show business has become a bigger factor in the economy than analysts ever expected."[4] The production boom continues into the new century. In the end, Hollywood's economic success is displayed by the growth of its coffers: U.S. Distributor revenues from the worldwide release of theatrical movies have increased from about $1.1 billion in 1970 to $39.8 billion in 2003— more than a tripling as a proportion of total economic activity in the United States, as measured by GDP.[5] A comparable growth in movie industry production investments has naturally followed.

A large chunk—nearly half in recent years—of Hollywood's film income comes from outside the United States, especially western Europe and Japan. As they have in America, these markets have grown as new movie exhibition media have diffused and as television systems have been expanded and privatized in many countries. Of most significance, though, the terms of trade have turned sharply in the United States' favor: a larger and larger share of those bigger pies has flowed to U.S. distributors. The net result has been a growth rate in the foreign income of U.S. distributors that is at least as great as that from domestic sources (see Appendix C).

As the economies of Europe and Japan recovered from World War II in the 1950s, their film production industries enjoyed a period of unprecedented creativity and prosperity. In the "Golden Age" of European cinema, for example, great directors—among them Jean-Luc Godard and François Truffaut in France; Federico Fellini, Luchino

Visconti, and Michaelangelo Antonioni in Italy; John Schlesinger and Stanley Kubrick in Britain; Luis Buñuel in Spain; Ingmar Bergman in Sweden—achieved prominence in their home countries and throughout Europe. In Japan, a comparable era of artistic achievement was led by Akira Kurosawa. Famous movie stars emerged from all these countries: Sophia Loren, Catherine Deneuve, Jean-Paul Belmondo, Max von Sydow, Anouk Amée, Brigitte Bardot, Marcello Mastroianni, and Toshirô Mifune among them. Of course, the greatest artists did not always produce the highest-grossing movies, and the creative flames of the 1950s and early '60s died down as well. But the domestic film production industries in much of Europe and Asia were at least commercially prosperous into the 1970s.

While Hollywood struggled, a long list of foreign films—including *La Dolce Vita* (Italy, 1960), *Marriage Italian Style* (Italy, 1964), *A Man and a Woman* (France, 1966), *Z* (France, 1969), *Cousin, Cousine* (France, 1976), *Elvira Madigan* (Sweden, 1967), and *Seven Samurai* (Japan, 1954)—achieved notable, albeit modest, box office success in America during these years. Along with the economic acceptance of their movies, the major European directors and stars achieved celebrity status in the United States as well as at home.

The doldrums of Hollywood and the relative glory of the foreign cinema in those days even led some to speculate that European production centers were on track to replace Hollywood as the dominant world center for movies. But thirty years later, very much the opposite has happened.

A European Union report estimated that in 1968 American movies earned about 35 percent of the total European box office, while European-produced films accounted for 60 percent.[6] Today, those numbers have reversed. In 2003, American films earned 72 percent of the European box office, European movies 26 percent.[7] In Japan, the domestic box office share fell from its peak of more than 80 percent in 1960 to 33 percent in 2003, the large majority of the remaining two thirds undoubtedly accounted for by American movies. In fact, American films now earn more than half the box office in nearly all major markets of the world, and the U.S. share routinely exceeds 80 percent in several major countries, including Germany and Britain. Hollywood's dominance of foreign prerecorded video rentals and sales is probably even more lopsided, and American films have a strong presence on the expanded and newly privatized television systems appearing around the world. The most overwhelming performance of American films is, of course, in the United States itself, where Hollywood's fare has usually earned about 95 percent of the box office since at least the 1980s. (See Chapter 5 and Appendix F.)

Today, Hollywood's products—led by massively financed, special-effects-laden films—*Titanic* (1997), *The Lord of the Rings: The Fellowship of the Ring* (2001), *The Matrix Reloaded* (2003), *Spiderman 2* (2004), and *Star Wars, Episode III: The Revenge of the Sith* (2005) are just a few examples—dominate not only theaters and other movie exhibition media in America, but wash like great waves over international borders throughout the world. Hollywood's top-of-the-line international movies have now graduated from "blockbuster" to "tentpole" status—an industry term coined to describe films such as the *Harry Potter, Lord of the Rings,* and *Matrix* series, which are originally conceived as copyrighted franchises of stories and characters that will involve sequels and large-scale spin-offs of video games, music, and commercial products. By all appearances, the technological glitz of these movies far outshines that of top productions in earlier decades.

As the box office records imply, film industries worldwide have not shared in Hollywood's success. Film production activity in some major countries, notably France and Japan, remains at a relatively high level.

And there have been some well-publicized individual movies that have been hits at home and around the world, including in the United States—for example, *Crouching Tiger, Hidden Dragon* (2001), *Life Is Beautiful* (Italy, 1998), *The Fifth Element* (France, 1997), and *The Full Monty* (Britain, 1997). But throughout Europe and in many other countries, production industries have become heavily dependent on government subsidy. The movie stars and famous directors in Europe and Japan are mostly gone. A great many of them, in fact, have moved to Hollywood.

As film production industries around the world weakened, Hollywood's strengthened. Today, probably over 80 percent of all money spent by consumers on movies worldwide is spent on American films.[8] Hollywood has truly become the King of Content.

Questions We Ask

What can explain the extraordinary economic achievements of the American theatrical film industry, both in its home market and worldwide? How have the Hollywood studios been able to use the various television and video media to multiply their revenue in the United States so successfully? How has Hollywood overwhelmed its foreign competitors to dominate the world market for movies? And how have the economic forces of audience demand, technology, and the environment of high risk combined to change the kinds of movies Hollywood produces?

In this book, we address these questions from an economic perspective. They are, of course, large and difficult questions, and their answers involve much more than just economics. This book is hardly the first to concern itself with these issues. The movie industry is a popular topic in the media, both print and nonprint. A great many people, including academics studying the industry, have written about similar questions, especially on Hollywood's dominance of the world market for movies. In recent years we have seen an accelerating stream of useful academic research in movie industry economics. The present book criticizes some of this research, as well as some of the industry commentary and analysis from other quarters. Throughout these pages, though, we build upon the work of others in striving to make a unique and valuable contribution.

The prevalence of movie industry scrutiny, in the media as well as bookstores, is testimony to the significance of the questions this book addresses. Movie production and distribution is not an especially prominent part of the American economy (though it is important to Southern California). It looms large, though, among positive net contributors to the U.S. balance of payments, in the same company with aerospace and aircraft equipment, and chemical products. The movie industry's contribution comes not so much from the size of its exports as from an unusually lopsided ratio of exports to imports—roughly ten to one.[9] Also, movies (and entertainment more generally) have long been thought to have a marketing impact for the American goods and services they display that is greater than the foreign revenue they earn themselves. Though now a sensitive subject to discuss publicly, the Motion Picture Producers and Distributors Association (ancestor of the Motion Picture Association of America, or MPAA) in an earlier era repeatedly cited a Department of Commerce "estimate" that for every foot of film sent abroad, one dollar's worth of other goods was exported.[10] In any case, the stellar export performance of the American movie industry has endeared Hollywood to the U.S. Congress and various administrations, and they have pursued American movie industry interests worldwide with great vigor.

We suspect that most of our readers have not picked this book up out of concern about the economic impact of the film industry. Most of the volumes of words written and read about the industry merely reflect the general public's fascination with movies. But there are some more serious reasons, besides economics, to be concerned about the pervasive influence of American movies. Both in the United States and around the world, many people worry about the violent, sexual, or political content of popular movies. The kind of worry varies greatly from one country to another, but one position seems to be shared by most foreign politicians and social commentators (though obviously not most audiences) outside the United States: a general disdain for American movies.

From the earliest days of the industry, the dominance of American films and television programs has generated anger and resentment worldwide. The archetypal critique was expressed by Jack Lang, French Minister of Culture, in the early 1980s. Lang condemned American entertainment as "a financial and cultural imperialism that no longer or rarely grabs territory, but grabs consciousness, ways of thinking, ways of living."[11] Notice the basic message in this quote. For the most part, critiques of American movies by foreign observers have been not so much a condemnation of specific content as they have been lamentations over the notion that the commentators' lands have become swamped with American culture at the expense of their country's own. The French have probably been most extreme in their moral crusade against American films. But a chorus of resentment that American movies are invading the cultural sovereignty of many nations has only intensified as worldwide market shares of American films have increased.

One result of these culture wars has been a long history of attempts in countries around the world to impose import quotas, tariffs, currency controls, and a variety of other trade barriers to limit imports of American movies and television programs.[12] Perhaps a more important

motive behind these trade barriers has been simple industry protec-
tionism. As indigenous film industries have dwindled, political pressure to limit unemployment in the film production and related industries has increased—inspiring the same economic measures that we
often see in other industries, from cement to electronics. Still, there is
no doubt that resistance to the importation of American media products has been intensified by cultural motives. At least in the more lucrative markets, the trade barriers imposed on American movies have
mostly either proven to be ineffectual or have been discarded. A not-
insignificant reason for this has been the bare-knuckle efforts of the
MPAA and the U.S. government to break down the barriers by threatening boycotts or general trade sanctions. These aggressive tactics have
hardly mollified those who desire to protect the cultural integrity of
their country and restore the glory of their film industry. On the contrary: much of the world has come to feel that American film people
and government officials are extremely arrogant. The Americans, for
their part, are unapologetic. Whether appropriate or not, the feelings
stirred up by American movies, on screen and off, are often intense.

Plan of the Book

Our analysis of the American film industry in this book is both economic and historical. Simply put, we attempt to explain the remarkable
development of the American movie industry since about the end of
World War II, using simple economic principles.

One such principle used throughout this book is *price discrimination*—which just means charging different prices to different people according to their willingness to pay. To illustrate, imagine that one potential patron of a movie theater will pay a high price to see a certain
film playing there, while a second is willing to pay a lower price, but

still enough to cover the operator's cost of serving one more person. If the theater is forced to set a single admission price, there is no way to avoid forfeiting some money—either from the high-value patron if the price is low enough to attract the low-value patron—or from exclusion of the low-value patron if the price is set high enough to collect all that the high-value consumer is willing to pay. Thus, at least potentially, the theater operator can always make more money by price discriminating—charging a high price to the high-value consumer and a low price to the low-value consumer.

How does one accomplish this price discrimination in practice? That question leads us to a second economic principle, closely related to the first: *market segmentation*. To successfully price discriminate, the movie seller must find a way to separate consumers. Otherwise, the high-value consumer will simply take advantage of the lower price offered to the low-value patron. One way to segment the markets might be to charge a high price the first night, then a lower price the second night, on the expectation that the more intense desire of the high-value patron will induce him or her to attend the earlier showing. Or, to consider the studio's overall pricing strategy more broadly, the movie might be released in theaters first for a high price and later on video for a lower price. A major theme of the economic success story we tell in this book is how the movie studios have taken advantage of different movie media to segment their markets and thus to efficiently and accurately price discriminate among movie patrons.

A third economic principle we employ is fundamental to any economic analysis of media products; like other media, movies have "public good" characteristics. Analogous to public parks, for example, movies have a high cost of creation, or "first copy" cost, that is unaffected by the number of people who watch it, but a relatively low, or even zero, marginal cost of serving additional viewers. One more person coming into a theater to watch a film, for example, has a negligible effect on costs, and one more viewer of a free TV movie has no effect on the broadcaster's costs at all. Of course, the cost of operating a theater for one more showing of a movie is significant, as is the cost to a video store of renting a DVD to one more person, or the cost to a cable system of selling and processing a subscription to HBO. So the public good analogy is imperfect. But any of these costs of duplicating and distributing movies to additional patrons pale in comparison to the first copy creation cost—namely the $60 million or so it costs to produce the average major Hollywood feature.

The public good, or high first copy creation cost / low distribution cost, feature of the movie industry has important implications. One is that price discrimination tends to be a more significant business strategy in the film industry than in other industries because there is such a wide range of price demands that are worth serving. Demands on the high end can be very intense, and thus very lucrative if high enough prices can be charged. But someone having an extremely low interest in seeing a certain movie may still be worth serving, because an even lower cost distribution method (for example, broadcast television) could be cost effective.

A second implication of the public good characteristic of movies is that the market offers a trade-off between the number (or variety) of different movies that can be produced and the first-copy cost (production or "negative" cost) of those movies. For roughly the same level of industry spending, we can either have a large variety of relatively inexpensive movies or a small variety of more expensive movies. This market choice is important because there is generally a positive relationship between a movie's production cost and its attractiveness to audiences.

Of course, many expensive movies flop with audiences, and cheap movies can attract great crowds. But in general, the better the acting, the writing, and the directing, and the more impressive the special effects, the exotic locations, and so on, the more attractive the movie generally is to its potential audiences. In economic terms, then, a studio's or an individual producer's decision to make a greater negative-cost investment means higher product "quality"—a term we use in this book to indicate production values and audience attractiveness, *not* aesthetic quality. The end result is that if studios as a whole respond to consumer demand with more expensive, and thus higher-quality, movies, then, other things equal, variety must be sacrificed.

The public good characteristic of movies, and the relationships between cost, quality, and variety that result, are germane to our explanation of how American movies have become increasingly dominant worldwide, and to our analysis of how changing demand and new production technologies over the past several decades have influenced movie variety and production costs.

In the pages to follow, we develop these key economic principles more fully, and introduce some others as needed. No economic study of the movie industry and its products, for example, could omit consideration of the notoriously high risk of movie production, for which principles such as risk aversion and risk diversification are relevant. At various points in this book, especially in our analysis of television's impact on the industry and of the types of movies Hollywood now produces, we consider risk and its effects.

Nevertheless, while much popular commentary, as well as a number of academic studies of the movie industry, focus on risk and how the studios confront or avoid it, this book is more about the *return* side of the equation.[13] Movie production risk is an exciting and analytically interesting subject, but companies that face high risk, like movie studios, can keep it in the background via fairly straightforward means—such as corporate diversification or sharing risk with others, much like buying insurance. More challenging, in our view, are decisions about what movies will be successful on balance, and how to distribute those movies in the most lucrative possible way.

A word at this point about boundaries. This book is almost entirely concerned with theatrical feature films and the firms that are involved in their production, distribution, and exhibition. The 400 or 500 feature films that get some kind of theatrical release in the United States each year (excluding pornographic films) are in one way like the tip of an iceberg. Thousands more feature-length movies are produced and exhibited on video, pay TV systems, or broadcast television, but never have a theatrical run. The theatrical films, while a minority in number, are generally far more expensive to make and account for the vast majority of industry revenues worldwide, as well as the bulk of attention from critics, industry observers, and the general public. In this book we consider nontheatrical features and the firms that make them primarily in the context of contrasting them with theatrical films.

Chapter 1, "The Players," is an overview of the Hollywood studios and their functions, and how the competitive environment of the industry has evolved over time. Chapter 2, "Television: A Parting of the Ways," analyzes the period between about 1948 and 1975. Its main subject is how television's devastating effects on movie theater admissions transformed the theatrical film industry into its modern form. Chapter 3, "The Pay Media: A Shower of Money" covers the period from about 1975 to the present, during which pay television systems and the home video industry revolutionized the theatrical movie release system. Chapter 4, "Controlling the Release Sequence," explains how the studios have dealt with two different challenges to the development of price discrimination in the United States: piracy and home copying, and challenges to their "windows"—the time intervals between the industry's release of a product from one medium to the next. Chapter 5, "Rising American Dominance," is concerned with Hollywood's increasing control of foreign markets for movies, and the accompanying decline of indigenous production industries in most countries of the world. Chapter 6—"What Has Hollywood Done with the Money?"—discusses changing demand and evolving production technologies, and how these have affected the balance between the quality and variety, as well as the content, of Hollywood's movies. In the concluding chapter, "Hollywood's Digital Future," we apply the models developed in earlier chapters in an attempt to predict how digital production, distribution, and exhibition, and digital rights management (DRM) technologies of the future will affect the economic prosperity of Hollywood, the dominance of its films in foreign markets, and the types of movies it is likely to produce. Finally, for those interested, the several appendixes elaborate on the sources and methods used in the creation of this book.

Chapter 1

The Players

Who are the players who make the decisions and come up with the movies that have propelled the American film industry to its achievements? In this chapter we introduce the Hollywood studios and their most important economic functions, and we investigate how the competitive environment within which they produce and distribute movies has developed over time.

The Hollywood Studios and What They Do

People usually refer to the six or seven major Southern California–based companies that produce and distribute theatrical movies as the "Hollywood studios" or sometimes the "majors," and we also use those terms.[1] The major companies belong to the Motion Picture Association of America, or the MPAA, and together they consistently account for 80 to 90 percent or more of the total receipts from the distribution of theatrical movies to theaters and the variety of other media in the United States. The majors also dominate the distribution of American movies to foreign markets. All of these companies are household names: Universal Pictures, Paramount Pictures, MGM, Fox Film Corporation, Columbia Pictures, Disney, and Warner Brothers.

From our perspective, the most important feature of the studios is their role as *distributors,* and we often refer to them by that term. By controlling distribution, the studios act as gatekeepers: they decide which movies get produced and how they are made, and they also largely determine when and at what prices viewers get to see them on which media. The studios have several business functions that derive from their control as gatekeepers. If not engaged in the actual production of a film, they decide whether or not a film is produced and they usually arrange for financing. The studios also negotiate the contracts with theaters and other media that will exhibit the movie, and when the film is completed they physically deliver prints or videos for exhibition. In the process, the studios are mostly responsible for promoting and marketing the movies to the public worldwide.

The ideas for movies that get produced come from many sources. Tens of thousands of movie scripts are written and passed around each year. The studios evaluate them with small armies of readers they hire, but scripts routed to the decision-making executives via agents, writers, producers, and actors with track records or business connections have a much better chance. A relatively small percentage of movies are "pitched" to the studios as ideas before any script is written. Most of the time, scripts are either written in advance of their being shopped around, or scripts are commissioned, the latter often based on successful books, foreign movies, or other art forms. Each of the major studios keeps a slate of films or film ideas, usually between 100 and 400 of them at a time, in "development." For these projects, the ideas or scripts are worked and reworked and tentatively filled out with potential talent. At any stage in the development process, which can last for years, the studio can give up on a project and put its creators or promoters back into the open market. In these ways, the majors and their subsidiaries winnow movie ideas into the approximately 200 to 250 theatrical releases they distribute each year.

In effect, the major studios actually produce or control production of the great majority of the feature films they end up distributing. Often they produce films "in house" by engaging the services of producers or production companies that maintain offices on their studio lot or with whom they have long-term option contracts. In other cases, the studios contract with unaffiliated, "independent" producers on a film-by-film basis. Producers, directors, and other talent make their movies with varying degrees of creative autonomy. But in nearly all cases, the studios maintain overall control of the production process by holding the purse strings.[2] Generally, the studios finance directly from earnings or from revolving lines of credit that they maintain with banks, guarantee production loans made by banks or other parties to the producer, or facilitate the raising of venture capital, the returns on which are dependent on the performance of the movie in question. Very often, production budgets are cobbled together from a variety of these resources. A critical ingredient in the great majority of all cases that non-studio funds are involved, however, is an explicit advance guarantee by the studio to distribute and market the movie.

In some other cases, the studios arrive very late in the process. In so-called negative pickup deals, the studio may buy the rights to distribute an independently produced film that is already developed, or that is partially or even completely finished. In such instances, production control is obviously more in the hands of the independent production company. Such deals, however, are uncommon, and in any case the studio remains the gatekeeper by means of its selection power.

In substance, these basic elements of studio control in the movie production process have changed little over time. Probably the main change has been that actors, actresses, and most other agents of production are now much more likely to be independent contractors than in earlier days. In the old "studio system" that faded away in the mid-1950s, a high percentage of production agents were salaried employees of the studios and were simply assigned to work on different films over time. That more factory-like system probably resulted in somewhat tighter control over production outcomes. (We return to this subject in Chapter 2.)

Ordinarily, the studios contract with producers to buy the rights to distribute and market each film not only to theaters, but also to home video, pay television, broadcasting, airlines, and all of the other venues that theatrical features usually find their way to. Most often, the studios obtain these rights in both the United States and foreign markets. In a number of cases, though, studios have divided those rights. U.S. and foreign market rights to *Titanic* (1997), for example, were divided between Paramount Pictures and Fox Film Corporation. In other instances, the film's producer may retain the distribution rights to certain media within the U.S. or certain foreign markets. Spyglass Entertainment, the producer of *Seabiscuit* (2003), shared its production costs with two studios, Universal and DreamWorks, and retained rights to some foreign territories as a result.[3] In the great majority of cases, though, one or more studios retain the rights to distribute a movie to all media worldwide.

Another circumstance in which the studio may explicitly forgo control of the movie release process is via a grant to the producer of discretion over creative or other elements of the film's advertising campaign. In unusual cases, very prominent producers obtain all their own financing and retain most or all film ownership rights for themselves. George Lucas, for example, employed this model in contracting with Fox Films to release *Star Wars* episodes for a percentage of the gross theatrical rentals less expenses.[4] In almost all cases, though, the studios maintain broad contractual control over the timing and other terms and conditions of each movie's release and its marketing. As we discuss in Chapters 2 and 3, U.S. copyright and antitrust laws stop short of granting carte blanche to the studios in some important aspects of film distribution, notably pricing; but their overall degree of control is high.

Besides the majors, there are a number of studios or film distributors usually known as "independents" (e.g., Samuel Goldwyn Films and Lions Gate) that have the same basic functions, although they are more likely to subcontract distribution to foreign markets or certain media to other distributors. Together, the independents release more movies in the United States than do the majors—250 to 300 on average in recent years. As individual companies, though, the independents tend to release relatively few movies per year, and those films generally have lower budgets and often serve niche markets, such as the "art" or foreign films segments. Probably the most well-known "independent" studio as of this writing is DreamWorks, which entered the market in the mid-1990s and models itself much more after the majors in terms of film budgets and other business aspects. DreamWorks is mostly a producer, however, and it has contracted with Universal to distribute its films theatrically.

There are now several other U.S. film distributors that one may have thought were independents, but that are in fact wholly owned subsidiaries of the major studios or of their corporate parents. Among these are Miramax (owned by Disney) and New Line (owned by Time Warner). In fact, both Miramax and New Line were formerly independents that achieved a measure of success before being acquired by their major studio parents in the 1980s and 1990s. In other cases, the studios have started their own "classics" divisions, such as Fox Searchlight and

Sony Classics, which usually release the same kind of smaller or niche-market films as independents. Although subsidiary distributors operate with varying degrees of autonomy from the major studios that own them, they are subject to central decision-making control, and thus for our purposes are considered to be part of the major studios.

A Historical Perspective

In order to better follow the discussion in the following chapters, we must examine the market structure of theatrical film distribution and how the Hollywood distribution establishment has developed over time. A history of distributor market shares of the domestic theater market since the late 1940s, assembled mostly from *Variety* records, is shown in Figure 1.1. (For details on the sources used for this figure, see Appendix A.)

Given the dramatic changes in demand and technology over that long time, the relative stability of membership in the Hollywood "majors club" is remarkable. Six of the seven major studios in business as of 2003 are the same companies that led the industry in the 1940s, or they are descendants of these firms. One of the original eight, RKO, went out of business in 1957, but that was largely the doing of its eccentric owner, Howard Hughes. Both MGM and United Artists have had rocky histories, but they have at least continued to exist in merged form. Only one new major studio, Disney, managed to enter distribution during this period, in 1955, and after a long period on the periphery, rose in the 1980s under the leadership of Michael Eisner to firmly place itself within the major studio establishment.[5] The number of majors is set to decline by one with the acquisition in mid-2005 of MGM by Sony Corporation, which also owns Columbia.[6]

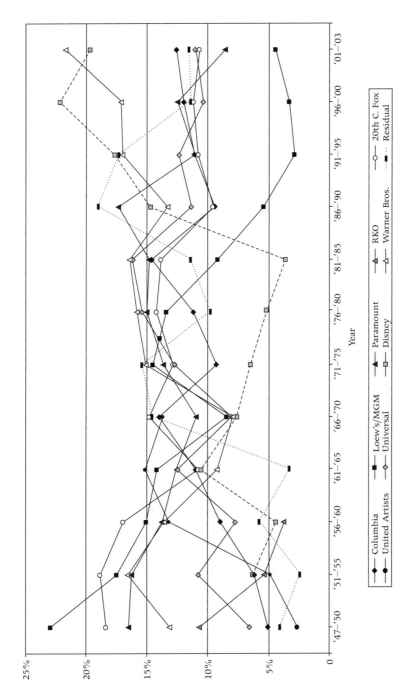

FIGURE 1.1 Distributor market shares of domestic box office/rentals, five-year averages, 1947–2003. (For sources, see Appendix A.)

As the "residual" category indicates, independent distributors have entered the industry and, at least as a group, have claimed a significant market share over time, especially after the early 1960s. A few smaller companies, such as American International Pictures, Allied Artists, and Orion, existed along with the majors for long stretches of time on the economic margins of the industry.[7] Others, such as Cinerama Releasing and National General in the 1960s and '70s, and "mini-majors," such as the Cannon Group in the late 1970s and '80s, launched ambitious, but more short-lived, attempts to enter the ranks of the majors. Some other independents that entered the industry in the 1960s and '70s, including Miramax and New Line, have survived in the sense that they were among those acquired by one of the majors and still exist as subsidiaries.

One significant change in market structure evident from Figure 1.1 is a narrowing in the spread of studio market shares from the late 1940s until the early 1960s. The five studios generally having the highest market shares in the 1940s—Fox, MGM, Warner, Paramount, and RKO, known at that time as the five majors—were vertically integrated into production and theater exhibition and had consistently dominated the industry since the mid-1930s.[8] The three others—Universal, Columbia, and United Artists, known as "the minors" at the time—owned no theaters and earned lower market shares. All eight of these studios were brought to trial by the U.S. Justice Department in the 1940s, and an eventual Supreme Court decision in 1948, *United States v. Paramount Pictures, Inc. et al.,* ruled that the eight distributors had violated the Sherman Act and other antitrust laws by attempting to monopolize the industry to the exclusion of independent producers, distributors, and exhibitors.[9] The Court ordered the five major distributors to divest their extensive theater holdings, a process that was completed in the mid-1950s. The Court also established a number of regulations on the contractual relationships between distributors and theaters that were intended to level the playing field for independent companies. These included a prohibition on the practice of block booking (conditioning the rights to exhibit one movie on acceptance of another) and on "master agreements," by which studios made a single deal with a theater circuit to show a movie in several or all of its theaters.

After the *Paramount* decision, the prewar stability of industry structure among the eight Paramount defendants began to crumble. Industry positions of the majors and minors converged, and the extent of independent entry increased. We argue in the following chapter that the almost coincident diffusion of broadcast television had more profound long-range effects on the movie industry than did *Paramount,* but it is likely that the ascendance of all three of the minor studios into the majors' ranks, and perhaps the rise of independents in the 1960s, were related to the Court's intervention.

In any case, the long history behind most of the major studios suggests there is a lot of inertia, or barriers to entry, in theatrical film distribution. One source of this inertia is probably economies of scale in the physical process of theatrical distribution. With the telling exception of chronically troubled MGM/UA, which released between 8 and 16 films annually from 1992 through 2003, each of the major studios (not including their subsidiaries) has typically released 15 to 30 movies per annum in recent years.[10] An infrastructure of production, marketing, and sales personnel, including networks of regional sales offices, is underutilized with too few movies on the schedule. The reputation of the studio with producers, theaters, and other media (though probably not much with consumers) is no doubt also affected.

Another source of firm inertia in movie distribution is surely risk bearing. The notorious unpredictability of the movie selection, production, and distribution process tends to drive the financing function into the hands of companies that can diversify the risk by distributing a slate of different movies. Few independent producers, in fact, are able to raise funds on their own at favorable rates, and the cost of capital for almost any producer is likely to decline with the underwriting of a major distributor.

The historical record, then, suggests that the time and investment required for a potential player to get up to speed with a large enough slate of major films to accomplish such things as cover fixed costs, build a reputation and relationships with producers and exhibitors, and calm down bankers are important obstacles to potential entrants in film distribution. Nevertheless, as illustrated in Figure 1.1, individual studios have rarely been able to sustain more than a 20 percent to 25 percent share of the domestic theater rental market, evidence that limits to these economies of large scale in film distribution are reached at levels far below total industry demand.[11]

As the contribution of theaters themselves to total studio revenues from theatrical film distribution has declined over time, theater market share has become a less certain reflection of total market share. As Figure 1.2 shows, independent video distributors (the "residual" line in Figure 1.2) have steadily lost share as the industry has matured. Although comparisons between Figures 1.1 and 1.2 are imprecise,[12] it can be seen that the same seven major distributors, all of which operate their own home video divisions, have also come to dominate video. Movies that do well in theaters generally also do well on video (and other media), as reflected by the similar pecking order of the majors' shares in both theater and video distribution. Disney has been something of an exception to this rule, especially before the 2000s, in terms of its greater dominance of the video market.

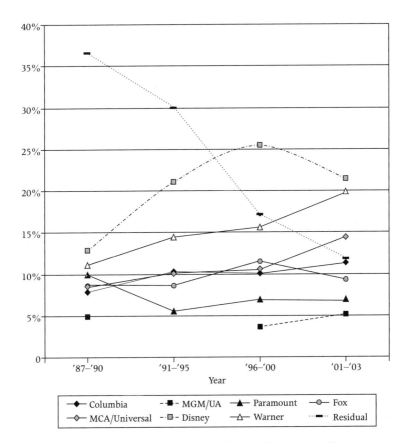

FIGURE 1.2   Market shares of domestic video supplier revenues, five-year averages, 1987–2003. (For sources, see Appendix A.)

Competition, Coordination, and Conglomeration

As a stable, oligopolistic industry, the major studios recognize their market interdependence and behave strategically.

In the process of selecting which movies to produce and when to release them, interactive jockeying among the major studios is clearly evident. If a studio is considering a green light for an expensive earthquake disaster movie, it may decide against the project if it learns another studio has a similar earthquake disaster movie in the works. Or it may proceed if it believes that the other studio can be intimidated into canceling its project. Major projects in development at the various studios are usually not very well guarded secrets. In addition, industry trade publications routinely report actual film production starts, so once a project is in production, major details are often a matter of record. Approximate release dates for major films are often planned in conjunction with production decisions. One studio, for example, may be more inclined to produce a comedy for Christmas if it believes that all the other studios are preparing to release dramas. This interactive process, however, works very imperfectly. Film critics and observers routinely lament the imbalance of Christmas or summer movie subject matter. The media have on several occasions taken the studios to task for their apparent inability to avoid producing and releasing similarly themed blockbuster films at about the same time, as happened with *Dante's Peak* (Universal) and *Volcano* (Fox), both released in 1997; *Deep Impact* (DreamWorks/Paramount) and *Armageddon* (Disney) in 1998; and *Red Planet* (Warner) and *Mission to Mars* (Disney) in 2000.[13]

In the actual scheduling of release dates, a more organized process of industry coordination takes place. In any one month, only a dozen or so major films are released, and it is well documented that the box office performance of any one of them can be dramatically affected by the opening dates and advertising campaigns of competing films.[14] Tentative theater release dates for a year or more in advance are collected and published by the Exhibitor Relations Company. Using this information, studios and theater operators juggle dates to avoid being entrapped in a logjam of too many releases at the same time, to maximize differentiation from other releases, and the like.[15] There was discussion in the trade press, for example, in 1997 about how Universal's impending Memorial Day release of *The Lost World: Jurassic Park* intimidated other studios into avoiding that weekend to open their summer pictures.[16] A similar system of announcing and then rearranging video release dates also takes place (as discussed further in Chapter 4). Finally, the process by which movies are licensed to theaters within local geographic areas appears to involve a good deal of mutual interaction among studios and theater operators to extend runs for more successful movies, move unexpected flops out of the area, and otherwise smooth an inherently uncertain market process.

A 1970s' economic analysis by Robert Crandall covering the 1948–1966 period argued that, in spite of the *Paramount* decision, the major studios were able to tacitly collude to restrain their levels of theatrical feature output until the wave of independent distributor entry in the mid-1960s.[17] They were able to do this, he claimed, mainly by taking advantage of the industry's advance public announcements of film production plans. Although it is true that nearly the same seven major companies successfully maintained control of the distribution industry for many years after Crandall's article was published, it is hard to imagine that any such tacit collusion could have persisted in the midst of rapidly rising demand for movies after the 1970s.

As Crandall also acknowledged, aggressive studio competition in terms of movie production investments characterized the period he studied, which resulted in studios' tending to bid away excess profits gained from any restriction in the number of movies released. In those earlier days and since, the president of the MPAA has periodically made speeches urging the studios to restrain "excessive" or "out of control" production costs,[18] but the nature of movie production seems to leave no objective basis on which they could cooperate to do so. The value of various film ideas and talent brought to market is highly subjective; whatever collusive hopes might be harbored among the major studios, movie budgets are not subject to reliable verification by competitors—and, with the prevalence of participation payments, they are not even known in advance.[19]

At least over the long term, then, there seems no question that the studios compete fiercely in the production market. In this respect, the movie industry is a lot like professional sports. The L.A. Lakers organization hires a team of basketball players, trains them to work together, produces a schedule of games and, through their coach, orders them on and off the court during each game. But the ultimate market power in the industry lies with its top talent. Everything depends on whether the team is able to contract with the best players, and with a top coach. As reflected by the huge salaries that Shaquille O'Neal, Michael Jordan, and other, more "ordinary," NBA stars have made, top talent is rare. The athletes thus call the shots by forcing the teams to compete furiously to persuade them to join one team instead of another. In a similar way, the Hollywood studios are forced to scramble to engage the services of the best writers, the top stars like Brad Pitt or Julia Roberts, directors like Steven Spielberg or Martin Scorsese, producers like Jerry Bruckheimer or George Lucas, and even top executive talent like Barry Diller (former CEO of Twentieth Century Fox) or Sherry Lansing (former CEO of Paramount). In sports, antitrust exemptions permit bizarre collusive agreements among team owners, notably salary caps, to help control their "production" costs, but no such luxuries can be found in the movie industry.

So far, we have barely mentioned the well-known fact that most of the studios are subsidiaries of larger conglomerate organizations, most of which own a variety of other media properties. Table 1.1 describes these relationships as of 1998. Since then, Seagram has sold Universal Pictures to Vivendi, which in turn sold it to GE in 2003. Sony' acquisition of MGM in 2005 effectively buries the latter studio's operations

Table 1.1 Conglomerate ownership of theatrical feature film distribution, 1998

(1) Studio	(2) Parent corporation	(3) Other primary media businesses	(4) Revenue from all sources (in billions)	(5) Theatrical film revenue as a % of total corp. revenues
Disney	Walt Disney	Television, cable, radio, music, books, magazines	$23.0	27%
Warner Bros.	Time Warner	Television, cable, music, books, magazines	$26.8	15%
Fox	News Corp.	Television, newspapers, books, magazines	$20.4	20%
Sony Pictures (Columbia)	Sony	Television, music, games	$51.9	5%
MGM-UA	MGM-UA	Television	$1.2	75%
Universal	Seagram	Television, music, books	$9.4	21%
Paramount	Viacom	Television, cable, books	$12.1	21%

Source: Author's estimates based on annual financial reports and Paul Kagan Associates data.

into the machinery of that conglomerate's far larger, hardware-based organization.

The significance of these corporate relationships to studio behavior and the types of movies Hollywood produces has been variously interpreted and is not easily subject to empirical verification. The financial success of movie studios has in some cases been attributed to the brilliance of the conglomerate executives overseeing them, such as Michael Eisner's turnaround of Disney in the 1980s;[20] it is plausible that bringing a movie studio under the wing of a well-regarded CEO, such as Rupert Murdoch of News Corporation or Sumner Redstone of Viacom, benefits its vision. Other commentators have lamented the rarity of entertainment industry executives that can "strike the right balance between the artists and the suits."[21] As we discuss further in Chapter 6, excessive movie budgets and an overreliance on sequels or derivative movies have also been associated unfavorably with conglomerate organization and the mentality of the top executives in charge.

When merger plans are announced, industry analysts often cite efficiencies, such as workforce combinations, or marketing advantages, such as the ability to cross-promote movies using television, magazines, or other media assets also owned by the conglomerate. Also commonly mentioned are the advantages of vertical integration, such as the ownership of television or cable networks that can serve as guaranteed outlets for movies produced by the conglomerate's studio branch. A related benefit is the ability to consolidate exploitation of a single story idea or character through books, magazines, television shows, music publishing, Internet Web sites, or other media within a single corporation. The economic advantages of such operating efficiencies (often called *economies of scope*) are plausible. However, real multimedia exploitation within the same conglomerate is apparently infrequent, and other efficiency claims have come into recent disrepute—notably in the cases of the AOL–Time Warner and the ABC-Disney mergers.[22]

Perhaps the most compelling economic advantage to movie studios of conglomeration is finance related. It is well known that even with a slate of 20 to 30 releases per year, the high risk of movie production and distribution can lead to serious year-to-year fluctuations in studio income.[23] Affiliation with reliable cash cow businesses like soft drinks or television stations can provide a steady internal flow of investment funds to compensate. Also, income fluctuations are unwelcome to bankers, who provide rolling lines of credit, and to the stock market, which rewards income predictability with higher stock values. As we discuss in Chapter 2, increasing fluctuation in studio revenues after television probably contributed to the widespread acquisition of major studios by larger corporations during the 1960s and 1970s, including Paramount by Gulf & Western (1966), United Artists by Transamerica (1967), Universal by MCA (1962), and Columbia by Coca-Cola (1982). As the last column of Table 1.1 displays, most of the major studios have come to account for relatively small proportions of the total revenues of their corporate parents.[24] Even so, the fate of individual blockbuster films can apparently have a sizable impact on the income and stock prices of some conglomerates. Disappointing box office returns for *Treasure Planet* in the fall of 2002, for example, was largely blamed for a 41 percent fall in Disney's net income for the quarter.[25] MGM's avoidance of high-budget tentpole movies has been attributed to the excessive risks it would face, and related concerns have been expressed about the future of DreamWorks, given its taste for high-budget films.[26]

It remains unclear how much credit the deep pockets of media conglomerates should really be given for freeing the studios to engage in high-budget, high-risk projects with good profit potential. An especially successful period for films released by Warner Brothers—probably the industry leader in its proclivity for high-budget, "event" movies—coincided with the disastrous financial effects of the AOL–Time Warner merger in the 2000–2003 period. In this case, the film studio has been widely credited with propping up its parent during this period, rather than the other way around.[27] A similar situation occurred at Universal Pictures, which had a string of successful high-budget films and made ambitious production investments in spite of financial scandals at Vivendi, Universal's parent company at the time, that left Vivendi essentially bankrupt.[28]

The uncertainty of management, operating efficiency, and even risk-diversification effects of conglomerate ownership on movie studios leads to us assume that the studios basically stand on their own in their moviemaking decisions and in their competitive battles. Meddling from above surely takes place. Certainly, the "greater good" of conglomerate objectives can trump those of studio subsidiaries. Like other holdings of major media conglomerates, though, the movie studios appear to operate in most cases with a high degree of autonomy in their decision making.[29]

In the following pages, we thus focus on the basic economic forces of demand, technology, and competition in order to explain the market performance and the output of the movie industry.

Chapter 2

Television: A Parting of the Ways

One cannot understand the modern theatrical film industry without considering the effects that television had on it in the 1950s and 1960s. In important respects, the high-rolling, blockbuster-driven Hollywood establishment we see today was created by broadcast television.

Two well-known effects of television on the movie industry are that it devastated movie theater admissions and it eventually created an aftermarket for old movies. We focus on two related, but less obvious, effects. One is that it turned an albeit glamorous, but still rather predictable, industry into a much more high-stakes environment, in which the major studios scramble to outdo each other with ever grander and more expensive movies. The second thing television did was to radically reform the timed movie release system that studios used to extract money from movie viewers. TV sharply segmented the consumer market for theatrical movies into high-value and low-value components. Overall, television was bad for the theatrical movie business in economic terms because it drew away so many customers. The blows were softened,

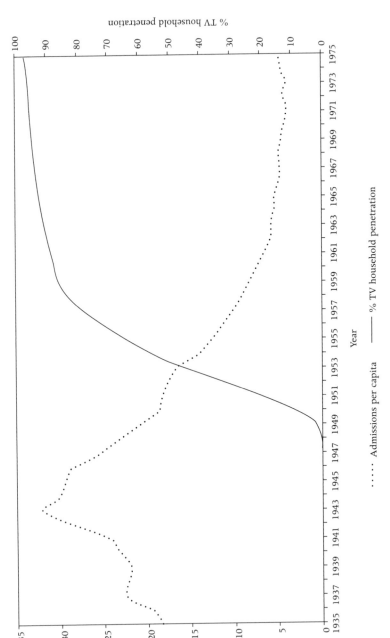

FIGURE 2.1 U.S. annual movie theater admissions per capita versus TV household penetration, 1935–1975. *Sources: International Motion Picture Almanac* (Quigley Publications, annual); *Statistical Abstract of the United States* (annual); Christopher H. Sterling, *Electronic Media: A Guide to Trends in Broadcasting and Newer Technologies, 1920–1983* (New York: Praeger, 1984).

though, by the beneficial effects of market segmentation on movie pricing and by the greater efficiency of television delivery.

The admissions decline, as shown in Figure 2.1, started before significant commercial television came on the scene. But no one denies that the rapid, coincident diffusion of broadcast TV was mostly responsible for the drastic fall in U.S. theater admissions.[1] It is sobering to note how precipitously theater attendance fell in those years. Adult per capita admissions declined from a high of about 32 per year in 1943 to a nadir of 4 per year in 1971. Inevitably, the theater audience for movies was left greatly changed.

In this chapter, we focus mainly on the period from 1948 to about 1975, a time we identify as the "broadcast television era." In 1975, HBO's satellite debut launched the "pay media era," which is the subject of Chapter 3.

Television, B Movies, and Blockbusters

Classic films remind us of the glamour and colorful figures of the old Hollywood. In fact, the movie industry of the 1930s, '40s, and into the '50s was much more in the limelight than it is today. Think of all the attention that television now attracts—not only in terms of the time one spends watching it (four hours daily per person, on average),[2] but also in terms of all the press coverage concerning TV stars and directors, mergers, violent programming, and even government policy, from V-chips to HDTV conversion. Before television overwhelmed the movies, all that attention was directed at the film industry. In those days movies, along with radio, were the only show in town—and thanks to the more dramatic impact of the visual image, movies easily won over radio. Even in the relatively boring sphere of government policy, the *United States v. Paramount Pictures* antitrust trial of the late 1940s got headlines rivaling those of *United States v. Microsoft,* and highly publicized congressional hearings on movie industry trade practices like block booking extended into the mid-1950s.[3] Much social activism was focused on movies. An effort to effectively ban double features in the state of Illinois in 1938 (opponents of the double feature argued that unacceptably poor films were paired with good films, the practice caused eyestrain and fatigue, and it was bad for kids) failed to become law only when the governor refused to sign the bill.[4]

In a sense, the movie industry of earlier days was really the movies and television of later years rolled into one. As the two industries essentially split off in the 1950s and 1960s, television co-opted a lot of entertainment that used to be the province of movies and induced theatrical film producers to sharply differentiate their products from TV programs. The result for movies was higher production values, along with greater risk and industry volatility.

Production Values in Movies and Television

In the period from the 1930s to the early 1950s, popularly known as the "studio system" era, seven or eight film production and distribution companies (mostly the same ones we have today), plus two or three long-surviving but fairly marginal studios, dominated the U.S. movie industry.[5] Together these companies typically produced somewhere between 250 and 400 films per year, and these movies were generally classified either as A or B. The A movies were basically "one-off," "custom," top-of-the-line films, like *Gone with the Wind* and *Stagecoach.* They combined the best scripts, the best directors and talent, and the best technical resources—in short, they were in the same vein as the movies produced by major Hollywood studios today. The B pictures were typically lower-budget, routinized, formula films that used mostly second-tier performers and directors. Many of the B movies were destined to be part of double feature exhibitions, usually paired with A films in their later theater runs. Actual serials, such as Columbia's *Batman* and *The Shadow,* were also produced and exhibited, often as Saturday matinees. Feature-length class B series, such as *Blondie* (28 movies) and *The Lone Wolf* (14 movies), were commonly available as well.[6]

In these years, individual studios tended to specialize in certain genres, or were known for certain qualities of movies. For example, MGM was renowned for producing the highest-quality movies, especially musicals, and their output included few B movies. RKO produced mostly cheaper movies, but was well known for its thrillers and mysteries. Warner Brothers and Universal produced many westerns and crime dramas, lots of them B's. The product lines of two minor distributors, Columbia and Universal, included a high proportion of B films. Some of the more marginal distributors, such as Republic Pictures and later American International Pictures (AIP), produced nearly all B's.

The character of many pretelevision movies, especially the worst ones, is revealed by their production process, often described as a factory system. The prevailing practice of the Hollywood studios was to engage high-level talent on long-term contracts, typically extending seven years, and to hire producers, other talent, and other agents of production, such as cinematographers and film editors, as salaried employees of the studio. Lower-quality movies tended to be made on relatively short, set production schedules, and often relied on the same major players from film to film and on recycled scripts with the most perfunctory changes. The classic example of the Hollywood B movies was the "factory westerns" produced by Warner, Columbia, and some other studios, known as "oaters" in the industry.[7] This production method—which earned the studio system label—was a form of vertical integration of production with distribution. The studios often contracted with unaffiliated individuals, such as character actors, for example, for individual movies. Mostly, though, they relied on employees or people under contract, especially for the B movies, rearranging them into different productions.

As television moved into American homes in the 1950s, all this changed. In some ways, television was adapted from radio, as Bob Hope, Milton Berle, Jack Benny, and other radio stars of the 1940s moved their weekly series from radio to television. And of course television became a creative medium in its own right with the development of new formats specific to TV. But a lot of television was essentially lifted from the movies. Serials or B-movie series found a natural home on television as weekly series. The first stars to migrate to television were the "B-movie cowboys," including Roy Rogers, Gene Autry, and Hopalong Cassidy, who started weekly TV series—some remarkably successful and long lasting—that were little different from their films.[8] By the time TV became a major commercial force in the early 1950s, the classic B movie was already in decline; but, broadly speaking, television took over the role of the B movie. Essentially, these formula-based movies were transformed into the sequential episodes of dramatic television series.[9]

While this transition was taking place, the old studio system of movie production declined and by the late 1950s had virtually disappeared. Production became vertically disintegrated from distribution as the studios abandoned salaried employment of most agents of production, as well as long-term contracting. The dominant mode of movie production became the one-off method, in which collections of individual agents of production were assembled by a separate company, which contracted with the studio to deliver a single movie. Independent production companies, such as Samuel Goldwyn Productions and many others, became prominent in Hollywood.[10]

In one sense, the factory system of production remained alive and well in Hollywood. It simply moved to television along with the B movie. From a studio's perspective, it makes sense to retain agents of production as studio employees or under long-term contracts when the same basic group of people can be reliably rearranged to produce different movies over time. This system is much less likely to be workable, though, with more creative, higher-quality one-of-a-kind productions. For those movies, the required agents of production might come from anywhere, in any combination.[11]

The weekly television series, by contrast, is the very essence of the talent-rearrangement model. Perhaps the most vivid example of this change in production was Warner Brothers. Under the leadership of Jack Warner, that studio literally converted its B-movie lot into a television production lot and adopted the same basic production-line system for cranking out weekly series, including the retainer of talent on long-term contracts.[12]

As audiences defected, Hollywood's film production volume steadily declined. The seven major companies released an average of 278 new features per year in the 1950–1954 period, but only 147 per year from 1970–1974, reaching a historical low of 85 films in 1977.[13] The main casualties were the lower-quality B movies, which were essentially taken over by television. Concurrent with the B movies' decline was the virtual demise of double features; in the mid-1930s, double bills were almost ubiquitous outside of exclusive first-run theaters, but by the late 1950s, they had practically disappeared. As mentioned, the prevailing practice was usually to pair an A movie with a B movie. As television eliminated the low-value demands, people quit staying inside theaters for so long, and the double feature died.

The movie industry that emerged from television's devastation of the old Hollywood was thus in one sense what was left over—the "high end" of the old movie industry, or the A movies. In addition, movie producers attempted to differentiate their products from television in the 1950s and 60s with Cinerama, the Todd-AO process, and production of wide-screen "spectaculars." The A movies, that is, became more elaborate. These decisions contributed to the decline in film production as investments were channeled into fewer, more expensive movies. The beginnings of Hollywood's blockbuster era are often associated with the dramatic worldwide success of Steven Spielberg's *Jaws* in 1975. Leading up to *Jaws,* though, were many precursors designed to distance movies from small-screen TV: *The Robe* (Fox, 1953), *The Ten Commandments* (Paramount, 1956), *Ben-Hur* (MGM, 1959), *Around the World in 80 Days* (United Artists, 1963), *Cleopatra* (Fox, 1963), *The Godfather* (Paramount, 1972), and a number of road-show productions that traveled the country from city to city at high prices in the 1960s.[14]

These spectaculars, as well as the more recent blockbusters, have accentuated the most important economic difference between theatrical movies and television programs, one that persists to this day: production quality. Movies are expensive and television is cheap, and the differences are extreme.

The wide cost dichotomy was established from the first days of television. The average budget for theatrical features released by Warner Brothers in 1950–1954 was reported to be $1 to $2 million.[15] The average budget for one-hour episodes of Warner's signature television series, *Warner Brothers Presents,* was approximately $50,000–$75,000 in the 1954–1955 season—roughly one tenth as much as its movies on a per-hour basis. As producers and critics were well aware, these differences were reflected in production values.[16] A $4.3 million movie of Jack Webb's *Dragnet* was produced in 1954,[17] while half-hour episodes of the successful TV series presumably cost around $25,000, the prevailing network television rate at the time. Although these contrasts were surely exacerbated in early years because of low household penetration of television (approximately 60 percent in 1955), the great differences in movie and TV program production values transcended these constraints. One result was that top movie talent could not be attracted to television, and a stigma persists today that "doing television" will lower a movie actor's prestige. The most direct contrast is in the cost of theatrical features and made-for-TV movies. In 1975, for example, after television had long achieved virtually total household penetration, these weekly two-hour films were consistently budgeted by the three networks at $775,000 each, while MPAA-produced theatrical features averaged $3.1 million.[18] There have recently been some highly publicized, unusually expensive TV series, such as the $10 million per episode licensing fee reported for *Friends*.[19] But by the turn of the new century, the average cost of a one-hour broadcast television drama program was in the $1 to $2 million range, in comparison to over $50 million for MPAA-produced feature films.[20]

In spite of these extreme contrasts, broadcast television has of course one overwhelming economic attribute in its favor: it's free. Given this fact, the challenge of making a trip to the movie theater more attractive than watching television required extreme measures on the part of moviemakers. Judging from the persistent decline in theater admissions into the 1970s, their efforts were only moderately successful at best.

The attempts to differentiate movies from television during the period of the 1950s to the 1970s apparently resulted in higher-production-quality movies, at least on average. In a competitive industry, trends in studio theatrical film production investments are bound to be roughly reflected by trends in studio revenues from the distribution of these movies. Average world theater rentals per film for the six major studios for which continuous data could be obtained rose from $1.9 million in the 1950–1954 period to $6.1 million for the 1970–1974 period, a 93 percent increase in real dollar terms (CPI-deflated).[21] That increase understates the rise in total studio revenues per film because television revenues, which had come to account for 15 to 20 percent of total studio worldwide revenues from theatrical features by the mid-1970s, are not included.[22] The implied increase in studio costs per film over this period may simply reflect the dropping of lower-quality movies from studio production slates, which (as we discuss below) undoubtedly occurred over this period. The studio per-film revenue increases, however, are consistent with abundant anecdotal evidence of studio attempts to outspend television by stretching the limits on top-end features in the 1950s and '60s.[23]

The Transition to Higher Risk and Market Volatility

Changes in movie production risk and industry stability from the individual studio's perspective are illustrated in Figure 2.2 for the 1949–1975 period.[24] The trend line shows the average year-to-year variation in worldwide theatrical film rentals earned by individual major studios, relative to the overall change in rentals for all the companies combined. (See Appendix B for details.) From the late 1940s until at least the early 1960s, studio revenues were remarkably steady from year to year, suggesting a predictable industry environment.[25] During that period, film rental revenues of the individual major studios deviated on average by no more than 13 percent from the change in total worldwide rentals of all eight (later seven) studios combined. In the 1960s, this average annual variation was much as 21 percent; and by the early 1970s, annual

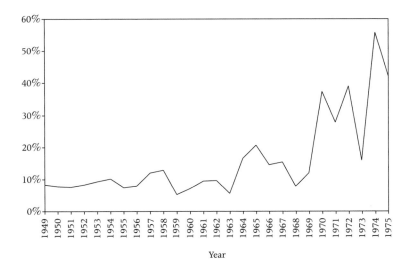

FIGURE 2.2 Stability of world theatrical rentals, average percentage variation around the mean annual change, major distributors, 1948–1975. (For sources, see Appendix B.)

deviations from the average had become erratic, reaching 40 percent to over 50 percent in some years.

The company-by-company financial records (Appendix B) show that the studios were broadly affected by these changes in the risk environment. The worldwide theatrical revenues of MGM, for example, never varied outside the range of $98 billion to $110 billion from 1948 until 1960, but fluctuated between $80 billion and $140 billion in the 1967–1974 period. In the most extreme case, Warner revenues stayed between $63 billion and $75 billion from 1948 to 1960, but moved erratically between $64 billion and $276 billion in 1967–1974. The sharper fluctuations can often be identified with one or two hit movies: Fox's *MASH* and *Patton in* 1970–1971 led to a 29 percent revenue increase for 1971, followed by a 25 percent fall the next; Warner's *The Exorcist* in 1973–1974 led to an 80 percent rise for 1974, followed by a 27 percent fall the next. These fluctuations in the late 1960s and 1970s thus began to reflect the blockbuster-driven uncertainty of the modern theatrical film industry.

How did television contribute to this change? Certainly the studios took many production risks in earlier days. Performance of the B pictures or lower-budget films, however, were likely more predictable in the marketplace than the higher-end theatrical film productions that were left to the studios after the advent of television. Statistical evidence based on the actual financial records of at least one studio, Warner Brothers, over the 1921–1941 period supports this conjecture, although its reported differences in profit variability by budget level were not extreme.[26]

Another reason for the increased volatility was simply a sustained decline in the number of movies produced by the major studios. From averages of 30 to 40 releases per studio in the early 1950s, output declined to the 10 to 20 range in the 1970s. Even if variability of returns to individual movies did not change, performance on a studio-by-studio basis will be more erratic when fewer tosses of the coin are made. Finally, as the studios dropped lower-quality films and made conscious decisions to shift resources into fewer, higher-budget movies to compete with TV, they put more of their eggs in single, high-cost baskets.[27] At a cost of $17 million (including $5.5 million for the story rights alone), Warner's production of *My Fair Lady* (1964) was said to have single-handedly put the studio into the red while its filming took place.[28] In perhaps the most extreme case, the $37 million cost of *Cleopatra* (1963) apparently absorbed a very large proportion of Twentieth Century Fox's production budget and nearly bankrupted the studio.[29] The credibility of these anecdotes is supported by statistical evidence that the skew of domestic box office revenues (which are inevitably related to production spending on average) strongly shifted toward a relatively few top-performing films from the mid-1940s to the mid-1960s.[30]

Thus the high-rolling, blockbuster era of movie production was ushered in. Everyone is fascinated with risk—the thrill of winning or losing. Add to that the inherent drama of the movie industry and the glamorous characters involved, and the public's adrenaline runs. It is return, though, not risk, that most preoccupies the movie studios, because high risk can be managed. As we saw in Chapter 1, most of the major studios were acquired or merged into larger conglomerate organizations in the 1960s and 1970s; these moves presumably led to lower borrowing costs and to more stable stock prices. The practice of "laying off" risk by bringing in outside investors apparently has also become much more common in the past two or three decades. "Split rights" and other cofinancing deals, in which the studios share risk with rival studios, the movie's producers, or foreign distributors, have became more prevalent as well.[31] These strategies accomplish basically the same risk-reduction purpose as conglomerate ownership.

The high uncertainty of movie production has implications for the behavior of movie studios and for the types of movies that get produced (subjects we return to later). The effect that television had on movie production values, and the resulting segmentation of movie and television audiences that we discuss later in this chapter, however, are more significant to our story of Hollywood's transition to prosperity.

The *Paramount* Decision

The effects of the great changes in movie industry structure and trade practices that the *Paramount* case mandated (see Chapter 1) have been studied extensively, and a wide range of industry outcomes have been attributed or related to that decision. These include the entry of independent producers, distributors, and theater operators after the decision; the decline of the B picture and the double feature (due to the prohibition on block booking by the defendants, and because vertical disintegration of distribution and exhibition removed "guaranteed markets" for bad movies); the demise of the old studio system (due in turn to vertical disintegration and the decline of block-booked B pictures); increasing production quality of movies (due to vertical disintegration, the decline of B pictures, and breakdown of the cartel that served to exclude independent producers, distributors, and theaters); and the greater volatility of market shares (due to vertical disintegration of distribution and exhibition, and breakdown of the cartel's control of markets).[32]

Though not all have agreed, plausible evidence has been advanced that *Paramount* lowered barriers to entry by independent distributors and exhibitors.[33] Nevertheless, the most significant economic changes that we have discussed in this chapter—the decline of B pictures and double features, the increase in the volatility of industry market shares, the transformation of the old studio system, and an increase in movies' production quality—can all be explained by television. *Paramount* may have facilitated these changes, for example, by stimulating industry competition. As we argued in Chapter 1, *Paramount* plausibly opened the way to all three of the minors—Columbia, Universal, and United Artists—joining the five majors in the big league.

It is hard to imagine, though, that the year-to-year volatility of studio revenues, changes in the nature of the film product, modes of industry production, or the entry of independent producers had much to do with *Paramount*. The defendants were not accused of attempting to coordinate production investment decisions, and the government presented no evidence at the trial to support such an allegation. In any case, it would not have been in the *Paramount* cartel's interest to curtail the market success of a box office hit at the expense of a worse-performing movie offered by another member of the cartel. So it seems implausible that growing year-to-year instability of box office market shares after the early 1950s would be related to the legal decision of *Paramount* in a substantial way. Vertical disintegration of production and distribution was also not mandated by the Court, so it is not evident how the demise of the old studio system could be related to these legal events.

Finally, the decline of B pictures and double features, the move to more elaborate production values, and the higher quality of the exhibition experience are also hard to connect persuasively to *Paramount*. For example, there are viable economic models that explain how the studios might have profitably tied their B pictures to their A movies as a device to exclude from the market independent distributors with only B's to sell.[34] It is a stretch, though, to argue that the market for B pictures *existed* because of block booking.

In its more than fifty years of commercial experience, television programming has now greatly evolved in its own right. The origins of the theatrical movie industry's transition into the expensive and unpredictable high-end segment of the entertainment market, though, are rooted in the early development of broadcast television.

Television and the Price Discrimination System

The story of the studios' initial reluctance, then embrace of television as an exhibition medium for theatrical features in the mid-1950s is well chronicled.[35] From its first tiny contribution to distributor income recorded in 1949, television went on to become the second most important source of revenue to movie distributors until pay television surpassed it in the late 1970s and early '80s.

The overall financial effects of television on the movie industry were negative by any reasonable measure. Between the 1947–1949 and 1973–1975, consumer spending on theater tickets declined sharply, from .88 percent of all U.S. consumer spending to only .20 percent.[36] In spite of welcome new revenues from television exhibition of old theatrical films, which by the early 1970s accounted for over 25 percent of studio income from domestic sources, total studio revenue from distribution of theatrical films in the United States still fell, from .14 percent of total economic activity in 1947–1949 (as measured by GDP) to .05 percent in 1973–1975. All things considered, though, the studios still fared quite a bit better in the theater market than the 72 percent fall in annual U.S. admissions (from 3.4 billion to 1.0 billion) over the 1947–1975 period would suggest. In CPI-deflated terms, consumer spending on theater tickets fell by only 42 percent, and total distributor revenue from theaters by only 19 percent. The economic blows from television were thus cushioned by more than television's income alone. How was this possible?

The answer is fundamental to the nature of market segmentation and price discrimination. To explain the mitigating effects of television in these terms, we must first set out the economics of the old movie release system that it changed. The intertemporal price discrimination model we describe in the following pages will be a useful lens through which to interpret a variety of movie industry trade practices and developments to the present day.

The Old Theater System and Price Discrimination

When the now classic John Wayne movie *Stagecoach* opened at the plush Roosevelt Theater in downtown Chicago on February 25, 1939, it began a complex progression through eleven separate tiers, or runs, of Chicago-area movie theaters that continued until early June of that year, for a total theater life of fourteen weeks. The Roosevelt was in those days one of seven large and luxurious downtown Chicago Loop district theaters which premiered "A-class" theatrical features. After a two-week run at the Roosevelt, *Stagecoach* disappeared from the market for twenty-one days. Then, on March 31, it reopened at the Granada, the Uptown, and the Tivoli, three downtown "A pre-release" theaters just outside the Loop, for a one-week stint. Then it went directly to four more Chicago theaters, one on each of the North, West, East, and South sides of Chicago, for another week. After an eighth, a ninth, and a tenth week at other sets of Chicago theaters, *Stagecoach* opened on May 10 simultaneously at twenty-one "general neighborhood release" theaters, most of them in the Chicago suburbs. After only a three-day run in this group, the movie moved through four more sets of suburban or neighborhood theaters, and was last seen (at least for that year) on June 8 at the Community and the Coed, two obscure seventh-week, general-release movie theaters somewhere in the suburbs of Chicago. For all but its Loop first run, *Stagecoach* was paired with a variety of other current, but mostly forgettable, movies, including *Cafe Society* and *My Son Is a Criminal,* as part of double-feature attractions.[37]

Stagecoach's theater journey was typical of "A-class" features released in major cities by the studios at the time. As movies made their way from downtown Chicago in wider and wider circles away from the city center, the admission price was reduced, from 75 cents at the Loop theaters, to 50 cents in A-prerelease, to 40 cents in the third tier, and so on, finally reaching 20 cents or even less at the end. In most of those cases, the double billing meant that the viewer got two movies for one price, though one of them was usually a less desirable B film. The system was not entirely rigid. Although all movies were still withdrawn from the market for two to three weeks following their Loop first run, the length of the Loop run itself generally varied from one week to as much as four weeks, depending on audience response. "Held over by popular demand!" was a common phrase on the ad copy in newspaper movie sections. Also, very popular movies were sometimes later re-released midway in the sequence after their initial run.

In smaller cities, of course, there were fewer tiers in the theater sequence; the smallest towns would have only one. Also, smaller cities and towns often had to wait until prints became available from the waning major-city release. And in the larger cities, "B-class" movies typically opened at a later stage of the sequence, usually general neighborhood release, and went down from there. Or they were relegated to second billing in double features to begin with. Apart from such variations in detail, though, the sequential price-tiered exhibition system was the rule of the day.

This old movie release sequence appears to have the essential, underlying economic element of price discrimination.[38] That is, the system is designed to induce consumers to pay for movies according to their willingness and ability to do so. Higher-value consumers were attracted to travel to the first runs in downtown Chicago, while lower-value consumers (those with less interest or money to spend) waited for the more convenient later runs, many of which were in suburban areas.

Price discrimination schemes are common in many industries. The idea appeals to any business for evident reasons. As long as the marginal cost of producing and selling a product is at least covered, making another sale is worthwhile. The challenge is how to avoid leaving money on the table—that is, to charge the highest-value customers the most they are willing to pay. The key is to devise an effective way to *segment the market*—which basically just means preventing the high-value viewers from taking advantage of the lowest prices. Often segmentation is not easy. Once customers show up at your local hardware store, for example, the merchant would be hard pressed to charge one shopper $3 and another $2 for the same screwdriver.

Businesses thus rely on a great variety of tricks to segment markets in order to price discriminate. A simple one for the hardware store is to occasionally put screwdrivers regularly priced at $3 on sale for $2. The more price conscious, low-value consumers will tend to watch the newspaper for sales, while less-price-conscious consumers will just walk in and (most of the time) pay the $3. The familiar airline practice of charging far lower prices to people willing to make reservations more than one or two weeks in advance, or to stay over on a Saturday night, is a well-known device for separating business travelers, who tend to have a high willingness to pay, from low-value vacation travelers. Automobile manufacturers discriminate by offering expensive models with high-markup amenities to high-value buyers and stripped-down, low-markup models to low-value buyers. Software retailers discriminate by offering rebates, knowing that only low-value customers are willing to go though the complicated process of cutting out the cardboard packaging containing the bar code, filling out a microscopic form with address and other information, mailing all the materials in, and then waiting months for the rebate to actually arrive. Even then, the customer needs to be vigilant in order to spot the rebate check, which often resembles junk mail.

Fundamentally, all of these schemes depend on successful segmentation of high-value from low-value consumers. They simply use different devices for doing so. The dominant device in the Chicago movie-release system was time. Those with an intense desire to see *Stagecoach*, and the cash to back it up, went to the Loop, while those with lower-value demands decided to wait. A second segmentation device in the old movie system was geography, or distance. High-value patrons were willing to travel into the central city, while those with low value would choose not to incur this time and expense. A third segmentation device in the movie case was the quality of exhibition. First-run Loop theaters in Chicago were lavishly appointed and used state-of-the-art equipment. At the far end of the sequence were ten- or twenty-cent theaters with few comforts. In general, higher-value consumers will pay more for higher-quality products, so the differences in theater quality served to reinforce the segmentation of high- and low-value consumers.[39]

Like all price discrimination schemes, the movie system was necessarily imperfect and the parameters were set at compromise levels. The "clearances," notably the two- to three-week disappearance from the Chicago market after a movie's exclusive first run, provided extra encouragement for patrons to attend the most expensive showings. But if the lag were too long, the freshness of the movie would diminish and the impact of the initial advertising campaign would fade. Also, the distributor clearly is interested in collecting rental income (which is generally paid when the exhibition actually occurs) as soon as possible. Wherever the clearance was set, it could never be ideal for extracting maximum value from all patrons. Also, price discrimination was not the sole motive behind the release sequence. A lavish display of publicity, including personal appearances by the major stars in big city premiers, klieg lights and all, would be used to generate downstream demand for later runs. The timed sequence also allowed word of mouth to have its effect on risk-averse patrons unwilling to attend a movie in advance of hearing trusted personal advice. It further allowed distributors to adjust their marketing strategies depending on initial consumer response.

Television and the Movie Release System

As television spread like a wildfire, the old system of movie release crumbled. Later-run exhibitions vanished. In Chicago, for example, the usual number of stages in the pattern had been reduced to three or four by the mid-1970s. Nonexclusive, "limited engagement" first runs became more common. In Los Angeles in the 1970s, for example, major films were often released simultaneously in as many as sixty or seventy "neighborhood first run" theaters spread throughout the region. These often followed an exclusive "showcase" first run in the Westwood or Hollywood areas; but for lower-quality movies, there was often no prior run. The whole theatrical exhibition sequence took less and less time, usually ending in four to six weeks or less. Time clearances between theater runs essentially disappeared. Concurrent with these changes, a far greater number of theaters moved up to first-run status. While less than 10 percent of theaters, for example, had first-run status in Chicago, New York, Atlanta, and other major cities in the 1930s and '40s, often more than half were first run in major cities by the early 1970s. In suburban areas and smaller communities, most or all of the theaters had attained first-run status (exclusive and nonexclusive) by this time.[40]

These great shifts in theatrical exhibition patterns were driven not only by television's reduction of demand but by the massive population movement after World War II from cities to the suburbs. As those demographic shifts took place, urban theaters went into material decline along with the city centers they were in, and were replaced by smaller suburban theaters, many of them in the multiplex buildings that dominate theater exhibition today. Overall, though, the number of theater screens declined steadily, from over 18,000 in 1948 to a post–World War II low of about 11,000 screens in 1967.[41]

Although the general decline of theater exhibition in this period obviously reflected the devastating effects of television on demand for movies as a whole, two mitigating benefits emerged. First, television became the "last window" for movie exhibition. Second, admission prices rose substantially, along with an increase in the share of box office revenues that theaters remitted back to studios.

Television as the Last Window

The major studios had started selling old movies to TV from their vaults by the mid-1950s, but by the mid-1960s routine exhibition of recent theatrical features on the three commercial broadcast networks (CBS, NBC, and ABC, which in those days attracted 90 percent of all TV watching) became a mainstay of the networks' prime-time schedules.[42] Through the 1970s, nearly every major theatrical film received a major network television release after its theater release. In the 1960s and 1970s, usually two or three "Movie of the Week" prime-time showings of a given film were spread over a two- to three-year interval. Then the movie was typically syndicated to independent television stations, allowing perhaps a dozen more showings over the following three to five years.

Although the theatrical exhibition cycle had become much shorter, there was an extremely long clearance, or window, between the end of a movie's theatrical exhibition and its television exhibition. An analysis of release dates for theatrical features that were exhibited on broadcast television between September 1970 and August 1980 showed an average window length of 46.1 months, or nearly 4 years, although during this interval the average window fell steadily from almost 5 years (57.6 months) in the 1970–1972 period to a little over 3 years in the 1978–1980 period (38.3 months).[43] There was a great deal of variation in this interval. Near the high end, *Ben-Hur* (1959) was not released to television until 1971. Near the low end, *Serpico* (1974) waited only 19 months for television exhibition. While a few movies had shorter windows, release in less than 18 months from theatrical release was quite rare in those days. A number of the longer windows, such as in the case of *Ben-Hur,* involved a theatrical rerelease during the window interval.

What explains the changes in the theatrical release sequence after the advent of television? First, to the distributor's advantage, television replaced the later-run theaters in the exhibition sequence with a much more efficient distribution system than those brick-and-mortar theaters could ever deliver. According to Federal Communications Commission (FCC) data, the cost per TV household of operating the entire national television broadcasting system in 1975, including all local station operations but excluding programming costs, was less than 2 cents per hour (or a delivery cost of 3 to 4 cents per movie per person)—practically nothing when compared to theater exhibition.[44]

Major theatrical features exhibited on the networks in the 1970s typically attracted 15 to 20 percent of the prime-time television audience, which amounted to a total of 20 to 25 million people—several times as many people as would usually see the film in a theater.[45] Thus, free television vastly increased the audience for most movies. Television's distribution efficiency, however, was accompanied by an extremely inefficient pricing system. Television advertisers are basically interested only in body counts, though they attach somewhat higher values to people with certain demographic characteristics. Those advertisers will pay only so much to expose their messages to viewers regardless of whether or not they are high- or low-value customers in terms of their willingness to pay.

A summary of how television changed the economics of studio price discrimination is illustrated in Table 2.1. Though the data are not precise, the overall effect is not in doubt. While theater attendance shrunk dramatically, theatrical movie viewing on television went up so much that the total per capita consumption of theatrical movies by U.S. adults more than doubled. The importance of theaters in the total share of theatrical film viewing thus shrunk to a small fraction of what it had been before TV. But by the time the broadcaster's share was taken out, the studio was paid barely more than a penny per viewer, a tiny fraction of

Table 2.1   Prices, revenue, and viewing of theatrical feature films, 1948 and 1975

Year	Average realized price per viewing	Gross studio revenue per viewing	Annual number of U.S. viewings per capita
1948			
Theaters	$0.44	$ 0.10	30–35
Total			30–35
1975			
Theaters	$2.05	$0.67	5
Broadcast networks	0	$\left\{0.01-0.02\right\}$	23
Independent stations	0		35–45
Total			65–75

Source: See Appendix D.

the revenue from a theater patron. The per capita revenue to studios from TV was so tiny that theaters still brought in nearly four fifths of distributor income from the domestic market. (See Appendix C.) Of course, many of the theatrical movies being watched on television were first made and released before TV was introduced. Virtually all of the network showings, and an increasingly large fraction of the syndicated movies, though, were by the 1970s current-release movies following the theaters-to-TV release pattern.[46] Under the circumstances, it is no surprise that studios set a broadcast window that was so long and protective of theatrical exhibition.

Many people preferred watching films on television to going out. Television thus provided a degree of product differentiation that increased the sum total of movie consumption via its appeal to new consumers. In this way, television extended the reach of movie viewing in a meaningful way, essentially creating a different product (the movie and the exhibition medium combined) for consumers. To that extent, the audiences for movie theaters and television were naturally segmented.

Probably for most potential theatergoers, though, watching a movie in theaters versus on television was a substitution. To that extent, television facilitated audience segmentation by distributors based on quality differences between the dramatic experience of theatrical exhibition and the commercial-ridden experience of watching movies on a small TV screen, which until the mid-1960s was in black and white for most people. Basically, television took the place of the shabbier sub-run theaters, which in earlier days had served to segment movie audiences in terms of product quality. With television, people having a higher preference for quality continued to be attracted to theaters and those with a tolerance for low quality waited for the television showings.

Admission Prices, Changing Demand, and the Rental Rate

After keeping close pace with the general rate of inflation since the mid-1930s, average ticket prices headed sharply upward around 1948 and between that date and their historical peak in 1972 rose almost twice as fast as the general rate of inflation (Figure 2.3).[47] Thus, while the total number of theater admissions fell to approximately one third their former level from 1948 to 1975, theater box office receipts fell by less than 50 percent in inflation-adjusted terms. The rise in prices has been widely noted, and is all the more remarkable because it occurred during a period of declining consumer demand. As we discussed earlier, the prevalence of double features also declined from their near ubiquity outside of first-run exhibitions to negligible levels. Thus, fewer movies were offered for the higher prices.

The most prominent explanation of rising prices in the economic lit-

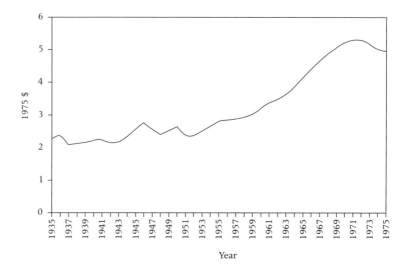

FIGURE 2.3   Real theater admission price trends, United States, 1935–1975. (Realized average admission prices deflated by the CPI. *Sources:* MPAA; *International Motion Picture Almanac;* U.S. Bureau of Labor Statistics.)

erature has been that they reflected a rising quality of the theatergoing experience as theater crowds thinned out due to declining capacity utilization.[48] This seems to us an odd explanation. During this period of falling demand and dim hopes for the future, the number of theater screens in operation declined by a third. When the multiplex theater building boom began in the 1970s, most of the older theaters that remained became more and more shabby and found themselves in declining neighborhoods.[49] The newer theaters that were built tended to be much smaller and more modest. These are not trends that suggest an enhanced viewing experience. Also, more recent research shows there is a "contagion effect": crowds tend to enhance one's enjoyment of entertainment events.[50]

The price discrimination model offers a more plausible explanation for rising ticket prices. One aspect of the change was probably just mechanical. As the old price discrimination system crumbled and the number of stages became fewer, it was the lower-priced exhibitions that were eliminated from the market—leaving only the higher-priced first and second runs to figure into the admission price average. In the pretelevision era, movie distributors earned half or less of their total rental income from first-run theaters.[51] By the mid-1970s, exclusive and nonexclusive first-run theaters probably accounted for 80 to 90 percent of total distributor receipts. Thus, the low-priced later-run theaters were replaced by free television, leaving the higher-priced market intact.

It is also likely that as free television took away the low-value, more price-conscious movie consumers, it left a core of high-value, less price-conscious theatergoers, allowing theater owners to raise ticket prices. This idea is consistent with the changing nature of the film product and the film audience. Along with the industry's B movies and other mediocre productions, television took over the movie theater's habitual consumer. Into the 1950s, a large proportion of the movie audience went to a theater at least once a week and often sat through a three- to four-hour double feature presentation. People often attended on certain days of the week, making a choice of movies among whatever happened to be available. Or they would regularly patronize a certain local theater and accept what was delivered that week. This type of behavior is similar to the standard model of television watching in recent years—except, of course, that people spend far more time watching TV because it's free.

The more cynical film critics of that day echoed the famous "vast wasteland" criticism of broadcast television that Newton Minow delivered in 1961, and that broadcast television has still not entirely shaken.

Consider, for example, these comments on movies in the years around 1950:

> The [motion picture] product must have no special quality, it must be average, because it is offered to a large, fairly homogeneous group of buyers, who would no more accept an unusual picture under the familiar trademarks than they would accept an occasional bar of green soap in an Ivory wrapper.[52]

> The average mental age of audiences has been worked out by one producer at $13\frac{1}{2}$ years and he shapes his films accordingly.[53]

> Cinema audiences are conditioned to like what they get, and even though the more critical film fan may despise some of the twice weekly syrup ladled out to him, he has caught the habit.[54]

And this observation, from 1957:

> It is the small local houses that have suffered. For they have lost the "habituals," those patrons who regularly went to the movies several times per week regardless of what was being shown.[55]

By the 1960s, the television's habit had become totally entrenched in America, and at least until the 1980s and 1990s, most critics shifted their hostility to small-screen fare. The routine, frequent attendance behavior of the pretelevision theater audience implies a price responsive, or price-elastic, audience member on the margin. That is, frequent theatergoers were more likely to shift their patronage to other theaters or to other movies if the price fell. When this low-value segment of the theater audience was absorbed by television, theater owners could accommodate a less price-responsive audience member who selected films with more regard to content.

Besides admission prices, the percentage share of total box office receipts that distributors collected from theaters (called the "rental rate") also rose between the late 1940s to the mid-1970s. The indicated rise in Table 2.1 was from 23 percent in 1948 ($.10/$.44) to 33 percent in 1975 ($.67/$2.05). That increase further cushioned the negative effects of television on distributor revenues. This rental rate increase began during the early 1950s and was a subject of attention in congressional hearings in 1956 and in later economic analyses.[56]

One explanation for this trend offered in a 1958 economic study was that prior to the divorcement of theaters from distribution, vertically integrated firms made accounting transfers that underrepresented the rental rates that would have been set by the market.[57] That is possible although, as we discuss later, the upward trend in the rate proved to be sustained well after divorcement was complete in the late 1950s, eventually reaching about 50 percent by the 1990s. Another explanation offered was that the lower court's institution of competitive bidding by theaters forced rates up.[58] Competitive bidding by theaters proved to be short lived and ineffective, though, and has apparently never accounted for more than a very small percentage of total transactions in the theater market.[59]

In searching for an alternative explanation, consider that the rental rate is really just an accounting ratio. The average rate for the industry in a given year is by definition the ratio of total producer-distributor

expenses plus producer-distributor profits (the numerator) to total theater box office revenues (the denominator). The latter consists of theater operating expenses plus profits in addition to the money paid back
to distributors. Thus, for example, the rental rate could rise if distributor marketing expenses were to increase relative to those of theaters, or
if there were other cost (or profit) shifts over time.

Viewed from the accounting-ratio perspective, a rise in the rental
rate from the late 1940s to the 1970s seems especially curious because
theater capacity utilization fell significantly during that time,[60] implying higher theater costs per patron, which would in turn lead to a fall
in the rental rate. Rental rates might also have risen because more intense theater competition shifted bargaining power from theaters to
studios. During this period, though, times were hard for both industry
branches.[61]

An alternative explanation for the rise in rental rates follows from
the price discrimination model. That is, theatrical exhibition became
more cost efficient as television eliminated the lower-priced runs in
lower-quality theaters. Before television, average rental rates were consistently higher in earlier-run theaters. In 1946, for example, Chicago
Loop first-run theaters owned by Balaban & Katz paid an average of
31.7 percent of box office revenues to distributors, but outlying sec-
ond- and later-run theaters paid only 24.4 percent.[62] Before television,
distributors were motivated to completely exhaust theater demand by
releasing films to lower and lower priced theaters until the marginal
contribution of the last exhibition just covered incremental distribution and exhibition costs. When more efficient distribution via television offered an alternative to later theater runs, distributors considered
the interdependent demand between theater and television audiences
and had an incentive to remove a film before the lowest value demands,
served by relatively inefficient theaters, were exhausted.

The shift toward more efficient movie exhibition systems has apparently contributed to further rises in the rental rate during the pay media era. We take up that subject in the following chapter, and we consider how newer movie delivery systems have furthered the multimedia market segmentation process that broadcast TV began.

Chapter 3

The Pay Media: A Shower of Money

How have the Hollywood studios managed to use pay television, video, and other direct payment media so successfully in the United States? It would be easy to say simply that these technologies have expanded the market for movies; that they provide more choices, plus flexibility and control, for the consumer; and that these new media appeal to different demographic groups.

The pay media have indeed done these things, but we would not be saying anything new to make these points. Our focus is rather on the economic performance of the studios as sellers of movies. To a large extent, the pay media have been extraordinarily lucrative for the studios because they have improved the studios' ability to segment markets and price discriminate—that is, to extract money more efficiently from people according to their willingness to pay. In this chapter, we use the price discrimination model developed in Chapter 2 to show how an explosion in the variety of these pay media has dramatically changed the movie release system and enhanced its efficiency. After outlining the changes in movie release patterns and pricing that have taken place since the 1970s, we examine the economics of pay television and then home video systems. As we do so, we identify basic assumptions about consumer behavior that are necessary for intertemporal and product-quality segmentation to be used profitably.

Evolution of the Modern Release System

The pay media era began with the commercial emergence of monthly subscription ("premium") television channels. The first of the pay media, these channels proliferated and gained acceptance in the late 1970s after the 1975 satellite launch of HBO, eventually counting over two fifths of U.S. TV households among their subscribers.[1] Pay-per-view (PPV) systems became commercially practical shortly afterward. Now supplemented by "true" video-on-demand (VOD), so-called à la carte systems are available to the majority of cable and direct broadcast satellite (DBS) subscribers, but at this writing remain of minor economic significance. The growth of the home video industry, though nominally launched with the first Sony videocassette recorder in 1976, was slower to gain popularity than pay TV. But as VCR household penetration grew from about 4 percent in 1980 to over 75 percent by the mid-1990s, prerecorded cassette rentals and sales exploded. Beginning with the first significant diffusion of digital video disc (DVD) players in about 1997, the DVD software revolution has followed, with household penetration of DVD players rapidly heading toward saturation levels by the mid-2000s.

To a great extent, theatrical movies drive these media. In spite of the notoriety of original series like HBO's *The Sopranos* and *Sex in the City,* over four fifths of premium subscription channel viewing is for feature films, the great majority of those theatrical. Over two thirds of all prere-corded video use, and about two fifths of all PPV and VOD spending, is for theatrical features.[2]

The economic results of the pay media boom are reflected in con-sumer spending statistics. In 1975, Americans spent $2.1 billion for movie theater tickets (up from the historical nadir in 1971 of $1.4 bil-lion). In 2004, consumers spent about $9.6 billion on theater tickets, $9.3 billion on premium subscription movie channels and PPV/VOD movie purchases, and $20.3 billion on video sales and rentals of feature films, for a combined total of $39.1 billion.[3] Of course, much general economic growth and inflation has taken place in that quarter century–plus. But movie media spending as a percentage of all U.S. consumption expenditure has more than doubled (from .21 percent in 1975 to .52 in 2003), and the increase as a percentage of total recreational spending has been nearly as great.[4]

Our interest in this chapter is less in consumer spending on movies than in the increased movie production resources that spending has provided to the studios. A picture of how Hollywood's domestic reve-nues have expanded since 1970 is displayed in Figure 3.1. The graph in-cludes income to U.S. studios from distribution of theatrical feature films to all domestic movie media, deflated by the Consumer Price In-dex.[5] (For notes on sources, see Appendix C.)

The most remarkable feature of this figure is that while some media have fared better than others, revenues from pay TV, video, theaters, basic cable, and even broadcast television have essentially just stacked on top of one another. This "stacking" phenomenon is evidence of ef-fective market segmentation, the main prerequisite for successful price discrimination. The end result is that from 1975 to 2003, domestic movie studio revenues as a fraction of overall U.S. economic activity, as measured by GDP, increased fourfold (.05 percent to .20 percent),

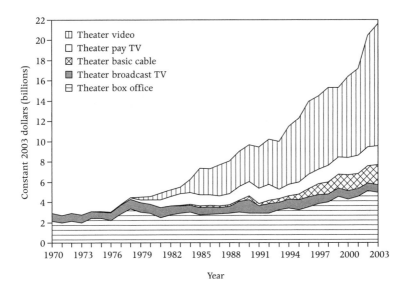

FIGURE 3.1 U.S. theatrical distributor revenue from domestic sources, constant $, 1970–2003. (For sources, see Appendix C.)

reversing the decline the industry suffered in the broadcast television era.

How did the old multitiered theater release system evolve into the multimedia release sequence typical of major films in the mid-2000s? The six main theatrical feature window periods are illustrated in Figure 3.2. The film begins its life in theaters, a market that is usually exhausted within one to three months. Sub-run theaters still exist, but they play a very minor economic role. Since the late 1990s, though, the huge-screen IMAX theaters have begun to emerge as a distinct market segment. At least until 2003, IMAX release has been a few weeks after standard theater release.[6] Except for fairly unimportant airline and hotel PPV showings (which, along with military, college, and other nontheatrical types of release, usually open and close within about a month), the typical movie is left completely out of circulation until the

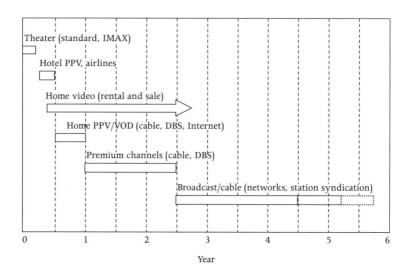

FIGURE 3.2   Typical domestic theatrical release sequence, early to mid-2000s. (Source: author's compilation from trade literature.)

fourth or fifth month, when it appears in stores for both DVD and VHS sale and rental. Release on cable or DBS pay-per-view networks, such as iN DEMAND, generally follows about 45 days after home video release. Emerging from experimental stages, VOD release to multichannel media and on the Internet (via *movielink.com,* for example) has sometimes preceded, but generally shares, the home PPV window. Then, about one year after their theatrical release, movies appear on HBO, Showtime, or other monthly subscription premium cable channels. Subscription video-on-demand (SVOD), which allows subscribers to select precise viewing times for movies included in basically the same monthly menu, is an emerging market segment within this window. At about the two- to three-year mark, the premium channel window ends, and often after a "back window holdback" of a few months, the film may appear on one of the four major national broadcast networks (ABC, CBS, NBC, and

Fox), followed by release on cable networks. Commonly, though, the movie is licensed directly to basic cable networks like TBS or TNT, or syndicated to local broadcast stations, at the two- to three-year mark. Broadcast or basic cable contracts usually last for several years, and by the time its cycle is ended, a film may be anywhere from five to fifteen or more years old.

There are many variations to this pattern, and as we discuss in Chapter 4, a movement to shorter video windows after 2002 has been condensing the process in general. But this sequence—theaters–video–PPV/VOD–premium channel–broadcast/basic cable—is currently followed by the great majority of significant theatrical features in the United States. A few very successful films, such as some of Disney's animated classics, have never been on broadcast television, but are rereleased in theaters or recycled through PPV or premium networks indefinitely. More typically, better movies do appear at some point on broadcast television or the basic cable networks, but are then recycled through part or all of the sequence. After they complete their initial broadcast/basic cable run, many better films end up shifting over time between premium cable networks and broadcast television indefinitely. And as any late-night-TV addict knows, even Hollywood's worst efforts often show up on independent broadcast stations or basic cable networks decades after they are made. Another similarity to the old release system is that lower-quality products, among them direct-to-video, made-for-PPV, made-for-pay, made-for-(basic) cable, and made-for-broadcast features, start at their designated medium and flow down from there (though frequently with an upstream video release first).

Although the initial pecking order of theatrical movie media in the first two or three years of the release sequence is fairly consistent, there is a good deal of film-to-film variation in the timing of these windows.

The regularity of the sequence in terms of window order and timing is a topic to which we return in Chapter 4.

A look at how the modern release sequence appears to be a price discrimination device is displayed in Table 3.1. The first column indicates average retail prices per transaction. The second column translates these "raw" prices into realized retail prices paid per individual viewing, based on survey data showing the average (or, in the case of video, the median) number of individuals who actually end up watching a movie as a result of a single transaction (for details on the calculations and sources, see Appendix D). The statistics in Table 3.1 are only estimates, however, and there are tremendous variations across consumers for all the movie media except theaters. Those variations occur because of great differences in the actual number of people who watch a rented or purchased video or a PPV exhibition, the number of movies that a premium channel subscriber decides to watch, and so on. Also, prices are difficult to define toward the end of the sequence. Premium network subscriptions are usually sold together with basic networks and other programming, and while watching broadcast stations with an antenna is free, most people watch them as part of a basic cable or DBS subscription.

Elements of the same market segmentation devices used in the old theater system are recognizable in this economic picture of the modern release system. Retail prices per transaction are a motley collection of numbers that reflect the different systems and bundling strategies now used for retailing films. More or less declining retail prices over time on a per-viewing basis, however, suggest price discrimination that is preserved by means of the intertemporal segmentation of high- and low-value consumers.

A tendency for unbundled (that is, à la carte) pricing systems to be toward the front of the system is also apparent. Bundling of movies on

Table 3.1 Prices and viewing of theatrical films in the release sequence, United States, 2002

	Retail price per transaction	Realized retail price per viewing	Annual number of viewings per capita
Theaters	$5.81	$5.81	6
Video sales	$14.77	$3.69	}25–30
Video rentals	$2.84	$1.13	
PPV/VOD	$3.50–$4.00	$1.50	}25–30
Premium channels	$7.64/mo.	$0.76	
Basic cable	$34.52/mo.	$0.46	}35–45
Broadcast TV	0	0	
Total			90–110

Sources: See Appendix D.

Notes: Viewing per transaction assumptions: video sales, 4; video rentals, 2.5; PPV/VOD, 2.5; premium channels and basic cable, see Appendix D.

individual premium channels is now well down the pipe, and the even broader bundling of channels that show movies into basic cable subscriptions comes later, followed by the free broadcast exhibitions at the end.

Product quality segmentation is also evident in the modern system, though it is more complicated than before. Theaters, for example, deliver the highest aesthetic quality viewing experience, but PPV/VOD and home video (especially DVD) have desirable control features that many consumers may prefer to theaters. Traditional monthly subscriptions to premium channels offer less viewer control, and basic cable still less because of fewer repetitions per time period. Basic cable exhibitions are also cluttered with commercials, but with generally fewer per hour than broadcast networks or stations, which are unambiguously at the low end of the quality spectrum. The geographic segmentation element in the old theater system has been replaced at least in part by media access. As new media diffuse, for example, the fraction of the total population they reach offers a natural segmentation device. A variety of other factors, some similar to the old multitheater system and some new, influence the pecking order, timing, and prices of media in the modern sequence. These include the marketing and information collection value of the first-run exhibition and, as we explain in Chapter 4, the presence of piracy and copying devices.

The last column of Table 3.1 echoes the stacking phenomenon apparent in the financial data and testifies to the expansion of movie markets that the pay media have fostered. Video and pay TV systems have come to account for more than half of all theatrical movie watching in the United States, but theater viewings per capita have also increased since 1975 (from 5 to 6; see Table 2.1). Broadcast television, in combination with ad-supported basic cable networks, accounts for considerably fewer theatrical film viewings than it did in the mid-1970s (35–45 compared to 65–75). Overall, though, theatrical movie viewing per person in the United States is half again greater than it was at the end of the broadcast TV era and has roughly tripled since the pretelevision heyday of old Hollywood.

Pay Television

No one can say that the movie studios failed to recognize television's potential as a way for viewers to pay directly for movies. From broadcasting TV's earliest days, the studios pushed for development of commercial pay TV systems that could show movies.[7] In the 1960s and 1970s, studios participated in pay TV experiments conducted in Hartford, Connecticut, and other cities.[8] Following the launches of subscription networks in the mid-1970s, pay TV has proliferated into a maze of familiar and still developing forms: dozens of monthly subscription networks, ranging from "full pay" networks like HBO that show recent major films to "mini-pays" like Flix or Sundance that show older or more obscure movies for much lower monthly rates; PPV networks (sometimes called "near video on demand," or NVOD, systems if they stagger the start times of the same movies on different channels); true VOD systems; and the hybrid SVOD systems, which allow subscribers to control individual program viewing within a given menu for a set monthly price.

Early forecasts that theaters would disappear if pay TV succeeded commercially were accompanied by other claims that it would replace ad-supported TV as a movie exhibitor—and perhaps even destroy free TV as a medium altogether.[9] Predictably, warnings about the demise of ad-supported TV were mostly made by broadcast network executives, who advocated—successfully until the late 1970s—crippling legal restrictions on pay TV programming content that prevented the subscription networks from much success.[10] The buzzword in those days for the evils of pay TV was "siphoning." These systems, it was said, would simply vacuum up programs, especially movies, from ad-supported broadcast channels, so that these programs would no longer be free to viewers.

After pay TV regulations were abolished in the late 1970s, theatrical movies were indeed siphoned into an earlier release cycle on premium networks, and the studios siphoned money from viewers in the process. In 1980, subscribers paid an average of $7.41 per month per network (in addition to a basic cable subscription), which worked out to an average of about 66 cents per household per movie actually watched.[11] Although this system yielded only about a third of the monthly price back to the studio after the cable operator and the network took their cut, that was far better than the few pennies that ad-supported broadcast TV could manage. In the mid-1970s, before the explosion of video, subscription pay TV channels accounted for as much as 20 percent of domestic revenues of U.S. theatrical distributors (see Appendix C).

Premium networks created value for consumers because the movies were available sooner and with no commercials; there was greater selection, including foreign and other obscure movies; and the films were frequently repeated. These time-of-release and quality attributes also served as a device for the studios to segment the TV market and price discriminate between viewers who were willing to pay for them and those who preferred to wait for free TV exhibition. Thus, in effect, pay TV took advantage of the efficient distribution technology of free TV, but replaced its woefully inefficient pricing mechanism with direct charges.

In the end, audience segmentation using pay TV has apparently cost consumers little in comparison to the opportunities they already had to watch theatrical movies on television. The major broadcast networks eventually lost their role as routine exhibitors of theatrical features, but the movie window for nearly all major features on broadcast stations and ad-supported cable channels has become even shorter, down from its three-to-four-year level in the mid-1970s (Chapter 2) to the typically two- to three-year cycle of recent years.

Subscription versus Pay-per-View

It may seem that, as a revenue raising device, à la carte pricing is inherently superior to monthly subscription because it can efficiently target the highest-value consumers. It is remarkable, in fact, that from the beginning of the policy debates in the 1950s, nearly everyone apparently assumed that any commercial pay TV systems coming on line would naturally be pay-per-view.[12]

These assumptions turned out to be incorrect, as have relentlessly optimistic projections by some industry analysts for the future of PPV or VOD systems. Even though commercial à la carte systems have been on the market for nearly as long as subscription channels, consumers spent about ten times as much for the latter as they did for PPV movies in 2003.[13] A mitigating factor for the studios is that both retail prices and program supplier margins are higher for PPV/VOD systems: suppliers generally get about half of PPV final sales; but by the time cable and DBS operators and the networks get their share, suppliers receive only about one quarter of retail-level payments for premium services.[14] Despite these facts, movie distributors still got less than one quarter of their total pay TV revenues from PPV and VOD sales in 2003.[15]

Clumsy technology for ordering and delivering movies, inadequate selection due to the limited capacity of servers, and the threat of piracy and copying have all been blamed for the slow growth of PPV/VOD systems. They may well have a bright future. Also, an inherent disadvantage of subscription networks is that bundling a month's worth of movies together for one price prohibits the metering of actual use. That is, higher-value consumers who want to watch a lot of movies end up paying the same price as those who want to watch only a few—not a system that one would think is conducive to successful price discrimination.

Monthly subscription networks, though, have pricing advantages in their own right that may justify their superior performance. First, high-value households can subscribe to multiple networks, and many do.[16] Multipay network subscribers will thus tend to pay higher effective prices for the movies that they actually watch.[17]

A second factor in favor of subscription networks is that consumers seem to desire subscription pricing in itself. In a variety of contexts, people have demonstrated a strong preference for a fixed monthly rate over à la carte pricing plans.[18] The dominant service plans for Internet service providers (ISPs) and cell phone operators, for example, are flat rate. One reason that people may prefer subscription plans is budget certainty. Another, more interesting explanation is that subscription plans offer a kind of "option value" for consumers.[19] It is not a small point that movie channel subscribers do not actually buy the movies they watch, but the *right* to watch them at any time during the month, at no marginal cost. Of course, most consumers make a mental accounting of how much they expect to watch a given network as a guide to their subscription decision. Recent economic research in other contexts, though, suggests that significant numbers of subscribers may overestimate the actual number of movies they will watch on subscription channels, thus paying more than they would if the same films were selected on an à la carte basis. One study, for example, showed that 80 percent of individuals who elected to pay a monthly health club membership fee rather than paying on an à la carte basis for actual visits ended up paying more money than if they had used the posted à la carte rate.[20] The true value of subscription-based services, though, does not necessarily boil down to such a mechanical cost-benefit calculation. The option value of having four subscription channels available for viewing at any time can itself be a luxury that high-value consumers desire in the same way that the owner of four cars may enjoy having all four at the ready. In any case, though, the bottom line is that monthly subscription plans generate a surplus to the seller that is generally *above* the value to the consumer of actually using the products themselves—in the movie case, a free lunch of sorts to the provider that could not be exploited by free television or theaters.

A third advantage of subscription television in particular is that it allows more efficient price discrimination among pay TV users than à la carte pricing by means of its "value averaging" effect.[21] Say that two families, the Norths and the Wests, have the following price demands for two televised movies, *Daredevil* and *Chicago*:

	West family	North family
Daredevil	$4	$6
Chicago	$6	$4
Total	$10	$10

Assume also that the pay TV operator has no way to determine which households value which movies the most, but has a good idea of what families will pay on average. In that case, the operator has two pricing options:

1. An à la carte price of $4, yielding 4 sales; total revenue: $16.
2. A bundled price of $10 for A and B together, yielding 2 sales; total revenue: $20.

With à la carte pricing, the seller makes less money, forfeiting (or "leaving on the table") a total of $4 that these consumers would have been willing to pay. Bundling the two movies together serves to average out the unknown variations in taste. Bundling thus improves price discrimination, since more of the consumer's surplus (in this case all of it) is now extracted by the seller. Certainly people have different tastes, and subscription TV yielded a new way for studios to extract consumer value that was unavailable to them with either theaters or ad-supported TV.[22]

The One-Two Punch of Subscription and Pay-per-View

While subscription networks thus have pricing and segmentation advantages of their own, subscription pay TV can most efficiently segment higher- and lower-value consumers when used in tandem with pay-per-view. Bundling does not work so well when some people have relatively extreme values for movies. Both extreme and modest values can be extracted, though, by offering à la carte prices to everyone first, and then offering the bundle at a later time.[23]

To illustrate, let's modify our earlier example by letting the North family be an extremely high-value consumer for *Daredevil*, but with no interest at all in *Chicago*. In this case a price of $21 would be the best à la carte pricing strategy, even though this would result in only one sale, with all of the West family's value left on the table. The bundling alternative, with both movies offered for $10, would result in two sales, but only $20 revenue.

	West family	North family
Daredevil	$4	$21
Chicago	$6	$0
Total	$10	$21

Let us also assume that after a period of time, say six months, the two families' price demands to watch the movie have changed to these:

	West family	North family
Daredevil	$3	$7
Chicago	$5	$0
Total	$8	$7

Since the movies are now older, it makes sense that they will both be worth less money to everyone. The extreme value to the North family for *Daredevil*, though, has declined the most: the Norths' demand for *Daredevil* is only a third of what it was, a decline of $14, while the Wests' valuations for the two movies have fallen by much less, only $1 each.

In this case, an à la carte price of $21 can be collected from the Norths at the time of initial release, and then the bundle can be sold to the West family six months later for $8. That strategy yields a total revenue of $29—$8 more than the next best alternative of simple à la carte pricing at $21 in the first period.

The success of this intertemporal price discrimination example depends on a basic assumption about human nature embedded in the numbers: consumers having the highest-value demands for individual movies (here, the Norths) are *more impatient* than the low-value consumers (the Wests). Basically, intertemporal separation solves a fundamental problem; if the bundle and the à la carte options were offered at the same time (called "mixed bundling"), the North family would not pay the full $21 for *Daredevil* because they could get a far better deal by buying the bundle for $10—yielding a *net* benefit to them of $21 − $10, or $11). The North family, that is, makes their purchase choice by weighing each option's net benefit, which is arrived at by subtracting the actual price offered from their maximum willingness to pay. In this example, the à la carte price for *Daredevil* would have to be below $10 to induce the Norths to take the à la carte option when both are offered at the same time. But that strategy would again yield total revenues to the seller of no more than $20, the amount that would be collected by the bundling option of $10 that we already established as being inferior to the $21 à la carte price. As the model illustrates, intertemporal segmentation *always* involves a sacrifice to the seller, because everybody's demand for a movie will decline somewhat as the movie gets older. But as long as the high-value consumer's demand declines fastest, intertemporal segmentation can be profitable.

The "one-two punch" of à la carte pricing followed by subscription network movie release also offers a general explanation of why unbundled pricing systems—like theaters, most video rentals and sales, and PPV—tend to be positioned at the front of the movie release sequence. Of course, numerical examples can be manipulated to show all sorts of possibilities. We should point out that intertemporal segmentation of movie media is not necessarily required for effective market segmentation and price discrimination. Examples can easily be constructed in which simultaneous mixed bundling (that is, offering *Daredevil* and *Chicago* as a bundle for one price and also à la carte for separate prices at the same time) would be profitable.[24] In fact, we consider a form of simultaneous mixed bundling in the video market later in this chapter.

Digital Technology and Pay TV: A Primer

Since the 1970s, pay TV systems have steadily improved, with faster and more efficient transmission and payment mechanisms, greater movie variety, and enhanced viewer control over movie exhibition times. Higher-capacity coaxial cable and, later, fiber-optic cable led the way to steady increases in the number of available pay TV or PPV channels that cable systems could offer. Behind most of the recent economic improvement in pay systems, though, is digital technology. We should take a brief detour at this point to explain the fundamental advantages that digital technologies offer to movie distributors. These technologies create value by improving quality and variety and enhancing viewer control at lower costs; they also, from the distributor's perspective, create new opportunities for market segmentation and price discrimination, not only in pay television but also, as we shall see later, in home video, the Internet, and other media. Some of these opportunities involve a new landscape of distributor controls over consumer copying and piracy made possible by digital encoding—as we discuss in greater detail in Chapters 4 and 7.

Instead of creating, sending, and receiving visual images as continuous "waves" (the familiar metaphor used to describe analog systems), an end-to-end digital television system records, transmits, and receives pictures as streams of 0-or-1, on-off pulses. Digital production and transmission systems for TV are actually almost as old as television. Analog systems, however, which include 35 mm film as well as standard broadcast television, developed first and dominated the film and television industries because cost-effective analog hardware and software were the first to be developed.[25] It is at least technically possible to do almost anything in television with analog technology, including PPV, VOD, interactive TV, and high-definition TV (HDTV). The accelerating diffusion of digital systems in the 1990s mostly reflects recent advances in technology that have put the cost-quality trade-offs for these systems overwhelmingly in favor of the digital option.

The digital transition in television has been slowed by a maze of technical standards, complicated by market coordination problems. For broadcast TV in the United States, the government-set NTSC (National Television Standards Committee) standard of the 1940s has proven infamously difficult to replace with a digital broadcast system, although that effort was begun by the FCC in the 1980s. Broadcast stations and networks, as well as cable operators and other players, have reacted slowly because the incentive to make the necessary investment often does not exist until other players also make investments, and especially until the public buys enough sets.[26]

Many profitable aspects of digital conversion have still occurred, though, because complete end-to-end digital TV systems are not essential. For example, an analog 35 mm film print can be converted to a digital file for more efficient electronic transmission to PPV homes and then reconverted to analog form with a set-top box at the consumer's home for reception by a standard analog TV set. Similar methods are employed for broadcast and other cable signals.

What features of digital transmission are most important for today's movie-based pay TV systems? One remarkable feature of digital technology is the continuous trade-off it permits between picture quality and system capacity. To an engineer, movies are just bits, and a system's capacity to deliver bits can be expressed in terms of the speed with which they are transmitted—whether that is through the air on broadcast TV, via a cable, or to a DVD player. At the very top end, a full-motion digital transmission of an HDTV-quality signal requires a transmission speed of up to 100 megabits per second (Mbps), which ends up absorbing 45–60 megahertz (MHz) of bandwidth—-far more than the 6 MHz that a standard NTSC-quality analog TV channel provides. Digital compression however, can generally squeeze one HDTV signal into a 6-MHz bandwidth space without noticeable video quality degradation when viewed on a 36-inch digital HDTV set. Progressively more compression can squeeze more and more digital channels into a given bandwidth—but they will be of progressively lower and lower visual quality. A respectable-looking movie with a reasonable amount of action requires only about 3 Mbps for a standard TV, while a minimum "VCR-quality" transmission requires about 1.5 Mbps.

The bottom line for cable or DBS operators is that digital technology magnifies their potential channel capacity and gives them quality choices. They can generally squeeze roughly 6–12 digitally compressed channels having quality comparable to a standard NTSC signal into one 6 MHz channel. Or they could take advantage of digital transmission by using that same 6 MHz channel to send one HDTV-quality signal. They could also choose a middle ground, such as two "near-HDTV quality" signals in one standard channel space, and so on.

Up to now, cable and DBS operators have mostly taken the high-capacity route (though some would call this the "low road"). DirecTV, for example, was compressing most of its DBS satellite channels, all of which are digitally transmitted, at about a 6-to-1 ratio, on average, in the early 2000s. Most channels delivered by cable systems are still analog, but the "digital tiers" they have offered in the past several years have generally been compressed about 12 to 1. More recently, DBS and cable operators have been responding to increasing diffusion of digital HDTV sets by opting for more bandwidth-hungry HDTV transmissions on some of their digital channels. Thus, digital technology has allowed multichannel operators to choose a blend of transmission qualities: some low, NTSC-quality channels, along with some other HDTV-quality channels.

A second key advantage of digital technology is more efficient control by both subscribers and operators. "Addressable" cable systems use a computer at the "head end" to send out digital codes to subscriber set-top boxes that instantly descramble or rescramble designated channels for individual subscribers. From the subscriber's perspective, the same boxes can transmit channel or PPV orders to the operator. From the operator's perspective, addressability makes subscription-channel sales more efficient by eliminating the need for a "truck roll" to the subscriber's home to do the switching; and addressability is virtually essential for any à la carte services to be offered. In these ways, digital technology allows cable or DBS operators to bundle or unbundle various channels and market them to subscribers for different prices. SVOD and true VOD systems on cable or DBS also require more sophisticated digital set-top boxes, along with digital transmission of the programs themselves.

Digital technology has thus aided both subscription and à la carte PPV and VOD systems. The expansion of cable and DBS channel capacity made possible by digital compression has allowed a growing proliferation of premium channels, including "multiplex" versions of some networks that simply time shift the same schedule or programs. Many more channels can also be used for NVOD systems. In addition to SVOD systems, personal video recorders (PVRs) are an equivalent technology. Using a set-top box, the subscriber can select a scheduled HBO movie, for example, and shift it to a convenient time much more seamlessly than a VCR can do. VOD systems, in which subscribers can literally select a movie at any chosen time and have DVD-like control of its exhibition, are becoming more viable as server capacities and fiber-optic networks expand and as digitally based ordering and payment systems become more efficient.

In sum, digital television technologies are creating value that consumers will pay for, reducing costs, and allowing more efficient market segmentation and price discrimination. More options, combined with on/off channel controls in the hands of subscribers and sellers, mean more ways for sellers to accurately calculate and extract value with differently priced network or program bundles or different control features. Some cable operators, for example, have levied an extra surcharge to premium channel subscribers for SVOD capability, thus segmenting out higher-value consumers within pay network subscriber roles. Higher-priced HDTV exhibitions segment both pay network subscribers and PPV buyers in terms of their demands for signal quality, using the limited diffusion of digital HDTV sets as a natural segmentation device.

Many observers have seen VOD as a kind of Holy Grail for movie distributors because of the "anything at any time" power it grants to consumers. Digital technology has indeed opened the door for VOD. So far, though, digital as well as other technological advances have tended less to replace one pay TV system with another as they have served to enhance the variety of alternative pay systems. Studios have benefited from this proliferation through increased opportunities to subdivide the pay TV market into different segments according to consumers' willingness to pay.

Home Video

Driving to the store to get a video is an inelegant delivery system for the information age. That fact has long led some Wall Street and other analysts to write off the long-term future of video retailing, especially rentals, in favor of PPV or VOD systems.[27] But home video has remarkable economic attributes in its own right, and at least for the present, it has become by far the most successful and lucrative of the movie media. And, like pay television, video revenues have mostly just amended, rather than replaced, those of existing movie media.

Why has home video, especially DVD, been so successful? From the consumer's perspective, an obvious answer is that videos create a great deal of value. When prerecorded VHS tapes were introduced in the 1970s, VCR owners (especially those with children) quickly discovered the pleasures of controlling the flow of the movie and the far greater access to movie variety that videocassettes provided. The movies also came out sooner—about six to nine months after the theater opening as opposed to a year or longer wait for subscription pay TV. As the second generation of video, DVDs are an improvement over the VHS format: they increase both exhibition quality and flow control, and newer releases routinely provide "bonus" material like deleted scenes, interviews, and special-effects information.

From the studios' perspective, this greater consumer value obviously creates revenue opportunities, because people will pay more for better things. Also, though, the retailing of videos, both for rental and sale, provides movie distributors with a terrific new way to extract value through better market segmentation and more effective price discrimination—opportunities they could take advantage of clumsily at best using just theaters and television. And while we have seen that videos and pay TV systems account for about the same amount of theatrical film viewing in the United States (Table 3.1), video is far more lucrative for the distributors, producing several times the dollar volume of revenues that suppliers earn from all pay TV systems (Appendix C).

One Window, Multiple Media

Video rentals and video sales, although they make use of the same physical objects and are released at the same time, are to the distributors different media. Both employ mainly unbundled pricing, but they each appeal to consumers with different valuations of the movie product.[28] Similarly, the main formats in place as of the mid-2000s, VHS and DVD, appeal to consumer segments desiring different cost and quality features. From the studios' perspective, DVD and VHS are seen as four different video media: DVD rentals, DVD sales, VHS rentals, and VHS sales. Movie distributors have benefited from keeping the consumers for these four "media" as separated as possible to facilitate price discrimination. Like the various forms of pay TV, the various video media subdivide the video market. In general, video buyers are higher-value users than renters, and DVD consumers are higher-value consumers than VHS.

With high-definition DVDs approaching market introduction and VHS falling off rapidly, the specific breakdowns of spending, transactions, and revenues for the video media shown in Table 3.2 as of 2002 are a snapshot in time, but they provide a basic picture of the market that underlies this chapter's story about how video segmentation works. As the consumer spending numbers show (row 1), all four media have registered significant market appeal; but the economics of rentals and sales are very different. The great majority of retail transactions (row 2)—about 80 percent—are video rentals. Retail revenue volume of both DVD and VHS sales, however, are much closer to their respective rental volumes because as the "average retail price per trans-

Table 3.2   Home video consumer spending and supplier revenue summary, United States, 2002

	DVD		VHS	
Category	Rentals	Sales	Rentals[a]	Sales
(1) Consumer spending (billions)	$3.6	$8.4	$6.4	$3.9
(2) Retail transactions (millions)	1,091	491	2,434	342
(3) Average retail price/transaction	$3.25	$17.19	$2.64	$11.26
(4) Supplier net revenue (billions)	$1.2	$7.2	$1.4	$3.1
(5) Supplier receipts per transaction	$1.12[b]	$14.72	$0.57[b]	$9.09

Source: Author calculations based on *Hollywood Aftermarket* (Adams Media Research), Feb. 28, 2003, p. 3.

Notes: (3) = (1) ÷ (2); (5) = (4) ÷ (2).

a. Includes rental priced tapes only.

b. Ignores resale value of used DVD and VHS units.

action" figures show (row 3), sale prices are considerably higher than rental rates.

Movie distributors are especially fond of video sales. As the "supplier net revenue" figures show (row 4), sales—especially DVD sales—are a much more important revenue source for the studios, generating more than four times the revenues from rentals in 2002. Studio earnings on a per-transaction basis (row 5) are even more dramatically skewed toward sales, and the contrast would be even greater if the resale value of used rental units were considered (a market we discuss in more detail later). Mostly, the rental-versus-sales-revenue-per-transaction contrasts reflect retail costs. The great majority of new video sales to consumers (now mostly DVDs) are made through low-cost general-merchandise discount stores like Wal-Mart and Target, which simply mark them up 15 or 20 percent and scan them through a checkout line. Rentals, most of them made by specialty stores like Blockbuster or Hollywood Video, are by contrast a transactions-intensive business. The average rental video turned over about 25 times in 2002, and efficient as these big video rental chains may be, a calculation based on the information in

Table 3.2 reveals that the studios only grossed 26 percent of the aggregate retail rental volume in that year, versus 84 percent of the sale volume.[29]

Finally, notice from Table 3.2 that DVDs command higher effective retail prices than VHS, both in the sales and rental markets, and that the studios earn more per transaction from both DVD sales and rentals. These DVD-versus-VHS differences reflect market segmentation; but they also reflect bizarre twists to the movie pricing and distribution system as a result of the first-sale doctrine of U.S. copyright law, a subject we return to shortly.[30]

The Economic Marvel of Home Video Sales

To understand the success of video sales for movie studios really requires just three words: kids, collections, and gifts.

Kids

One of the main reasons people buy videos is that they expect to watch the movie enough times that it becomes cheaper to buy than rent. The leading high video usage group is families with young children. In a 2002 *Video Store Magazine (VSM)* survey, 38 percent of respondents reported that their usual intention in buying videocassettes was for children under twelve.[31] Studies have documented how children will watch the same movie or other video again and again.[32] In the *VSM* survey, 33 percent of respondents with children under twelve reported that the average videocassette they purchased was watched more than ten times, compared to only 20 percent for families having no children under twelve.[33]

The influence of children is vividly reflected in video sales data. Disney's market share of video sales dominated that of other studios in the early 1990s, and by 1996, six of the ten biggest video sellers in U.S. history were Disney animated theatrical features.[34] Contrasts in intensity of video use by children versus adults are not as extreme with DVDs (which at least so far are not as easy for younger kids to use), but children's use still accounts for a sizable proportion of DVD sales.[35] As shown in Figure 1.1, Disney continued to lead the video industry overall through the 2000–2003 period in spite of the market shift to DVDs.[36]

Watching the same movie over and over indicates high-value demand. Before videos, the insatiable repeat-viewing demands of children could not be served effectively. Small children are not easily portable to theaters. In fact, while Nielsen Media Research reported in the late 1990s that kids aged two to eleven were the heaviest VCR-using demographic, this group typically does not even show up on theater attendance surveys, and this was true even before video.[37] Before home video, the Disney classics were usually given public exposure only through their rerelease to theaters in seven-year cycles—a very cost-ineffective method by comparison. The eighteen-fold increase in Walt Disney stock value since 1984[38] no doubt owes a debt to the vision of Michael Eisner, who became CEO of Disney in that year. But the advent of home video technology (including synergistic effects on theme-park attendance and merchandise sales) surely deserves a healthy part of the credit for Disney's stellar performance in the 1980s and '90s.

From a price discrimination perspective, frequent viewing of purchased videos means that video purchase is really less of a gold mine than the $14.72 and $9.09 supplier receipts per transaction data for DVD and VHS sales from Table 3.2 imply. If a family with children watches a DVD or video ten times, that works out to only $1.47 and $.91 per individual viewing, respectively. Like a pay TV subscription, the highest-value, most frequent users pay least on a per-view basis. Some of that high-frequency viewing of purchased videos could be replaced by repeated rentals or use of other media to watch the same movie. Before video sales, though, distributors had little opportunity to efficiently extract such high-value demand from repeat consumers, whether kids or adults, and the reduction in the consumers' transaction costs is undoubtedly a major factor in their preference for sales over repeated rentals.

Collections

At the other end of the buyer spectrum are people who watch a video they buy only once, or perhaps not at all. A *Variety* editorial, effusing over the explosion of DVD sales in 2002, identified "cults" of DVD buyers—people who purchase many videos in a certain genre, but who "have dozens of DVDs still in their wrapper, years after purchase."[39] A recent *New York Times* article reporting on passionate DVD collectors described one person with a collection of 1,462 Italian horror movies, and another who claimed to have spent over $20,000 on DVDs in the past five years.[40] While cult consumers are by definition a thin slice of the total market, 11 percent of respondents in the 2002 *VSM* survey said their primary reason for purchasing a DVD was "for their video collection."[41]

Cross-tabulations in the 2002 *VSM* survey offer a fascinating glimpse of video collectors. For example, 14 percent of respondents reported that they or someone in their household usually watch a DVD they purchase only once or not at all, and another 20 percent reported only two viewings.[42] These are individuals who would be very unlikely to use their DVD purchase as a way to avoid buying the movie elsewhere in the sequence, thus paying effective prices per viewing ranging to the $15-plus average retail price of DVDs.

For the studios, such collectors are the ultimate movie consumer. They get pleasure from simply owning a video or, like pay TV subscribers, they may have "option demand"—a desire to have a certain movie *in case* they want to watch it. Whatever their cognitive motivations, these accumulation-minded, low-usage consumers were simply inaccessible to studios in theater and television days.

Of course, those who do watch a purchased video frequently, like families with small children, can also have ownership or option demand for the video in addition to the pleasure of actually watching it. As the health club research mentioned earlier implies, it is also a good guess that many consumers systematically overestimate the number of times they will actually watch a video they buy. Still others may simply buy to avoid the inconvenience of returning a rental video.

Whether accumulated to use, to reflect upon, or just to avoid hassle, a broad spectrum of people now have large video collections, and they have shifted rapidly toward acquiring the more compact and durable DVD format. In the 2002 survey, respondent households with VCRs reported owning an average of 50 videocassettes; DVD-player households had 24 DVDs.[43] By mid-2004, the average DVD collection size had reportedly reached 43.[44] Children are well represented in these collections; video units intended for kids under twelve accounted for about 39 percent and 22 percent, respectively, of VHS and DVD collections in the 2002 survey. In building these video collections—undoubtedly costing well over $1,000 for a large segment of the U.S. population—extraordinary sums of money are flowing to the movie studios.

Gifts

A third group of high-value video buyers are gift givers. Video gifts—especially DVDs—are big business. Major space is devoted to gift sets at video stores, and they are heavily advertised. DVD sales shoot up at holidays, and video retailers are reported to be heavily reliant on pre-Christmas, fourth-quarter DVD sales.[45]

Studios could take little advantage of gift giving before video retailing. And in a real sense, movie studios get something for nothing with gifts. In general, the recipient of a video gift can be expected to have lower-value demand for that movie than does someone who buys the same video for his or her own use. There is, in fact, some empirical evidence on this subject. In an academic journal article with the Grinch-inspired title "The Deadweight Loss of Christmas," Joel Waldfogel estimated that the average recipient of a noncash gift values the gift at only about 90 percent of its price.[46] This makes sense; after all, the receiver did not choose to buy the product for him- or herself. Gift giving is a wonderful thing, but the only people who get a benefit at least as great as the price are the givers of the gift; and chances are, those givers will never watch that video unit. From the movie studios' perspective, that's all easy money that goes right into their pockets.

At the retail level, a large sale market for used videos has also developed. We will consider the used market after describing the rental pricing system that produces most of it. First, though, we offer some further analysis of why the survival of alternative video formats can be to the studios' advantage.

Video Formats and Quality Segmentation

The extraordinary growth of DVD since the late 1990s put movie distributors in a euphoric mood. Consumers started buying DVDs in droves because the software gives greater value and the hardware became much cheaper. Surveys confirm that not only have people been buying new DVD movies, but they have also been "turning over" their collections of classic and other older movies they have on VHS. From the studios' perspective, there has been another advantage: DVDs cost less to manufacture, package, ship, and hold in inventory.[47]

The VHS format entered a period of rapid decline in the early 2000s, and by 2004 there was widespread industry sentiment that the format is doomed.[48] Exhibition technologies that prove to be overwhelmingly inferior to newer ones, or that serve a niche so small that a significant level of software production cannot be sustained, are destined to disappear or become too obscure to matter. The DVD's digital predecessor, the fourteen-inch laserdisc, managed to serve about a 1 percent market slice of video enthusiasts for over twenty years—evidence that even thin movie markets can survive over time. Eventually, though, laserdiscs were overcome by the smaller, more cost-efficient DVD, and laserdisc production for new movies was effectively shut down.[49] Yet as we have seen, other established movie media, from theaters to broadcast TV, have managed to confound industry soothsayers in their persistent survival, if not continued prosperity.

There is no evidence that VHS will not go the way of the old laserdiscs, or of LP music albums, perhaps soon. The video format survival issue, though, provides a good illustration of one reason for the stubborn persistence of many established movie media. Studios benefit from having all but the most hopelessly outmoded channels left in place because they facilitate segmentation between high- and low-value consumers in terms of their demand for exhibition quality.

A simple numerical model illustrates this point, and in the process demonstrates the fundamental principle of product quality segmentation.[50] In the spirit of what seems sure to develop as high-definition DVDs become available, what we call the "quality segmentation" model below shows the price demands of two types of consumers, labeled high-value and low-value, in purchasing the standard DVD and the "high-def" format of a given movie. Assume for the illustration that all costs (manufacturing, shipping, etc.) are zero and that hardware availability is not a constraint—assumptions that permit us to focus on the central feature of the model.

	High-value consumer	Low-value consumer
High-def DVD	$20	$10
Standard DVD	$12	$ 8

Now consider the following possibilities:

Case 1: only standard DVD available

Optimal price = $8; profit = $16

Case 2: Both standard DVD and high-def DVD available

Optimal prices: standard DVD = $8; high-def DVD = $14;

      profit = $22

Case 3: Only high-def DVD available

Optimal price = $20 (or $10); profit = $20

    For the initial case, say that only the lower-quality standard DVD format is available. The optimal price for the seller is then $8. At that price, both the high- and the low-value consumers will buy the standard DVD, for total revenues (and profits) of $16. (If the price were set at $12, only the high-value consumer would buy at all, resulting in a profit of just $12.)

    Now say that high-definition DVDs become available along with standard DVD. The seller can profitably price discriminate by selling the DVD version of the movie at $8 as before and the high-def format at $14, for a total profit of $22 (Case 2). Note that the $8 standard DVD sale extracts all of the benefit from the low-value consumer, but the $14 high-definition video price extracts only some of the potential from the high-value consumer. Without the standard DVD alternative, the high-value consumer would be willing to pay $20 to realize the $20 in benefit from buying the high-def version. As in the intertemporal segmentation model presented earlier in this chapter, the high-value consumer chooses the alternative that gives that greatest net benefit—that is, the value received less the price paid. With the standard DVD also available at $8, though, the high-value consumer could realize a $4 net benefit by buying that version instead (i.e., $12 in gross benefit less the $8 price). So the seller is forced to offer the high-value consumer a bargain on the high-definition DVD. Still, though, the seller's profits rise by $6.

So far, the example shows that if both high-and low-quality products are available, sellers can make more money. The central feature of our model, however, is that market segmentation *by itself*—independent of the increased value to consumers of higher quality per se—is profitable. If only high-definition DVDs were available (Case 3), the seller's maximum profit would be just $20 (from sales to both consumers at $10 each, or from only the high-value consumer at $20).[51] Note also that although more limited diffusion of high-definition hardware can facilitate discrimination, that is not required for the segmentation to work.

The retail video price structure for VHS and DVD shown in Table 3.2 is evidence of price discrimination that has already been taking place, based on video format quality segmentation. DVDs have higher retail prices than VHS tapes, in spite of the fact that the average cost for manufacturing, packaging, and distributing DVDs is less than for VHS. While First Sale–related legal considerations affect retail sale prices of both formats, the most plausible explanation for this cost-price paradox is simply that DVD buyers are higher-value customers than VHS buyers, and the studios successfully discriminate just by charging them higher prices, in spite of their lower per-unit costs. As they enter the market, high-definition DVDs will almost surely have higher prices than standard DVDs, but the production and distribution costs will not be much greater for the former format.

Movie distributors thus gain not only from the higher prices they can charge for higher-quality movie-watching experiences, but also from having a spectrum of different-quality media so as to segment markets and effectively price discriminate. Of course, producing and stocking the same movies in multiple video formats is costly to the industry. To overcome these costs, quality or other differences between the formats must be great enough for them to appeal to consumer groups having distinctly different willingness to pay.[52] If that condition is satisfied, an interesting implication of this model is that if movie studios could prevent it, they might be better off slowing down, rather than speeding up, the march of technology to a 100 percent digital, high-definition DVD world of home video. That assertion is uncertain in practice because other factors, like the collection-turnover effect, may dominate, thus shifting the balance to greater studio benefit from faster standard DVD diffusion at the expense of VHS, then faster high-def DVD diffusion at the expense of standard DVDs. Also, the latest generation of video technologies, notably high-definition DVDs, offer new ways to segment video demand that, once significantly diffused, would probably outmode the usefulness of VHS as a market segmentation device. In any case, the example demonstrates that from the studio's perspective, there is more to technological improvement in movie exhibition than meets the eye.

The DVD-VHS cost-price paradox also shows that the effect of cost-reducing technological advances in movie distribution is not necessarily lower prices for consumers or the elimination of lower-quality technologies. Because of their market segmentation advantages, maintaining an array of technologies, with higher prices for higher-quality media—even if the higher-quality media are cheaper to produce—is profitable for studios.

Video Rentals: The Studios' Misunderstood Child

Since the VCR was invented, the studios have griped about movie rentals, leaving an impression that they would like to be rid of them. In early years, it was said that the studios tried hard to kill the rental market because they assumed that sales would predominate.[53] More recently, the studios have come to make so much more money from DVD sales, who could blame them for wishing everyone would just buy the movie (for a far higher price than a DVD rental). In fact, in 2002 Warren Leiberfarb, an executive of Warner Brothers, tried to force down retail DVD prices in order to convert renters to buyers.[54]

It would be a mistake, though, to interpret these complaints or business initiatives literally as a desire to eliminate video rentals in favor of sales. While renters are lower-value video consumers than buyers— usually only interested enough in the movie to watch it once, without enough option or ownership demand to warrant a purchase—video rentals permit unbundled pricing and appeal to the same relatively high-value market as PPV or VOD. Once in hand, a rental video offers the consumer the same control over exhibition and the like as does a sale. The video rental market is also huge in numbers. In spite of a strong DVD-driven trend toward sales in the early 2000s, rental transactions were more than two and a half times the number of sales transactions in 2004.[55] Video rentals, like sales, have also helped expand the market for movies to important niches of new consumers, especially small children.[56]

From the studios' perspective, rentals pick up the lower half of the generally high-value home video market. It would never make sense to try to turn all renters into buyers because to reach the vast majority of them would mean lowering video sale prices so much that the high-value consumers with strong ownership, option value, or repeat viewing demands would not be paying the premiums to buy that they are willing to. The studio's problem with video rentals has not been how to get rid of them, but how to serve this huge market *efficiently*.

Fundamentally, video rental is a clumsy, transactions-intensive business. Price discrimination among renters takes place, however, and technology has steadily improved the efficiency of rental systems.

Flat Pricing versus Revenue Sharing

The studios make money from video rentals by two methods. In one method, "flat pricing," videos are sold outright to stores for a fixed price per tape or disc—ranging widely from about $10 to $60 or higher, and the retailer rents it at will. In the other, more recently adopted, method of "revenue sharing," the studios collect a small fee up front for each unit that a retailer contracts for, and then they take a percentage cut, usually 40 to 50 percent, from each rental turn.

Revenue sharing improves the profitability of rental by providing a more efficient method of contracting between studios and retailers. It was made practical by PCs and advances in computer software that allow cost-efficient tracking of retail transactions, and it began to grow rapidly in the mid-1990s. At the end of 2002, revenue sharing accounted for nearly half of all video rental market transactions.[57]

It may seem that better contracting methods would be of minor significance; but by one estimate, revenue sharing results in up to 6 percent higher retail profits, and has made it much more likely that you will be able to find a video on the rental shelf during its period of peak demand.[58]

To see why revenue sharing can have large benefits to both distributors and consumers, consider an example.[59] Say initially that videos are sold wholesale for a flat $60 price; this means that it requires 20 rental turns by the store at $3 per rental for the store to break even on each one. (We are assuming that the store's costs to make rental transactions are zero to make the example simpler.) The store will therefore buy videos of *Attack of the Killer Tomatoes,* say, until the last one bought is expected to yield at least 20 additional turns in total.

To demonstrate the inefficiency of this flat pricing system, say that one video of *Killer Tomatoes* on the shelf would in fact result in 20 turns (store revenue = $60), but that because of better availability, a second would produce 30 total turns (2 copies @ 15 turns each), yielding a store revenue of $90. If each unit is wholesaled at $60, the store will buy only one because the second would only generate an extra $30. The basic problem with this system is that the studio's *true* cost of distributing each additional video to a retailer is very low—essentially just the $1 or $2 cost of making and distributing the video itself. Thus it would basically make sense for both the studios and the store for the store to have the second copy. A way to do this is revenue sharing. For example, say the studio *gives* two *Killer Tomato* videos to the store, but demands 83 percent of total store revenues. In this case, the store turns the two videos a total of 30 times at $3 as assumed earlier; the result is $75 for the studio (.83 x $90) and $15 for the store (17 x $90). With revenue sharing, studio revenues have gone from $60 to $90 and net store revenues from $0 to $15, a net industry gain of $30 less the $1–$2 true video cost. While there are different ways to divide the pie in the revenue sharing system, the point is that the size of the pie to divide goes up.

Basically, revenue sharing is a wholesale price discrimination technique, which can be understood as being equivalent to a quantity discounting scheme in which the store's cost per video falls as more are purchased. The studio, the retailer, and the consumers (who find more videos on the shelves) are all better off as a result.

Retail Discrimination at the Store Level

In either a flat rate or a revenue sharing system, the studios also benefit indirectly from rental price discrimination that takes place at the store level, because the higher the consumer revenue potential, the more videos the retailers obtain and the more money the studios make. DVDs and VHS have typically been priced by stores at the same rate for rental; but, like the studios with their release of new movies, most retailers discriminate over time by charging higher effective rental prices for new releases and lower prices for older tapes. Some stores charge $3 to $4 for new releases and as little as $1 for older, "catalog" rentals.[60] The Blockbuster model has been to charge the same price for most rentals, but to vary the number of days the rental is good for, thus changing the effective rental price per night. And of course, there are coupons, discount days, senior discounts, lower prices of kid videos, and a myriad of other retail gimmicks, many of them having their antecedents in theater days.

Rentals also aid price discrimination in ways that were not available to theaters. First, high-value consumers may choose to rent several movies at once to make sure they have plenty of options. To encourage this practice, some stores give quantity discounts—such as five videos at once for a set price. A novel way that video stores price discriminate is via late fees. In the early 2000s, these accounted for a major chunk—usually 10 to 20 percent—of total video specialty store revenues.[61] To some extent, these fees simply compensate the store for not having a video in stock to rent to someone else. They are also convenient discrimination devices because higher-value consumers are less willing to go out in the middle of the night to return their movies.

Late fees do make some people angry—not an advantage to any seller. Some of Blockbuster's customers got so angry about late fees that they filed a class action law suit in 2000 against the company alleging that the fees amounted to a deceptive business practice.[62] Blockbuster settled by agreeing that the company would no longer charge more than the effective daily rate at which the original rental was made, and changing the label on the videos to read "extended rental fees"— which is what they were in the first place.

In December 2004, Blockbuster announced that it would terminate all late fees in favor of a new system. The new plan effectively extended rental return deadlines, but if no return is made by the deadline, the subscriber's credit card is charged the difference between the sale price and the rental payment already made, thus turning ownership of the video over to the consumer.[63] This system can be interpreted as a price discrimination device similar to late fees. High-value consumers are less likely than others to return videos within the rental period, acquiescing to higher prices by turning themselves into (probably low-usage) buyers.

Internet retailing has taken a significant share of the video rental market and is apparently improving its efficiency.[64] Netflix and other services that use the postal mail for distribution apparently have lower distribution costs than brick-and-mortar stores. The subscription pricing plans that dominate these services (for example, unlimited rentals for a set rate of $19.95 per month, on a one-to-one exchange basis, with no late fees) also reduce transactions costs. More recently, competing subscription plans have been adopted by Blockbuster and other major video chains. These pricing plans preclude the use of late fees as discrimination devices, and more frequent renters undoubtedly tend to self-select into them. It is likely, though, that these plans also attract many less frequent renters who value the certainty of a fixed rate in itself, who benefit from the option value, or who systematically underestimate the extent to which they actually use them. It was reported in

2002, for example, that the average Netflix customer on a subscription plan obtained five videos per month, a price point that at a $19.95 monthly rate approximately works out to an à la carte rental rate of $4—not an indication that frequent renters exploit these plans on average.[65] Some subscription plans explicitly discriminate among high- and low-usage consumers by offering different prices depending on the number of videos the subscriber is permitted to have at any one time.

The video rental market could undergo a more profound efficiency development with the development of nonreturnable, "disposable" DVDs; we will have more to say about this in Chapter 7. For now, we turn to a major by-product of video rentals that may well benefit distributors by serving yet another distinct video market segment: used video buyers.

The Market for Used Videos

Used videos have been called the "nuclear waste" of the movie industry because of their potential to undermine the demand for new videos.[66] Used products of a wide variety—cars, refrigerators, and recorded music, to name a few examples—are an inherent problem for sellers in durable-goods industries.[67] High-value consumers will potentially pay high prices for new items, but if used prices are low enough, they may be able to get a better deal in the used market, causing the seller to leave money on the table. This problem can thus undermine the price discrimination system of the movie studios.

Potentially, used videos are a huge problem in movies because of the vast numbers of them generated by the rental market. A large Blockbuster store, for example, may need hundreds of copies of a major new release on its rental shelves to satisfy peak demand within the first few weeks, but will eventually retain only one or two copies for catalog rentals down the road. This short-term need for large numbers of videos is known in the industry as the "copy depth" problem. Used rental units start coming off the shelves within a few weeks, and by the second or third month of release, a flood of them has become available.

An active market for "previously viewed" videos (earning another industry acronym, PVs), especially DVDs, has resulted. The resale of used rental videos began to boom in the early 2000s, and by 2003 they were estimated to account for about 8 percent of total U.S. video sales volume.[68] While the great majority of used videos come from the rental shedding process, a growing source is people who bring their own videos back to market for sale or trade, via Internet sites or retailer-sponsored trade-in markets. In 2003 and 2004, Blockbuster developed a used video trade-in system that allowed customers to get store credit for their turn-ins.[69] Also reported is a growing level of consumer activity in trading their growing DVD collections among themselves.[70] The recent growth of these markets is again attributable to the greater durability, compact design, and value of the DVD.

Undoubtedly, these activities interfere with new-sales video demand, attracting some buyers who would otherwise have bought the same video as new, seen the movie in a theater, and so on. On the upside, though, the used market benefits studios by providing an opportunity for them to extract value from a distinct, new market segment. Used video buyers in general probably have lower value than new video buyers, but higher value than renters.

How can studios extract value from used video buyers?

For rental videos provided to retailers, the mechanism is relatively straightforward: studios can raise the wholesale price of DVD and VHS units sold to video rental stores to account for their used sale value. Judging from the $5 to $15 prices for used DVDs and videocassettes charged by many retailers, those values are substantial. Also, most distributors have in recent years offered retailers "buy-back" programs that specify offers to repurchase used rental units after an interval of time sufficient to ensure that most demand for new videos of a given movie have been exhausted. Apparently, a lot of repurchased rental VHS units, at least, have ended up in landfills.[71] Apart from the costs of collecting and bulldozing, buybacks are not very expensive to studios because they can simply add the guaranteed repurchase value to the new videos. Revenue sharing contracts have provisions that permit retailers to sell off used stock, but only after a certain time. In 2002, for example, one studio permitted DVD sell-off after 30 days, though such contracts averaged 45 to 60 days.[72] Of course, studios cannot control consumer-initiated resale and trading markets. These markets are more problematical because studios have no way to control the flow of these videos coming from consumers. Again, however, the studios can extract at least some of their resale value simply by building that into the wholesale prices of new sales videos.

These value extraction methods are far from precise. Many consumers, for example, do not want to resell, which raises the issue of how studios can discriminate between resellers and non-resellers in the retail market for new videos. On the whole, though, this problem may not be so bad. It is reasonable to expect that individuals who take the trouble to resell videos tend to be lower-value consumers who would never have bought the new video without the resale opportunity—making the built-in resale pricing strategy something like publishing a "cents off" coupon that only they will bother with. Another problem affecting used value extraction is that the studios are constrained by the first-sale doctrine from separately pricing rental and sales videos to retailers, and thus from separately targeting used rental buyers and consumer resellers.

In sum, studios have some evident protection from the "nuclear waste" downside of the used video market. Without a detailed study, it cannot be determined whether the value extraction benefits outweigh the undermining effects of used video markets, but it is seems likely that the studios benefit on net. A related efficiency advantage may result as well. By siphoning off some higher-transactions rental demand, the used video market may streamline efficiency of the overall movie release system—a subject we return to near the end of this chapter.

We have alluded several times to legal constraints on video distribution imposed by the first-sale doctrine of the U.S. Copyright Act. Although the studios have devised some interesting strategies to evade this law, its effects have been misunderstood, and bear some exploration.

Effects of the First-Sale Doctrine

It's hard to complain about a commercial-free, remote-controlled movie at home for $3 or $4, especially if you have some friends or a family to join you. Without the first-sale doctrine of the Copyright Act, though, video rentals might not be such a bargain. Rental prices would probably be higher, sales prices lower, and the steep contrasts between revenues per transaction generated for sales versus rentals in Table 3.2 less extreme. Unconstrained by the first-sale doctrine, the studios could almost certainly make even more money from video.

In effect, the first-sale doctrine prevents the studios from efficiently segmenting the rental and sales video markets, and thus efficiently price discriminating between them.[73] Basically, First Sale says that if the owner of a copyright (here, the movie studio) assigns that copyright to a second party (here, the video store), the copyright owner may not control the second party's disposition of that product. In practice, this means that once a video retailer buys a video unit from a studio, the studio cannot control whether the retailer rents it or sells it. The result is that even though video rentals and sales are from the distributor's perspective different media that warrant different pricing and distribution strategies, the first-sale doctrine inhibits that. In practical terms, video distributors are constrained to choose a single wholesale price for DVDs, and similarly for VHS. The studio is thus forced to aim for either the rental or the sales market, ignoring the other, or to offer a compromise pricing strategy that accommodates both markets to some degree. The studios are also effectively constrained by First Sale to release movies for video rental and sale on the same date.

The original intent of First Sale, which first appeared in U.S. law as part of the 1909 Copyright Act, was to promote education, literacy, and the distribution of knowledge, apparently by protecting the rights of libraries to loan out books.[74] Of course, the framers of the law could hardly have anticipated home video. As the video rental market began to boom in the early 1980s, the MPAA tried to persuade Congress to modify the most recent Copyright Law revision of 1976 to exempt videos from First Sale. The VSDA and the Home Recording Rights Coalition (HRRC), a consumer-advocacy group, argued against the exemption. Their basic argument was not that cheap videos had the same socially redeeming value as Leo Tolstoy novels, but that the studios' intention was to eliminate the cassette rental market or to raise rental prices.[75] The studios lost, and no exemption for videos was made. The political reality was that a lot of people had already bought VCRs by then, they loved cheap rentals, and the VSDA and HRRC witnesses were persuasive.

It would not have made sense for the studios to kill off the booming rental market, however, as some people feared they would do, because rentals had by then revealed themselves to be the overwhelming source of consumer demand for home video—then accounting for 9 in 10 transactions.[76] Another misconception about First Sale is that the studios objected to it because it prevented them from making revenue sharing contracts with stores similar to those they routinely made with theaters to give them a share of each admission ticket. As a witness from the U.S. Copyright Office made clear at the hearings, such deals, in which the studio leases the movie for a period of time to the retailer, either for a cut of each rental or for a flat rate per month, were entirely legal. Vigorous objections by video retailers to a number of experimental revenue sharing and video leasing programs that the studios attempted to impose on them in the early 1980s were motivated mainly by the hassles of record keeping and, apparently to some extent, by general worry that the studios, not the retailers, would own the video.[77] From the studios' perspective, record keeping by retailers risked fraud, and the plans were soon abandoned, not to be revived until advances in computer software made them cost effective in the 1990s.

As Alan Hirschfield, President of 20th Century Fox, and other studio representatives testified in 1983 congressional hearings, what the studios really wanted was just to put "for sale" videos in black boxes and "for rent" videos in red boxes, and charge the store different wholesale prices—which they proposed to be on flat, per unit terms—for these tapes.[78] In other words, the studios just wanted to *separate* the rental and sale markets. From the beginning, they had devised one marketing scheme after another to accomplish this, but they all proved to violate First Sale, or to be impractical.[79]

The Byzantine wholesale pricing system that evolved for videocassettes puts the effects of the first-sale doctrine into relief. For VHS tapes of most movies, studios have chosen either a "rental price" or a "sell-through" strategy. In the rental price strategy, tapes usually have a flat per unit wholesale price in the $20 to $60 range, a level that virtually eliminates consumer sales. The specialty stores just put them on the shelf and turn them over to renters as many times as they can. Alternatively, rental pricing can be achieved through revenue sharing contracts, which by committing the retailer to return a certain percentage of each rental transaction to the studio, removes the video from the sale market by contract. Although the practice is fading from the market with the decline of VHS sales, rental priced tapes in the early 2000s were typically "repriced" down to $8 or $10 by studios for the sale market, but not for about six months, by which time rental demand is virtually exhausted. In contrast, the sell-through strategy for VHS tapes has usually been reserved for mass market films that have been relatively successful at the box office. In this system, the tapes are wholesaled to stores for the sale market, generally at $10 to $15, with suggested retail prices of $14.95 to $24.95. As First Sale frees them to do, video specialty stores both sell and rent these tapes from the outset, although the major discount retailers like Wal-Mart usually do not choose to rent.

For DVDs, many observers have predicted that the studios will eventually revert to a similar two-tiered pricing strategy. At this writing, DVDs of virtually all movies are wholesale priced to stores at relatively low sell-through levels, although as Table 3.2 indicates, these price levels have been higher than those for sell-through VHS tapes. Again, video specialty stores both rent and sell these DVD units. Like cassettes, DVDs are typically repriced to lower levels a few months later, although the price drop is not as drastic as that from VHS rental to VHS sell-through.

Market complexities make prediction difficult, but if studios were able to use the red box–black box separate pricing method that First Sale precludes, there would almost certainly be upward pressure on retail rental prices and downward pressure on retail sale prices.

A simple numerical example illustrates why. To focus on the main idea, assume for simplicity that video retailers are reasonably competitive so that any excess profits at the store level are eliminated. Also say that there is no used video market and that the rental and sales markets are independent—that is, that sales prices do not affect rentals and vice versa. Now studios cannot by law designate retail prices of videos in either the rental or sales markets, but they indirectly control them through wholesale pricing decisions. Let's say that given the market forces governing their own competitive environment, demand conditions are such that studios would all like to see DVD rental prices at $5 and sales prices at $12. For the sales market, the mechanism is straight-forward. If stores add a $3 markup to cover transactions and other operating costs, a per unit wholesale DVD price of $9 would result in the $12 optimal retail price ($9 + $3). Though slightly more complicated, the same principle applies to studio control of rental prices. If retailer costs per rental transaction are $1, let's say, and we assume that each DVD turns over an average of 20 times before rental demand is exhausted, a $5 average rental price could be achieved by setting wholesale DVD prices per unit at $80 (that is, $80 spread over 20 turns, plus $1 per transaction, or $80/20 + $1 = $5).

The effective pricing constraint of First Sale is that the studio can choose only one wholesale price that makes the best of both markets. Drawing on the numerical model, if the single wholesale DVD price were $20, retail sales prices would be $23 ($20 + $3), with resulting rental prices at $2 ($20/20 turns + $1). From the distributor's perspective, First Sale in this example thus forces video sales prices to be higher than desired and rental prices lower than desired.

While this example undoubtedly exaggerates the effects of First Sale on video prices for practical reasons we explain later, the studios' schizophrenic VHS pricing system makes it evident that their preferred wholesale prices for video rental units are in fact much higher than for sale units. In fact, optimal wholesale prices for rental and sale are apparently so different that studios have decided to pursue either a sell-through strategy that practically ignores the VHS rental market or a rental strategy that essentially postpones the sale market for a few months via the "repricing" mechanism. Flat prices of $20 to $50 for VHS rental tapes in the early 2000s have presumably been near the optimal rental level, since virtually no new sales can be made at these price points anyway. Optimal wholesale prices for the sales market are dictated by the level at which consumers will buy en masse, which is far lower. It is unclear why two-tiered wholesale pricing has not yet evolved for DVDs, but it is apparent that the DVD sales market has proven too lucrative relative to rentals to overcome widespread resistance from video rental retailers, who anticipate a decline in their core business from two-tier pricing.

The dimensions of these economic forces in the current market for DVDs are indicated by Table 3.3. About 14 percent of the total number of DVDs distributed in 2002, or 79 million units, were placed in rental service in that year. These were all priced at roughly the same $15.44 wholesale level shown. Presumably, though, the studios would have preferred to price the DVDs used for rental at least at the $22.95 average realized level for new VHS rental-priced units—and probably more due to the higher quality of DVDs. Such a move would tend to force DVD rental prices up. Even without differential pricing, the studios benefit

Table 3.3   Video supplier receipts from rental units, 2002

	DVD	VHS
(1) Units placed in rental service (millions)	79	61
(2) Net supplier receipts from rental service units (billions)	$1.2	$1.4
(3) Net supplier receipts per unit placed in rental service	$15.44	$22.95

Source: Author's calculations based on *Hollywood Aftermarket* (Adams Media Research), Feb. 28, 2003, p. 3.

   Note: (3) = (2) ÷ (1).

from a natural form of market segmentation at the retail level, since the large discount retailers that account for the great majority of video sales are not equipped to rent. Meanwhile, though, the video specialists, such as Blockbuster, make a killing from renting DVDs. If we conservatively assume that studios would prefer to price DVDs used for rental at the $22.95 VHS rental-price level and that the same number of DVDs were used for rentals, the studios would have earned an additional $593 million from the DVD rental market in 2002, or about half again their actual total revenues from this sector. Of course, fewer DVDs would have been used for rental at these higher prices, but it appears that these losses are significant. As DVD sales have continued to boom in the early 2000s, nearly doubling studio revenues from that market between 2002 and 2004, these losses have evidently been magnified.

For VHS, the price pressures and studio losses have evidently been less. Only about 6 percent of all sell-through-priced VHS tapes were shipped to video rental stores in 2002, and a large percentage of those were surely sold to consumers anyway.[80] Probably a larger loss to the studios and consumers is that retail VHS sales of rental priced movies have been effectively postponed until about the six month repricing interval, by which time sales demand is surely diminished far below its street date potential.

The actual magnitude of upward pressure on video sales prices is uncertain, but the direction of that pressure is almost surely up. While it is evident that DVDs are wholesale priced primarily for the sell-through market already, studio profit maximization dictates that their optimal wholesale price under First Sale is higher than if the rental and sales markets could be priced separately.[81] Consistent with the numerical example, that also implies lower retail sale prices in the absence of the first-sale doctrine.

The idea that elimination of the first-sale doctrine would result in higher rental prices and lower sale prices depends on one other variable: the practical feasibility of the two-tier, color-coded box method at the retailer level. Since 1995, the European Commission's Rental Rights Directive has banned First Sale–like provisions in the European Union video market. Some nations, including France and the Scandinavian countries, have never had such laws to begin with.

Video distributors have responded with attempts to convert to two-tiered simultaneous pricing in Europe, releasing videos at the same time in low-priced blue boxes for sale and high-priced silver boxes for rental. Progress has been slow, partly due to retailer resistance, especially in the U.K. The main factors are apparently the strength of copyright law and the state of business conduct. In Scandinavia, two-tiered simultaneous pricing by the studios has apparently been practiced successfully with major releases for a number of years. In most of the rest of Europe, including France, those forces have apparently been insufficient to deter retailers form ignoring the law and simply renting the cheaper videos intended for resale. Recent press reports, however, indicate growing success with two-tiered pricing in a number of countries.[82] Given its strong copyright law tradition and the presence of large video rental chains, it seems likely that a regime of separately priced and distributed videos could be sustained in the United States, although the explosion of more difficult-to-police Internet retailing calls that assumption into question.

In the broader scheme of things, the nagging inefficiencies of the first-sale doctrine are surely a secondary element in the remarkable explosion of home video in the United States. To some extent, First Sale may even have helped the studios historically by promoting the rapid household penetration of VCRs in the 1980s. Before DVDs put video sales in the forefront in the 1990s, the video market was much more driven by rentals, and artificially low rental rates were undoubtedly a factor in consumers' VCR purchase decisions. In any case, although video rentals play second fiddle to sales from the studios' perspective for evident reasons, the role of rentals has been integral to the studios' market segmentation and price discrimination strategies.

Differentiation, Repeat Viewing, and Cost Efficiency in the Release Sequence

Although the most important economic developments in the movie release system have involved pay television systems and home video, those media are not the full story. Airlines, hotels, the military, colleges, and other more obscure outlets could also be dissected. Still other segments are emerging. For example, though they are still serving a small niche, IMAX theaters charge an average price of several dollars above that of first-run, standard theaters, and they are subdividing the theater market by demand for quality. HDTV pay network subscriptions, such as HBO HD and Showtime HD, and HD PPV exhibitions, are typically on higher-priced optional tiers, similarly segmenting the pay TV market.

Of course, the segmentation and discrimination process in the movie release system as it has evolved is far from perfect. Interdependent demand in the sequence always tempts higher-value consumers to take advantage of prices intended for those with low demand. As we have also seen, consumers resist à la carte payments for watching individual movies on TV, and the bundled pricing plans most people opt for are second-best solutions for movie sellers. Theaters and video stores also generally charge the same retail price to see or rent movies of obviously different attractiveness to audiences, a curiosity that seems to defy standard economic models of profit maximization.[83]

The unexpected survival and prosperity of so many different movie media and the extent to which the "stacking" phenomenon has served to greatly expand studio revenues testify to the success of audience segmentation in the new media environment. The achievement of this segmentation, though, is not just an accident of technology and history. It can be viewed as a contrivance of movie distributors.

The press often portrays movie media such as theaters, for example, as struggling to differentiate their products to survive the competition from home theater systems and other high-quality media—just as theaters in the 1950s were said to struggle to survive television by adopting Cinerama and other big-screen technologies. From the perspective of those media, that is indeed an accurate picture. But from the movie distributors' perspective—and they after all have final say over the survival of movie media by means of their distribution and marketing choices—these attempts to differentiate can be viewed as deliberate efforts to separate audiences as sharply as possible with respect to product quality in order to facilitate price discrimination. An analogy can be made with an example offered by a nineteenth-century French economist, Jules Dupuit, who argued that railroads intentionally exaggerated the differences in comfort between superfluously luxurious first-class coaches and crowded, roofless third-class cars beyond what consumers would otherwise prefer, just to separate the markets.[84]

Similarly, the recent success of IMAX theater exhibitions probably reflects technological advance only in part. IMAX technology, after all, has been in use for many years at museums and other out-of-the-mainstream locations (out of the mainstream, at least, for moviegoers). The recent explosion of IMAX revenues for some major films mostly reflects a new distributor willingness to produce, promote, and distribute IMAX versions of those films as a method to more sharply differentiate the quality of theater exhibition from HDTV-based home theater systems. Behind the stacking phenomenon is the will of movie sellers.

A related improvement of the modern movie release system is that it surely encourages more repeat viewing of the same film than did the old system. Repeat viewing reflects high-value demand and is thus in effect a price discrimination mechanism. A movie and its medium—that is, a movie in a theater, a movie on DVD, and so on—are really joint products of medium and message. The more differentiated that any pair of them are, the more likely a consumer is to choose both media rather than just one. Of course, high-value consumers in early days could see the same movie in its first run and then in the neighborhood run, but those experiences had limited potential for differentiation. The modern sequence also lasts far longer than it once did, encouraging a film's more ardent fans to re-experience it.

Patrons who revisit theaters to see the same movie are apparently a thin slice of the market today.[85] Repeat viewing of one movie on different media, however, is apparently more common. The broadcast networks, for example, although they offer a far fewer number of theatrical films than in the past, choose to show more popular blockbuster movies that have been heavily exposed because they get larger audiences.[86]

Another more lucrative repeat viewing phenomenon is theater attendance and video sales. Many video buyers report in surveys that they have already seen the movie in a theater.[87] While this behavior has often been interpreted as complementary demand effect, in which theater attendance actually promotes the video market, it is also effective price discrimination. Consumers who see a certain movie in a theater and also purchase the video are the highest-value consumers for that movie; by using both markets they generate the highest total studio revenues.

The efficiency of digital media for bundling and unbundling information has led to a now-common studio strategy of rereleasing movies in theaters or, more commonly, on DVD with the addition of new footage that had originally landed on the cutting-room floor. In some cases, the initial DVD release of major films has added new footage to the theatrical version. For example, the "Special Expanded Edition" of *The Lord of the Rings: The Two Towers,* released on DVD in November 2003, included 43 added minutes.[88] Disney rereleased its original theatrical film *Beauty and the Beast* (1991) to IMAX theaters in 2003 with extra footage, and Francis Ford Coppola added 49 minutes to his original 1979 classic film for an IMAX version entitled *Apocalypse Now Redux.*[89] In the context of the price discrimination model, these strategies combine intertemporal and quality segmentation strategies to encourage repeat viewing of the same film.

From the distributor's perspective, the movie release system has become progressively more cost efficient, continuing the trend that started with the replacement of sub-run theaters by television distribution. One element of greater efficiency is a shift toward media, especially video sales, that give distributors higher percentages of retail value by eliminating transactions intensity or costly hardware. Pay television systems and video have also contributed to exhibition efficiency by allowing individual moviegoer demands to cumulate over much longer periods of time at lower cost. For a single first-run theater exhibition, perhaps 100 people had to be simultaneously attracted to travel to the same place at the same time. The continued increase in theater rental rates from around 35 percent in the 1970s to about 50 percent may reflect a continued shift toward more efficient theater exhibition. Multiplex theaters, for example, can respond to unexpected demand by quickly increasing or reducing the number of screens a movie shows on.

In sum, the diffusion of pay media in the United States has transformed the revenue earning power of theatrical films not only by expanding markets to new consumers, like small children, but by allowing the studios to segment markets and extract far more of the demand that essentially had lain dormant within the queue of consumers waiting in a theater line of the 1940s. More efficient movie distribution technologies have increased our access to movies, and they have also provided the movie studios with new methods to serve high-value demands that were largely inaccessible to them in the past.

The market segmentation system that these media have found their place in, though, is not without its problems. In the following chapter, we consider the challenges that studios have faced in maintaining a consistent pecking order and timing in the sequence, and especially in preventing a loss of control to the ravages of piracy and consumer copying and sharing of movies.

Chapter 4

Controlling the Release Sequence

We have seen how the movie studios use their choices of media and the timing of release to segment markets and price discriminate. On the surface, this may seem easy for distributors to do because their copyright (or distribution contract) allows them to authorize media and timing choices. In reality, though, studios have faced two difficult challenges in effectively controlling the movie release process.

One of these challenges—piracy and copying—has been highly publicized. In terms of the pricing model, segmentation fails and revenues fall if individuals who would have paid to see the movie at some point in the sequence instead take advantage of lower (or zero) prices for pirated or copied goods. A second, more obscure, but also important challenge has been to prevent collapse of the time intervals that separate release to the various media in the sequence.

In this chapter, we investigate how the studios have met these challenges. Both have required the studios to coordinate their behavior, through trade associations and other means. So far, they appear to have done so successfully. Distributors now face the glaring threat of digital piracy and copying, especially via the Internet. They also face the potential collapse of the video window, as studios have moved to substantially shorter time lags between theater and video release beginning in 2003. No one can know the outcome of the powerful forces for change now in the works. The uncertainty may diminish, though, if we can better understand how the industry has coped in the past with earlier versions of the same threats.

The Challenge of Maintaining Windows: Movies as Durable Goods

In March 1999, *The Matrix* was released by Warner Brothers. A highly successful film, it earned $171.4 million over a relatively long U.S. theatrical run of 176 days, or about 25 weeks. This movie was released on video two days before the end of its run in theaters, 174 days after its theatrical opening. In the same year, Warner also released *Goodbye Lover,* a lower-budget feature that remained in theaters for only 41 days, earning $1.9 million at the box office. This movie did not appear on video, however, for another 138 days, or a total of 179 days after its theatrical release.[1] What induced Warner Brothers to wait so long, to release *Goodbye Lover* on video at roughly the same six-month window as *The Matrix?* This example is not unique. As we discuss later, the median time gap between close of the theater run and video release for theatrical features is substantial, about 89 days for major films released from 1988–2002, and much longer when sub-run theater engagements contributing relatively negligible revenues are ignored.[2] The result has been a clustering of video "street dates" during this time frame at around the fifth or sixth month after theatrical release.

The long wait from the opening of theatrical release until the video street date presumably persuades many patrons to open their wallets for an expensive first-run ticket instead of waiting for the video, thus preserving intertemporal segmentation of these markets. To maintain this long window, though, movie studios face an interesting dilemma. Attraction of potential video consumers to theaters relies on their *expectations* of how long the wait for video will probably be. Those expectations are evidently formed on the basis of some average of video windows observed in the past. But what is to prevent Warner, or any distributor of a poorly performing movie, from relying on those expectations to attract the largest possible crowd to the theater and then, when the theater audience starts to tail off—within one or two months for most movies—immediately releasing it to video?

As industry executives publicly acknowledge, there are real temptations to follow this strategy.[3] The earlier the video release, the fresher are the impressions of an expensive theatrical advertising campaign in the minds of consumers, and the fresher is the movie itself. Also, the sooner the video release, the sooner the studio gets paid—not a minor consideration for a $100 million production, whose carrying costs can be millions per month. The pressures are especially great during not-uncommon periods of studio financial duress.

Adding to the temptation in a competitive environment is the likelihood that if a studio gives in to an early video release strategy for one or a few movies, such opportunism would likely have a minor effect on consumers' perceptions of the average video window. If short video windows become a general practice, though, consumers will adopt the mindset that any movie they are thinking about seeing in a theater will probably be available on video quite soon. Without some mechanism to prevent studios from indulging in the temptation to release films to video as soon as the theater market is exhausted, this logic implies a tendency for video windows to collapse over time to a shorter length than distributors as a whole would prefer, thus undermining their price discrimination strategies.

The movie industry's window-setting dilemma is actually an example of a classic economic problem for durable-good producers first identified by Ronald Coase that has come to be called "time consistency."[4] How, for example, does the buyer of a lithograph know that after he or she buys one, say for $100, the artist won't later decide to run off another thousand copies at $10 each once the $100 market has been exhausted? Or, to cite another example, how does a company that buys a newly introduced copy machine model know that the manufacturer is not "skimming the cream" from high-value buyers with the intention of chopping the price a week later to pick up the low-value market? In both cases, the result can be that no one at all will buy these products because everyone knows that once the cream has been skimmed from the high-value market, the seller's rational strategy is to immediately start lowering the price until it eventually reaches the cost of manufacturing the product. So, at least theoretically, everyone would wait for the low prices, and no sales can be made above what buyers believe to be the marginal cost of production.

Sellers of durable goods have devised a variety of methods, with varying success, to cope with the time consistency problem.[5] One way is for the seller to make some kind of commitment that the price will not be lowered, at least for some period of time. In the case of the lithographer, a common strategy is to make a limited run and then publicly destroy the original—an extreme measure, but one that guarantees prices will never be lowered in the future. In the copy machine case, a common strategy is to lease rather than sell. The buyer then faces no risk that the price will be dropped because no purchase has been made. Perhaps most commonly, individual sellers try to establish a reputation that they just don't engage in exploitative price-reducing behavior, but this is surely an imperfect mechanism. People know, for example, that at any time a camera manufacturer might come out with a new model and use that as an excuse to immediately close out the one you just bought and steeply discount the price. Nevertheless, since we observe what looks like effective price discrimination over time in many durable goods markets, industries must have found more or less effective solutions to the time consistency problem.[6]

How have movie studios dealt with the time consistency problem?

Time Consistency in the Movie Release Sequence

If movie distribution were a monopoly, time consistency might be easily resolved, since consumer expectations could be molded at will by a centrally controlled release sequence. Before a series of legal challenges in the 1930s and '40s outlawed them in the United States, the multi-tiered theater release systems described in Chapter 2 were apparently organized by a close approximation of a monopoly: cartels of the major movie distributors and exhibitors.[7] In the 1920s and '30s, Clearance and Zoning Boards established and controlled the release systems in major cities of the United States. These cartels consisted of representatives of the major distributors and major theater owners operating in the local market. After an early period, these organizations were arranged by the Hays Office (the industry's trade association of movie studios of the time) into thirty-two Film Boards of Trade serving major urban areas in the United States. Their basic function was to assign the run stage, run length intervals, a minimum admission price, and geographic and temporal clearances to each theater in the area. Theater owners could file an appeal to the board for a better position in the system, and this was a common way that adjustments were made. The end result was a lengthy manual for distributors that included every theater in the urban area. Presumably, coordination of this system was facilitated by the extensive vertical integration in those days between major distributors and theater chains, most of which were in turn heavily concentrated within local market areas.[8]

The release system was based on minimum runs and clearances and was not inflexible to variations in market demand. Movies that did poorly in first run tended to cycle through the system more quickly. For example, *Stagecoach* took over four months to completely play off its eleven-run theater sequence (February 25 until the week of June 8, 1939), including three full weeks playing at the Chicago. A long-forgotten film, *Stand Up and Fight,* played its minimum one week at the Roosevelt (beginning February 24, 1939), but after being out of the market for its three-week mandatory clearance period, was quickly moved through to the end, skipping four of the eleven run stages, last appearing in the Chicago area during the week of April 21. In general, the more popular a movie was in its initial runs, the more different theaters played it over a longer total period of time.[9]

After reorganizing to adapt to antitrust challenges in the 1930s, the Film Boards were finally ruled to be in violation of the Sherman Act in the Supreme Court's 1948 *Paramount* decision.[10] The Court determined that the boards had the intent and result of excluding independent exhibitors and distributors from the industry. Scholars of *Paramount* and other antitrust decisions of the period have presented evidence that the boards, along with broader collusive activities of the *Paramount* defendants, indeed had this effect (See also Chapter 2.)[11]

Whatever anticompetitive effects the boards may have had, we advance the theory, based on the price discrimination model, that one benign function of the boards may have been to maintain time consistency in the movie release system so that consumers could develop reliable expectations of when movies would be available to them at what prices.[12]

As a variety of electronic media have replaced the old multitier the-
ater-run system, the absence of formal coordination mechanisms and
generally sparse levels of vertical integration have created new challenges for the studios to maintain consistent windows. In this environment, how can studios not only prevent windows from collapsing, but
effectively commit to consumers that they will be consistent in length?

One coordinating device is contracts with preceding media in the sequence. The PPV window, for example, typically appears in video retailer contracts as a "PPV holdback," specified as the minimum number
of days, generally 45 to 60 days in the early 2000s, between the movie's
video street date and its PPV premiere. Retailers demand these terms
because national PPV release is close enough to the video street date to
directly affect video demand for individual movies, and thus the retailers' wholesale order volume. The major distributors may also coordinate the PPV window among themselves by means of public announcements of what their holdback policies will be. Paramount Pictures, for
example, announced to the trade in 1993 that it intended to lengthen
its PPV window range due to renewed concerns about the level of piracy on that medium.[13] Like the announcements by steel companies of
what their price structures will be, this behavior facilities consistent industry action.

The video window, by far the most important in economic terms, appears to pose especially difficult challenges.

To our knowledge, theater exhibition contracts in the United States
never specify a video window. One reason is that the need for a simultaneous national video release date has forced the video window to be
defined in terms of the interval from the beginning, rather than the
end, of theater release. The local nature of theater exhibition results
in inconsistent theater closing dates, rendering them an impractical

benchmark. The high prerelease uncertainty of theater performance then makes video window commitments risky, since distributors may want to vary the window for individual movies depending on box office results. Distributors can generally benefit from quicker video release of movies that end their theater releases early because publicity from the theatrical release fades quickly. Another reason for the absence of video window holdbacks in theater exhibition is that in the modern market, consumers probably do not blame individual theaters for showing movies that might appear on video sooner than they expected. While theaters as a whole lose from shorter video windows, theater ownership in the United States is fairly diverse, the largest circuit having only about a 17 percent share of box office revenues in 2003, and all others under 10 percent.[14] Thus, individual theatrical exhibitors would seem to have little incentive to demand minimum video windows in their contracts. And perhaps with the exception of Disney, the public seems not to identify movies with the particular studios that release them. Thus the reputation among consumers of the particular studio that chooses an early window may not suffer much as a result.

In European countries, where antitrust laws tend to be weaker than in the United States, the video window coordination problem has been addressed by industrywide agreements or in some cases legal statutes that mandate a minimum video window.[15] Though they have been relaxed in the past several years, an industry study of fifteen European countries in the mid-1990s indicated that in most cases the window was set at either 6 or 8 months, but it was 12 months in the two countries having statutory windows, France and Portugal.[16] The industry agreements were reported to vary in their rigidity, some of them "strictly adhered to" (Norway) with others labeled as "not compulsory" (Switzerland) or "fixed on a case-by-case within guidelines" (Spain). In countries with statutory windows, producers or distributors could apply for a "derogation" that permits an earlier interval for movies that do poorly at the box office.[17]

In the United States, no legislation governs movie windows, but at least in the past, the industry in that country may have cooperated to control the video window. Press reports describe one attempt by the National Association of Theater Owners (NATO) in 1996 to coordinate a minimum video window. In 1995 and 1996, four major features, *Twister, Eraser, The Nutty Professor,* and *Independence Day,* were released to video less than 5 months after their theatrical opening—unprecedented for major films at the time.[18] NATO complained vigorously, and according to the *Hollywood Reporter* in early 1996:

> The National Association of Theater Owners drafted a resolution calling for a stricter adherence to the unspoken agreement between distributors and exhibitors to wait six months after a movie's theatrical release before putting it out on video.
>
> During a speech at the ShowEast Convention at the Trump Taj Mahal on Wednesday, NATO president Bill Kartozian said if the resolution were honored, it would not only benefit the exhibitors, who would sell more tickets, but also the distributors and the rest of the industry.[19]

It was reported that Mr. Kartozian then began making visits to the major studios to discuss the resolution.[20] Of course, theater owners have an obvious interest in the longest possible video windows, but there was at least some sympathetic response from distributors. As a Paramount Pictures executive was quoted to say a few days after the Kartozian initiative, "What we don't want is to have the consumer think they can pick up a movie on video in three months. It's a very dangerous trend."[21]

No press reports on the results of Kartozian's studio visits were evident, and there have been no outward signs of similar attempts at industry coordination of video windows since these incidents. The international comparisons and the actions of theater owners in the United States nevertheless indicate the plausibility of some form of industry coordination to substitute for the old Film Boards.

The Empirical Record

How successful have the studios been in maintaining the video window? And is there evidence of coordinated behavior among studios and theater operators?

Trends over time in the median video window for major theatrical films are shown in Figure 4.1. (See Appendix E for details and discus-

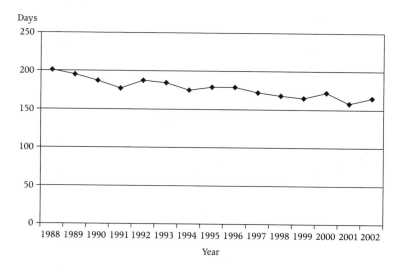

FIGURE 4.1   Median video window, major theatrical features, 1988–2002. (For sources, see Appendix E.)

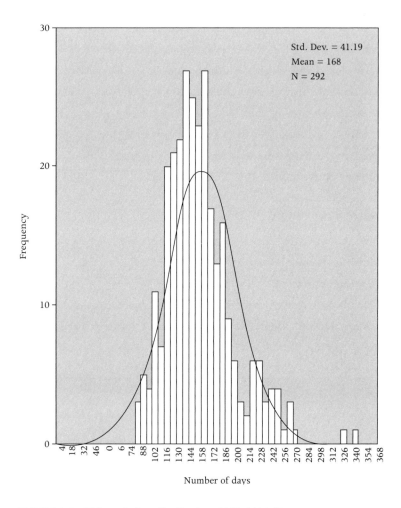

FIGURE 4.2   Video window distribution, 2001–2002. (For sources, see Appendix E.)

sion of data in this section.) The window has slowly declined since 1988, but remained well within the five- to six-month range until the end of 2002 (the latest date for which we have systematic data). Overall, relative stability in the window and certainly no evidence of collapse are shown by these trends.

Turning to movie-by-movie data, the distribution of windows for major theatrical film video releases in 2001–2002 (Figure 4.2) shows that there is quite a bit of variation in windows around the mean of 168 days, including a number of extreme cases. There is a marked tendency, though, for the windows to cluster around the mean.[22]

Finally, Figure 4.3 illustrates the relationship between movie theater run lengths and the median "out-of-market" gap—the period of time between the end of a movie's theater run and its video street date—for major theatrical movies released on video from 1988 to 2002.[23] Only theater run lengths of up to 26 weeks are shown, since there seems lit-

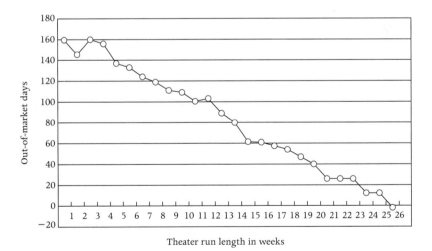

FIGURE 4.3   Median out-of-market days versus length of theater runs, 1988–2001. (For sources, see Appendix E.)

tle question of industry coordination for movies that stay in theaters longer. Many of the video windows over 180 days, for example, probably result because very high theater demand simply pushes them beyond the six-month period (For example, the 2001 film *Dinosaur* had a video window of 256 days and a theater run of 267 days.) In other cases, delays in "authoring" (production) of DVD bonus materials appear to have delayed video releases.[24]

Figure 4.3 shows a strong and consistent inverse relationship between the two variables. For movies that remained in theaters for 26 weeks (180 days), for example—unusually successful films for the most part—the mean out-of-market gap was −2 days, resulting in a mean video window of 178 days. At the other end of the spectrum, the average movie that lasted only one week in theaters was withheld from the market for 168 days, resulting in a video window of 175 days. In the middle, movies that had a theater run length of thirteen weeks (99 days) had an average out-of-market period of 82 days, resulting in an average video window of 190 days.

This relationship between average run lengths and average out-of-market gaps is not entirely smooth; and, as we have seen, there are considerable variations from movie to movie. Overall, however, the data show that while there has been a clustering of video windows in the five- to six-month range, there is practically no statistical relationship between how long a movie stays in theaters and the date that it is released to video.[25] Movies that were relatively successful and stayed in theaters for nearly the full five- to six-month period were quickly released to video and thus have few out-of-market days. Movies that dropped from the theater market quickly were essentially warehoused by their distributors until the five- or six-month interval.

What can we conclude about how well the window setting process has worked from the industry's perspective? Because we do not know what the industry's optimal pattern of windows is to begin with—that is, what windows the players would choose if we allowed them to reform the old Film Boards of Trade—no definitive conclusion can be reached. Yet the relative stability in the window over the 1988–2002 interval and the presence of long out-of-market gaps on average suggest a level of success among distributors in avoiding self-destructive behavior and maintaining windows at levels satisfactory to the industry as a whole.

Just how the industry has managed to maintain the out-of-market gaps is not clear. The window variations in Figure 4.2 indicate no minimum benchmark, such as 180 days, that the window always or consistently tends to exceed, although no movies at all among the 2001–2002 major film releases appeared on video sooner than 95 days after their theater opening. First, however, institutional realities would constrain the precision of any such agreed-upon window benchmark. The studios typically float potential video street dates to their large retail buyers in advance of committing to a final date. For a given movie, these buyers report back the street dates floated by other distributors; as a result, distributor adjustments ranging from a week to perhaps a month or more are commonly made to avoid undesired competitive conflicts.[26] This trial-and-error process is similar to that by which major distributors finalize theatrical release dates, and serves to smooth market flow.[27] Marketing strategies involving holiday release dates also constrain video release strategies. Press reports, for example, indicate that studios often bend the window one way or another to get videos out in time to meet Christmas demand.

Using data for 1,429 major theatrical features released to U.S. theaters between 1988 and 1997, we conducted a separate econometric study to measure the extent to which economic factors, including interest rate, VCR penetration, and movie-specific factors such as box office performance and the season of theater release could account for the variations we observe in the video windows of individual movies.[28] These and some other economic variables had a statistically significant influence. Higher interest rates tended to encourage shorter windows, for example, and higher box office performance led to longer windows. The slow decline in the median window up to 1997 can be accounted for by increased VCR penetration, which moves the economic trade-off between the studio's incentives to encourage theater patronage with long windows versus their incentive to capitalize on the larger video market with shorter windows in favor of the latter. Altogether, though, these economic variables could account for no more than about 20 percent of the movie-to-movie window variations we observed. By far the strongest statistical relationship we observed was the inverse correlation (illustrated in Figure 4.3 for the longer 1988–2002 sample period) between a movie's length of theater run and its out-of-market gap.

We are left without direct evidence that the movie studios and the theater operators have colluded or otherwise coordinated their behavior to maintain video windows longer than a truly competitive market would produce. It is conceivable that if an individual studio adopted a policy of short windows on its own, it would be identified by movie-goers and expectations adjusted for that one studio's output. In that circumstance, long windows might be sustained over time by a competitive market with entirely independent firm behavior. Persuasive explanations for the out-of-market gaps apart from market interaction and coordination of studios, however, are not obvious.

Whether industry coordination has been practiced or not, individual firm reputation established by repeated market interaction over time surely plays an important role. A telling example of what can happen

when the pressures of repeated market involvement are minimal involves Francis Ford Coppola and the distribution of *Apocalypse Now,*
his highly successful Vietnam War epic film. Coppola mostly financed
the $32 million film himself and, in his deal with the distributor,
United Artists, retained control over the television exhibition rights, an
unusual situation for a major theatrical film's producer to be in. According to a *Variety* report, when *Apocalypse Now* was released to theaters in 1979 Coppola publicly declared that he did not intend to sell it
to television because of the diminishing aesthetic effects of the small
screen. But in November 1980, about a year after its theatrical release,
Coppola announced that he had changed his mind and was planning a
TV version that would incorporate unused footage from the original
production.[29] In May 1983, *Apocalypse Now* premiered on ABC, and has
since appeared in videocassette and DVD editions.

Press reports of the time discourage conjecture that Coppola's change
of course was motivated by anything other than artistic integrity.[30] But
if one of the major studios, invested as they are in repeated dealings
with theaters and television, had owned the television rights, would it
have been willing to change such a commitment? Perhaps; but Coppola
himself, as an unlikely repeat player in the movie distribution market,
apparently had little to lose in doing so.

In late 2002 and early 2003, there were some radical experiments, led
by Columbia Pictures, with video windows of little more than three
months for some major theatrical features, including *Maid in Man-
hattan* (2002, 102 days) and *Tears of the Sun* (2003, 95 days).[31] Other studios have followed. Press reports suggest that a relatively high film-to-
film dispersion persists into 2005, but one industry tabulation shows a
drop in the average window from 168 days in 2001 and 165 days in
2002 to 142 days in 2003 and 138 days in 2004.[32]

Whether these changes indicate a breakdown of industry coordination of the video window or simply a transition to some new industry optimum is unclear. Certainly, the explosion of DVD sales has put downward pressure on video windows by making the video market more lucrative relative to theater revenues (see Appendix C). That change in revenue potential shifts the optimal trade-off between encouraging theater attendance and tapping the video market to a shorter out-of-market interval. The rather abrupt change in the average window to a lower plateau in 2003 and 2004 is at least consistent with the theory that some kind of industry cooperation has been occurring in this market.

The Challenge of Piracy, Copying, and Sharing

In 1975, the FBI raided the home of actor Roddy McDowall (of *Lassie Come Home* and *My Friend Flicka* fame) and seized 500 copies of movies and TV programs on 16 mm film that he had made from borrowed studio prints.[33] Although McDowall was later cleared of copyright infringement when he persuaded authorities he was copying for personal use, not for sale or profit, the historical contrasts are telling.[34] In those days of innocence, studio angst over piracy or copying of movies (at least in the United States) usually went little further than this sort of celebrity naughtiness, or its counterpart among soldiers in the military. Studios were protected because it was a glaring crime for a commercial theater to exhibit a stolen movie print, and few people had the home equipment to show one.

Pay TV and VCRs, of course, dramatically changed all that. With home video, pirates now had plenty of time to turn out bogus videocassettes from a stolen or "borrowed" 35 mm print before the studios released their own cassettes six months later. Within private homes, pay TV movies could be copied by subscribers, or access obtained illegally with a rigged decoder box. Prerecorded cassettes could themselves be copied with a dual-deck VCR or two VCRs in tandem. And once in hand by whatever means, a video movie could be shared among uncontrollable numbers of people. Digital technologies and the Internet have, of course, added a new dimension to these problems, dramatically magnifying the potential for copying and sharing of movies to take place. In this section, we explore how successfully the Hollywood studios have so far met these challenges in their domestic market. To do so, we interpret the effects of piracy, copying, and sharing in terms of the price discrimination model.

Piracy, copying, and sharing have often been portrayed by the movie industry and the media that exhibit movies as rampant and crippling problems. The record shows, though, that in spite of still-nagging difficulties, the studios have adroitly used their political influence, the law, and a variety of pricing and distribution strategies to greatly limit the negative effects of these practices in the United States. In some ways, the studios appear to have turned copying, sharing, and even piracy to their advantage by using them to improve their price discrimination system.

We distinguish three categories of piracy, copying, and sharing issues in this chapter: one, "hard goods" commercial piracy; two, stealing pay TV signals; and three, home copying and sharing of pay TV and video movies.[35] The first two are unambiguously illegal, while the third is subject to hazy legal interpretation. Internet file sharing of movies is a fourth category presently in its early stages; we postpone that analysis until our concluding discussion of Hollywood's digital future in Chapter 7. We should also note that in the present chapter we focus almost entirely on the United States. Piracy in foreign markets is a very different story, which we consider briefly in Chapter 5.

Hard Goods Commercial Piracy

Apart from the manufacture of pay TV decoder boxes and other hardware or software that can be used as illegal circumvention devices, nearly all commercial piracy of theatrical features within the United States has involved the manufacture and distribution of counterfeit DVDs or videocassettes. Counterfeit videos can originate from several different sources, including illegally acquired theater film prints, recordings made with handheld devices pointed at the screen by theater patrons, or duplication of legitimate videos. Besides street merchants, stores or Internet sites sell bogus videos, perhaps unwittingly if the piracy takes place upstream in the distribution chain.

The economic consequences of commercial piracy are unambiguously bad for the studios. While industry executives have been criticized for failing to foresee the commercial value of VCRs, they certainly saw their destructive potential for piracy. The MPAA attacked video pirates early and hard on two fronts. In 1975, the first year VCRs were sold to the public and three years before they reached even 1 percent penetration in the United States, the MPAA hired four FBI agents and a former chief of police for the city of Paris to open the Film Security Office in the United States. Its mission was to seek out movie pirates and assist law enforcement officers in their prosecution (in the United States and worldwide). On the legislative front, the MPAA vigorously lobbied Congress for stiffer U.S. penalties, and in 1982 President Reagan signed a revision to the 1976 Copyright Act mandating long jail sentences for commercial video pirates. Seizures and prosecutions followed rapidly.[36] As of the mid-1990s, the MPAA's private investigation force had grown to 100 people in the United States.[37] Following the model of federal drug enforcement authorities, the MPAA publishes statistics on piracy seizures and prosecutions and seems to seek out as much publicity for its efforts as possible.[38] Parallel to this legal enforcement was the development of encryption technology for videocassettes. Mostly through proprietary systems developed by Macrovision Corporation, studios began using anticopy encoding of cassettes in the 1990s to reduce the ability of retail store owners to illegally duplicate them and to identify the origin of counterfeits. Consolidation since the 1980s of video retailers into publicly visible chains undoubtedly reduced the sale of counterfeit videocassettes.

These developments apparently reduced once-rampant commercial videocassette piracy in the United States to low levels. In the early days of VCR diffusion, piracy was reportedly so widespread in the United States that some studios would not release movies on cassettes at all.[39] In 1987, the MPAA estimated losses from video piracy to be $200 to $300 million, which amounted to 10 or 15 percent of total studio revenues from the distribution of prerecorded videocassettes in that year.[40] The MPAA apparently does not publish its methodology for calculating piracy losses.[41] The studios continued to make basically the same $250 million loss claim until 2001, however, while their legitimate video revenues more than quadrupled, implying that U.S. piracy losses had dropped to about 5 percent by 1995 and 3 percent in 2001.[42]

DVD piracy is more threatening to copyright holders than analog VHS because DVDs can be manufactured and distributed faster and more cheaply, and the copies themselves can be essentially perfect. In economic terms, the higher quality of digital reproduction increases potential studio losses from copying or piracy because higher-value consumers may now prefer to take advantage of them.

The studios have several advantages, though, in their battle against hard goods DVD pirates. One is the use of "digital rights management," or DRM, which has become a blanket term covering a variety of devices that owners of digitally distributed information products can employ to control their use.[43] Legitimate DVDs can be encoded with "watermarks" or "fingerprints" that allow copyright owners to trace phony copies to their original source. DVDs can also be encoded with signals that prevent them from being copied or that greatly degrade the quality of copies that can be made. Although copy protection has also been applied to analog VHS, digital systems work better and they are used by studios more frequently.[44] As we discuss later, the most significant use of these and other copy-control technologies is to manipulate consumer home use. Watermarking and DVD copy prevention, however, have proven useful for studios to handicap hard goods piracy attempts and to improve enforcement.

Parallel to the development of DRM technologies have been studio efforts to limit the potential U.S. market for phony DVDs by legal means and via their initiatives with equipment manufacturers. The studios coordinate their antipiracy efforts through the MPAA. A key aspect of these joint efforts has been use of the studios' collective economic leverage over software licensing rights to force hardware manufacturers to produce equipment that includes copy control or anticircumvention devices. A fundamental limitation of any copy prevention technology is that encoded software only works if player hardware is manufactured to recognize those codes. In the DVD case, for example, studios insisted that the major electronics manufacturers agree to produce players with watermark detection capability as part of the DVD copyright protection system.[45] A major legal reinforcement has been enactment in 1998 of the renowned Digital Millennium Copyright Act (DMCA), which prohibits attempts to circumvent hardware or software devices that are designed to protect copyright holders from infringement. It is thus illegal to defeat the devices on DVD players that reject "unauthorized" discs.

The MPAA has furthermore had a running start in its campaign to limit the potential for massive retail sales of counterfeit DVDs in the United States. Their VHS enforcement system is already in place; DVD copy protection R&D is well funded; and, as mentioned earlier, most retail video transactions are handled by large public corporations. The MPAA has reported an increase in seizure of illegal DVDs in the United States.[46] Since 2001, however, the MPAA has apparently ceased making claims of either DVD or VHS piracy for the United States alone, reverting to a single estimate for worldwide losses. There are other suggestions that losses from DVD piracy in the United States are minor. First, although industry spokespersons repeatedly refer to the specter of "perfect" pirated DVD copies, that has apparently not always been the case. In reporting on a 2002 raid of a CD burner factory in New York, for example, the MPAA chastised the criminals for their attempt to "dupe consumers into purchasing a wholly inferior product."[47] An article discussing the MPAA's efforts to close illegal DVD plants referred to stopping the manufacture of videos "sold on street corners and alleys in America."[48] Such reports not only imply low transactions volume in the United States, but they also suggest an important characteristic of pirated, copied, or shared movie users: they tend to be low-value consumers who would not otherwise take advantage of legitimate channels.[49]

In sum, while hard goods DVD piracy is undoubtedly a crippling problem in many countries, especially in Asia, hard goods video piracy in the United States seems to have been well controlled.

Consumer Theft of Pay Television

A thornier piracy problem for the studios in the United States has been illegal reception of subscription pay TV networks or PPV services. The multichannel operators who offer these pay TV services at the retail level are in the best position to control piracy, but they have weaker incentives to do so. The evidence is nevertheless that pay TV piracy is not as bad as it has been made to appear, and that it is diminishing.

Theft of basic and premium cable subscriptions can be accomplished by physically tapping into wires running down a street or by moving into living quarters already wired for cable without notifying the cable operator. Legitimate basic cable subscribers can obtain premium cable services by using illegal "black boxes" that have been programmed to descramble signals. On older cable systems, traps that block certain channels at or near the home premises can be physically removed by the resident. Piracy of DBS services is usually accomplished by obtaining illegally manufactured "smart cards" that descramble the satellite-fed transmissions.

Based on a 1999 survey of its membership, the National Cable Television Association (NCTA) estimated that 9.5 percent of all homes passed (that is, all homes that have cable service available) received premium or PPV networks illegally.[50] Those homes included both legal and illegal receivers of basic service. Roughly the same proportion of homes passed by cable, 11.5 percent, was reported to be stealing their basic service. Recent reports of DBS piracy rates, which usually involves getting all the basic, premium, and PPV services at once, are mixed, ranging from about 5 percent up to 16 percent of all households that receive the service.[51]

Rates of piracy in these ranges translate into much less severe losses for the studios. Cable operators generally discover "unauthorized users" of either basic or premium services by means of periodic electronic "tap audits." These are typically followed by "amnesty" campaigns, in which the operator offers illegal subscribers an opportunity to sign up for paid service to avoid prosecution. The NCTA's piracy estimates are based on the assumption that in lieu of the theft opportunity, all of the thieves would have bought legitimate service. A number of case studies published by antipiracy organizations including the NCTA itself, however, indicate that illegal-to-legal basic subscriber "conversion rates" from cable operators' tap audits are typically in the 25 to 40 percent range.[52] In other words, roughly two thirds of basic cable thieves are low-value consumers who prove unwilling to pay the retail price when they are caught stealing.

Conversion rates for premium cable services alone do not appear to be published.[53] Accepting the NCTA's official piracy incidence estimates at face value, however, and assuming conversion rates for premium services comparable to those for basic, implies cable industry revenue losses from subscription pay and PPV piracy of about one third what the NCTA claims, or in the range of 3 to 4 percent of their total net revenues from pay TV (one third of 9.5 percent). Since contracts are structured to give the movie studios a percentage of the total take, the studios' percentage losses would be in this range as well.

For practical purposes, this estimate of studio losses is probably still on the high side because cable operators appear to use piracy as a marketing device to increase subscribership over the long term. Typically, tap audits are conducted periodically at discrete intervals (e.g., several months or years), rather than continuously. Illegal subscribers thus accumulate during the intervals; and after the audit, the offer to become a legitimate subscriber is made. This process is similar to a traditional market penetration strategy in which cable or DBS operators offer basic service, or certain premium networks, at no charge for the first one or two months in an attempt to get subscribers hooked before payment is required. As the dealer of a "satellite piracy store" in Windsor, Canada, recently declared in connection with their sale of reprogrammed access cards for DBS service, "It's like heroin. Once you have access to all those channels, all those movies, you can't give it up."[54] The implication of this interpretation of the multichannel enforcement system is that at any given time, some of the households classified as illegal pirates by the cable operators are actually subscribers-to-be who are participating in "free trials" of basic or premium service.

From the studios' perspective, piracy deterrence against premium service channel theft in the United States still falls short. The power of enforcement against cable or other multichannel pirates rests almost entirely in the hands of the operators who deal directly with consumers. A long history of anecdotal evidence suggests that the enthusiasm of cable operators for piracy enforcement, especially against premium channel theft, has contrasted sharply with that of the MPAA. As one cable executive was recently quoted as saying in a trade article about the cable industry's "long-neglected scourge": "We left the key in the car. We were looking the other way."[55]

A basic reason that cable operators are tempted to look the other way is that if a legitimate basic service subscriber steals a premium network or PPV movie, the latter products do not legally exist and no payment is made to the network or program supplier. Of course, operators do get a cut of every legitimate premium channel or PPV sale. Their marginal incentive to enforce, however, is reduced because they weigh only their percentage share of a legitimate sale (usually about half), not the full market value of the product. As cable operators frequently point out, tap audits and other enforcement efforts are expensive to conduct; and, as the cable industry's own case studies make obvious, operator enforcement decisions are made on a cost-effectiveness basis.

A related factor discouraging cable operator enforcement is that legal basic subscribers who are enjoying premium networks or PPV programs for no additional charge are more likely to be satisfied with their cable service and thus less inclined to switch to DBS or decide to disconnect and live with a broadcast antenna.

In spite of these nagging frustrations for studios, pay TV piracy has followed a pattern of diminishing importance over time similar to that of counterfeit hard goods. In the early years of subscription pay TV, piracy was reported to be rampant.[56] Before 1980, penalties for unauthorized reception of subscription pay TV signals were mild, and the practice was not even clearly illegal. In fact, a once thriving industry, Home Satellite Dishes (HSD), was largely built on a loophole in the law that allowed owners of these three- to four-foot satellite dishes to get all the programs they wanted for free. Amendments to the 1934 Communications Act, followed by the 1984 Cable Act, specifically declared unauthorized cable and satellite reception to be illegal, and penalties were greatly increased to include potential prison terms.[57] The 1984 act also made illegal the manufacture or alteration of decoder boxes for the purpose of stealing pay TV signals via cable or other wireless systems.[58] These laws were further strengthened by the DMCA, which increased penalties for making or selling black boxes and other circumvention equipment, as well as permitting multichannel providers to demand restitution from pirates they catch.[59]

On the technology front, HBO and other operators began encrypting their satellite signals in the early 1980s, and cable systems began converting to addressable technology that controls legitimate pay network access from the headend, rather than by easily removed mechanical traps on the customer's premises. Addressable systems in conjunction with digital technology can also support "electronic bullets" to catch PPV pirates red-handed. In 1993, for example, Time Warner's Staten Island cable system offered a free T-shirt to subscribers during the Holyfield vs. Bowe PPV boxing match, but all legitimate boxes were programmed to scramble the ad. Thus, only those receiving the match illegally could see the ad. Four hundred people who responded to the ad got a bill for $2,000 in the mail and an order to pay up or confess where they got the boxes.[60] In other cases, electronic bullets have been used to directly identify and disable illegal boxes.[61]

The result of these legal and technological developments is that the cost effectiveness of piracy enforcement at the multichannel operator level is steadily improving. Although no hard data are available, press reports and an increased use of restitution payment demands by cable operators suggest that the operators are in fact becoming more aggressive in pursuing pirates.[62] At least some cable operators, such as Media One, have dropped amnesty or restitution attempts and begun campaigns that attempt to arrest pirates outright.[63]

Our analysis of the cost of pay TV piracy remains incomplete in that one reason studios have been unwilling to grant a more favorable window to PPV is apparently their assumption that black box and other piracy would increase if they were to do so. The most important consideration in this and other such decisions, however, appears to be home copying and sharing, a problem to which we now turn.

Home Copying and Sharing of Pay TV and Video Movies

Copying a movie at home for later use or for sharing with friends and acquaintances—or even just the sharing of a rented or purchased video—can undermine studio profits in basically the same way that piracy can: without that copy, the user may have paid to watch the movie somewhere in the release sequence. As the studios have frequently declared, DVDs and other digital technologies exacerbate the threat of losses from home copying and sharing for basically the same reasons that that they escalate the piracy threat. Digital copies are higher quality, they attract higher-value consumers, and with the right home equipment at hand, they can be copied and physically shared more quickly and conveniently.

So far at least, the studios have managed to limit their losses from home copying and sharing in the United States to low levels. To do so, they have pursued a variety of legal, political, technological, and economic strategies. In at least some ways, the studios have likely been able to use consumer copying and sharing as a device to better segment high- and low-value users and thus more effectively price discriminate. While digital technologies have raised the stakes, DRM has also equipped the studios with improved ways to segment markets and extract value from consumers.

The Law and Politics of Copying and Sharing

Media industry critics have lamented that the strategy of movie and music copyright owners seems to be to gain total legal control over the copying and distribution of their products, with little regard for privacy or other individual rights.[64] While this may well be an accurate description, that strategy does not mean, as often imagined, that they want to snuff out all copying and sharing—only that they want to have the authority of *granting permission.* As copyright owners, they want the flexibility of being able to say no when copying is not in their interest, but permitting or encouraging copying when it can improve their profits. In striving for this objective, the studios have not won every battle, but they have mostly done well on the legal front.

The legality of movie copying and sharing revolves around the interpretation of "fair use." The 1976 Copyright Act mandates that intellectual property may be duplicated by individuals for some purposes, but the specific boundaries of what qualifies as fair use have been a matter of court precedent. In a famous case involving Sony Corporation and the now-defunct Betamax video recorder, the Supreme Court ruled in 1981 that copying of over-the-air broadcast television programs by individuals for personal use (that is, for later exhibition or sharing with others if no personal gain to the copier is involved) is fair use. The case was originally brought by MCA (whose subsidiary, Universal, had television programming as well as theatrical movie interests), on the theory that later exhibitions of copied programs (including movies) would be purged of advertisements and thus diminish the copyright owner's profits.[65] For theatrical film distributors, at least, zapping of commercials has proven to be of little importance since few revenues come from that source.

Copyright law specifically prohibits duplication by users of prerecorded videos. Copying for personal use off of cable television, including premium networks and PPV, has, however, generally gone unchallenged in court and is thus presumed legal as fair use.

The de facto legality of pay TV movie recording has been a frustration for the studios, at least in the case of PPV. They have fruitfully focused their efforts, however, on public information campaigns against back-to-back copying of prerecorded videos, and on forcing hardware and software manufacturers to integrate technological restraints that prevent or control copying. As discussed below, paralleling the latter efforts has been successful lobbying for antipiracy legislation (notably the DMCA) and for FCC regulations that legally mandate DRM copy controls over digital programs delivered via multichannel systems.

Back-to-Back Video Copying

Though it is now fading into the background, the precursor to consumer duplication of rented or purchased DVDs using a computer or DVD burner is copying VHS tapes with two VCRs in tandem, or with a dual-deck VCR. DVDs can also be copied to VHS with a DVD-VHS combo machine.[66] All of these procedures are illegal, and apparently they have not led to much back-to-back copying of legitimate video movies.

Although well over half of U.S. households own multiple VCRs, few of their owners (11 percent of VCR households by one report in 2000) have ever taken the trouble to connect their machines.[67] When Go-Video, a small electronics company, patented a dual-deck VCR design in the mid-1980s, the MPAA foresaw a threat and opposed its import into the United States.[68] Go-Video later sued the MPAA and nine or more Japanese and Korean electronics manufacturers under the antitrust laws, alleging that the MPAA had used its leverage over licensing rights to persuade the manufacturers to refuse to supply components for Go-Video's machine. In 1988, the suit was settled. Go-Video agreed that all dual-deck VCRs it sold in the United States would have anticopying devices, and the MPAA dropped its opposition to the machine's importation. Dual-deck machines never reached significant market penetration in the United States, but the basic copy-control agreement was later extended to all VCRs (and later to all DVD-to-VHS recorders) that are sold in the United States. The DMCA codified these restrictions by mandating that all VCRs sold in the United States be equipped with copy-protection technology patented by Macrovision Corp.[69]

Copy-protection codes can be defeated by savvy consumers, but the MPAA's video-control efforts have again been enhanced by the DMCA's prohibition of attempts to defeat them. Besides these maneuvers, the familiar FBI warnings at the beginning of every video movie have apparently had an effect. In a 1996 survey, only 4 percent of respondents agreed with the statement "People should be allowed to tape and sell prerecorded videos to other people."[70]

The result of these efforts to date has been fairly minor back-to-back video copying and sharing in the United States. Surveys indicate that between 4 percent and 7 percent of adults with access to a VCR have admitted to successfully making a back-to-back copy of a prerecorded videocassette in the past year.[71] (Attempts to make copies were reported to fail about half the time.)[72] Most tapes appeared to be made with the copier's intending to keep them, but some sharing goes on. A 1989 Office of Technology survey reported that 70 percent of adults who made tapes did so with the intent of keeping them, but 42 percent of the originals had been obtained from friends, versus only 23 percent from stores.[73] Sharing also occurs after the fact. A 1993 survey found that while only 7 percent of households had themselves made a copy from a prerecorded video in the past year, 18 percent said that others had made copies for them.[74]

These surveys also suggest that users of illegal home video copies, like pay TV pirates, tend to be relatively low-value consumers who offer few other significant revenue opportunities for the studios.[75] Respondents who used the back-to-back copies said that they would otherwise have rented the same video about two-thirds of the time, and would have purchased the same video only about one-third of the time.[76] Taking these statements at face value, we calculate total industry losses from back-to-back video copying and sharing, as a percentage of total retail video revenues, to be in the 1 percent to 3 percent range during the 1990s.[77]

The rapid diffusion of consumer hardware that can quickly create high-quality DVD copies raises the stakes of back-to-back copying; but so far, the equally rapid development of anticopy technology has apparently left that activity in the hands of a relatively few technologically savvy individuals.

Copying from PPV and Subscription Pay Television

All indications are that consumer copying of PPV movies has been much more prevalent than back-to-back video duplication. Surveys done since the late 1980s report that about one quarter to one third of PPV subscribers say that they copy at least some movies.[78] A 2000 survey estimated that about 15 percent of all PPV movie exhibitions were taped.[79] A closer look, however, suggests that the negative effects of this pay TV copying are less than these statistics may suggest.

Because movie distributor revenues from PPV and VOD are tiny relative to home video, the direct financial effect of any à la carte pay TV copying is certainly a very small part of total studio revenues. The full impact on the studios may be greater, though, because of the studios' claim that the propensity for PPV copying, as well as piracy, is a major factor inducing them to maintain a PPV window that is 45-plus days later than the video window.

The rather lame history of PPV (Chapter 3), plus the likelihood that an earlier window would have negative effects on home video demand, should temper any estimate of how lucrative an earlier, copy-protected PPV/VOD window would be for the studios. They have demonstrated, in fact, an apparent ambivalence to PPV piracy protection. Since the late 1990s, the overwhelming proportion of legitimate black boxes that cable subscribers use to order and decode PPV programs have been equipped with Macrovision copy-protection technology. PPV digital encryption is reportedly difficult to defeat, giving the studios a potentially high degree of control over PPV copying, especially in light of the DMCA. At least as of 2003, though, cable and DBS operators had reportedly not enabled the anticopy encoding on their set-top boxes, and apparently no studios had chosen to encrypt their PPV movies with the Macrovision codes that would prevent copying.[80] Dormancy of the anticopy encoding for PPV has apparently been the result of a standoff between the studios and the cable operators, who want a commitment that the PPV window will be moved forward in exchange for enabling the black boxes. Recent trade press reports indicate that due to their increasing optimism for VOD, studios have been reconsidering their options of having PPV and VOD copy protection in conjunction with an earlier window.[81] Time may tell if such a development revitalizes à la carte pay TV, but studios' actions to date suggest that they have not believed that an earlier, copy-protected PPV window would increase their profits.[82]

Undoubtedly, subscribers to premium movie channels frequently make copies. Surveys have shown that by far the most frequently copied type of television programming by all VCR owners is movies, and the most widely available source for commercial-free films is these subscription networks.[83] As we discuss later, the premium subscription release window is far enough down in the release sequence that copying and sharing of movies apparently have only a minor effect on demand for movies on other media.

Studio Benefits from Copying and Sharing

How can the studios mitigate losses from the home copying and sharing of movies that does take place, or even turn copying and sharing to their economic advantage? In general, video renters and purchasers, PPV buyers, and subscription pay TV subscribers who copy or share movies do so because they receive at least some value beyond just their own one-time enjoyment of the movie. To that extent, studios can earn greater revenues because copying and sharing consumers have higher price demands for the video and PPV media they copy.[84] In the 1980s, for example, the demand-enhancing benefits of subscription pay television copying were demonstrated by network advertising campaigns that promoted copying as a reason to subscribe.[85]

In the case of individuals who copy movies from these sources and retain the copies for their own later use, the studio's ability to extract higher demand is straightforward. Those people are willing to pay higher prices to reflect both their one-time enjoyment and their prospect of future viewings—or at least the option demand of having the movie available. In the case of sharing outside the household, either of a copied movie or of a rented or purchased "original" video, the ability to extract value is more problematic. Potentially, though, copying and sharing can be advantaged as a price discrimination device to tap low-value demands that were previously inaccessible.

Consider the following example (which will come in handy to our later discussion of how Internet file sharing can potentially benefit studios). Say that Consumer A is willing to pay $5 to watch a PPV movie, while Consumer B will pay only $2. If no copying or sharing is possible, the PPV operator's best price is $5. Only A will buy, yielding revenues of $5.

Now say that it becomes possible for Consumer A to copy and then physically share the movie with B. Copying and sharing has a cost, however, to the person who makes and delivers the copy. Say that this cost is $1. If A and B could make an advance plan to pool their resources with the sharing in mind, the seller could potentially charge $6 for the PPV exhibition ($5 + $2 − $1), thus extracting all the potential value.

More commonly, perhaps, such pooling of resources does not take place. In that case, the most that the PPV operator can charge is the value to A of actually watching the movie *plus the value to A of sharing it with B*. Ordinarily, one would expect, the latter value will be smaller than the benefit that B actually gets from watching the movie. Still, though, the PPV operator may at least be able to extract more total value than when copying and sharing is not possible at all. Say that the value to A from sharing with B is $1.50. In this case, the operator can charge $5.50 (A's value of $5 plus $1.50, less the $1 cost). Essentially, the seller has used copying and sharing as a price discrimination device by attracting a low-value consumer into the market who otherwise would not have watched the movie at all.

In many cases, of course, the users of copied or shared "originals" will be higher-value consumers who decide as a result not to buy or rent the video, PPV exhibition, or premium network. It is a good guess that the studios lose money on net from copying and sharing activities. The point of our example is simply that there is a silver lining to the already fairly low incidence of home copying and sharing activities.

DRM as Ideal Price Discrimination

We have noted that as the transition to digital movie media proceeds—DVDs, digital PPV, VOD, and their variations—the higher quality of copied and shared movies increases the likelihood that their users will in fact be the higher-value customers who decide to cancel demands for "original" movies as a result. Recent political activity of the MPAA, though, demonstrates how DRM controls also offer studios the prospect of more efficient price discrimination via selective harnessing of home copying and sharing.

DRM is remarkably versatile. Copying of DVDs, PPV, or broadcast transmissions can not only be prevented, but also be limited to one or to some other particular number of copies via digital encoding. Through DRM, these capabilities open up pricing possibilities foreclosed to the studios in an analog world.

The potential of DRM for effective price discrimination is illustrated by legislative and regulatory initiatives the studios have pursued. In 1996, the MPAA helped prepare the Digital Video Recording Act, legislation that would have required consumer hardware sold in the United States to prohibit any copies of a digitally prerecorded video or of a digitally transmitted PPV, to allow only one copy of a premium channel program, and to allow unlimited copies of broadcast or basic cable exhibitions. That bill was abandoned, but a very similar proposal soon resurfaced with efforts by the MPAA to induce five major equipment manufacturers (known as the "5C") to incorporate technology in their hardware that would control copying of digital programming distributed by multichannel operators (e.g., cable and DBS). These controls would block all PPV or VOD copying, permit one copy of a premium or basic cable network program, and permit unlimited copies from unencrypted broadcast exhibitions.[86]

Meanwhile, the MPAA has continued to lobby for regulations or congressional legislation that would legally force all equipment manufacturers to include copy protection devices conforming to the software restrictions. In 2003, the FCC adopted "Plug and Play" rules that classify certain digital transmissions by multichannel operators (such as cable or DBS) according to how copyright owners can restrict consumer copying of them. The FCC rules mandate that digital PPV or VOD programs can be restricted to no copies, that premium subscription channels, nonpremium subscription TV (i.e., basic channels), and other "conditional access" programming can be restricted to one copy, but that no copy restrictions on unencrypted digital broadcast programming can be imposed.[87] Modifications or legal challenges of the FCC rules remain possible.[88] Essentially, however, the FCC adopted in 2003 nearly the same rules for digital TV transmissions over multichannel systems tha the MPAA had advocated since 1996.

Of course, it is difficult to judge what particular rules the MPAA might advocate outside of a political environment in which both home copying advocates and equipment manufacturers exert their influence. Yet the MPAA's initial proposals and the 2003 FCC rules appear to make economic sense as a way to enhance the efficiency of pricing within the release sequence. Any copies made from PPV, VOD, or DVD, especially if the former window is moved up, would tend to appeal to higher-value viewers, thus undermining the sequence. It is reasonable to expect, though, that allowing a single copy of a subscription pay TV movie would enhance the subscription's value to the buyer by more than it undermines demands for other media in the sequence. That is, the pay TV window is far enough down the line so that the impact of copying and sharing is surely low, and permission for only a single copy would seem to discourage any rampant sharing among friends. Allowing unlimited copies of commercial-ridden broadcast programs, while not ostensibly in the interest of the MPAA, would seem at most a low-cost political concession to recording rights advocates.

The Plug and Play rules do not apply to encrypted broadcast television programming. Although recent court action has not been in the MPAA's favor, that leaves open the possibility for suppliers of over-the-air HDTV transmissions to prevent copying (via the "Broadcast Flag"), thus laying the groundwork for segmentation of high-value HDTV consumers from low-value receivers of standard-quality television broadcasts.[89]

As an MPAA official commented, "What we have with copy-once content protection technology is the ability to go beyond just a pay-per-view business model to a pay-per-copy business model."[90] Or, from the perspective of one home copying rights advocate: "If content has its way, the 'play' button will become the 'pay' button."[91]

The potential of digital technologies to create pay buttons is limited by the apparent disinclination of consumers to pay at every turn. It is evident, though, that while the stakes are higher, the studios stand to gain much more from copying activity in the digital world than they could in the analog world. We return to DRM technology in Chapter 7 as we discuss the challenge to the studios of uncontrolled Internet distribution of movies.

Chapter 5

Rising American Dominance

We have so far focused almost entirely on Hollywood's domestic market. As we noted in the Introduction, though,
foreign markets for Hollywood's theatrical films account for nearly half
of U.S. studio income and have made a contribution at least as great as
the domestic market to revenue growth since at least the early 1980s
(see Appendix C).

One source of this growth has been expansion of the foreign markets
themselves. As in the United States, countries around the world have
seen their mix of movie revenue sources transformed by the lucrative pay television and video technologies. Foreign movie markets have
on the whole, however, grown more slowly than the U.S. market. The
main source of foreign revenue growth has been a steady rise since the
1970s in the market shares that American movies have captured. In the
process, Hollywood's blockbusters and other movies have become the
world's common denominators, submerging many countries' indigenous film industries.

In this chapter we explore this pattern of change. Why have Hollywood movies done so much better in the world marketplace over the past three decades than the products of other countries? The general subject of American film industry dominance has attracted an extraordinary amount of attention from industry observers and academics in a variety of disciplines. Although most of these works have not been concerned with the trend of rising American dominance per se, their efforts have made it evident that cultural, social, and political, as well as economic, factors have contributed to the imbalance.

Our focus in this chapter is on the contribution that economic development of movie exhibition media has made to growing American dominance. In essence, the United States' faster and more successful development of the pay media since the 1970s has increased the size of the American "home market" for movies relative to that of its foreign trading partners. Because a country's home market is comparatively more important than its foreign markets as a means to support movie production investments, American producers have been able to supply a larger number of more attractive movies for the international market than have indigenous producers. In turn, the more successful development of the domestic movie market in the United States can partly be attributed to government policies more conducive to movie media development.

The Pattern of Dominance

In studying American performance in other countries, we focus on the United States and five of its major movie trading partners: Japan and the four most populous countries in Europe—Germany, the United Kingdom, France, and Italy (for convenience, we'll refer to them as the EUJ5). Not only were we able to assemble extensive data for these countries; we also note that Japan, Germany, the U.K., France, and Italy were, respectively, the first, second, third, fourth, and eighth largest export markets for U.S. movies in 1999.[1] Together, these five countries accounted for nearly half (47 percent) of all MPAA-company theatrical film rentals from foreign markets in that year. As one would expect, the EUJ5, along with the United States, also make up most of the total world box office. The United States is definitely the 800-pound gorilla here, however, accounting by itself for 44 percent of world box office revenues in 2001, while the United States and the EUJ5 together garnered 73 percent of all world movie ticket revenues.[2] Thus, even though most foreign countries receive little attention in this chapter, the few that we focus on make up a large majority of the overall world market for movies.

Movies at the Box Office

A broad picture of rising American dominance is painted by Figure 5.1, which shows box office market share data for American movies in the EUJ5 since the 1950s. (See Appendix F for a discussion of these data and their sources.)

At least for Germany, Italy, and France (the three countries having continuous data) American movies have claimed a major portion of the box office throughout the half century since World War II. The fortunes of American films generally declined or remained steady in these three countries until about the early 1970s. Since then, American market shares increased markedly before stabilizing in the mid-1990s, at a point where they routinely account for more than half the box office in these nations as well as in Britain.

An accompanying decline in the fortunes of domestically produced movies in all of the EUJ5 countries is shown in Figure 5.2. In roughly a mirror image to Figure 5.1, the prosperity of each country's films increased or held steady until about the mid-1970s in the four European

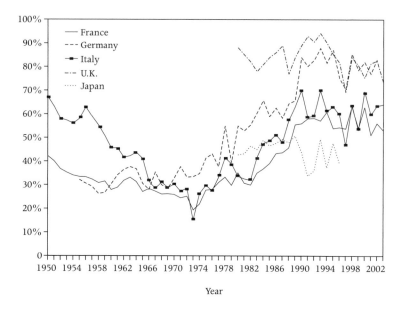

FIGURE 5.1   Box office market shares of U.S. films in the EUJ5, 1950–2003.
(For sources, see Appendix F.)

nations, but then steadily declined into the 1990s. Japan shows the same general pattern, although the strength of its domestic production industry began to ebb earlier. Over time, Japan and France have sustained the strongest domestic film industries among the EUJ5, but still had domestic market shares of only about one third in 2003.[3] The fall from glory has perhaps been greatest for the Italian film industry, which at its peak in 1971 accounted for 64 percent of the Italian box office, the highest in Europe, but for only 22 percent in 2003.

Although the limited data in Figure 5.1 for U.S. market shares in the United Kingdom show little trend, it is apparent from Figure 5.2 that American movies in Britain experienced the same general pattern of declining shares until about 1970, and then rising fortunes thereafter;

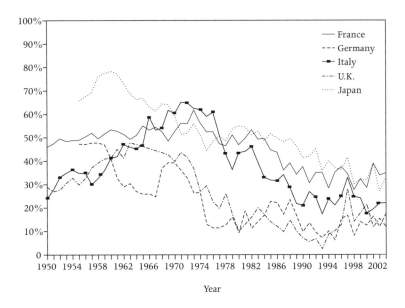

FIGURE 5.2   Box office market shares of domestic films in the EUJ5, 1950–2003. (For sources, see Appendix F.)

similarly for Japan, although the implied turning point was earlier. A factor in the sustained decline of domestic market shares in Europe shown in Figure 5.2 has been the loss of a fairly active interregional trade that some of the major European nations had in the 1960s and 1970s.[4] Since American movies account for consistently high fractions of all imported movies in Britain and Japan for the years for which we have separate data, however, it is likely that U.S. market shares in those countries have followed a generally inverse pattern to the domestic share trends shown in Figure 5.2.[5]

By contrast, Americans have always had a notorious distaste for foreign movies, but their lack of interest appears to have become even more pronounced in recent years. U.S. box office market shares of imported films averaged about 5 percent in the 1980s and '90s. Available data for the 1958–64 period indicate a 7 to 10 percent average foreign share, not including historically important imports from Britain. (See Appendix F.)

As noted in the Introduction, the greater prosperity of foreign films in former times reflects the high visibility that European and Japanese movie stars and directors had in America from the late 1950s to the mid-1970s. Of course, in recent years there have been several successful foreign movies, including *The Full Monty* (1997) from Britain, *Life Is Beautiful* (1998) from Italy, and the Chinese language film *Crouching Tiger, Hidden Dragon* (2000), a coproduction of Taiwan, Hong Kong, China, and the United States. But appearances can be deceiving. Since at least 1990, no foreign movie has made it onto the list of top ten American box office films.

The pattern of American movie dominance as it has evolved is shown by cross-country comparisons of the top ten movies in the United States and each of the EUJ5 countries in 1999 (Table 5.1). Comparing the rankings of particular movies in different countries can be misleading because of time lags in their dates of theatrical release. Several key points, though, emerge from Table 5.1. One, American movies dominate the American box office and have, to varying degrees, a very high presence in all of the other five countries. Two, the best-performing American movies—most of them special-effects-laden science-fiction, action-adventure, or animated blockbusters—tend to appear not only on the U.S. list, but also on the lists of several different countries. That is, they are common denominators for audiences worldwide. Third, at least some domestically produced films, which at least in the Table 5.1 list tend more toward the comedy genre, or animation in Japan— do very well in their countries of origin. With some rather unusual exceptions, however—notably the French-German-Italian coproduc-

Table 5.1   Top ten box office films in the United States and the EUJ5, 1999

Country	Rank	Title	Producing country	Genre
U.S.	1	Star Wars: Episode 1	U.S.	Sci-fi/adventure/action
	2	The Sixth Sense	U.S.	Thriller/drama/horror
	3	Toy Story 2	U.S.	Animation
	4	The Spy Who Shagged Me	U.S.	Comedy
	5	The Matrix	U.S.	Action/thriller/sci-fi
	6	Tarzan	U.S.	Animation
	7	Big Daddy	U.S.	Comedy
	8	The Mummy	U.S.	Adventure/action/horror
	9	Runaway Bride	U.S.	Comedy/romance
	10	The Blair Witch Project	U.S.	Horror/thriller
Germany	1	Star Wars: Episode 1	U.S.	Sci-fi/adventure/action
	2	Notting Hill	U.K.-U.S.	Comedy/romance/drama
	3	The Mummy	U.S.	Adventure/action/horror
	4	Runaway Bride	U.S.	Comedy/romance
	5	Tarzan	U.S.	Animation
	6	The Matrix	U.S.	Action/thriller/sci-fi
	7	A Bug's Life	U.S.	Animation
	8	The World Is Not Enough	U.K.-U.S.	Action/thriller
	9	Astérix et Obélix contre César	Fr.-Ger.-It.	Adventure/fantasy/comedy
	10	You've Got Mail	U.S.	[not available]
U.K.	1	Star Wars: Episode 1	U.S.	Sci-fi/adventure/action
	2	Notting Hill	U.K.-U.S.	Comedy/romance/drama
	3	A Bug's Life	U.S.	Animation
	4	The Spy Who Shagged Me	U.S.	Comedy
	5	The World Is Not Enough	U.K.-U.S.	Action/thriller
	6	Shakespeare in Love	U.S.	Romance/comedy
	7	The Mummy	U.S.	Adventure/action/horror
	8	The Matrix	U.S.	Action/thriller/sci-fi
	9	Tarzan	U.S.	Animation
	10	The Blair Witch Project	U.S.	Horror/thriller
France	1	Astérix et Obélix contre César	Fr.-Ger.-It.	Adventure/fantasy/comedy
	2	Star Wars: Episode 1	U.S.	Sci-fi/adventure/action
	3	Tarzan	U.S.	Animation
	4	The Matrix	U.S.	Action/thriller/sci-fi
	5	Notting Hill	U.K.-U.S.	Comedy/romance/drama
	6	A Bug's Life	U.S.	Animation

Table 5.1 (continued)

Country	Rank	Title	Producing country	Genre
	7	The Mummy	U.S.	Adventure/action/horror
	8	Wild, Wild West	U.S.	Action/western/adventure/ comedy/sci-fi
	9	Jeanne d'Arc	Fr.	[not available]
	10	The World Is Not Enough	U.K.-U.S.	Action/thriller
Italy	1	Notting Hill	U.K.-U.S.	Comedy/romance/drama
	2	Shakespeare in Love	U.S.	Romance/comedy
	3	The Sixth Sense	U.S.	Thriller/drama/horror
	4	Tarzan	U.S.	Animation
	5	Cosi' e la vita	It.	Comedy
	6	The Mummy	U.S.	Adventure/action/horror
	7	Star Wars: Episode 1	U.S.	Sci-fi/adventure/action
	8	Eyes Wide Shut	U.S.	Thriller/drama
	9	Astérix et Obélix contre César	Fr.-Ger.-It.	Adventure/fantasy/comedy
	10	Runaway Bride	U.S.	Comedy/romance
Japan	1	Armageddon	U.S.	Action/romance/sci-fi/thriller
	2	Star Wars: Episode 1	U.S.	Sci-fi/adventure/action
	3	The Matrix	U.S.	Action/thriller/sci-fi
	4	Pokemon	Japan	Animation
	5	The Sixth Sense	U.S.	Thriller/drama/horror
	6	Ringu-2	Japan	Thriller
	7	Poppoya	Japan	Animation
	8	Doraemon	Japan	Animation
	9	The Mummy	U.S.	Adventure/action/horror
	10	Eyes Wide Shut	U.S.	Thriller/drama

Sources: EAO, *Focus 2000: World Film Market Trends* (Strasbourg, France, 2000), *www.imdb.com.*

tion *Astérix et Obélix contre César,* and the British-U.S. coproduction *Notting Hill*—these films tend to do poorly outside their countries of origin. The overwhelming overall American advantage at the box office is emphatically demonstrated by the fact that in 1999, 24 out of the top 25 movies ranked by total world box office were American-produced. Similarly lopsided fractions have persisted in the 1990s and early 2000s.[6] For early years, box office information like this is available only in bits and pieces, but to illustrate the great changes, nine of the top ten films of 1975 in France were French produced. In 1969–1970, six of the top ten German films were German, with one Italian, one British, and two American productions making up the rest.[7]

For countries outside the EUJ5, most of them much smaller, sketchier and shorter-term information shows parallel trends in box office market shares.[8] American shares have increased in nearly all European countries since at least the early or mid-1980s, though in most of the smallest nations, domestic shares have been so low historically that trends are barely observable. National films in Switzerland, Belgium, and Luxembourg, for example, have not earned more than 5 percent of the box office since at least 1985, and most of the rest of the films are American. Comparable patterns of rising American dominance are seen in Latin America and most of Asia, although the receptivity of Asian populations to American movies has been generally less than in other regions.[9]

There remain some notable exceptions to the pattern of American dominance of the world theatrical box office. Tiny Hong Kong managed to produce movies attracting 42 percent of its theater audience in 2000, and its producers earn movie export revenues way out of proportion to the country's size and wealth. (Hong Kong's box office share has declined, however; it was 58 percent in 1990.) In India, American movies are reported to earn only 5 to 8 percent of the theater box office, though it remains unclear how much effect trade barriers to the import of American films have had in that country.[10] Another exception, the Korean film industry, is reported to be booming, its domestic box office share rising from 25 percent in 1996 to over 50 percent in 2003, and its export markets expanding.[11]

In several countries, notably China and the Eastern European nations, strict trade barriers to theatrical exhibition of American films were relaxed in the 1990s, and those changes are responsible in part for an increased American movie presence.[12] In most countries, though, including the EUJ5, trade barriers to movie imports for theater or home video exhibition have been minor, or at least ineffective, since at least World War II.

Movies on Other Media

American movies seem to be even more dominant on video in countries outside the United States than they are in theaters. In Europe, domestic films are reported to be more underrepresented on video than in theaters, and scraps of data seem to confirm this. A French government report, for example, stated that only 10 to 15 percent of wholesale income from video movies in 1994–1995 was for French films, compared to about double that for theater revenues.[13] Available lists of top-performing movies on video in Europe show an even greater prevalence of American films than do the box office lists, with the same U.S. blockbusters topping the lists from country to country.[14] Anecdotal reports have indicated that American movies also dominate the Japanese video market, though to a lesser extent.[15]

Video market share trends over time probably follow box office market share trends, since movies that do well in theaters tend to do well on video. Furthermore, since the video market did not exist thirty years ago and seems at least as U.S.-dominated as the theater market, this market could only have added to the upward trend in American movie industry control worldwide.

On foreign television systems, American movies are less dominant than they are in theaters or video stores, but they have a strong presence in most countries. In nearly all the world, including the EUJ5, government influence, via direct control, legislation, or political pressure, has actively restricted the proportion of American movies and other programs on publicly and privately operated broadcast television systems, so it is difficult to determine the influence of market forces directly. Content studies of European free television generally show that U.S. movies account for about half of the theatrical feature films exhibited.[16] In Japan, the majority of imported fiction programming is American, although the overall percentages of program imports on free Japanese broadcast channels are too low for Japan to be a very significant television market for U.S. movies.[17] On the earliest and largest pay television system in Europe, Canal Plus, French government quotas have actively restricted non-European programs (namely American movies) to no more than 50 percent of total programming hours since the service began in 1984. The proportions of American films on other majorpremium movie services in Europe and Japan, most of them starting after 1990 and less restrained by quotas, are probably as high or higher.

Trends over time in the market shares of American movies on foreign television systems could not be documented. As we discuss later, television outlets worldwide have exploded since the early 1980s due to privatization of public systems and channel capacity expansion, most of which has gone into private hands. Certainly the absolute supply of American movies on all foreign television has vastly grown as a result. The earliest reports from the 1960s and 1970s indicate a strong American presence among the relatively few theatrical films that were shown on European and Japanese TV.[18] It seems likely that the recent technological and policy changes have served to maintain or expand the American share. In Europe, the newer private, free broadcast channels, including Channel 5 in Britain; K1, Pro 7, and RTL 2 in Germany; Italia 1 and Rete 4 in Italy; and M6 in France, have tended to carry American

movies in high doses.[19] The newer pay television systems in these countries have followed a similar path.

American Dominance in Perspective

The increasing world prevalence of American movies has dealt a double blow to film production industries outside the United States. Not
only have larger slices of their domestic markets been taken by American films, but also, as the market share trend data indicate, the export markets they once relied on—mostly regional, but including the
United States—have also been squeezed by the rising worldwide American dominance.

European, Japanese, and other film industries around the world are
still, of course, a source of vibrant and creative—as well as commercially successful—movies. In the United States, several foreign movies
have been nominated for Best Picture at the Academy Awards, and in
1998, the Italian film *La Vita è Bella (Life Is Beautiful)* actually won. A
series of European Union and other government reports in the 1990s,
however, have documented the economic decline of film industries in
Europe, and discussed their increasing dependence on state subsidies.[20]
Only a small minority of the films produced in Europe ever cross international borders in trade.[21] About half of all European films produced
in 1993–1994 were reported to receive direct state subsidies, and the
level of these subsidies has apparently increased since then.[22] Although
available data are ambiguous, one critic of European subsidy programs
has claimed that a majority of many European theatrical film budgets
are essentially state subsidies.[23]

American supremacy in the world trade of movie products is not
unique; but in economic terms it is an extreme, as well as a very significant, case. In 2000, U.S. exports of "audiovisual products" (all the-

atrical, video, and television software, the large majority of which are theatrical features) to the fifteen countries of the European Union were put at $9.0 billion, while imports were only $851 million—a roughly 10-to-1 ratio that has more than tripled in dollar terms since the first comparable data were reported for 1988.[24] The audiovisual export-to-import ratio is probably just as lopsided for non-European countries. If so, the net balance of trade accounted for by U.S exports of these products worldwide was probably around $14 billion in 2000.[25] That is not only a major net contribution to the U.S. balance of payments, but very few if any significant U.S. industries seem to have such a skewed export-import ratio.[26]

Among media products other than movies, American television series and other made-for-TV programming dominate world television program trade volume. That trade is much less important in economic terms, however, and U.S. programs produced for television rarely account for more than half the fiction televised in major countries.[27] In the only other media sector with substantial trade volume, recorded music, a trade association report showed "domestic repertoire" to account for 93 percent of recorded music sales in the United States in 2002 and for 59 percent in France, 45 percent in Germany, 45 percent in Italy, 54 percent in the U.K., and 74 percent in Japan. Except for the United States, these numbers (along with comparable data for sixty-five other countries in the study) indicate that domestic market shares in music tend to be much higher than that of the theater box office.[28] In book publishing, American products are also prominent internationally, but what skimpy data there are indicate that in most countries (including the United States) home-grown authors account for most sales of fictional works.[29] Certainly in newspapers, magazines, and radio, the origin of content around the world is overwhelmingly domestic.[30]

Explanations for American Dominance

How have American movies (and television) come to dominate the world market? Here we distill the most plausible explanations that have been advanced. Some of these involve economics; others do not.[31]

1. *The Home Market Advantage.* An economic element favoring the United States is the inherent advantage of having a large and lucrative home market to support its production industry.[32] The United States has a much bigger home market for movies than any of its trading partners, and this fact has much to do with the arguments we develop later in this chapter.

2. *The Lure of Things American and the Prevalence of the English Language.* If audiences around the world are fascinated with America in some sense—its glitzy economic success, its worldwide political and military might, or its political and cultural freedoms—they are likely to be drawn to see its movies or other media products. A more specific cause may be the "Madison Avenue" effect: the idea that relentless advertising of American products, and of course the products themselves (Coca-Cola, Disneyland, McDonald's, et al.), are so prevalent around the world that audiences develop an Americanized consumer consciousness that lures them to American movies and television.[33]

Related to an Americanized consumer consciousness is that English is the world's most widely understood language. The better international audiences around the world can understand American movie dialog, the higher the demand for American movies should presumably be.[34] Dubbing is routine in larger countries outside the United States, but language may also be correlated with the notion of "cultural proximity" as an explanation of the receptivity of American movies and TV programs in different regions of the world.[35] Certainly, the native-English-speaking populations of Britain, Australia, Ireland, and Canada have always been among the most receptive to American movie exports.

3. *Cultural Advantages of the United States as a Producing Nation.* Many have observed that American producers have a remarkable talent for making movies and TV programs that transcend geographic boundaries. In the words of Scott Robert Olson, Americans are skilled in making "transparent texts"—stories that can be enjoyed by diverse peoples, though perhaps interpreted in quite different ways.[36]

As an immigrant nation, America is the great melting pot. Perhaps this is what gives American producers a special understanding of how to make movies that appeal to a wide range of audiences in other countries. American producers have at least had to learn how to make movies that appeal to the diverse social and cultural heritages that American audiences have. That experience translates into the knack of making movies having worldwide appeal.[37]

4. *Differences in "the System": Business Culture and Practices, Infrastructure, and Technology.* While European and other foreign film industries have been modeled on the "auteur" theory, in which the film's director has a high degree of control of the end product, the American studio system is perceived to use a much more bottom-line-oriented method, in which creative control is more firmly in the hands of business executives.[38] Especially when compared to Europe, Hollywood has far more efficient machinery for distribution and marketing, and European systems for financing films one by one are not as efficient as the

American arrangement, in which studios tend to fund slates of movies all at once through revolving bank credit.[39] In addition, at least until recently, European countries as a whole have been said to have an outdated infrastructure of movie theaters to exhibit films, thus weakening the best opportunities that European producers have to launch their own wares into the market.

Another system-related factor is that the United States is a world leader in technology and innovation (of particular value in developing special effects) and has an abundance of support industries (such as film processing and special effects contractors), favorable production conditions (including the Hollywood weather), and the advantages of intense firm rivalry (that is, among the seven major studios) for honing the competitive skills of the participants in the Hollywood industry.[40]

5. *Political and Economic Aggression of Hollywood and the U.S. Government.* The "cultural imperialism" school of thought argues that movie and other mass media flows are unbalanced and unidirectional—that is, coming from the United States—because they reflect the exploitative structure of world power in American hands. In this model, powerful multinational corporations, in league with the U.S. government, use the media as an instrument to maintain and expand the American empire.[41] A more transparent version of the same general idea is that American movie dominance is due to extremely aggressive behavior by the MPAA, hand in hand with the U.S government, to promote Hollywood's business interests abroad.[42] These basic arguments have been the most prevalent and enduring theme of a long history of treatises on American media dominance.

The equally long history of hard-fought attempts by governments around the world to limit the importation of American movies and TV programs has been largely one of frustration for those countries, due to boycotts organized by the Motion Picture Association (MPA, a legal cartel of MPAA members, formerly called the Motion Picture Export Association) or, especially in recent years, by U.S. government threats that if trade barriers to movies and TV programs are not relaxed or if copyright laws are not strictly enforced to limit piracy, a penalty of wider trade sanctions would be imposed.

These MPAA–U.S. government efforts have for the most part been successful.[43] Given the sizable contributions that Hollywood products make to the U.S. balance of payments—as well as the vague idea that American movies may serve to promote other American products or even democratic values—it is easy to imagine the political enthusiasm in Washington on behalf of Hollywood. Especially due to the success of these efforts, foreign nationals have expressed indignation at what is perceived to be great arrogance on the part of Hollywood and the U.S. government.

Often coupled with claims of political maneuvering have been abundant assertions that the Hollywood studios engage in collusive, anticompetitive behavior to insure that their films dominate distribution and exhibition networks worldwide. Outside the United States, it is argued, these tactics disadvantage domestic film industries, while within the United States, they help prevent foreign films from gaining a foothold with American audiences.[44]

6. *Inadequate or Misdirected Protectionist Policies.* There are two lines of thought that blame government policies for the extent of American domination of media flow. The traditional criticism has been that trade barriers such as quotas, duties, currency controls, or subsidies to domestic production industries are inadequate or too easily evaded to be effective.[45] For example, it is widely acknowledged that Hollywood studios can often avoid quotas or other restrictions on American im-

ports by forming coproduction alliances with indigenous producers that are in name only. A second, more recent wave of criticism has claimed that media policies are part of the problem. At least in Europe, a widely shared view among industry observers is that extensive film subsidy systems insulate producers from the discipline of the marketplace, weakening their incentives to make films that are commercially viable.[46] Thus, subsidies are seen to contribute in the longer term to exactly what they attempt to prevent: the excessive import of American movies.

It would be a book in itself to evaluate these arguments. All are plausible, and together they surely help to explain the world dominance of American feature films. From our perspective, however, two general critiques of the list are called for.

First, the explanations have mostly been advanced to explain why the United States has generally dominated film or media product trade—not to account for the rising tide of American control. Of course, one can extend these arguments to include the notion that gaps between the United States and other countries have widened because of the increased sophistication of marketing and distribution practices, or because of increasingly misdirected national film policies. Or perhaps American producers have been able to widen the production technology gap in spite of pressures toward the international diffusion of knowledge. A change in demand can be explained by the progressively greater receptivity to American cultural values throughout the world. Since World War II, English proficiency has steadily expanded worldwide.[47] Moreover, there has been a generational shift in moviegoing populations (primarily those who are under twenty-five) throughout Europe and elsewhere; and these moviegoers are more fluent in English, are more likely to have traveled to the United States, and are less steeped in their national or ethnic traditions.[48] It remains puzzling, however, why we should see the post–World War II pattern of shifting fortunes in the world film market, first in favor of America's trading partners, and then since the 1970s, in favor of Hollywood. And if the world is becoming smaller and more culturally homogenized, why have Americans themselves become less receptive to foreign movies?

A second critique is that some of these explanations must themselves be the result of more fundamental causes for American dominance. How, for example, could Hollywood have gained the political power to sustain its aggressive "foreign policy" if it had not had an inherent trade advantage potential in the first place? And although a consortium of U.S. distributors controlling half to nearly 100 percent market share in most countries probably has the power to behave anticompetitively, they could not do so without gaining high market shares to begin with. Similarly, such factors as superior business practices, plentiful support industries, efficient systems of financing, marketing, distributing, and exhibiting movies, and the remarkable ability of American filmmakers to produce common-denominator products surely derive in part from the higher volume of American film output for honing these systems and skills. Further, any arguments involving inadequate or misdirected film policies beg the question of why governments thought it necessary to impose such policies in the first place.[49] It can certainly be concluded that many of the explanations put forward for American film dominance are relevant to its inertia and sustainability, a subject we return to in Chapter 7. For now, we will concentrate on fundamental economic causes and focus our analysis on the home market advantage and the role that media development has played in its enhancement.

The Home Market Advantage

That a country with a large and lucrative home market for some product or service should have a natural advantage in the market for its export is an intuitively appealing idea. Home market effects are commonly observed. Various assumptions about demand or technology have been shown to lead to home market effects.[50] With some twists, these ideas can be applied to movies or other media products.

The logic of the home market theory for movies begins with the idea that movie producers in any given country make investment decisions based on the total potential market for their products—which consists of both their own and foreign countries. It is reasonable to believe, though, that a producer's home market is most important because of a "cultural discount" factor. That is, we assume that other things equal, audiences prefer movies in their own language or that reflect their own cultural values. Thus, a producer in a certain country has a natural advantage in assembling a movie script, actors, actresses, and other agents of production that can appeal to its native audiences. The result is that producers operating in larger or more lucrative domestic markets effectively have larger potential markets. In a two-country world, for example, producers in the larger market have a full slice of the large market and (due to the cultural discount) a partial slice of the smaller market, while those in the smaller country have a full slice of the smaller market and a partial slice of the larger market.

A second assumption about audience demand for movies in this theory is that films with bigger production budgets will, other things equal, generally be more attractive to audiences and also that a greater variety of movies will draw a larger total audience. Under these circumstances, producers with more lucrative home markets (and thus larger total potential markets) can spread production costs over a larger number of potential patrons and will have an incentive to produce films with higher production budgets.[51] Competitive forces will also induce producers with larger potential markets to create a larger number of movies.

The end result is that to the extent film producers are responsive to economic incentives and free trade prevails, the market shares of domestic films in countries with relatively large and lucrative home markets will be relatively high, while those in smaller and less lucrative home markets will be low. In Cyprus, let's say, a basic audience preference for movies that reflect Cypriot cultural values is always present, but working against that are the higher production values and greater variety offered by U.S. and other foreign movies. In the world's largest market, the United States, foreign films face a double disadvantage. They not only reflect cultural values alien to those of mainstream American audiences, but they also have lower production budgets and are fewer in number. In other words, the home market theory as applied to U.S. movie industry dominance basically means that American producers succeed around the world by "buying" audiences away from the inherently more interesting—but also more cheaply produced—domestic material that those audiences would really prefer to watch.

Does higher spending on movies really result in larger audiences, as the home market theory assumes? Certainly there are notorious examples of very cheap, starless movies that attract very large audiences. Every year in the United States, it seems, industry critics or analysts gloat over the box office success of a *Blair Witch Project* (1999: $1 million production cost, $141 million U.S. box office), *My Big Fat Greek Wedding* (2002: $5 million cost, $241 million box office), or *Farenheit 911* (2004: $6 million cost, $119 million box office), and the flops of expensive films, from *Heaven's Gate* (1980: $44 million cost, $3.5 million box office) to *Waterworld* (1995: $175 million cost, $88 million box office) and *Treasure Planet* (2002: $140 million cost, $38 million box office).[52] For the great majority of films, though, and certainly on average, numerous statistical studies have shown that more expensive movies with high-priced stars systematically make more money.[53] Even a simple statistical correlation shows that in spite of a lot of film-to-film variation, there is a strong positive relationship between production costs and U.S. box office revenues.[54] The raw audience appeal of high production values and big stars comes through even for many big-budget failures. Though judged to be a terrible movie by almost every critic, for example, *Waterworld*'s U.S. theater performance still ranked it eleventh for the year and it earned $255 million worldwide, somewhat more than *Blair Witch Project's* worldwide gross of $220 million.[55] We return to the relationship between production budgets and movie "quality" in the next chapter.

Perhaps the best circumstantial evidence of the existence of a cultural discount factor is the extensive international trade in television formats. The widely distributed TV series *Dallas,* for example, was remade into numerous, obviously much cheaper local versions around the world that often received higher ratings than the American original. More recently, the British-originated *How to Marry a Millionaire* has been locally produced, again with obviously lower budgets, in 79 countries. A number of other recent programs have followed suit.[56]

A rough idea of the size of cultural discount factors for movies produced in the United States, France, and Germany in the mid-1990s is provided in Table 5.2. Basically, these numbers measure the cost effectiveness of film production investments in the indicated export markets by comparing the ratio of total production investments to the ratio of box office revenues earned in each pair of countries. (See Appendix G

Table 5.2 Estimated cultural discount factors in the United States, France, and Germany, 1994–1996 averages

	Country of destination		
Country of origin	U.S.	France	Germany
U.S. films	1.00	0.14	0.32
French films	0.04	1.00	0.07
German films	0.01	0.05	1.00

Source: See Appendix G.

for the derivation.) The .14 discount factor for American movies distributed in France, for example, means that the ratio of total theatrical film production investments by producers in the United States to total investments by producers in France is approximately seven times (100/ .14) higher than the ratio of box office revenues in France earned by domestically produced French movies to revenues earned in France by American-produced movies. Other things equal, that is, the estimated cultural discount factor in this case indicates that $1 invested by an American producer returns, on average, seven times more from a typical moviegoer in the United States than it does in France.

The estimates in Table 5.2 suggest that cultural discounts for movies are generally large, though the handicaps are greater for French and German movies imported into the United States than for U.S. movies exported to these countries. As might be expected, American movies travel more freely in Germany (where American market shares consistently exceed 80 percent) than in France. These calculations are admittedly crude and for several reasons are almost surely biased downward (thus overestimating the actual severity of the cultural discount).[57] At the least, however, the estimates lend credence to the cultural discount phenomenon.

Table 5.3 Consumer movie media spending and related data in the United States, Europe, and Japan, 2002

	U.S.	France	Germany	Italy	U.K.	Japan	EUJ5	EU13
GDP (U.S. $ billions)	10,481	1,435	1,991	1,189	1,557	3,972	10,144	8,904
Population (millions)	291.0	59.9	82.4	57.5	59.1	127.5	386.3	379.1
Primary movie media spending (U.S. $ millions)	41,999.9	4,519.3	2,498.6	1,519.5	7,526.6	9,011.4	25,075.4	NA
Per capita primary movie media spending (U.S. $)								
Theatrical box office	32.7	16.2	11.0	10.4	20.3	12.3	13.6	13.3
Pay TV (premium + PPV)	35.7	26.9	3.3	6.7	42.9	20.8	19.3	NA
Video rentals and sales	71.7	32.4	16.0	9.3	64.2	37.6	32.0	12.3
Total	140.1	75.5	30.3	26.4	127.4	70.7	64.9	NA
Films produced	543	200	116	130	84	293	739	634
Average production cost (U.S. $ millions)	27.0	4.1	5.9	2.0	10.1	4.4	5.3	NA

Sources: See Appendix F.

Cross-Country Comparisons

Turning to relationships between consumer spending and market out-comes, Table 5.3 shows comparisons of consumer spending on movie exhibition media and movie output in the EUJ5, and, for perspective, the thirteen largest western European countries (EU13). The pattern is consistent with the home market explanation of U.S. dominance. The United States has the largest population and the largest economy (as measured by GDP) of the six individual countries, and also has by far the largest total of primary movie media spending. The latter consists of total consumer spending on the three main media—theaters, pay TV, and home video—that exhibit movies with direct payment support; we use this figure to represent the total size of the domestic consumer movie market that producers have available.

The middle rows of the table show that with little exception (notably pay television in the U.K.), American consumers compound their popu-lation advantage by spending more per capita on all three primary movie media than do consumers in the EUJ5 countries, or in western Europe as a whole. The U.S. advantage thus derives not just from the country's greater economic resources, but also from Americans' will-ingness to spend a higher proportion of those resources on movie media when compared to citizens of other countries.

As the home market model would predict, the estimated total vol-ume of movie investment at the bottom of the table shows that U.S. firms also produce many more movies, and invest more in each of them, than do producers in other countries. To illustrate, French government data show that of the 89 national or majority coproduction French films released in 1994, 10 had budgets above $9 million and two were "mega-budget" productions exceeding $16 million.[58] By contrast, at least 83 U.S.-produced films in that year cost $16 million or more and 11 had budgets of $50 million or more, the latter group including the internationally successful *Forrest Gump, Clear and Present Danger,* and *Stargate.*[59] The average cost of American movies reported in Table 5.3 is brought down considerably by a large number of independently (non-MPAA) distributed features, which generally account for only 10 to 20 percent of U.S. box office receipts and probably for a comparably small minority of all foreign receipts. In 2002, the average cost of MPAA-member-produced feature films was $58.8 million.[60]

Watching practically any selection of European and other foreign films reveals dramatic contrasts in the economic resources invested in them compared to those of major U.S. studio productions. While many foreign movies are beautifully crafted given their constraints, few employ anything close to the time, talent, and technology that are poured into major Hollywood features.

Finally, it is consistent with the home market idea that countries like the U.S. should be more dominant in movies than in other media products, such as recorded music or books. A cultural advantage may apply to any media product, but the effects on demand from increasing production investments in books or CDs seem likely to reach diminishing returns much earlier than movies, thus reducing the importance of having a large home market to support high quality products. Also, even though many countries run large deficits with the U.S. in movie and television trade, and their export markets have greatly diminished, the larger and more prosperous among these trading partners—including all of the EUJ5—still maintain substantial export businesses in television and film. At least the U.K. and Japan report overall net trade surpluses in this sector.[61]

Of course, the real world could hardly fit perfectly into such a simple model. Overall, though, the home market model offers a logically consistent framework, based on reasonably plausible assumptions, to explain why the United States tends to dominate world trade in movies.

Historical Trends in Market Shares and Movie Spending

If the home market theory is right, there should be a correspondence between the long-term shifts seen in the market shares of domestic versus U.S. movies and shifts over time in the relative amounts of home market consumer spending on movies in those countries. To measure these relationships, we assembled consumer spending and related data for the three primary movie exhibition media—theaters, pay TV (monthly subscription and PPV movie channels), and prerecorded home video—for each of the EUJ5 countries and the United States from the 1950s up to the early 2000s, to correspond with the box office market share data presented earlier (see Appendix F).

Statistical tests that confirm significance of the hypothesized relationship between movie spending and box office market shares are reported in Appendix G.[62] Here we summarize some essential features of those results in graphical terms. Figure 5.3 shows the correspondence between the average U.S. box office market share and the average ratio of total primary movie spending (converted at current exchange rates) for France, Italy, and Germany combined—the three countries for which we had essentially complete data over the half century period. Up until the mid-1970s, as U.S. market shares declined in these countries, their consumer spending on movie media (in those days entirely theater tickets) was generally rising compared to that of American consumers. Then, after the mid-1970s, as spending by American consumers increased in relative terms, U.S. market shares in these coun-

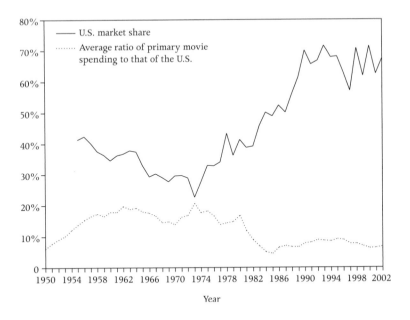

FIGURE 5.3   Average U.S. box office market share in France, Germany, and Italy versus average ratio of French, German, and Italian to U.S. primary movie spending, 1950–2002 (at current exchange rate).

tries also began increasing. Certainly, as Figure 5.3 shows, the correspondence between these trends is only broad but, as shown statistically in Appendix G, is generally consistent with the home market model.

An alternative perspective that avoids pitfalls of long-run financial comparisons in terms of current exchange rates is shown in Figure 5.4.[63] All six countries (the United States and the EUJ5) have undergone the same basic economic cycle in terms of falling, then rising primary movie spending as a fraction of total economic activity. U.S. movie spending, however, generally lagged that of the other countries during the early period when U.S. market shares were relatively low. Since the 1970s, the situation has generally reversed, as the home market model would predict. The gap has generally narrowed since about 2000, but with the very recent exception of Britain, U.S. movie media spending has continued to lead that of the EUJ5 countries in GDP-adjusted terms.

How can these long-run changes be related to the diffusion and development of movie media in the United States and other countries during this period? As we shall see, all of the movie media, including broadcast television, diffused most quickly or most successfully in the United States—in the broadcast TV case to the disadvantage of American producers, but in the case of pay media, at least, to the advantage of American producers.

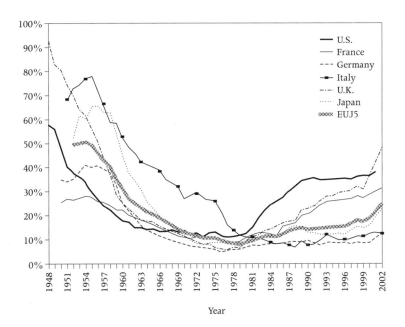

FIGURE 5.4 Primary movie spending as a percentage of GDP in the United States and the EUJ5, 1948–2002. (For sources, see Appendix F.)

The Role of Movie Media Development

Theater Admissions and the Blows from Television

Broadcast television spread much more quickly in the United States than in any of the EUJ5 countries, although its diffusion followed most closely in Britain and Japan (Figure 5.5). It was not until the mid-1960s, when TV household penetration had reached over 90 percent in the United States, that television even began sizable diffusion in Italy and France.

Throughout the world, including the United States and the EUJ5, television's diffusion was accompanied by dramatic declines in movie theater admissions in the post–World War II period. Trends to the mid-1970s in movie theater admissions in the United States and the EUJ5,

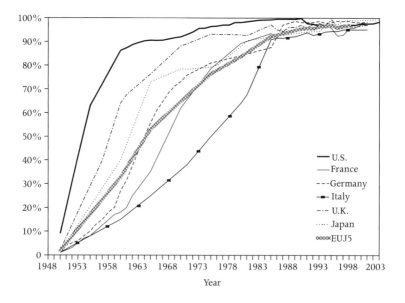

FIGURE 5.5   Household penetration of television sets in the United States and the EUJ5, 1948–2003. (For sources, see Appendix F.)

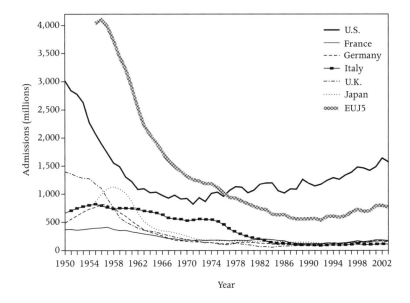

FIGURE 5.6   Movie theater admissions in the United States and the EUJ5, 1950–2003. (For sources, see Appendix F.)

shown in Figure 5.6, reflect basically the same pattern seen in the movie spending per GDP comparisons given earlier: a sharp decline for all six countries from their levels in the late 1940s or early 1950s.

Reasons for the postwar trends are complex. In some countries, initial increases in theater ticket sales probably reflected recovery from wartime destruction and restrictions on film production.[64] There is little question, though, that television played the central role throughout Europe and Japan, as it did in the United States, in devastating movie theater attendance.

The timing of TV's blow to theater attendance, however, was tellingly different from country to country. In the United States, where television diffused earliest and most rapidly, theater admissions also declined the fastest. At its widest gap in 1956, EUJ5 admissions were more than double those in the United States, and the EUJ5 lead persisted until the mid-1970s. In France and Italy, the two countries with the lowest penetration of television into the 1960s, theater admissions remained robust until about that time.

Television's impact outside the United States was probably also less because TV programming was less attractive to audiences. American television was from the beginning overwhelmingly driven by commercial forces, with three audience-driven, ad-supported networks in place by the early 1950s. In Europe and Japan, one- or two-channel, publicly operated broadcast systems were the norm throughout most of this period.

What these comparisons suggest is that the "Golden Age" of cinema in much of Europe, and a similar period of creativity and prosperity in Japan, was aided by a "calm before the storm" preceding the mass diffusion of television outside the United States. During this time, Hollywood, with its production capacity more weakened by television than that of its trading partners, struggled to compete with the more television-insulated, still-prosperous movie production industries in Europe and Japan. Both at home and in overseas markets, Hollywood's market shares reached their nadirs during this time.

Since the mid-1970s, as U.S. market shares in the EUJ5 have increased, the trends in theater admissions have reversed. American admissions have actually risen steadily while movie ticket sales in the other five countries continued to erode, at least until the early 1990s. In spite of recent upturns in Europe and Japan beginning in the 1990s, U.S. theater admissions were by 2003 still more than double those of the EUJ5 combined.

It appears that the negative effect of free broadcast television on moviegoing was more drawn out in Europe and Japan than it was in the United States. It was not until the mid-1970s and, in most cases, the

1980s and 1990s that state monopolies of television in Europe and Asia began relaxing controls that had limited both TV's economic resources and its responsiveness to viewer demands. The result was an explosive growth of channels in private hands and with that a dramatic growth in TV advertising—developments that have been sustained as cinema attendance continued to diminish until at least about 1990. Of course, there was also a great increase in channel variety in the United States during this same period—but without an accompanying decline in theater admissions. Whatever the causes, moviegoing in the United States emerged from the 1970s with a continuing vigor that has sustained it well above the levels of the EUJ5 countries.

Pay TV

Subscription premium channels that rely heavily on theatrical movies developed much earlier in the United States than in the EUJ5. The premiere U.S. service, HBO, achieved national distribution in 1975 and was soon joined by Showtime and other competitors in the late 1970s. It was not until 1984 that Canal Plus launched in France, becoming the first major movie-based premium service outside the United States. Other premium services in the EUJ5 followed a few years later: Sky Movies (1989) and the Movie Channel (1990) in Britain, Teleclub (1990) and Premiere (1991) in Germany, WOWOW in Japan (1990), and Telepiù in Italy (1991).[65]

We do not have systematic premium channel subscribership data outside the United States, but by the launch of Canal Plus in 1984, there were already 29 million premium network subscriptions in the United States, or .34 channels for every U.S. TV household; by 1990, the U.S. ratio was .44. Ever since its launch, Canal Plus has prospered in France, coming to account for about 3 million premium subscriptions by 1990 (but still only .15 subscriptions per French TV household).

During the 1990s and into the 2000s, premium channel take-up rates have risen briskly in France, Japan, and especially Britain.[66] On the whole, though, as indicated by the cross-country financial data of Table 5.3, the EUJ5 countries have lagged far behind the United States in premium channel development.

PPV and VOD movie systems have so far not been very successful in any country (accounting in 2003 for only about 2 percent of total movie distributor revenues even in the United States); but, like premium channels, they became available to American viewers much earlier than in Europe or Japan. By 1989, 32 percent of U.S. TV homes could receive PPV channels, but such services were essentially nonexistent in Europe and Asia until 1995. Growth of PPV access has been very rapid in some European countries, but by 2003 the United States still maintained a sizable lead.[67] À la carte spending inevitably reflects these differences. In 2002 total PPV and VOD spending for all content in the United States was about $2.2 billion versus an estimated $0.5 billion in all of Europe.[68]

Closely related to the growth of pay TV services around the world has been diffusion of multichannel cable or satellite systems to transport them. In the United States, premium channels have mostly been delivered by cable systems, which by 1985 had reached 43 percent household penetration in the United States, compared to 7 percent in Germany and less than 1 percent in France, Italy, and the U.K. In Japan, by 1990 only 5 percent of TV households were passed by cable wiring and thus able to subscribe.[69] In contrast, DBS systems capable of delivering premium movie channels began earlier in Europe and Japan than in America. The first European systems followed launch of the Astra satellite in 1986, and DBS began in Japan on a commercial basis soon after, while DirecTV, the first "true" American DBS system, did not launch until 1994. Overall, though, the diffusion of multichannel delivery systems in the United States has been considerably faster than in the EUJ5 countries. As of 2001, U.S. multichannel penetration of TV households was near saturation at 88 percent, compared to 42 percent in the U.K., 62 percent in Germany, 39 percent in France, and 12 percent in Italy. Japanese multichannel penetration was 46 percent in 1998 (the most recent year for which we had data) compared to 81 percent in the United States.[70]

In the absence of cable or satellite systems to deliver them, earlier pay TV systems in the EUJ5 relied upon less efficient distribution methods. Canal Plus, and later Telepiù, launched by means of single-channel, scrambled, terrestrial-broadcast systems. These were similar to early "STV" systems that operated in some U.S. cities during the late 1970s and early 1980s before they went out of business in the face of expanding cable diffusion.[71]

The slower diffusion of à la carte movie services in the EUJ5 can also be related to slower diffusion of efficient delivery systems. Commercially viable PPV or VOD requires digital transmission, whether via cable or DBS. Though originally all analog, cable systems in the United States have also converted to digital distribution more rapidly than have the EUJ5 countries.[72] The earlier DBS systems in Europe and Japan were also analog, and their digital conversion moved slowly. American DBS systems, although launched later, were all digital from the beginning.

In addition to platforms for premium and à la carte movie services, multichannel systems in the United States have also provided revenue to movie distributors via advertiser-supported (basic) cable networks such as TNT and the USA network. Although these networks share the broadcast window and provide relatively low levels of support in per viewer terms, a significant part of their revenue comes from direct viewer payments via the per subscriber fees these networks charge to

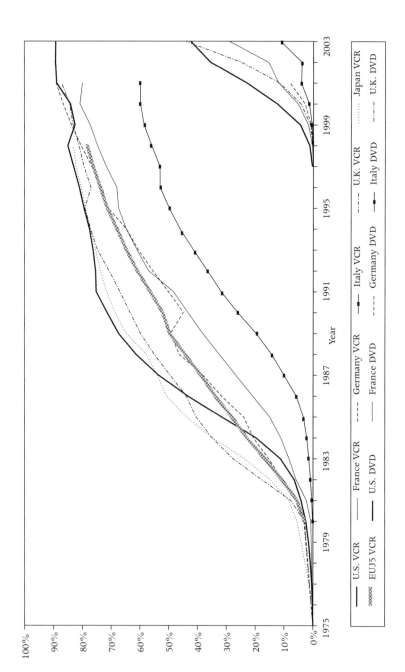

FIGURE 5.7 Percentage of households with VCRs and DVDs in the United States and the EUJ5, 1975–2003. (For sources, see Appendix F.)

cable and DBS operators. From very low levels in the early 1990s, the aggregate financial contribution of U.S. basic cable networks to the studios has steadily grown, and since 1999 it has exceeded that of premium networks (see Appendix C). In contrast, these types of networks have been of minor significance in Europe, at least until about 2000.[73]

Home Video

In contrast to pay television systems, VCRs took off rapidly throughout the EUJ5 as well as the United States after 1980, though since about 1985 American consumers have embraced these machines more than the EUJ5 as a whole (Figure 5.7).

Of most direct importance, the use of video machines to watch prerecorded movies has not caught on in most countries the way it has in America. As Figures 5.8 and 5.9 illustrate, there has been a common shift away from rentals toward sales transactions in both the United States and the EUJ5 countries, as the "sell-through" video market has developed worldwide. That trend has been accelerated in all six countries by the DVD revolution. Throughout the period, though, the United States has retained a large lead in both video rental and video sales transactions per household. At least in part, faster diffusion of DVD players (Figure 5.7) in the United States has surely contributed since the late 1990s, though by 2003 gaps had narrowed.

Like the movie spending and box office market share analysis given earlier, our comparisons of diffusion of the primary direct-payment movie exhibition media in the United States and in the EUJ5 countries are very broad. Patterns of development have varied greatly from country to country. Overall, though, it is evident that since the 1970s, as American dominance of the world movie industry began increasing,

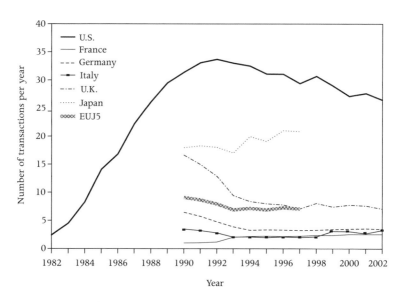

FIGURE 5.8   Video rental transactions per household in the United States and the EUJ5, 1982–2002. (For sources, see Appendix F.)

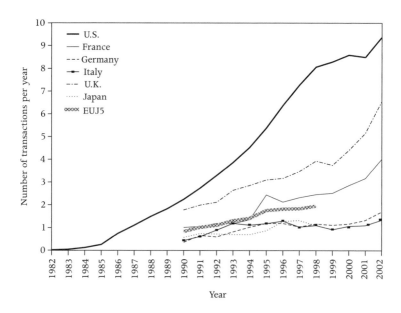

FIGURE 5.9   Video sales transactions per household in the United States and the EUJ5, 1982–2002. (For sources, see Appendix F.)

the United States also took the lead over all the EUJ5 countries, and almost surely most of the rest of the world, in developing pay media in the home market for theatrical feature film exhibition. Moreover, the United States has apparently avoided the demand substitution effect on theatrical admissions much more successfully, resulting in a more robust direct payment system for theatrical movies.

Reasons for the Movie Spending and Media Diffusion Trends

Why have the direct-payment media for movies proven so much more robust in the United States than in the EUJ5? This is a difficult, but important, question for understanding the movement toward American movie industry dominance.

Among some possible reasons, people around the world exhibit different habits of media use and entertainment. Changes in those habits might take place over time in some regions of the world and not others, leading to divergence in media adoption and use.[74] Change in relative income levels, in turn affecting consumer spending on movies, is another possibility. Income differences would not seem a major factor, though, since there has been a long-term post-1970s trend in Europe, and especially in Japan, toward increasing per capita wealth and consumer spending relative to that of the United States—the opposite of what would cause the trends we observe.[75]

As we discuss further in Chapter 6, some degree of reverse causation must also be recognized. The true home market model is surely interactive. That is, the decline of indigenous movie production in the EUJ5 countries and the rise of American production have themselves probably contributed to faster development of movie spending in the United States. If rising American dominance, and with it declining domestic film production output in U.S. trading partner countries, has occurred for some independent reason (such as an increasing "Americanization" of world cultures), then audiences outside the United States could be expected to reduce their movie consumption because they have fewer culturally compatible, high-production-value movies available to them. Similarly, Americans would increase their movie consumption, since they now have a larger supply of high-production-value, culturally compatible films available. This logic is consistent with the basic assumptions of the home market model that movies are subject to a cultural discount and that there is a positive relationship between production investments and the attractiveness of film products to audiences. The implication of an interactive model is that the total spending pie to be divided in any country is not predetermined, but rises or falls depending on the attractiveness of the offerings available. Such reverse causation likely contributes to the differences in U.S. and EUJ5 home video usage rates as well. Americans have more high-production-value, culturally compatible movie fare available to them than do the viewers of any other country in the world.

Government Policy and Movie Media Diffusion

Another possible reason for the more successful American market for movie support media since the 1970s is government regulation and other media policies. Free broadcast TV and the pay media have played quite different roles in the exhibition and financial support of theatrical features in the EUJ5 and the United States.

Broadcast Television

We have already seen that broadcast television makes only a minor contribution to the financial support of theatrical features in the United States. American television organizations have also had a fairly peripheral role in the actual production of theatrical movies.[76] Especially in Europe, free television's support of theatrical films has been much greater, and film finance has been closely integrated with the broadcast industry. The public-service traditions of broadcasting in the EUJ5 countries have inevitably led government to play a prominent role in decisions about the financing of theatrical features in those countries.

We were able to estimate the relative contribution that four media—theater rentals, pay television license fees, wholesale home video transactions, and broadcast television license fees—made in 1994 or 1995 to total domestic distributor receipts from the domestic exhibition of theatrical films in the United States, Italy, France, and Germany (Table 5.4). The importance of theater exhibition is within the same general range in all four countries, but the role of home video was far greater in the United States. Thanks to the early development of Canal Plus in France, the contribution of pay television was highest in France, though U.S. pay TV contributed proportionally more than in Italy or Germany. The greatest contrasts involve free broadcast television, which has played a much more important part in theatrical film exhibition in all three European countries—though especially in Italy and Germany.

Table 5.4   Sources of revenue to theatrical distributors from domestic media in the United States, France, Germany, and Italy, 1994–1995

Medium	U.S. (1994)	France (1994)	Germany (1995)	Italy (1995)
Theaters	30%	27%	17%	25%
Video	50	13	13	13
Pay TV[a]	13	32	3	8
Broadcast TV	8	28	68	53
Total	100%	100%	100%	100%

Sources: France, Germany, and Italy: Appendix F; United States: Appendix C.
a. Includes premium channels, PPV, and ad-supported cable channels.

These comparisons underestimate the actual contributions of broadcast TV to theatrical film support in Italy, France, and Germany. The public television systems in all three of these countries have also provided legally mandated production investment funds for domestically produced theatrical films that they contract to exhibit.[77] In France, these obligations have extended to private channels. To the extent that these investments are not fully returned, as has been widely claimed, that portion of the investment essentially amounts to a state subsidy. The amount of these subsidies is unknown, but the investment relationships between free television and film in these countries have been extensive. One study showed that from November 1992 to June 1994, 51 percent of the theatrical movies produced in western Europe were partially financed by television, including 73 percent of French and 63 percent of German, though only 13 percent of Italian productions.[78]

Broadcasters have not been legally required to invest in theatrical film production in either Britain or Japan, but the involvement of broadcast television in film finance and exhibition has reportedly been extensive. The percentage of U.K.-produced theatrical features with television investment during the early 1990s has been placed between 44 and 53 percent.[79] It has been claimed that Channel 4, a publicly owned broadcaster (though self-supported by advertising and other commercial activities) and the primary exhibitor of feature films on free television in Britain, has effectively subsidized theatrical film production. Little financial data on the importance of broadcast television in supporting feature films in the U.K. could be found, though one author described free TV as having become the "most significant source" of film finance in the 1980s.[80] In Japan, television channels were reported to be involved in the financing of about half of all theatrical features in the late 1990s. According to at least one estimate, though, the proportion of Japanese movie distributor income from television, while more than that in the United States, has been much less than in Europe.[81]

At least in Europe, the role of broadcast TV in the financial support of theatrical features is said to have risen dramatically from about 1980 to at least the mid-1990s.[82] As in the United States, television exhibition of theatrical films in the early years of TV contributed to the revenues of domestic producers. But before the move toward commercialization of TV and expanding broadcast channel capacity began in Italy in 1976, and followed in the rest of Europe during the 1980s and 1990s, those financial contributions must have been low (as the very small contributions of foreign television to American theatrical film distributors in the early 1980s suggest).[83] Before the moves to privatization, European television systems had few channels, they were mostly under tight state control, and advertiser support was low in comparison to license fee income collected from TV viewers. Liberalization resulted in an explosion in the number of TV channels and of commercial broadcast television advertising support during the 1980s and 1990s.[84] A similar trend took place in Japan for similar reasons. These expansions of broadcast television's economic resources in the EUJ5—much of those funds remaining in the hands of public service broadcasters—thus provided the means for much greater television involvement in film. In America, the opposite trend occurred, at least in proportionate terms. The contribution to U.S. theatrical distributor revenue from domestic broadcast television fell from 19 percent in 1980 to 8 percent in 1995 (Appendix C). Thus, while at least the European film industries were apparently becoming more dependent on free television, the American industry was reducing its broadcast TV reliance to very low levels.

It is hard to tell the extent to which government initiative in television's financial support of movie production may have pushed aside cinemas, pay television, or home video as film exhibition media in the EUJ5 countries. Certainly to a great extent, expanding broadcast television support of domestic film production has simply been motivated by widespread government mandates to preserve domestic film industries in the face of growing American dominance and the diminishing streams of producer income from theaters and the direct-payment-supported media.[85]

The reality in either case is that broadcast television has two important disadvantages as a means to support theatrical film production. One is that public-service-minded television organizations have an understandable incentive to direct the inevitable creative control they gain from providing a large fraction of the production money toward films that make good television or that enhance the reputation of their television organizations. At least some European observers have made such claims, though it is not clear how significant these problems are.[86]

The second and more important handicap of broadcast TV is fundamental: free television is simply an inefficient means to support theatrical film production. Television license fees in Europe and Japan have been set at low levels to encourage universal service, and advertisers are simply unwilling to pay more than a few cents per viewer for exposure to those audiences. As we saw in Chapter 3, broadcasting is a low-value medium from the distributor's perspective, which results in its being relegated to the end of the typical release sequence for theatrical features—behind cinemas, video, and pay television—everywhere in the world. Even with subsidies added in, the economic potential of broadcast television as support for domestic film industries is thus limited.

Pay Television

While low demand for movie-based pay TV services was evident throughout most of Europe and Japan until at least the mid-1990s, media policies have certainly been a factor in the slower diffusion of these services outside the United States.

In all of the EUJ5 countries, one economic force working against any commercial television service requiring a monthly payment or other charge has been the government-mandated license fees required of all television set owners. To the extent that households categorize their budget expenditures, they may already see themselves as subscribing to a form of pay TV. From that perspective, commercial multichannel services, and premium channels in particular, constitute an extra expense, limiting demand for them.[87]

A common force working against premium subscription TV in both the EUJ5 and the United States was the political influence of established media. In America, resistance from advertiser-supported TV stations and movie theater owners prevented the introduction of commercial pay TV systems until the early 1970s. As noted in Chapter 2, the U.S. courts opened a floodgate in the late 1970s by removing a variety of pay TV content restrictions that freed HBO, Showtime, and other competitors to diffuse rapidly.

Except for Italy, which essentially legalized pay TV in 1976, political resistance in Europe and Japan was more enduring. Legislation in France and Germany did not permit pay television services until 1982, and they remained heavily regulated in Britain until 1984. The slow introduction and diffusion of premium channels in Germany, Italy, and the U.K. after their enabling legislation suggests low consumer demand, but political obstacles and Byzantine regulations have also been blamed in all three of these cases. The slower diffusion of cable and DBS multichannel platforms in Europe and Japan and, later on, their slower digital conversion have also been attributed to political factors in part, including resistance from established media and a lack of politically co-ordinated decision making.[88] In the United States, the same forces of resistance were encountered, but were overcome more quickly.[89]

Home Video

At least in the early years of its diffusion, countries around the world imposed a variety of restraints on VCR hardware, including import restrictions and excise taxes in France, Italy, and some other countries of Europe. As the roughly comparable diffusion of VCRs in the United States and the EUJ5 countries makes evident, though, these constraints—most of them soon reduced or abandoned—must have had only a minor influence on the diffusion of VCRs.[90]

Apart from high taxes or duties on video software in a few countries, notably France, it is unlikely that government policies have had much effect on the lower consumer inclinations to rent or buy movies on video in the EUJ5.[91] Differences in the effectiveness of government piracy enforcement, however, have been more favorable to commercial development of the domestic video market in America.

In the earliest days of video distribution, piracy was reported to be rampant everywhere, but it has come under control in the United States more quickly. As Table 5.5 shows, estimates of "piracy rates" (the percentage of transactions that involve illegally reproduced videos) improved for VHS in all six countries over time, but have been consistently lower in the United States. The pattern of lower rates for DVD piracy in the United States is similar. It is apparent from Tables 5.4 and 5.5 that copyright enforcement could explain only part of the gap between U.S. and EUJ5 rates of legitimate home video use. Piracy enforce-

Table 5.5   Video piracy in the United States and the EUJ5, estimated
percentage rates, 1987 and 2002

| Country | 1987 | 2002 | |
		VHS	DVD
France	20%	7%	10%
Germany	25%	5%	22%
Italy	50%	20%	10%
U.K.	25%	8%	20%
Japan	50%	8%	3%
U.S.	10%–15%	< 3%	NA

Sources: EUJ5: Motion Picture Association of America, *Trade Barriers to Exports of U.S. Filmed Entertainment: Report to the United States Trade Representative* (Washington, D.C.), 1988, 2003; United States: author's estimates (Chapter 4).

ment has been a significant policy element, however, that has undoubtedly worked against the development of home video software markets in these countries.

The incidence of video piracy has been far higher in many other countries outside the EUJ5. Most of the worst cases are Third World nations that have little economic prospect as export markets. It is evident, however, that video and other movie piracy around the world substantially diminishes export revenues of U.S. movie distributors. Presumably, the inhibited development of video markets in these countries has also reduced opportunities for viable domestic movie production industries to be supported.[92]

In some other respects, policy may have advantaged movie media development in the EUJ5. The historical absence of a first-sale doctrine in most countries (and since the 1995 Rental Rights Directive, in all of the EU) and a legal environment apparently more conducive to the control of movie windows are cases in point. At least until very recently, however, the practical impact of rental rights has been minor; and legislated minimum video windows, at least in France, have apparently been too long to benefit distributors.[93]

Both Germany and Italy have taxed theater admissions or video transactions to subsidize local productions, a practice likely to inhibit demand in those countries. Regulations on video transactions have generally been absent in the United States, though this has also been true in the U.K. and Japan.[94] In the scheme of things, such practices probably have little effect in themselves. But an important element of the movie media infrastructure that may be affected by taxes or other regulations is theater construction. The more recent growth of movie theater demand in the United States and later in Europe has been attributed in part to the construction of modern multiplex theaters—a process that again began much earlier in the United States. At least in Italy, specific regulations limiting theater market entry are said to have slowed that construction.[95]

In this chapter, we have attempted to explain growing American dominance of the world theatrical film industry from an economic perspective, comparing long-term development of movie exhibition media in the United States and five of its major trading partners. Increasing world dominance of American movies since the 1970s can be related to a faster growth of America's home market for movie products, especially pay television systems and home video media. That faster growth has served to increase the economic resources of American movie producers in comparison to their foreign counterparts, providing the primary foundation for the vast investments that the high-production-value, internationally successful American blockbuster films require.

This economic analysis is certainly an incomplete explanation of U.S. dominance. The correspondences between market share trends and movie spending are broad. Some combination of other reasons, including the spread of English as a world language, an increasing receptivity to American cultural values around the world, a widening production technology or skill gap, and market distortions arising from film industry subsidies in some countries, have surely contributed to rising American dominance. As we have also hypothesized, the greater supply of high-production-value, culturally compatible movie products now available to American consumers probably stimulates their relatively high spending on movie media in the first place.

Not all countries—notably Hong Kong, India, and Korea—appear to fit the home market idea, or at least to follow the same recent trends. Our intention has been, however, to aim only at the broad picture. If a few countries, such as Hong Kong, have developed unusually prominent roles as regional movie exporters for historical or geographic reasons, or if their anomalous performances reflect extreme variations in cultural discounts or other variables not part of the theory at all, that is to be expected. In any case, India accounts for less than 3 percent of the world box office, Korea and Hong Kong for under 1 percent each.[96] These countries are worthy of detailed study. Yet if only those countries are the noticeable exceptions (apart from the obvious cases of countries that simply prohibit significant American imports), that is not discouraging to the general economic explanation.

Whatever the true complexities behind growing American dominance of movie trade, the economic reality remains that over the long term, theatrical film investments that are reasonably responsive to marketplace forces in any country must have a commercial support base of ticket buyers, pay television subscribers, and video renters and purchasers to return those investments. Other things equal, a country's domestic support base is disproportionately important to maintaining a viable theatrical film industry. Since the 1970s, the United States has gained a substantial competitive advantage over Japan, Italy, France,

Germany, and the U.K., and evidently nearly all the rest of the world, in building that domestic support base. A greater freedom from government regulation has likely contributed to the overall American lead in consumer spending on media. We emphasize that those regulations or other government policies may well have achieved other social benefits, such as the preservation of public service objectives of broadcast television systems. For better or worse, though, they have likely enhanced American dominance of the world movie industry.

Chapter 6

What Has Hollywood Done with the Money?

The remarkable growth in revenues of the movie studios from the distribution of theatrical features since the 1970s—both in the United States and from foreign markets—has had a predictable effect: a comparable growth in the volume of movie production investment. But what are the effects of this higher investment? Has it resulted in bigger and better movies—and more of them—or just wasteful spending along with fatter salaries for big stars, writers, directors, and other agents of production?

One part of the answer is shown in Figure 6.1. This graph indexes both the number of theatrical features released by MPAA companies and the average production cost of MPAA releases (to 100 in 1975) in order to compare rates of increase over time. Actual values at the beginning year (1975) and the ending year (2003) are also shown. Figure 6.1 shows clearly that Hollywood's overwhelming response has been to make more expensive movies rather than to increase the number of movies. Comparing 1975 to 2003, the average production cost of MPAA-company movie releases (in current dollars) went up more than

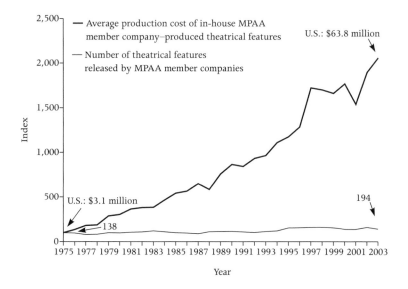

FIGURE 6.1   Trends in number of movies versus production costs, MPAA U.S. releases, 1975–2003. (1975 = 100; for sources, see Appendix H.)

nineteenfold. Meanwhile, the number of movies released by MPAA companies rose only by 41 percent, and a good fraction of that increase reflects the output of formerly independent distributors that became MPAA-member subsidiaries after their acquisition in the 1980s and 1990s. (See Appendix H for a discussion of these data.)

Of course, the somewhat larger number of movies suggests real value to movie audiences. But are the more expensive movies really better movies? Many movie critics seem to think that the money has poisoned the creative process. Renowned critic Pauline Kael wrote an article back in 1980 entitled "Why Are Movies So Bad?, or, The Numbers," which blasted what she perceived to be Hollywood's growing obsession with expensive, lowest-common-denominator blockbusters that avoided creative risks.[1] In 1997 Michiko Kakutani, in "Taking Out the Trash," ridiculed the prevalent export of U.S. blockbusters that are "right out of the junkyard" compared to the good old days when America "used to put its best cultural foot forward."[2] *New York Times* critic David Thomson, while never quite saying that the movies of 2001 were worse than those of 1971 in his year-end retrospective on the former year's films, made a case that the movies of thirty years earlier were more "about the world and everything in it."[3] Of course, many individual movies of recent date, including high-end blockbusters, have been honored; but it is difficult to find general praise. In 2002, Rick Lyman wrote, "The consensus is that, on average, Hollywood studio movies have gotten demonstrably worse in recent years—safer, more predictable, more likely to be sequels, franchises, or some other form of risk-averse pablum."[4] Neal Gabler has characterized recent Hollywood blockbusters as "the illusion of entertainment."[5] Joseph Lieberman and other politicians joined the chorus of disapproval in the 1996 and 2000 presidential campaigns with familiar claims that Hollywood produces excessively violent and otherwise socially unredeeming films.

Are theatrical movies returning us to the old "vast wasteland" of broadcast TV, or the worst of Hollywood's pretelevision efforts? We don't dare to argue with movie critics. But without disagreeing in aesthetic terms, we can address some interesting questions about movie quality and content from an economic perspective. Has the quality of movies risen in any meaningful sense, or do higher budgets just reflect inflation in costs of talent and other factors of production? How can we explain Hollywood's choice to produce more expensive movies instead of a greater variety of films? And finally, can we provide an economic rationale for what makes critics so unhappy about today's movies?

These are not simple questions, but we attempt some provocative, if incomplete, answers to them in this chapter. After reviewing evidence on the question of budget inflation, we explore how the expansion of Hollywood's markets, changing production technologies, and greater production risks has affected the economic trade-offs that determine the quality, variety, and content of movies.

Rising Movie Budgets: Inflation or Real Value?

It has been widely reported, apart from some recent acknowledgment of special effects costs, that the huge growth in movie budgets is due to inflated star and other "above-the-line" salaries.[6]

Certainly talent costs are a major factor in higher budgets. A 1978 *Newsweek* article reported top Hollywood star salaries to be in the $2 to $3 million range.[7] A compilation in that year of movie and TV star salaries listed the three largest single movie salaries in history to be $2,225,000 for Marlon Brando and $2 million for Gene Hackman (both in *Superman,* 1978) and (prospectively) $5 million plus a percentage of the profits for Burt Reynolds (*Cannonball Run,* released in 1981).[8] Star salaries accelerated in the 1980s and 1990s, and in 2002 *Variety* identified ten actors (among them, Jim Carrey, Tom Cruise, Harrison Ford, and Julia Roberts) in the "$25 Million Player's Club" and twelve more in the $20 million category, with actual compensations often running far higher when participation payments were included.[9] Routine megastar perks of $1 to 2 million per picture for private airplanes and retinues of bodyguards, chefs, personal hairstylists, various coaches, and the like are reported as well.[10] Dramatic increases in salaries of directors, screenwriters, and other "above-the-line" talent costs have tagged along.[11] Obviously, with salaries like these, stars account for a big chunk of a $50, $100, or even $150 million movie budget. Some examples are extreme. For *Legally Blonde 2* (2003), Reese Witherspoon was reported to receive $15 million of that movie's $45 million budget.[12] One industry commentator remarked in 1995 that while the split between budgets for "above-the-line" (cast, producers, story rights, writers, the director) and "below-the line" (production and postproduction salaries and expenses, and everything else) costs for major film and TV productions were once around one third and two thirds, respectively, the proportion had roughly reversed by the 1990s.[13]

It is surely true, though, that exploding Hollywood film budgets also reflect major increases in the economic resources that are invested in movie production. One indication of this is how long it takes to shoot movies. A 1995 *Variety* article reported that shooting schedules at major studios were then averaging 65 to 75 days and increasing, and that these levels were "roughly twice the level of a generation ago." The article referred to the "Hundred Day Club," a growing ledger of directors who have taken more than 100 days to shoot their movies.[14] Among some extremes, *Waterworld* (1995) took 166 days, and Stanley Kubrick was reported to take 300 days to film *Eyes Wide Shut* (1999).[15] More recently, the 102-day shooting schedule for *Terminator 3* (2003) was described in the press as a "relatively short time for one of today's mega-action movies."[16] More production days have some straightforward benefits: they permit more locations, more complicated scenes, and larger numbers of takes of any given scene for filmmakers to choose from in postproduction. Kubrick was said to frequently require more than fifty takes of a scene in *Eyes Wide Shut*.[17]

Filmmaking is heavily labor intensive. As shown by Figure 6.2, total employment in enterprises involved primarily in "motion picture production, except television" was flat during the era of broadcast television, but approximately tripled from its nadir in 1972 until 1997 (the latest year for which data are available). The number of major films produced, however, rose only slightly during the latter period—implying greater human resources per production. Increases in total reported em-

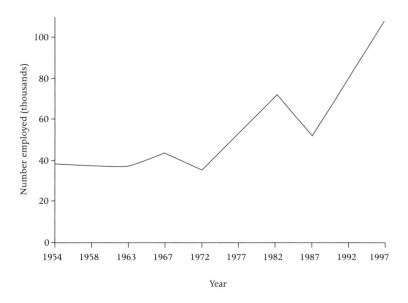

FIGURE 6.2   Motion picture industry employment, 1954–1997. (For sources, see Appendix I.)

ployment in other entertainment labor categories, including postproduction and related services, have also been great. (See Appendix I for discussion of employment data.)

Trends in movie screen credits offer a more vivid and dramatic, albeit much overstated, contrast in how the scope of Hollywood film production has changed in the past three decades.

We compiled a summary of the credits displayed on the ten highest U.S. box office movies in 2001 and compared them with those of the top ten in the "preblockbuster" year of 1971, the same years that David Thomson compared in aesthetic terms (see Table 6.1). In every category shown, there are increases, some very large, in the number of individuals who are listed. Two or three times as many cast members, writers, and producers were cited in 2001, but the largest percentage growth

Table 6.1 Change in number of end credits for top ten U.S. box office movies, 1971 and 2001

Average number of end credits

	1971	2001
Cast		
Stunts	0.2	43.7
Other	19.0	50.4
Total cast	19.2	94.2
Crew		
Producers	2.2	7.0
Writers	2.1	4.1
Sound effects	4.6	30.2
Special/visual effects	2.1	150.3
Other crew	24.9	364.5
Total crew	35.9	556.2
Total credits	55.1	650.4

Top ten movies (total number of end credits in parentheses)

1971		2001	
Rank	Title	Rank	Title
1	Love Story (51)	1	Harry Potter (820)
2	Little Big Man (100)	2	The Lord of the Rings (1,780)
3	Carnal Knowledge (33)	3	Shrek (491)
4	Aristocats (66)	4	Monsters, Inc. (252)
5	Summer of '42 (26)	5	Rush Hour 2 (421)
6	Willard (46)	6	The Mummy Returns (381)
7	Ryan's Daughter (62)	7	Pearl Harbor (1,108)
8	Andromeda Strain (60)	8	Ocean's Eleven (316)
9	The Owl and the Pussycat (53)	9	Jurassic Park 3 (581)
10	Big Jake (54)	10	Planet of the Apes (949)

Source: See Appendix J.

has been in stunt performers and postproduction categories, notably special effects (as well as "other crew"). As any movie viewer knows, credits for recent major Hollywood films usually run on for several minutes. *Titanic* (1997) got media attention for its landmark seven running minutes of end credits, in which over 1,200 individuals and small businesses are mentioned.[18]

Probably the main source of the huge growth in Hollywood credits is that many acting and other production jobs routinely credited today (such as stunt artists, minor cast members, drivers, caterers, various producers, assistant editors, etc.) were simply not mentioned in earlier times. One reason for this kind of credit inflation likely has to do with changes in the organization of production. In days of the old studio system, most actors, directors, and technicians were directly employed by the studios, and they would rely upon references from their former studio bosses when searching for another job. Today, film work is overwhelmingly carried out by individuals working as independent contractors. Largely through their craft unions, they have demanded screen credit as a way to build their résumés for future work. The result has been the creation of an elaborate manual for producers specifying who must be given screen credit for what.[19] In fact, such credits have literally become the currency of the entertainment industry job market, the manual often not a constraint. Studios often grant a credit in lieu of pay, or may buy out an individual's legal right to have a credit in order to give more prominence to someone else. The demands of savvy talent agents, bent on building résumés for their clients, have probably contributed as well.

Credits are a fairly cheap way to keep production personnel happy, although the extremes to which some studios have now gone to dole them out to drivers, babysitters, and extraneous producers have been ridiculed in the press.[20] Complaints that most producers listed contribute nothing substantive to the movie led the Producers Guild to negotiate a limit of eight to the number of producers that can receive a screen credit, and the Motion Picture Academy has ruled that no more than three producers can come on stage to accept an Academy Award for Best Picture.[21]

The great changes in industry crediting practices since the 1970s leave us unsure of the true extent to which modern movies may actually employ larger casts, crews, producers, and other workers. But anecdotal evidence suggests that the great expansion in movie credits reflects (in addition to industry antics) real increases in labor going into the making of Hollywood movies.

Most obvious are special/visual effects, usually considered part of the postproduction process. (We use the more popular term, "special effects," or simply "effects," to refer to both.)[22] Effects account for a large fraction of the credits for all eight of the live-action 2001 films in Table 6.1, but they were rare in earlier films. We all are aware of the dramatic strides in special effects since the paper puppets in *Wizard of Oz* (1939). Sophisticated effects on a major scale were pioneered in *Jaws* (1975), *Star Wars* (1977), and *Tron* (1982), and have been advanced dramatically in *Terminator 2* (1991), *Twister* (1996), *Men in Black* (1997), *Harry Potter and the Sorcerer's Stone* (2001), *The Matrix Reloaded* (2003), and many more. Of course, much of the growth in special-effects and stunt-work credits in the 1971–2001 comparison can be accounted for by a shift toward action-adventure, science fiction, and similar genres that use them best (a subject we return to shortly).

Effects and stunts have become routine in major Hollywood comedies of the late 1990s and early 2000s as well, including *There's Something about Mary* (1998), *Austin Powers in Goldmember* (2002), and *Bruce Almighty* (2003). A nostalgic viewing of the top ten movies of

1971 will make it evident that there are simply not very many stunts, and even fewer special effects, in these movies of the past. Even for modern blockbuster films, effects generally make up no more than 10 or 15 percent of the total budget, although there have been extremes.[23] Twenty percent or more of *Titanic*'s $200 million budget was reported to be for special effects.[24] The prevailing limit may be the $100 million for special effects out of an estimated $300 million combined budget for *The Matrix Reloaded* (2003) and *The Matrix Revolutions* (2003).[25]

Consider screenwriters, another focus of industry squabbling about who deserves credit. As the 1971–2001 comparison in Table 6.1 shows, more writers are credited now, in spite of stricter Writers Guild of America rules about who can receive on-screen writing credit.[26] In what Peter Bart and Peter Guber refer to in a recent book on Hollywood as the "multiple writers syndrome,"[27] more and more writers have apparently become involved in the preproduction process. In the most extreme case reported by the trade press, thirty-five different writers were said to have revised the script for *The Flintstones* (1994).[28] Bart and Guber also note that major films now spend more time, often years, in development. As they relate, "an ever mounting intrigue" has come to surround the development process, while in the 1960s and '70s it was "extremely rare for a project to be locked in development hell for more than a few months."[29] They report that some film projects now generate $5 million to $7 million just in expenditures for writers.[30]

Although there are few direct indications, longer shooting schedules, a preponderance of complex action scenes, and the need to integrate live action shots with special effects suggest that, at least for larger-scale films, the production process has also become more elaborate. A recent article about why films have come to cost so much to produce states that "a random survey of typical film costs reveals a staggering array of 'above scale' fees, star 'perk packages,' equipment rentals, crew overtime and vendor outlays that, when added up, begin to explain why movie-making has taken on all the appearances of a Pentagon operation."[31] A natural consequence of greater production complexity is more people to manage the process, including more staff personnel at the studio itself.

The greater number of producers credited on most films may be due largely to credit inflation, but it seems likely that the average of seven producers credited on the top ten films of 2001, including twelve for *Lord of the Rings* and thirteen for *Pearl Harbor,* compared to the one or two typically credited on films of the 1970s, reflects something more than just acknowledgment of the marginal fund-raisers, facilitators, and hangers-on who have always been around. In addition to the production and postproduction management and coordination work that producers are responsible for, modern high-budget productions also have more funding sources and thus require more fund-raising effort.

Of course, elaborate filmmaking exploits in Hollywood (always good media fodder to perk up audience interest) are hardly new. *Ben-Hur* (1959) and *Spartacus* (1960) each had a "cast of thousands"; the infamous *Cleopatra* (1963) cost $40 million and was in production for two years; and *Jaws* (1975) and *Lawrence of Arabia* (1962) had shooting schedules of 159 and 313 days respectively.[32] In those earlier days, though, such elaborate "super-colossals" (a term that gave way to "blockbusters" in the 1970s) were more the exception than the rule, and (as related in Chapter 2) these individual films apparently accounted for larger chunks of their studio's total annual production investments. And even these early extremes are now well surpassed. *Titanic* (1997) was widely described as a production on a scale never before seen, its centerpiece a full-scale model of the ship built with that film's $200 million budget.[33] The $135 million production *Pearl Harbor* involved blowing up 17 ships and exploding 350 bombs for one seven-second segment.[34] Or compare two films, one from each period. In a famous ten-minute sequence from *The French Connection,* the thirteenth highest-grossing film of 1971, Gene Hackman, as Detective Jimmy "Popeye" Doyle, pursues a subway train in downtown New York, driving at high speed under the tracks. Three or four cars were demolished in filming the chase, most of which was performed by a single stunt artist making a daredevil drive through a twenty-six-block stretch of Manhattan streets.[35] For a much more complex fourteen-minute chase scene in *The Matrix Reloaded,* a six-lane freeway in Alameda, California, was constructed at a cost of $2.5 million, and $2 million worth of cars were destroyed.[36]

Does Hollywood waste money? From an aesthetic or social perspective, it seems obvious that it does. From an economic perspective, however, the question is worth considering. To the extent that the higher budgets represent wasted resources, there would be no reason to believe that movies are any more attractive to film audiences than they were when they cost less to make.

The prevailing perception is that the higher film investments have been badly spent. Reflecting a common theme of movie industry critics, including Pauline Kael in her 1980 article, Bart and Guber contrast the modern industry with earlier times, when studio executives were in firm control of the production process.[37] Now, they and other observers say, CEOs of the media conglomerates that own the film studios are often distracted and uninformed. That, along with a corporate committee mentality within the studio's executive ranks, has effectively given directors more power over budgets. Naturally enough, most of them want to spend and spend. "Everyone wants to hit a home run," said one producer. "That enormous international market is beckoning to you. You start thinking special effects, big action scenes."[38] Aware of the need to hit a home run themselves, executives in the new environment become enamored with movie packages and are afraid to be the ones to say no to A-list star demands and ever bigger budgets for potential megahit films. Situations like the string of thirty-five writers on *The Flintstones* are typically cited as examples of wasteful, hand-wringing behavior that makes movies worse, not better. Bart and Guber's discussion of today's drawn-out development process has the same flavor.

Indeed, the press supplies us with examples of movie spending that seem to rival the infamous $600 Pentagon toilet seat: cockroaches that rent for $25 each for a horror movie, on-set "script doctors" earning salaries up to $125,000 per week, a Mercedes car rented for six weeks at $950 per day but used for only three or four days of shooting,[39] not to mention the publicity about do-nothing producers and the lavish salaries for superstars. Hollywood's critics can be especially strident when a movie fails: the lavish extravagances of *Waterworld* (1995) with its elaborate sets and 166 days of shooting; the notorious debacle of *Heaven's Gate* (1980); or *The Adventures of Pluto Nash* (2002), a sci-fi comedy with a $100 million budget, including star Eddie Murphy's "usual $20 million," that grossed $4.4 million at the box office.[40]

Examples like these have often been linked to the broader idea that film budgets are out of control and the studios the victims of their own excess. Especially in periods of rapid film-budget inflation, studios are admonished in the popular and trade press, as well as by the MPAA itself, for their failure to control costs, especially star salaries. In the 1980s and '90s, with articles carrying headlines like "Hollywood Battles Killer Budgets" and "In Denial, Studios Continue Lavish Ways," commentators have sternly warned of impending crisis.[41] As movie budgets stabilized for a few years in the late 1990s, the press backed off on these warnings and turned their attention to soaring marketing costs. There is, however, no mistaking the long-term anxiety. Attention to excessive budgets was renewed following the respective 23 percent and 9 percent increases in average MPAA film production costs in 2002 and 2003.[42]

Costs can get out of control in any industry, of course, especially in periods of high demand, and the movie studios are surely no exception. Portrayals of movie budgets as excessive have persisted at least since the 1960s, so the more recent situation is not unique.[43] Still, management inefficiencies are a well-known drawback of large and diverse corporate organizations, so the view that transformations in studio control have exacerbated wasteful spending is plausible. Creativity, and by implication the attractiveness of movies to audiences, also may suffer in the process. At the preproduction level, Bart and Guber say, "breakthrough ideas do not survive the trek through layers of executive committees."[44]

A more straightforward interpretation of higher spending on Hollywood movies nevertheless follows from economic principles. From the producers' financial point of view, increasing inputs into film production—more explosions, a new freeway for a single sequence, more cockroaches, more assistants for principal talent, more extras, higher prices for top talent—makes sense as long as the marginal attractiveness of their movies to audiences goes up enough to pay for them. Though questions are often raised about whether this or that star is overvalued in the market, there is little controversy about the viability of paying high salaries to talent in general. The frustration of studio executives who are forced to match escalating offers made by their competitors for top talent is a persistent theme of the industry commentary on movie budgets. The persistence of these higher salary rates for top stars over time, however, demonstrates their rationality. There is little reason to think that the same principle would not hold for $25 cockroaches or $125,000 script doctors. The same logic holds for evaluating film ideas in development for longer periods of time, rewriting scripts more thoroughly and more often, increasing the number of takes of each shot to make them perfect, or perhaps even engaging more committees to evaluate ideas at the preproduction stage.

Movie history is a gold mine for debaters to use in coming up with examples, often by the handful, for which generalizations do not hold. Of course, many cheaply produced films have made a fortune, and many expensive ones have lost a fortune. But as Pauline Kael admitted in her 1980 critique, "Even the lumpiest movies are better than television; at least, they're always bigger."[45] Hollywood's lavish expenditures may well make movies worse in an aesthetic sense, but they are responsible for the seamless and slick production values that seem to hypnotize audiences worldwide.

We should bear in mind that apparently wasteful spending on some components of movie production can be justified by the high cost of other components.[46] In a *Newsday* article about movie production costs, director Simon West explains how a broken screwdriver can bring a $20,000-an-hour production to a halt:

> If your Makita breaks and there are 100 people standing around watching you trying to mend the Makita—which is like a $30 electric screwdriver—and you're counting off the money as they're trying to recharge the battery or something, it's bizarre. You think, "Why don't you have 100 Makitas here because it would be cheaper to have 100 Makitas than to lose an hour of shooting." But if you had a 100 Makitas, they'd say, "What a waste! These film people have 100 Makitas lined up!"[47]

The same logic can apply to a report that Skywalker Sound intended to hire fifty film editors, instead of the usual six, to edit the "miles of footage" shot for *Titanic* in order to insure that the film would meet its July 1997 theatrical release date.[48]

Probably the largest single component of higher production costs—higher talent salaries—does not directly contribute anything to the real economic value of movies. But just as the multimillion-dollar salaries for NBA recruits seem to motivate countless young would-be basketball stars, extravagant Hollywood salaries probably benefit the quality of movies in the long run by tempting a wider range of potential top talent to take their shot at the Hollywood lottery rather than become lawyers, accountants, or entrepreneurs. It is surely these dreams of Hollywood riches that have helped inspire vast numbers of directors, producers, and other talent to migrate to Hollywood from around the world in the past twenty years.

Perhaps the most direct evidence that American movies have become more attractive to U.S. audiences is the rise in per capita movie theater attendance in the United States since the mid-1970s. In the first half of 2002, the press noted a 20 percent upsurge in theater attendance compared to the same period a year before. According to one article, the rise in attendance "has left Hollywood executives, marketers, analysts, and theater owners searching to explain their sudden, unexpected bounty—and why it seems to be affecting the movies almost exclusively."[49] The upsurge was variously explained by an increasing desire of movie audiences to escape from reality or bad times, by better and more comfortable theaters, and by higher movie marketing expenditures.[50] In reviewing possible explanations for this "mystery" of increasing theater attendance, one journalist commented that "some people even mention—with a straight face—that movies themselves have gotten better," to which one film industry critic was quoted in the article to respond "That's a hoot!"[51]

Attendance levels have since fallen back, but the longer-term growth in theater admissions—in spite of the dramatic growth of video and other competing media and a compression of movie windows—cannot easily be dismissed. To fully understand rising movie demand since the 1970s, we must consider the great increase in Hollywood's production investments, along with the magnificent technological improvements in movies that have taken place. Not to do so is really to say that Hollywood has accomplished nothing new from an economic perspective in thirty years.

Given the great rise in movie production investments as a whole, how can we explain the overwhelming imbalance of Hollywood's choice to produce more expensive movies, rather than a larger variety of movies? In the process of addressing this question, we also search for insights into why talent costs have risen so fast and, finally, how the pressures of expanding movie markets, advances in production technology, and increasing risk can indeed make movies worse from an aesthetic or a social perspective.

The Effects of Market Expansion

One likely reason for higher movie budgets since the 1970s is the continuing need to differentiate theatrical movies from cheaper original productions on pay TV networks and home video, like the "supercolossals" did in the broadcast TV era. Pay media content, though, is itself dominated by theatrical movies, making media competition much less of an issue. In looking further for an answer, we offer below an economic model of the trade-offs between movie quality and variety that recognizes the benefits of exhibiting the same movie on a variety of media.

Pay Media Proliferation

It is amusing to look back to the 1970s and see the expectations that came with the prospect of multichannel, pay-supported video media. A 1970 *Time* magazine article: "Some futurists, notably Alvin Toffler . . . argue that TV cassettes will quicken the already bewildering pace of change in American life, carrying the U.S. farther away from standardization in the arts, education, and cultural tastes."[52] *Newsweek* in 1978: "New markets for the [Hollywood movie industry's] 'software' are already opening up in video recorders, big-screen home-TV systems, and pay television—perhaps permitting a shift to lower budget movies."[53] These expectations were buttressed by economic models predicting that a larger number of television channels and the use of direct support mechanisms in place of advertiser support would lead to greater program variety and audience fragmentation.[54]

The pay media have in fact brought forth a huge supply of sharply focused, diverse programming, including some "made-for-pay" and "direct-to-video" fare, plus lots of programs involving the arts, education, and culture. But why has the predominant effect for theatrical films been larger-scale productions—many of them perhaps closer to "lowest common denominator" fare, as the critics assert, than to the elevation of "the arts, education, and cultural tastes?"

The movie industry's response to rising demand may be thought of in terms of an economic trade-off. Producers could respond to a doubling of the size of the market, let's say, either by producing twice as many movies at the same cost or by spending twice as much on the same number of movies. Because so much of movie costs are "first copy" outlays to create the product itself, there is a fairly pure practical trade-off between these choices.[55]

To see how even the development of a "niche" medium like pay TV or home video can induce studios to make more expensive, more "homogenized" movies rather than a greater variety of movies, consider an example of hypothetical revenue potentials for "high-cost" and "low-cost" movies under alternative scenarios. In the following table, we assume that a low-cost movie requires $5 million to produce, and a high-cost one requires $10 million. (For simplicity, say also that there are no distribution or other costs.)

Theater market revenue from . . .	Video market revenue from . . .	
(a)	(b)	(c)
High-cost theater movie: $9 million	High-cost video movie: $9 million	High-cost theater repeat: $7 million
Low-cost theater movie: $6 million	Low-cost video movie: $6 million	Low-cost theater repeat: $4 million

In a before-video initial case (column a), consider the choice of a single movie that can play only in theaters. Based on the demand potentials shown in that column, the film's producer will choose the low-cost option, earning $6 million in revenue, with a profit of $1 million (once the $5 million production cost is covered). Although the more attractive high-cost version would earn more revenue, the producer would lose $1 million ($9 million revenue against the $10 million cost).

Now say that home video comes on the scene and exactly doubles the size of the producer's potential market. The producer could now offer a second movie that is specialized to the tastes of video audiences (targeted to an older demographic, for example, or as Alvin Toffler perhaps imagined, a film of elevated cultural tastes). The revenue potential of those options is shown in column (b). Comparably to the theater-only case, the best option for the video movie is the low-cost version (also generating revenue of $6 million, less the $5 million cost). Combined profits for the low-cost theater movie and the low-cost video movie would be $2 million, with each movie's profit being $1 million.

Alternatively, however, the producer could respond to the new video market by adding, let's say, a spectacular car chase to the low-cost movie, to turn it into a $10 million high-cost movie, then exhibiting that film first in theaters and later on video. As the options set forth in column (c) show, that strategy yields higher profits than the low-cost differentiation strategy. For a single high-cost movie that is first shown in theaters and then repeated on video, total revenues are $9 million plus $7 million, less the $10 million cost, for a profit of $6 million. (Showing the low-cost version in theaters and then on video would yield only $6 million plus $4 million in revenue, less the $5 million cost, for a profit of only $5 million, so that option is out of the picture.)

An important feature of this model is that the high-cost option with repetition in both media is a lowest common denominator—that is, a movie that is at least satisfactory to all, but not everyone's preferred choice. Other things equal, namely cost, the video audience prefers content that is tailor-made for them. What drives the producer to offer the more expensive common denominator instead is that the appeal of higher production values dominates the video audience's demand for greater variety. Because movie producers realize such huge economies of scale by distributing the same movie to a larger potential audience, achieving greater variety thus turns into a costly, uphill battle.

In more practical terms, the model illustrates that the result of adding "niche" media, such as pay TV or home video, to the range of consumer options does not necessarily result in more specialized products, as both the tradition of economic program choice models and many futurists predicted would happen. It also illustrates the potentially content-homogenizing, idea-diluting effect of diverse media outlets. Diluting consumer tastes can be a good business if you spend enough money doing it. Of course, in the real world we do get original pay TV movies and video movies that are presumably focused toward pay TV or video tastes; but, as we have seen, the great proportion of pay TV and video movie demand is for repeated theatrical features.

International Market Expansion

A parallel analysis can be applied to the budget and content implications of the growth of Hollywood's foreign markets. Replace, for example, the words "video market" in our example with "France." With only the domestic market available, an American producer's most profitable choice is to make the low-cost (American) movie. With the French market added, the producer could choose to make an additional low-cost movie oriented to French tastes. As the model shows, though, production of a single higher-budget, homogenized movie for release in both markets would be more profitable.

In the international market context, the content-homogenization effect is surely more extreme than in the media proliferation case. Reflecting our analysis in Chapter 5, the American producer essentially "buys" the French audience with a high-budget film not oriented specifically to French tastes.

Of course, our numerical model is very simplistic. French producers do of course make lots of movies, albeit much less expensive ones, that cater to French tastes. Another simplification is that the model does not explicitly show how the opening of either new media or foreign markets might cause producers to homogenize content in a way that compromises demand of the original theater audiences. With the addition of some complexities, the model can be modified to show how expanding media or foreign markets can make a movie's content worse from the perspective of *all* audiences.[56]

To better understand the pressure of Hollywood's international markets on movie content, we compiled data on movie genres of top-performing movies in the United States, the EUJ5, and world markets. (Details of the study appear in Appendix K.) First we compared the genres of top twenty movies over the five-year period 1997–2001 (Table 6.2). All international coproductions were excluded from the study. The "Global" column of Table 6.2 shows the percentage of all movies appearing in the annual top twenty worldwide lists in each of the five most commonly appearing genres. (There were 6 international coproductions on the original list of 100 movies, yielding 94 movies for the study.) We also added a summary category that we call "violence-prone" genres. For example, 45 percent of the 94 top-performing global movies had "action" as at least one of their genre labels, and 73 percent of them were labeled with at least one of the seven "violence-prone"

Table 6.2   Genres of domestically produced movies in annual top twenty box office lists in the U.S., the EUJ5, and global markets, 1997–2001

	% of top twenty movies in genre		
Genre	Global	U.S.	EUJ5
Action	45	42	13
Comedy	44	48	59
Drama	34	27	29
Adventure	29	29	7
Thriller	25	28	9
"Violence-prone" index	73	77	29
Number of movies in sample	94	94	85

Source: See Appendix K.

Notes: The five genres cited are the top five global categories. The "violence-prone" index includes action, adventure, crime, horror, sci-fi, thriller, and war.

genre categories—action, adventure, science fiction, thriller, horror, crime, and war.

The next column shows the same data for all U.S.-produced movies that made the U.S. top twenty box office lists. Finally, the third column shows the same genre data for domestically produced top twenty movies in the individual EUJ5 countries. That is, the 85 movies included in the EUJ5 column consist of all the French-produced movies that finished in the top twenty within France, plus all the Italian movies finishing in the top twenty in Italy, and so on for the five countries. The other 415 movies on the top twenty lists of the EUJ5 countries were either foreign produced (nearly all of them U.S. productions), or international co-productions.

Of course, the top twenty movies are a small minority of all movie releases in any of the six countries. The top twenty, though, account for a disproportionate fraction of box office receipts. From 1997 to 2001, this group accounted for an average of 43.8 percent of all U.S. box-office receipts.[57] These top films are also the primary U.S. entries on the world market.

As Table 6.2 shows, genre labels for the global and the U.S. top twenty lists are very similar; nearly all of the top global movies (88 of the 94) are American-produced, and the American movies that do well internationally usually do well within the United States. The "action," "adventure," "thriller," and "violence-prone" categories are all much more prevalent on the U.S. and global lists than in the EUJ5. "Comedy" and "drama" are common on all three lists, but producers in the EUJ5 counties evidently have a comparative advantage in making movies in these genres for their home markets.

Although many U.S.-produced movies with elements of comedy or drama have a strong international presence, these comparisons confirm the conventional wisdom that action-oriented genres "travel well," and

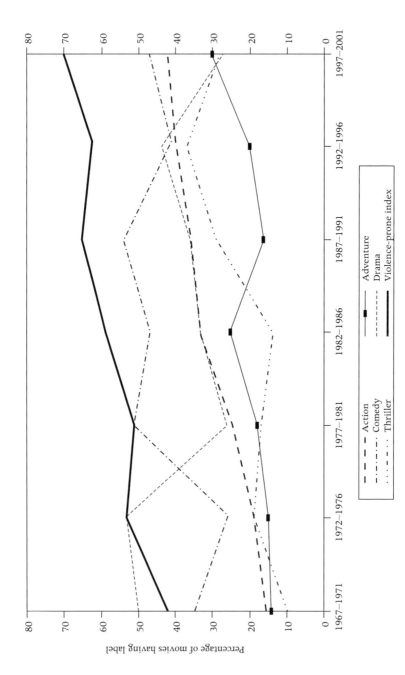

FIGURE 6.3 Trends in genres of top twenty box office movies in the United States, five-year averages, 1967–2001. (For sources, see Appendix K.)

that Hollywood dominates the world market for such movies. More interesting, the comparisons are consistent with the example we gave earlier. That is, the worldwide appeal of action or violence suggests that these may be "lowest common denominator" elements. Action and/or violence in themselves are not necessarily the most appealing elements to movie audiences—they are only the most *commonly* appealing.

We also compiled trends over a thirty-five-year period in the genres of top-performing U.S. movies.[58] (Trend data were not available for other countries.) Figure 6.3 shows trends in the same five genres (which were also the five most commonly appearing labels over the full 1967 to 2001 period)—along with our "violence-prone" index.[59] Over this time frame, the presence of "action" movies more than doubled (from 16 percent to 42 percent), as did the genres "adventure" (14 percent to 30 percent) and "thriller" (from 10 percent to 28 percent); and the violence-prone index rose steadily, from 42 percent to 70 percent. Over the same period, the presence of comedy also increased (from 35 percent to 47 percent). Drama, however, declined sharply, from 50 percent in the earliest period to 27 percent in the most recent. Our statistical analysis in Appendix K using annual data shows that these trends are all statistically significant and that the overall upward time trends in the action genre and the violence-prone index were the fastest of the top twelve genre categories we studied, while the decline in drama was the steepest of the twelve.

These trends are consistent with the conventional wisdom that Hollywood movies have become increasingly action-oriented and violent at the expense of "serious" subjects (as represented, perhaps, by the drama genre label). If action-oriented genres are indeed the lowest-common-denominator movies, the statistics thus provide some justification for the lament of some critics that America no longer puts its best cultural foot forward in the international marketplace.

The reasons behind these trends in top-performing U.S. movies are not obvious. Since the early 1980s, the significance of foreign markets as a share of the U.S. distributors' economic pie has increased substantially (Appendix C). This suggests a tempting explanation for more intense use in Hollywood movies of common-denominator production elements. Hollywood's "globalization," however, has a longer history. As also discussed in Appendix C, the relative economic significance of foreign markets to Hollywood has probably not increased by much, if at all, since the 1960s and 1970s. Our leading hypothesis is that the genre trends are related to advances in movie production technology, a subject that we take up later in this chapter. But first, a related question about an important piece of the budget inflation puzzle—one that implicitly involves the higher budgets versus higher variety trade-off.

Why Have Talent Costs Risen So Fast?

If top talent could get $20 to $25 million per movie in 2002, compared to $2 to $3 million in 1980, talent costs would seem to have risen even faster than total movie production costs (since MPAA-produced movie costs rose by a factor of 6.3 over the same interval). The apparent increase in above-the-line relative to below-the-line contributions to movie budgets implies that this would be the case.

As producers choose to add most inputs—whether more cars to crash, more assistant directors, and so on—the increased industry demand for production resources puts upward pressure on their prices (wages and salaries for people, purchase prices for cameras and editing machines, and so on) as they are bid away from other uses. In most cases, though, the end result will simply be a net inflow of new labor or other resources into the industry, rather than enduring (at least very large) increases in their prices.

Labor markets for top talent in entertainment and sports, though, don't seem to work that way. As demand for these individuals rises, the going rates for mostly the same group of people are bid up and up, while there is little increase in the actual number of these people that are employed. In professional sports, player costs have notoriously spiraled upward, while the number of teams and games played has risen far less. Given the marginal increase in the number of major movies produced in Hollywood since the 1970s and an assumption that the number of top stars employed per movie has not risen, talent cost inflation seems to have been the main result for the movie industry as well.

A plausible explanation for the unusual performance of labor markets in movies and sports is that athletic and entertainment talent is rare. In economic terms, this scarcity implies yawning gaps between the marginal contributions to a movie's box office performance that one individual can make over another. Those gaps can persist over time because only handfuls of these people are able to perform at top levels, or because only a few top stars or directors are able to capture the public imagination at a time.[60] As the potential market for movies increases with media proliferation, economies of scale in movie production and distribution magnify the economic importance of these revenue-earning differences, creating what we can call a "superstar effect."[61]

To illustrate the superstar effect, imagine two possible alternative movies that a studio can choose to make. First, say that the producer could combine a below-the-line investment of $900,000 with any one of dozens of would-be Hollywood stars available at $100,000 to star in an action-adventure movie that will break even by returning $1 million from the box office. (We ignore distribution and other cost components to keep things simple; this alternative is thus a break-even situation.) As the second alternative, say that if Tom Cruise can be hired as the star along with the same $900,000 in below-the-line inputs, this movie is expected to generate $2 million in distributor revenues. In this scenario, Tom Cruise can demand up to $1.1 million for his talents. From the studio's perspective, Cruise contributes a marginal value of $1 million in revenues over the next best alternative, plus the $100,000 "base" wage of the ordinary star.

Now say that demand doubles (due to video diffusion, for example). The producer could still make the garden-variety version of the no-name-talent movie for $1 million; other things equal, that movie would now earn $2 million due to the doubled demand base. In this case, though, a competing producer would surely see these extra potential profits and enter the market to produce another similar movie with one of the other would-be stars who are available for $100,000. Assuming for this example that the total audience for movies does not vary with the number of available movies (which is the same as saying that consumers as a whole do not place a value on variety), the result would be two generic action-adventure films splitting the audience and each bringing in $1 million at the box office as before.

With the Tom Cruise alternative still in play, though, doubling the potential audience base would mean that the potential studio revenues of the Tom Cruise movie would rise to $4 million. Because Cruise is a "unique" star, the increase in market size has magnified the economic effect of the talent gap between him and the next best alternative. Now Tom Cruise can demand a salary up to $3.1 million ($4 million, less the $900,000 below-the-line costs), and the producer still has as profitable an alternative as the two generic films. In the end, a doubling of audience demand leads to nearly a tripling of Tom Cruise's salary (from $1.1 million to $3.1 million).

In the real world, of course, audiences do value variety, there are alternatives to Tom Cruise, there is more to movies than their stars, prices of other inputs may go up, and so on. Conceptually, though, this example illustrates how superstar salaries can rise so fast in the movie business, accompanied by little increase in the variety of movies that are produced.

The Effects of Technology

There is a well-known reason that the costs of producing live theater, symphonies, television shows, and other performing arts products, including movies, should rise over time compared to the costs of producing "normal" goods like furniture. This theory, known unfortunately as "Baumol's cost disease," is premised on the assumption that the potential for improving labor productivity in the performing arts is limited or nonexistent.[62] Presentation of Shakespeare's *Much Ado about Nothing,* for example, takes precisely the same cast and other labor inputs as it did centuries before, and the potential for more efficient set construction and the like is very limited. Meanwhile, productivity in the rest of the economy rises steadily over time due to improved machinery and better education and training of workers. These contrasts of productivity growth potential in the performing arts sector cause wages in that sector to rise relative to those of the rest of the economy. For example, if higher productivity over a ten-year period permits one individual to double the number of wooden high chairs that can be produced in one day, wages in performing arts jobs would have to double relative to those of high-chair manufacturing to continue to attract labor into the former profession. The end result is relatively high growth in performing arts production costs.

While movie production is very labor intensive and thus subject to Baumol's cost disease, it seems certain that the superstar effect has far outstripped it in driving up labor costs in movie production.[63] Also, movie production has seen significant technological improvements over the past few decades, owing especially to the leaps and bounds of computer technology.

Movie producers, though, seem to have had the opposite response to technological improvements than we might expect. While computer use in filmmaking would seem to have real cost-saving potential, computer technology seems to have fueled, not mitigated, rising movie budgets.

Consider studio responses to recent developments in digital animation. The animation genre was dramatically, and rather suddenly, affected by advances in digital technology in the mid-1990s. Up to that time, "cell animation" (or "2-D") was the prevailing technology. In this method, an artist draws each frame of the movie separately, and then a camera turns them into full motion by filming twenty-four (more or less) of these frames per second to create the illusion of smooth movement. With the highly successful 1995 film *Toy Story*, the production company Pixar pioneered a new technique of computer-generated animation on a commercial level (called computer-generated imagery, or CGI).[64]

In the opinion of many observers, CGI permits a more engaging range of character movements as well as visual effects. What attracted particular attention in the trade press, however, was the notion that movies could be made far more cheaply with CGI technology.[65] As one press report recently observed:

> They [CGI movies] are particularly appealing to studios because they're much cheaper and quicker to produce. The rule of thumb, [Sony Pictures executive Penny Finkelman] Cox says, is that it takes 400 artists four years to bring a 2-D movie to theaters. It takes half that number in three years for a computer-generated movie. As a result, a digital movie typ-

ically costs about $80 million, compared with $150 million for a traditional animated feature.[66]

These cost differences and the creative possibilities led industry observers in the wake of *Toy Story* to predict a revolution in animation. *Toy Story*'s box-office success has indeed spawned a widespread industry shift toward CGI technology for major animated feature films. The next major CGI movies to appear (led by Disney's *A Bug's Life*) were released in 1998. Only 13 of the total of 48 major animated features released from 1998 to 2002 were CGI films, but they accounted for 40 percent of Hollywood's animated film production investments and for 51 percent of the total box-office revenues earned by animated movies. (See Appendix H for details.) We lack systematic data on movie production costs and revenues after 2002, but it is evident that the shift to CGI technology for major features has continued.[67]

The total number of major animated movies released in the wake of *Toy Story* has substantially increased. In the ten years from 1988 through 1997, 37 major animated features had been released, compared to 48 in the five years from 1998 through 2002. Trends in animated film production budgets, however, were the opposite of what many people seemed to expect. As Figure 6.4 shows, the average cost of animated features released in the United States generally tracked those of all movies until the mid-1990s, but since then, the cost of animated features has risen much faster than that of nonanimated movies.

The cost divergence began before any major CGI productions reached the market in 1998, and a handful of the higher-budget post-1997 animated productions, most of them produced by Disney, have been 2-D films, including *The Emperor's New Groove* (2000, $100 million cost), *Titan A.E.* (2000, $75 million), and *Treasure Planet* (2002, $140 million). Most of the higher-budget productions, however, includ-

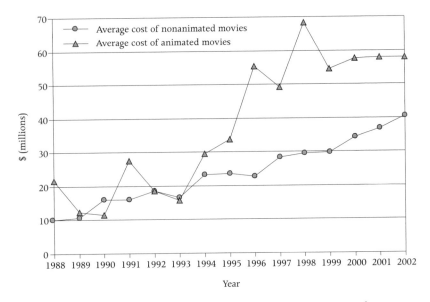

FIGURE 6.4   Trends in production costs of animated and nonanimated theatrical films released by all distributors in the United States, 1988–2002. (For sources, see Appendix K.)

ing *Monsters, Inc.* (2001, $115 million), *Dinosaur* (2000, $200 million), and *Finding Nemo* (2003, $80 million), have been the CGI entries.

Overall, the average cost of CGI movies released from 1998 to 2002 was $89.7 million, compared to $46.9 million for 2-D films. Movie producers switching to the "cheaper" CGI technology have thus chosen to spend more—not less—on their productions.

How can we explain these developments?

It is useful to think of technological change in movie production as either cost-reducing or quality-enhancing.[68] For example, digital recreation of movie extras, to the extent that they can pass for real people, is cost-reducing because it results in essentially equivalent outcomes for the movie viewer. Quality-enhancing technologies, on the other hand, include many special effects. For example, the dazzling visual effects of the ghosts in *Scooby Doo* (2002) and *Scooby Doo 2* (2004) are far better than could ever be achieved with the smoke and mirrors of films gone by. Of course, technological changes can be both cost reducing and quality enhancing, and computer animation is surely a good example. A computer-generated special effect might make a monster's dive off the top of a building look more real and dramatic than a stunt artist could accomplish and also be cheaper than paying that person to take the risk.

How advancing technology affects movie costs and variety is an empirical issue. A plausible theory, however, can be advanced to explain how either quality-enhancing or cost-reducing technological advances can in the end lead to increased costs for major films.

To begin, it is easy to imagine how producers might respond to quality-enhancing production technologies by increasing film budgets at the expense of variety. For example, a $1,000 special effects expenditure not undertaken in the past because its marginal effect on demand was perceived to be less than $1,000 now becomes worthwhile when better technology allows a more visceral audience response to be achieved with the same spending. The huge expansion in special effects into major Hollywood films, and the dramatic growth in the cost of action-adventure, sci-fi, and other genres of films that use them, is consistent with this interpretation.

It may seem, however, that cost-reducing production technologies would simply reduce costs, thus resulting in easier entry and greater product variety. Under some circumstances, such as a decline in the price of cameras or editing machines, perhaps, that is indeed likely to be the expected industry response. To the extent that cost-reducing technologies affect inputs that are also *potentially quality-enhancing*, however, the opposite may happen.

To illustrate these points, consider a simple example in which we hypothesize the effects of using more or fewer stunts in a certain movie production. Considering the initial case, in general the more stunts, the more attractive will be the movie to audiences. But there are diminishing returns, so that after the first stunt's incremental value of $4,000, each additional stunt leads to a smaller increment in audience response.

	1st stunt	2nd stunt	3rd stunt
Marginal value, initial case	$4,000	$3,000	$2,000
Marginal value, enhanced-value case	$8,000	$6,000	$4,000

In response to prospective demand, the producer selects the number of stunts so that the last one attracts additional demand that is at least equal to its cost. In the initial case, let us say that stunts cost $4,000. Thus, only one stunt will be used, at a total cost of $4,000. Now say that the marginal value of stunts doubles across the board to those on the second row of the table, due to technological advance following from computer enhancements. In that case, three stunts will be used, at a total cost of $12,000 ($4,000 × 3). The number of stunts used in the movie triples, as does the amount of money spent on them.

Consider now, however, a cost-reducing technology for stunts. That is, say the same stunt becomes only half as expensive to perform, dropping from $4,000 to $2,000 each. The best response in this case is also to increase the number of stunts in the movie from one to three. Total movie expenditures increase in this case as well, though only from $4,000 to $6,000 (3 stunts @ $2,000 each).

In both these cases, the response to improved movie production technology is to expand the scope of production, and at a greater total cost. Of course, the example is very simplistic. It is evident from industry reports that the pre–*Toy Story* success of Disney's *Lion King* (1994), and a competitive challenge to Disney's historical domination of the animation genre in the mid-1990s by Warner, DreamWorks, and other major studios using CGI technology contributed to the bidding up of labor prices for top Hollywood talent. That was followed by an apparent deflation of the animators' salary balloon after the late 1990s.[69]

Under reasonable assumptions, though, our examples show that both quality-enhancing and cost-reducing technologies can result in larger, not smaller, movie budgets for major films. In so many words, these movie technologies serve to put more toys in the hands of producers, and whatever the bean counters' expectations, the creative people respond with great imagination.

Our economic perspective on technological advances in movie production suggests a reason for the trend toward more action-oriented, violent movies at the expense of drama. Computer enhancements have made violence and death much more engaging to watch on screen, and other things equal, a spectacular explosion or a brutal murder is cheaper to present than it was ten or twenty years ago. Love scenes, tearful arguments, or other real-life portrayals are not so amenable to the computer's contribution. True, the comedy genre has also become more prominent among top films. But modern high-budget comedies, with their generous use of computer-enhanced visual effects and stunts, are also the frequent beneficiary of modern production technologies.

Uncertainty, Sequels, and Studio Management

If Hollywood is inclined to invest its money in sequels, remakes, and other safe, unimaginative products, can we blame that on the notoriously high uncertainty of movie production? In an obvious sense, yes—just as we could also sweep all the expensive flops that litter Hollywood's landscape into one box and blame them on natural risk. The story that *Raiders of the Lost Ark* was turned down by every studio before Paramount gave it the green light, and similar stories for *Gosford Park*[70] and other ultimately successful films, could be used here as well. There is more to be said, though, about the effects of risk on the movies Hollywood offers.

No one questions that movie production is subject to extreme uncertainty. It is a common misconception, though, that studios produce sequels, remakes, and other uncreative products for the purpose of avoiding risk. Notwithstanding the potentially numbing effects of bureaucratic corporate organization, studios are basically in the business of taking risks. What they seek is return, and return can be found throughout the spectrum of movie ideas, from completely original ideas to sequels and remakes.

Movie industry executives can be likened to a group of people wandering in a fog, looking for gold nuggets. When one person finds a nugget, others flock to the same area and search, because that area is more likely to have other, though perhaps smaller, nuggets. It makes sense to launch lonely forays into the dark to look for the big finds, but to bypass the more predictable areas would be foolish. It is hard to tell, too, if the discovered nuggets are real or fool's gold. So it is logical that we should see many eventually successful movie ideas turned away by their original finders only to be picked up by others later; and it is logical, too, that when a success is eventually proven, sequels and derivative films flow one after another until the expected marginal revenues from yet another bad movie fall below the required rate of return.

Our gold-digging analogy is limited because movie industry risk goes beyond simply finding the nuggets and turning them in to the bank. Even with the wisest of decisions at the executive level and the best of material and personnel, the movie production process can go awry for many unforeseeable reasons, much like a war can. As mentioned in Chapter 1, studies have also demonstrated statistically that box office returns vary greatly with the timing of release and what competing studios happen to come up with at the same time.

When a successful new idea is confirmed by the market, the money is phenomenal, but it is well known that for sequels and derivative films the returns are usually much lower. In most cases, sequels cost more than the original movie and earn less money at the box-office. A study of sixty original theatrical movies and their sequels released between 1970 and 1990 found that (corrected for inflation) the average sequel cost 20 percent more than the original, but earned only 70 percent of the original's theater rentals.[71] This pattern makes sense, because in the aftermath of a successful film, the producer and principal creative people are able to exploit the expected future returns in the same way that the producer and principals of a successful TV series are able to hike their salaries for a second season. Box office is lower because the rehash of an original idea is hard to make as enjoyable to audiences as the original. In exploiting the built-in demand, in fact, the studios seem usually not even to try to make sequels that are attractive as the original. Consider, for example, the stream of perfunctory animated direct-to-video films that Disney has produced to follow its successful original theatrical features, such as *The Return of Jafar* (1994) following *Aladdin* (1992) or *George of the Jungle 2* (2003).

There have been recent exceptions to the historical pattern of underperforming sequels, including the *Lord of the Rings: The Return of the King* (2003), *The Matrix Reloaded* (2003), and *Shrek 2* (2004), all of which outgrossed their predecessors at the box office. Yet industry commentators have attributed this trend to the tentpole concept: higher studio investments in sequel projects are induced by the expectation of releasing still more sequels to build upon the originals. "If you don't make a good sequel, you can kill a franchise," explained John Goldwyn of Paramount.[72]

Yet in spite of the attraction of sequels or derivative movies to the studios, there is little reason to believe that highly risky projects that are perceived to have the same average expected return are passed over by Hollywood. Even if a studio's slate of multiple productions or its parent company war chest fails to reduce risk to bankers' standards, venture capital markets are very effective at rounding up outside investors for the riskiest of business propositions. Witness the billions raised for Internet ventures in the mid-1990s. There is no shortage of this kind of money in the market.

The resulting popular impression of studio decision making under high risk is an unfortunate one. As the fog analogy conveys, rational decision making under conditions of extreme uncertainty has an inevitably comical, humiliating look to it. Copycats are not admired, and it is embarrassing to pick up a water bomb that explodes in your face. And, of course, all this is done in the public limelight. It seems to happen all the time in Hollywood, while in the less visible oil drilling industry, for example, debacles seem reasonably rare.

Does this logic exonerate studio management for *Heaven's Gate* (1980), *Ishtar* (1987), *The Adventures of Pluto Nash* (2002), and the long list of other unfortunate box office disasters that Hollywood has offered? Perhaps not entirely. Of course, in the movie or the cement industry, underqualified executives can find their way to the top, gaining the authority to make poor investment or marketing decisions, to allow costs to go out of control, and so on. Is it possible, though, that Hollywood is somehow more prone to mismanagement than "normal" industries? In spite of almost universal reverence for many of Hollywood's business leaders, from Louis B. Mayer and Walt Disney to Barry Diller and (at least until recently) Michael Eisner, there also seems no shortage of movies that the media or industry pundits claim should never have been attempted.[73]

Disastrous production decisions can always be attributed to bad luck or perhaps to the difficulty of successfully managing large-scale projects.[74] An economic rationale can be advanced, though, for why underqualified executives and bad decision making (and thus bad products) might in fact be more prevalent in Hollywood than in other industries due to high uncertainty and the difficulty of evaluating individual performance.[75]

While some of the most successful movie executives have sheepishly admitted to great uncertainty about the green-light decisions they make for their studios' film projects, the "nobody knows anything" syndrome of production decision making made famous by William Goldman should not be taken too literally.[76] Much the way that pro sports teams pursue managers or coaches, studios search for CEOs that they perceive can beat the odds, even slightly, and they pay very well for those that they believe can do it. Top studio decision makers, from production executive Louis B. Mayer in the 1930s to Disney CEO Michael Eisner in the 1980s and 1990s, have always been among the highest-paid executives in the United States.[77] Of course, studio executives' performance also relies on their ability to manage employees, their personal connections with top talent, and other attributes. Their high salaries seem mainly to testify, though, to the rarity of individuals who are perceived to see clearly enough through the fog to bat above the average on their go–don't go decisions.

In Hollywood, the inputs that go into decision making at the top levels are too complex and mysterious to be reliably parsed. Product, rather than process, takes precedence in evaluating the performance of studio executives as well as of creative talent. Essentially, the main output of top studio executives amounts to something like a won-loss record. A string of box office successes makes one the darling of the industry; a string of failures, whatever the particular circumstances, has the opposite effect. A 1998 *Wall Street Journal* article entitled "Universal Chief Quits in Wake of Movie Flops" chronicled the resignation of Universal Pictures president Casey Silver after three years in the job. The article went on to praise Mr. Silver's accomplishments in his first two years on the job, and said there seemed to be no specific grounds for his departure other than his losing streak of the past year. Ron Meyer, Universal CEO (and Silver's boss), was reported to say that "he [Meyer] isn't certain exactly what has gone wrong in the last eighteen months . . ."[78]

The key question is how many trials it takes to reach a reliable judgment about whether an executive does or doesn't have the elusive skill that can beat the odds, or whether he or she may have had the magic, but somehow lost it. Because there is such high uncertainty in selecting good film ideas, which then have to withstand the warlike uncertainty of the production process, plus unforeseeable competition at release time, it could take a long time for stockholders to determine whether an executive really does have that rare talent.

The implication of these circumstances is that at any given time we are likely to find a relatively high proportion of underqualified executives in Hollywood who will eventually be weeded out of their jobs once stockholders determine that a string of box office failures is not just bad luck or that a string of successes is not a beguiling result of unusually good luck. Consider the firing of Mark Canton, Sony's studio chief in 1996. A *Variety* article mused on why Sony kept him on so long after a string of box office failures, including *The Cable Guy* and *Last Action Hero*.[79] Were those movies just the usual bad luck, or would they have never been made if Sony had realized earlier that Canton was not a good executive choice?

The difficulty of evaluating performance in Hollywood extends beyond studio heads to others involved in the production and marketing of the film. Just as it's unclear in advance of production or even release whether a movie will be successful, it is often hard to determine why a given movie performed as it did after the fact. The success of *Independence Day* in 1996, for example, seemed to baffle even its distributor, Warner Brothers, which led to a variety of theories about whether special effects, the players, the director, the marketing people, or something else had created the magic.[80] Movie failures often lead to finger pointing. As a recent *Variety* article on the subject noted, "filmmakers frequently target marketing or distribution: 'They didn't know how to sell it' or 'They picked the wrong date.'" The article went on to remark: "Work can dry up for anyone associated with a B.O. clunker" and "the most dangerous aspect of a clunker is that the entire studio administration can come under fire."[81] Another *Variety* article on the subject noted, "They are the box-office bombs, bane of anyone with their names in the credits, but vindictive lifeblood of those who can prove no involvement—especially upward climbers at the studio in question."[82]

The marketplace thus applies rather brutal summary judgment to executives as well as artists in filmmaking, but for a logical reason.[83] The actual contribution of particular individuals or decision makers to a film's performance is very difficult to reliably determine. The implication is not only that numerous, rare executive as well as filmmaking talents have been unjustly rejected by Hollywood because those in charge deemed it too risky to give them a second chance, but also that at any given time the studios have more than their share of decision makers who should be elsewhere. The unfortunate by-product for moviegoers may be more bad movies than we might otherwise have to endure.

Before and After

The vast growth of Hollywood's financial and technological arsenals since the 1970s has resulted in some remarkable and critically acclaimed films, from *Independence Day* (1996), *Titanic* (1997), and *Shrek* (2001), to *Spiderman 2* (2004). Perhaps the pinnacle of what Hollywood can do with all its resources is *Lord of the Rings: The Return of the King* (2003), winner of eleven Academy Awards, including Best Picture.

A more telling example, perhaps, of what Hollywood has done with its great resources is the 2001 remake of *Planet of the Apes,* originally released by Twentieth Century Fox in 1968. *Planet* is an action-adventure, science-fiction story about space travel to a planet where the ship's crew finds apes in the role of humans, and humans as slaves of the apes. The original movie, starring Charlton Heston, was a high-end production in its day. Its negative cost of about $5 million may be compared to the $1.5 million average for MPAA-produced feature films two years later in 1970.[84] The movie was financially successful: it was the sixth highest grossing film at the U.S. box office in 1968, earning $15 million in that year, eventually reaching a total of $22 million.[85] The original *Planet* was widely praised by critics of the time, especially for the performances of Heston and others, and it has become a cult classic.

The 2001 remake, released under the same title, was directed by Tim Burton, stars Mark Wahlberg and Helena Bonham Carter, and was released by Fox. It cost an estimated $100 million to make, like its predecessor well above the average for MPAA movies of that year.[86] Although the setting and the basic story idea are similar (and much of the remake was filmed at the original location of Lake Powell, California), the differences in the scale of production and the viewing experiences of the two movies are striking.

In the 1968 version, several major players and scores of extras in some scenes wear ape costumes. For these, the original movie earned an Academy Award nomination for Best Costume Design. But while charming and admitting to suspension of disbelief, the ape characters in the movie do not seriously resemble real apes. The characters make no more than perfunctory attempts at walking or otherwise behaving like apes.

For the remake, 600 to 700 people were screened to go to a "Simian Academy," in which they were trained for weeks to move and act like real apes. One thousand ape costumes were constructed, several times more than ever appeared in the original. Elaborate cable rigs were made to create realistic tree-swinging shots. Up to four and one half hours per day were required just to apply the main actors' makeup.

There is a good deal of action and violence in the original, but nothing compared to the remake. Early on in the 1968 version, the spaceship dramatically sinks into the lake where it has landed. Later, in the course of two major battles that take place in the original, four ape characters meet violent deaths. In the new version, there are three major battles, each involving hundreds of apes, with roughly one hundred violent deaths shown on screen, some from the effects of huge explosions. The scale of the battles is notably greater in the remake. Aircraft are destroyed, tents and other structures are burned or damaged. The final battle scene goes on for more than seven minutes, involving scores of ape and human deaths and much destruction of property through special effects or live-action filming. There are 949 credits, including 109 stunt-artist and 136 special-effects credits, in the new version.

Film critics liked the extremely realistic apes and elaborate special effects of the *Planet* remake. Roger Ebert of the *Chicago Sun-Times* said: "The movie is great-looking. Rick Baker's makeup is convincing even in the extreme close-ups, and his apes sparkle with personality and presence."[87] As an aesthetic effort, though, the remake was widely panned as another failed Hollywood extravaganza.[88] Desson Howe of the *Washington Post* commented on "how tiring it was to watch apes perpetually pushing humans to the ground or sending them pirouetting into the air. It doesn't take a brain, or even opposable thumbs, to make a summer movie. Just a budget."[89] Some reviewers commented on the imaginativeness of the new ending, but others concluded that the ending was set up for a sequel.[90]

With these kinds of reviews, we might wonder, what was the bottom line for the studio? As the tenth highest grossing movie in 2001, the *Planet of the Apes* remake earned $180 million at the U.S. box office.[91] Using average ticket prices, that works out to about 36 million theater tickets sold in the United States for the remake, versus 17 million in 1968—almost twice the theater audience as the original. The video release of the new version kept it at the top of the sales and rental charts for several weeks, and it has now played on PPV and subscription pay TV. Even assuming a healthy stream of catalog video sales and rentals for the original *Planet of the Apes* around the world, probably several times as many people have seen the new version as the old. Although we have no comparative data for the original version, the remake was an international hit, finishing sixth in the global box office listings for its year with $358 million in revenue.[92]

Of course this is only one example, selected to make a point, and it may be that producers have a predilection for having a remake outdo the original in order to attract a fresh audience. The *Planet of the Apes* remake nevertheless embodies both the film critic's and the economist's story of Hollywood's transformation since the 1970s.

Can economic theory provide a happier ending to this chapter? Perhaps. Other things being equal, an expanding flow of resources into movie production in response to higher demand worldwide implies that audiences must be better off in some economic sense. But more can be said on this subject. One cause for the expanding movie production resources we have identified is more efficient price discrimination by the sellers. Although that may not sound good for consumers, price discrimination in the sale of information products, such as movies, has the benefit of increasing the ability of producers to support first copy creation costs of products for which demand is sufficiently high in the aggregate.[93] For example, if a music concert could be produced for $150 and one person would pay $50 to see it but another 100 people would pay only $1 each, the concert could only be offered if there is perfect price discrimination. In a sense, the high-value consumer subsidizes low-value patrons, just as Founders' Circle operagoers subsidize the students sitting in the back rows. Of course, seating-quality differences, time delays (in the case of movies) and other inconveniences required to preserve segmentation of high- and low-value demand detract from the benefits, but it is reasonable to suppose that the outcome in economic terms is positive on balance.

From this perspective, removing impediments to efficient movie audience segmentation by studios is, other things equal, favorable to economic welfare. For example, to the extent that the first-sale doctrine of the Copyright Act (Chapter 3) inhibits effective segmentation of video renters and buyers, we can say that studio revenues, and thus movie production resources and in turn the supply of movies, are reduced (although movie renters themselves would be worse off for the higher rental prices). We may conclude by the same logic that even overt collusion among studios to maintain a theater-to-video time window that maximizes total revenues from the theater and video markets combined (Chapter 4) would be socially desirable.

A caveat to the economic welfare story is the reality that much of the great increase in film production investments has evidently been devoted to higher salaries for big stars and other above-the-line talent. Such increases have little apparent social benefit beyond the vicarious pleasures we might take in watching the money being spent. Most important, though, consumers' economic welfare may pale in the face of the great cultural, social, and political forces unleashed by movies and the behavior of the companies that sell them to us.

Chapter 7

Hollywood's Digital Future

The world is going digital, and that includes movies. DBS and digital cable, DVDs, and the Internet are just the initial stages in a technological transition of movie exhibition that seems certain to continue. Electronic transmission of movies for digital presentation in theaters is on track toward widespread use. The rollout of digital production technologies for special effects, cameras, editing, and other production applications is well under way. Analog components, such as cameras and film stock, may hold a place into the future. Over the long term, though, digital production, transmission, and exhibition systems for movies generally offer higher quality, more versatility, and lower costs.

How will the digital transition affect Hollywood's fortunes? To answer that question, we must ask others. Which new media for movie exhibition will succeed, and which will not? Will revenue from the successful media be overwhelmed by accompanying piracy? Will digital technology promote or undermine Hollywood's world dominance? And what about the future of movies themselves—will there be more of the same big-budget blockbusters, or niches for specialized film content?

There is an old joke, probably referring to stock pickers, that there are two types of forecasters: those who don't know and those who know they don't know. We present this chapter in the spirit of the latter group, but with one upbeat caveat. The economic models presented in earlier chapters may be used as frameworks for thinking about answers to these broad questions. That is, readers should not look in this chapter for answers, only ways to get to them.

Digital Technology and Established Channels

How digital technologies will affect movie media in general is easy to imagine. Cable, DBS, and other multichannel systems will experience higher effective channel capacities. Higher-capacity servers and interconnected fiber networks will provide more choices for VOD-type systems. Addressing particular programs or bundles of programs to particular buyers will become cheaper and more efficient. The systems by which users can make choices and pay for them will become more seamless. The bit rate potential of digital video and other movie media will increase. Copy control mechanisms will be refined. The transition to digital broadcast television will provide a higher quality of transmission, potentially higher channel capacity, copy controls, and the possibility of direct payment for over-the-air transmissions. The viewer can expect better quality of exhibition, greater portability, more variety, and better control over movie choices and exhibition times, all at lower hardware costs.

It is much harder, of course, to predict the market acceptance of particular technologies that can enable all this to happen. Many movie exhibition technologies have fallen by the wayside. Still, DVDs in general and digital cable, DBS, SVOD, and even mail-order DVD rentals have been successful adaptations of digital technology.

It would be disingenuous to say in retrospect that we should have known what would succeed and what fail. History does show, however, that technologies that have succeeded in the movie release system have one or more of three characteristics: higher value for consumers; lower costs; and improved opportunities for market segmentation and price discrimination. Progress has not always been forward on all three fronts. Prerecorded videocassettes, for example, offered higher value and great potential for segmentation, but especially when consumer costs to obtain and return them are added in, they were a step backward in cost efficiency. In fits and starts, though, digital technology can be expected to continue the broad advances that movie distribution and exhibition technologies have made toward higher value for consumers, lower distributor and consumer costs, and more accurate pricing.

The growing proliferation of different movie exhibition media in the sequence also belies the notion that even if consumers overcome their apparent aversion to à la carte pricing, the "any movie at any time" promise of VOD would be destined to eliminate other media in the release sequence. Distributors earn the most money by dividing the total audience into boxes. The VOD box fits best for people whose relative valuation of its particular qualities is high. Other consumers have a relative preference for theater exhibition, video sales, or subscription networks. Distributors can make the most money by adjusting release windows and relative prices for a spectrum of movie media to serve all of these consumers at different effective price levels.

A case in point is high-definition DVD. How successful this generation of DVDs will be is a matter of speculation. Favoring the new generation from the studio's perspective is the groundwork being laid for more efficient digital rights management than can be accomplished with standard DVDs.[1] If hardware manufacturers cooperate, and if technical and legal obstacles are overcome, controls over the particular hardware units that high-definition disks can be played on, and the total number of times they can be viewed, will be more effective than is the case with standard DVDs. These controls will facilitate price discrimination within the base of high-definition DVD users.

We are in any case unlikely to see studios attempting to hasten the demise of standard DVD technology. Even if a format war is avoided, high-definition DVD sales will be constrained by the diffusion of HDTV sets, which remain expensive. Also, as the Betamax versus VHS war of the 1970s and '80s showed, the Hollywood studios are loath to preserve alternative video formats that are basically the same. As we showed in Chapter 3, however, the long-term coexistence of distinctly different video formats, like VHS and DVD, provides a natural device for studios to segment markets.

Disposable DVDs are a related development. In 2003 and 2004, Disney test marketed EZ-Ds, later known as "Flexplay," disks that self-destruct forty-eight hours after the seal is broken.[2] Although Flexplay is a chemically based technology, the concept was inherited from the DiVX format, which failed in 1999 after a brief period. DiVX was a DVD format that employed an early version of DRM. The number of times a disk could be played was electronically limited by means of encoding that was compatible with hardware also marketed by the format's sponsor, Circuit City.

Flexplay has not been well received,[3] but in one sense, an eventual success of disposable DVDs could prove correct those who have predicted the demise of video rentals. From an economic perspective, though, disposable disks are really just rentals without the return cost. Much like the Internet-based DVD rental system pioneered by Netflix, disposable disks have the potential to improve rental window efficiency for movie distributors.

Attracting much recent attention has been the prospect of using digital satellite transmission of films to theaters equipped with digital reception and projection technology. Potentially, that would replace the cumbersome and expensive process of physically shipping up to 3,000 prints to theaters for a national release. Conversion is expensive, coordination problems must be resolved, and piracy remains a threat. The end results, though, will also be a step toward greater cost efficiency in the movie release sequence.

Assuming that movie demand in general stays high, the march of digital technologies toward higher-value products, lower costs, and more efficient price discrimination will mean still higher net revenues for the Hollywood studios to devote to movie production.

Internet Movie Distribution

Internet protocol (IP), the standard for transmission of all information via the Internet, is digital. Streams of bits sent and received in IP format permit movies to be transported from central computer servers, such as Web sites, or between individual computer users, either by e-mail or by means of file sharing systems. Basically, the Internet can distribute movies in two different ways. One is via streaming, which permits the real-time viewing of a movie sent from a server at another node of the system. The other is downloading, a dumping of the whole stream of bits onto a computer hard drive or a portable disk for later viewing. Movies or other programming can be watched on a computer monitor; they can also be displayed on a digital television set or converted back to analog format for showing on an old-fashioned analog TV.

Beginning in the mid-1990s, experimentation with Internet broadband delivery of feature-length movies via streaming and downloading was pioneered by *sightsound.com, cinemanow.com,* and other sites that licensed exhibition rights for recent features from the major studios. A consortium of five studios followed with the 2002 launch of *movielink.com*. These and other Web sites have offered recent Hollywood features for outright sale (that is, unrestricted download, usually for $8–$15) or for "rent" (a one- or two-day license to access the movie before a digital code disables it, usually for $3–$5). Subscriptions, which allow unlimited access to certain subsets of the available movies, may also be purchased. The sale or rental options have generally been within the PPV/VOD window. Other Web sites have offered older Hollywood movies at cheaper à la carte download or streaming rates.

Everyone acknowledges that commercial viability of the Internet for any feature-length movie distribution depends on major long-term progress in its server capabilities, transmission capacity, usability of home premises equipment, and other technical features. In the long term, though, Internet technology has several characteristics that can increase consumer value, lower costs, and improve segmentation and discrimination—especially with VOD or other direct payment systems. In those respects, the Internet has high long-term promise as a movie distribution medium.

One comparative advantage of the Internet is lower delivery costs. As a means for the streaming of broadband content, such as movies, to large audiences at a time, it has been claimed that the Internet will never become as efficient as broadcasting, cable, or other multichannel distribution.[4] Downloading is another matter. An important delivery cost advantage of the Internet is the ability of consumers to download content rather than having to copy in real time off of a VOD exhibition or other PPV cable channel, or drive to the video store. Internet broadband is also generally free of geographic constraints, allowing cost-effective worldwide distribution from a central source.

A second advantage of the Internet it that it has the lowest capacity, or "carriage," costs of any current movie medium. Before the electronic media, increasing movie diversity in some given geographic area meant building a new theater. Those constraints have progressively diminished, first with broadcast television, then cable, DBS, and other multichannel systems. But an additional digitally compressed cable or DBS channel still requires a substantial capital investment. Home video has taken capacity a step further, but for video retailers, including mail-order firms, another DVD for rent or sale means inventory costs for as long as consumers wish to rent or buy it. The architecture of the Internet is fundamentally different. It permits a single Web site, or combination of sites, to "carry" a virtually unlimited variety of movies at virtually zero marginal cost.

A third benefit of the Internet for movie distribution is more efficient direct pricing and product bundling. Web sites can easily offer many individual movies at a variety of different à la carte prices, or in bundles that are either created by the seller or assembled by the user.[5] Any amount of ancillary information, such as talent interviews, outtakes, and the like, can be added or subtracted instantly. Varied options of movie bundles, or bundles of ancillary materials, can be presented in manageable form to subscribers and can be rearranged or repriced quickly and efficiently by the seller. Credit cards or micro payment systems can seamlessly charge subscribers for these services.

More efficient direct pricing means lower costs in making transactions, but also the ability to price discriminate more effectively. As we have seen, efficient bundling can serve as an efficient market segmentation device, and the more flexible the bundles, the greater the seller's opportunities to extract value. Effective use of other discrimination devices, such as reduction of prices over time for movies as they become older, or lower prices for repeat viewings, are also efficiently managed on the Internet. A plausible method of Internet TV pricing may involve consumer segmentation based on demand for different qualities of movie transmission. Consumers with higher-speed connections, for example, are likely to have higher valuations for high technical quality and will pay higher prices. Web sites can also engage in so-called dynamic pricing, by which consumers are charged different prices according to their perceived willingness to pay, based on prior Web purchasing habits, Web site visiting habits, or other information. Basically, dynamic pricing permits more efficient discrimination through better identification of high- versus low-value customers.

Another price discrimination advantage of Internet distribution can simply be different prices charged by different Web sites for authorized movie downloads. In July 2004, for example, *movielink.com* offered *Kill Bill, Vol. 1* as a PPV exhibition for $4.95, while *cinemanow.com* charged $3.99.

Like flexible pricing, low delivery costs and virtually unlimited capacity are key ingredients of cost-effective VOD or other direct-payment movie packaging systems. Of course, video retailers and cable or satellite-based television systems are competing hard to improve the efficiency of their services, and assertions of the eventual significance of such Internet attributes as dynamic pricing, flexible bundling, and micropayment systems for Internet movie distribution are of course speculative. The established movie media also have dramatic transmission capacity advantages that may persist for many years. It is a good guess, though, that enough of the Internet's remarkable potential will materialize for it eventually to earn a vital position in the intertemporal distribution of major theatrical feature films.

Free Internet Movies versus DRM

A fourth, and the most contentious, feature of Internet technology for movie distribution is the dramatically lower cost of copying and sharing of content. This attribute of the Internet is a double-edged sword, and its downside is very sharp. The cheaper and easier it is to copy or share movies, the deeper the cuts into legitimate demand for them on video and other media, including authorized Internet channels like *movielink*. In the long run, though, the lower copying and sharing costs create new revenue opportunities for the studios, including more efficient price discrimination—if they can devise a way to harness them.

Assuming for the moment that DRM controls are absent or circumvented, a movie downloaded via the Internet can be copied to the hard drive of a PC or burned onto a blank DVD for later viewing. File sharing systems allow virtual connections among PCs for the exchange of free movies as well as music. In the first-generation Napster model of peer-to-peer (P2P) file sharing, a central Web site displays the movies that are available from the PC hard drives of users who volunteer to share them. When a movie is selected from the list, the sharing transmission takes place between the individual PCs of the file sharer and the recipient. In more dangerous (to copyright holders) P2P versions, like the *kaaza* model, no central computer or server is involved. For P2P movie transfers to take place, participating users need only have the file sharing software installed and be connected to the Internet to create virtual connections among themselves.

The music file sharing explosion that began in the mid-1990s is the

MPAA's widely publicized nightmare model for the future of movies. Although the actual effects of P2P file sharing on record-industry revenues remain controversial, the retail sales of recorded music fell each year between 1999 and 2003, for a total decline of about 15 percent.[6]

The MPAA has claimed that hundreds of thousands of feature-length movies are already downloaded from file sharing systems each day in the United States. The greatest studio concerns are for the future; there is little evidence that movie file sharing has had a significant economic impact so far.[7] The much larger size of digital movies files has obviously helped shield Hollywood from a replay of the record industry's experience. Music files using the MP3 digital compression standard are small and quickly transmitted. The DVD of a feature-length movie usually contains 4 to 6 gigabytes, about 1,500 times the size of a typical MP3 file. Users ordinarily employ digital compression to reduce the size of movie files—typically to about 10 percent of the bits contained on a DVD, which ends up to be about the size of an uncompressed music CD. Still, it can take one to five hours or longer for a typical home cable modem or DSL broadband user to download a digitally compressed movie. Tests also show that movie file sharing doesn't work a good part of the time, and when it does, the results are virus-prone and often of unacceptable quality. While numerous episodes of successful unauthorized file sharing of recent movies have been documented, movie file sharing is not the mainstream consumer activity that music sharing has apparently become.[8]

In most foreign markets, the diffusion of PCs and broadband connections that can be used to engage in Internet movie exchange is less advanced than in the United States. In some countries, especially in western Europe, however, the frequency of video file sharing is reported to be greater than in the United States.[9] Foreign market problems for the studios seem certain to get worse before they get better. The Internet is also being used by commercial pirates to transfer movie files from the United States to foreign countries, where they are downloaded onto DVDs, duplicated, and sold as counterfeits in those markets.

No one can be certain whether Hollywood's worst-case scenario of movie revenue decimation due to P2P file sharing will materialize. The theory behind the studio apprehension is certainly plausible. The alarm bells should be tempered, however, by an inventory of the formidable legal, technological, political, and economic assets that studios bring to this battle—resources that they have successfully used to control or reduce earlier forms of movie piracy, copying, and sharing.

On the legal front in the United States, the MPAA has earnestly and successfully pursued individuals it claims are attempting to circumvent copyright control devices, including the now infamous lawsuit against the teenage hacker who broke the CSS (content scrambling system) encryption code for DVDs.[10] Makers of software that the MPAA claims to facilitate illegal P2P file sharing are also being sued. Internet surveillance to detect illegal movie transfer activity has been stepped up, and numerous lawsuits have been filed. The studios have earnestly lobbied Congress for stricter laws to limit P2P file sharing. They have also continued to use their political influence in attempts to induce PC manufacturers to adopt technology limiting the ability of users to illegally transfer movie files.[11] Rampant leaking of unfinished digital movie files from the production and postproduction process, and from Academy Award review, were uncovered in the early 2000s, bringing to mind the chaotic early days of videocassette piracy. The MPAA has moved to close these prerelease leaks. The various anti–file sharing actions undertaken by the MPAA have made the organization few friends among movie consumers or legal observers, and in 2003 it began a major advertising campaign to persuade the public that attempts to defeat movie copyrights through computer file sharing are immoral as well as illegal.[12]

On the technology front, the studios are investing heavily in new DVD and Internet-protocol encryption technologies that pirates or casual hackers will find harder to break.[13] Marking technologies that permit investigators to trace the original source of Internet-distributed movies are being improved. New generations of DRM copy protection built into computer software that plays movies, such as Microsoft's Windows Media Player and RealNetworks, are being launched.[14] The direct distribution of movies to consumers via authorized Web sites such as *movielink* is becoming more secure. Besides working to improve the efficiency of their own Internet movie distribution systems, the studios jam P2P sites with unusable movie files.

One technological element helping to protect established movie media (especially DVD sales and rentals) from illegal file sharing is movie transmission quality. Digital compression systems are generally designed to achieve faster transmission and efficient storage, while maintaining acceptable video quality. These systems have steadily improved, and many consumers may not care about, or may not notice, the differences in quality between a prerecorded DVD and a DVD burned from a compressed computer file when exhibited on the same NTSC TV screen.[15] Higher-value viewers may care, though, and none of the compressed video file users will have a nicely packaged DVD for their shelf. Also, high-definition TV sets are less forgiving than standard sets, not only of currently popular video compression systems, but of standard DVDs themselves.[16] As high-definition sets become more popular, studios have the opportunity to preserve these disparities by increasing DVD quality. High-definition DVD formats require a much higher digital bit rate than standard DVDs. Digitally compressing them below a certain level for speed of Internet transmission defeats the purpose of the format.

Apart from its use as a blunt instrument to prevent the copying and sharing of digital files, DRM also offers possible ways for studios to turn Internet file sharing to their advantage. Fundamentally, the lower consumer costs of copying and sharing of movies via the Internet create market value. The time-consuming process by which VHS tapes or DVDs are copied from pay TV or copied back to back, then physically transported to another user, is eliminated. As we discussed in Chapter 4, if studios can appropriate even a part of that created market value, their revenues and profits can rise.

To illustrate, recall the example we used in Chapter 4 to show how movie distributors can receive some benefit from the "old" system of copying and physical sharing of videos. In that example, Consumer A valued watching a certain movie at $5, while B was willing to pay only $2. The studio could collect $5.50 from A, however, under the assumption that A received a benefit of $1.50 for the copying and sharing privilege but also incurred a cost of $1 to copy and deliver the movie to B ($5 + $1.50 − $1 = $5.50). If that $1 cost disappears, the studio could potentially net $6.50 ($5 + $1.50) from A for a movie file that is DRM-controlled to allow transfer to one other user.[17]

It is also possible that studios could use P2P file sharing to price discriminate more efficiently. To illustrate, say that a certain film is available from the studio via *movielink* as a nontransferable file, but that a transferable file of the film is also posted to a P2P site (perhaps by a casual user or even by the studio itself). Price demands of A and B are $5 and $2 as before. Also assume, however, that Consumer A is unwilling to undergo the hassle of searching and downloading from a file sharing site, while computer-savvy Consumer B has no problem with doing so. Further imagine that an automatic electronic payment to the studio can be activated by any movie transfer from the P2P site. That is, the studio has established a business relationship with the file sharing site.

Under these circumstances, the studio can collect the full combined $7 value to both A and B of actually watching the movie by charging $5 at *movielink* (purchased by A) and $2 for the file transfer (purchased by B). One dollar of the $1.50 increase over the $5.50 net revenue in the old physical sharing system again comes from the more efficient system of copying and sharing via the Internet. The additional $.50 comes from more efficient price discrimination—the studio's ability to directly extract B's $2 value from watching the movie rather than having to rely only on the $1.50 benefit that A received from initiating the copying and sharing. In the end, the seller manages to extract all value from both consumers, even though they have different price demands for the same movie.

A key assumption in this model is that those who take advantage of Internet file sharing systems tend to have lower price demands and thus drop out of the market at the distributor's optimal price for the "original" movie. Segmentation is preserved because the high-value consumer is deterred from taking advantage of the low price due to higher perceived costs of file sharing. (In the model, the segmentation works as long as A's cost of using the file sharing site is anything greater than $3, while B's is zero.)

While this example is highly abstract and speculative, the technology behind it is not science fiction. A similar copyright control system was launched in late 2004 for marketing to the music industry by Shawn Fanning (the original architect of DeCSS). His "Snocap" software, if adopted by a file sharing site, recognizes DRM-fingerprinted songs swapped on its network and bills the recipient at a price set by the copyright owner.[18] Movie studios, like music distributors, could sell to lower-value consumers by charging lower prices for P2P shared files than for "original" files, such as those from industry-operated sites. To the extent that file-shared movies have lower transmission quality, market segmentation in terms of product quality could also be an element of P2P-based studio price discrimination.

In practice, such sophisticated forms of value extraction from private file sharing of movies may never be feasible. Monitoring usage of individual movie files and transacting with users may not prove cost effective. Abundant history, including the demise of Circuit City's DiVX video format, suggests that consumers may not accept such usage-based pricing. The most fundamental obstacle may be that by their nature, decentralized P2P systems—appropriately called "darknets" in some circles—are outside the control of copyright holders.[19] Like the proposed Snocap system for music, value extraction by copyright holders depends on cooperation by file sharing Web sites or software producers. It may thus prove impractical to monitor or control private Internet exchanges of movies, even if unauthorized sharing activities are illegal.

The studios may still not come out too badly. Lawrence Lessig has observed that as Internet direct payment systems become more seamless, troublesome methods like P2P file sharing will tend to be marginalized.[20] Certainly the legal and technological initiatives taken by the studios so far just to prevent any file sharing are intended to advance its marginalization. In economic terms, the studios' initiatives can be thought of as a market segmentation strategy similar to what they have pursued with piracy and illegal copying in the past. When file sharing is made more difficult to accomplish, is given a negative social stigma, and carries with it increased legal jeopardy, its perceived costs generally rise in comparison to the prices of legitimate media. Inevitably, computer-savvy individuals who consider these costs to be relatively low will continue to take advantage of illegal file sharing. As we have seen in the cases of piracy, copying, and sharing of pay TV and videos, however, the members of that group tend to be relatively low-value consumers who, if not for illegal file sharing opportunities, would drop out of the legitimate market. If the studios are successful with their current strategy, the file sharing segment will remain a relatively marginal group having a minor impact on industry revenues.

If all else fails for them, the studios may be resigned to supporting a noncommercial use levy, as first proposed by Neil Netanel.[21] In this system, individuals could freely transfer movie files using P2P systems, but copyright owners would be compensated from levies on hardware (such as DVD burners) according to usage rates metered by DRM technology.

In sum, the eventual outcome of Internet movie file sharing is highly uncertain, depending on technology, politics, and courtroom battles to come. DRM, however, gives movie distributors a powerful weapon in their struggle to preserve the traditional business model of movie release in the Internet age.

The Movie Release Sequence: Will Theaters Stay in Front?

As new movie media have come along, they have taken their place in the pecking order more or less according to the economic principles of market segmentation that govern that order. Media that offer higher exhibition quality have been positioned toward the front in the interest of price discrimination via quality segmentation. Unbundled pricing systems have come earlier because they are more efficient cream skimming devices. Piracy and copying have also played an important role in pushing more vulnerable media like PPV and VOD to a later time than they otherwise might be placed. Foreign theater release has been moved closer to, and is now commonly simultaneous with, U.S. theater release, in order to give pirates less time to work. As we have seen, struggles to coordinate consistent windows and to accommodate copyright quirks of the first-sale doctrine have also had their influence. The timing of advertising campaigns, word-of-mouth diffusion, and information collection play their roles in tweaking the system as well.

Exactly where VOD, SVOD, or media yet unimagined end up in the sequence will be resolved through a process of stumbling experimentation that new entrants of the past have always undergone before some regularity is established. While technology, piracy, and other forces of history have tested the system almost continuously since broadcast television entered the market, the economic incentive to preserve efficient price discrimination is a very powerful force. There may come to be heavier reliance on simultaneous release on certain media. But there is no reason to believe that any one medium will ever "take over" or, barring some catastrophic experience with piracy, that the intertemporal movie release process will simply collapse. The studios always benefit from some form of quality- or time-based segmentation among movie media.

Perhaps the most enduring single question about the release sequence is whether theaters have to be first. While they have never relinquished their position, speculation that one or another new medium would replace them has persisted, and there have been some probing attempts to actually do so. In the early 1980s, some saw PPV television as the new release sequence leader. In 1983, amid wide publicity, Universal released *The Pirates of Penzance* to PPV subscribers simultaneously with its theatrical release.[22] In 1993, TCI (a large cable system operator at that time) announced that it had acquired the rights from Carolco, a film producer, to exhibit a slate of major films, including sequels to *Terminator* and *Basic Instinct*, on PPV networks before their theatrical release.[23] Among recent experiments *Noel,* an independently distributed film, was given a limited 2004 theatrical release, simultaneous with its availability on disposable Flexplay DVDs.[24]

Critic Roger Ebert has speculated that Internet release could replace theaters at the front of the sequence.[25] DVD release dates that have moved closer to theater openings since 2003 have tempted speculation that video might share the spotlight with theaters in the simultaneous launch of major features. That idea is not entirely new. In the early days of video, some proposed that theater operators use their lobbies to sell a video version of the movie showing on screen.

So far at least, the speculations and experiments have come to little. *The Pirates of Penzance* did poorly both as a PPV event and in theaters. The TCI window reversal experiment apparently never materialized when studios refused to cooperate,[26] and *Noel* apparently generated minimal revenue either in theaters or with Flexplay DVDs.

The main explanation that has been advanced for the persistence of theaters at the front of the sequence is that they offer the highest exhibition quality, and thus are better suited than any other medium to effective publicity and strong word of mouth. In economic terms, though, there is nothing fundamental about the first-release position of theaters. As the models in Chapter 3 showed, it can be more profitable to separate media intertemporally under certain demand conditions, while in other cases simultaneous release to different media ("mixed bundling") may be more lucrative. VHS sales and rentals, and DVD sales and rentals, for example, while really four different media to the studios, are all simultaneous. If the revenue potential of DVD sales becomes still more important relative to theaters, considerations of carrying costs and movie freshness will weigh more in favor of simultaneous or even first release. And as high-definition home theater systems become ever more spectacular and affordable, there is no guarantee that even IMAX theaters will be able to offer a sensual experience enough better than regular theaters to justify the quality segmentation advantages that have kept theaters in the lead position.

Yet if the economic tables do turn against theaters—or, in fact, even if they have already—we may still see theaters at the front of the sequence for years to come. The reason is a form of inertia that can be traced back to the consumer's fundamental uncertainty about a movie's quality.

In order to decide whether a movie is worth seeing, potential patrons rely on a variety of information—who is in the movie, the ad campaign, reviews, what their friends say, and so forth. Patrons may have only some of this information, though, and even if they have it all, that may not be enough. People also use "market signals" to reduce their uncertainty about movie quality. Movies that debut in theaters are expected to have a higher production quality than direct-to-video, made-for-pay-TV, or made-for-broadcast movies, more or less in that order. This thinking is quite rational, since these expectations are in fact generally fulfilled, as evidenced by the sharply lower average production costs of movies that skip theater release. The average production cost for direct-to-video (DTV) movies, for example, was put at $4 million in mid-2004.[27]

The marketplace, in fact, puts a price on the value of the "released-in-theaters" quality signal. Theatrically released movies are said to automatically warrant a $1 million or greater bonus from subscription pay TV networks that license them, just for the fact of having had a theatrical release.[28] The existence of this bonus immediately raises a question: Why don't the distributors of low-production-quality films just release them to theaters to take advantage of its signaling advantage? On the margins, they surely do. Lower-quality films are often released to theaters with no real expectation of success in that market just so that their distributors can get critical reviews and later claim to video and pay TV consumers that they are "theatrical" movies.[29] As with all effective market signals, though, this behavior is self-limiting. It would be irrational for the distributor of a direct-to-video, or other "made-for" feature film to spend the tens of millions of dollars often required for a major theatrical ad campaign unless a certain level of expected theater demand can be achieved with it. Although they may not think about it explicitly, consumers know this and act accordingly. The result is that, on average, consumers' expectations become self-fulfilling and thus are indeed rational.

A distributor that tries to overcome the quality signal of a theatrical debut thus starts with a major strike against its guinea-pig movie. Consumers will reasonably assume that a video, PPV, or Internet premiere means that the movie is not worth paying a theater ticket price for. Of course, Hollywood studios might, with a few winks and nods, decide to launch enough high-production-quality movies with video, VOD, or Internet debuts to overcome the signal. That is more difficult, though, than it might seem. Behind each movie in a major distributor's release slate is a single producer, for which the idea of being part of any kind of an experiment is grounds for revolt.

There has been some progress in reducing the negative quality signal of direct-to-video movies—mostly, it appears, due to unilateral action by Disney. In 1997, Disney released *Honey, We Shrunk Ourselves,* a sequel to the theatrical hit *Honey, I Shrunk the Kids* (1989), direct to video. That film was by far the highest-production-value Hollywood feature ever to go direct to video. Other relatively high-production-value sequels followed, notably the DTV release in 1994 of *The Return of Jafar* (sequel to the successful theatrical release *Aladdin*). In making these experiments, Disney acknowledged that direct-to-video releases were generally "treated with the suspicion of a beggar in a royal palace," and the company proclaimed its intent to erase this negative image.[30]

It seems logical that of all the studios, Disney would have the most to gain from reducing or eliminating the negative-quality sign of DTV release, because of that studio's higher reliance on videos as the route to the children's market. Disney might also incur the lowest costs in leading the charge, if the formation of quality expectations by kids is somehow less reliant upon the market signal of theatrical release. So far, though—given the fact that DTV's top ten list for 2003–2004 consisted entirely of sequels, beginning with *The Lion King 1½, Bring It On Again, Blue Collar Comedy Tour,* and *Springtime with Roo,* in that order—we may safely say that at this writing we are in the realm of expectations fulfilled.[31]

Hollywood's World Dominance

Since the dominant worldwide market shares of Hollywood movies stabilized in the mid-1990s, there have been periodic upticks in favor of domestically produced European or Asian films. These have kindled optimism that a long-term recovery of the economic and cultural vitality of indigenous film production industries may be underway. But headlines since the mid-1990s like "Film Redux in Europe: Action!" and "H'wood Battles Local Heroes" have been followed by *Variety* banners like "H'wood Buries Overseas Pix" and "Yanks Rank but Locals Tank."[32] Since the early 1990s Hollywood's dominant market shares have stabilized, rising in one year with the worldwide success of one or two American movies like *Titanic* in 1998, falling the next. In the U.S. market, foreign-produced films like *Life Is Beautiful* (1997) have shimmered in the United States briefly, only to be overwhelmed by a raft of Hollywood blockbusters the next year.

Apart from the confluence of economic, cultural, and political forces that have propelled Hollywood to its world dominance, there is no doubt that a powerful inertia works in favor of sustaining it.[33] Even in an era of electronic communication, when movie stars or directors can live on ranches in Montana and stay in the limelight, physical proximity is generally an essential feature of movie production. A great pool of acting and craft labor—much of it already imported from countries around the world—resides in southern California and a few other satellite regions. A vast network of preproduction and postproduction support industries in Hollywood is important not only because of these firms' physical proximity. They also serve as a huge R&D lab that helps sustain Hollywood's technological leadership. The sophisticated financial and marketing infrastructures that support American movie production and distribution play similar roles. On the other side of the oceans, weaker infrastructures, as well as entrenched subsidy systems that seem to distort the financial incentives of European and other producers, contribute to the inertia.

Another contributor to Hollywood inertia is consumers themselves. In the fall of 2003 the video specialty chain *Movie Gallery* began to paste non-Hollywood video boxes in their "New Releases" section with two-inch-wide, bright yellow stickers containing the words "Foreign film." These stickers doubtless help foreign film aficionados find the movies they are looking for. But perhaps to a greater extent, these garish labels serve to warn the bulk of the store's customers that they are in danger of taking home a strange, cheaply produced, subtitled movie in which the main character may die at any time. Viewers' expectations of movie enjoyment are heavily based on past experience with movies that seem similar. Elsewhere in the world, expectations that a Hollywood movie will have high production values and a happy, inspiring ending work to the American advantage. European producers complain about the handicaps they face in overcoming the opposite stereotypes of their own movies. Even some European movie critics are said to have become prejudiced against their own country's output.[34]

While Hollywood's tanker may thus be slow to turn, our analysis of American dominance in Chapter 5 nevertheless showed that long-term shifts in the fortunes of American vis-à-vis foreign production industries can and do occur. The home market model implies that an important ingredient in the balance of movie trade is the relative size of domestic movie markets in terms of consumer spending. If, other things equal, movie patrons prefer domestically produced movie content, then higher movie spending in a given country should in the long term help its domestic movie production industry relatively more than it does American or other foreign producers.

Since the mid-1970s, the United States has built and sustained its lead over major trading partner nations in terms of consumer movie spending. Since the mid-1990s, however, the domestic spending gaps have been narrowing, especially in the U.K. and France. The home market model implies that a continuation of these spending trends will provide an economic foundation for recovery of indigenous production industries that can in turn shift the terms of trade away from American movies. Prediction requires caution, however, since there are many variables. As we discussed in Chapter 5, technology, politics, language skills, and cultural attitudes are also determinants of the relative attractiveness of American versus indigenously produced movies to audiences worldwide. What the model and the historical experience show with little doubt is that without a strong domestic infrastructure of direct-payment media to support consumer spending on movies, it will be difficult for any domestic production industry outside the United States to sustain a recovery.

Movie Content: Blockbusters versus Niche Movies

Of any mass medium yet, perhaps none has raised greater hopes for niche content than the Internet. That anticipation has extended to broadband entertainment, and a small explosion of commercial experimentation with Internet-original broadband content has taken place. Most of the original Internet broadband programming has taken the form of one- to fifteen-minute short films, "webisodes" (serialized shorts), or other short subjects, although experiments have included at least one Internet-original feature film, *Quantum Project,* thirty-six minutes in length and reported to have cost $3 million.[35] Among other Internet broadband experiments have been high-quality short features made by well-known Hollywood directors that integrate specific products, such as BMW autos and SKYY vodka, into their plots.[36]

The outlines of a dichotomy in Internet broadband content have emerged. At one end of the spectrum, Web sites such as *atomfilms.com* have displayed a burgeoning creative industry of innovative short films. On the whole, these films seem to have a distinctive, risqué flavor that are a natural fit to the freewheeling, independent atmosphere of the Internet. The great majority of this content is very cheaply produced, usually by amateur or struggling professional filmmakers, but it appears to attract a narrow contingent of loyal followers. At the other end of the spectrum is the emerging Internet window for high-budget Hollywood feature films on the studio-licensed Web sites we discussed earlier in this chapter.

As Internet broadband capacity and related hardware develops and broadband penetration rises, the economic viability of Internet original movies will be enhanced. Higher budgets and presumably longer features, independently produced from outside the Hollywood mainstream, can be supported. As the evolution of cable and video has demonstrated, Internet technology development and diffusion will similarly magnify the economic advantages of multimedia syndication of high-budget Hollywood features. As the predominance of theatrical features over "made-for" cable products on PPV systems, premium networks, and basic cable networks suggests, the economic cards are stacked in favor of the theatrical film syndication model for the Internet. Overall, at least, movie audiences seem to prefer older versions of high-production-quality movies to newer versions of low-production-quality movies, even though the latter are presumably more sharply focused to the specialized tastes of audiences on the "original" medium. To the extent that the Internet becomes a successful medium for feature film distribution, the result will be higher net revenues to support ever higher-budget Hollywood features.

The homogenizing effect of the multimedia price discrimination model will also influence the content of Internet-distributed movies. To the extent that the movie tastes of Internet users are distinct, they enter the blend of multimedia and multinational tastes that determines the content of Hollywood's theatrical blockbusters. The most noticeable homogenization effect is likely to be on Internet-original movies or shorts. As made-for-cable and direct-to-video movie producers have discovered, economic pressures to syndicate their products to other media are very strong. Typically, these made-for products run through the gamut of other movie media downstream in the release sequence. The most successful Internet distributor of original short films, *atomfilms.com,* has aggressively repackaged its products for cable networks, airlines, and video.[37] Inevitably, these market pressures will work to diminish the distinctiveness of Internet-original productions.

As for the effects of technology on movie production, it is safe to predict that the advance of digital production technologies will continue to make movie production more cost efficient and that these technologies will open up still more opportunities to enhance the visual experience of audiences. How are these changes likely to affect the balance of production quality and variety in the film menu that Hollywood makes available?

In 2000, an article about how the latest generation of digital camera and editing equipment would affect filmmaking appeared in *Scientific American*. Citing a decline in the cost of shooting and editing with 35 mm film of $4,865 per hour to $20 per hour with a mini-DV camera and video editing equipment, the article extolled an independent film production revolution in the making, noting, "It is now possible for all of us to try to become desktop Scorseses."[38] As widely reported in the trade press, costs of digital animation, film editing, and other postproduction hardware and software are plummeting as well—making possible, for example, realistic computer-generated backgrounds that can substitute for expensive on-location shooting.

One apparent result of cheaper digital cameras and related equipment has been a boost to the independent filmmakers who work on shoestring budgets. Presentable movies can now be produced that were not possible to make with 35 mm film simply because of the cost barriers. In a typical story, for example, executive producer Brian Labelle claimed that he could not afford the film stock to make his 2004 independent film, *Somewhere,* but that by using a Panasonic VariCam HD camera, "we made a $500,000 movie for $50,000."[39]

The relative cost savings for major Hollywood productions, however, are bound to be smaller because cameras and editing equipment make up a much lower proportion of major film budgets. The key to predicting how technological advances embodied in production and postproduction equipment will affect major Hollywood productions is whether or not those technologies are potentially quality enhancing. Can cheaper and better cameras, for example, allow more creative camera work, or more takes of a shot? Do new generations of digital editing equipment allow editors only to process larger amounts of footage more efficiently, or do they enable more creative editing? To the extent the answers to those questions are yes, our analysis in Chapter 6 suggests that the end result is likely to be more, rather than less, spending, on major features. In any case, it is a good bet that as cheaper equipment puts film production within closer reach of the next generation of Scorseses, we won't be seeing many of their shoestring efforts in theaters. Instead, aspiring filmmakers will use those efficiently produced movies to display their talents to the major studios. With a good dose of luck, they will then be drawn into the mainstream system of big-budget Hollywood film production that can apply those rare talents most cost effectively.

Attracting much more public attention than the price of equipment has been the possibility of replacing human actors and actresses in major roles with virtual reality characters. Release of the milestone 2001 film *Final Fantasy,* whose protagonist, Aki Ross, was computer generated, inspired speculation that Hollywood's elite stars might someday be put out of business and, in the process, their exorbitant salary demands given the deep freeze.[40] On an ABC *Nightline* program in the wake of *Final Fantasy*'s theatrical release, host Chris Bury led off a discussion with the question "How far will this technology go? Can unreliable or overpriced actors really be replaced by high-tech doubles?"[41]

The Hollywood guests on *Nightline* generally scoffed at the idea that this would happen, at least any time soon. For the sake of argument, though, let us say that Hollywood stars can indeed someday be replaced by digitally generated actors. What would happen to star salaries, movie budgets, and movies themselves? Star salaries surely would fall, but they would almost certainly be replaced by equally outrageous demands from the creators of the virtual characters. If talent to capture the public imagination is rare, it is probably just as rare for computer artists to do so as for anyone else. There is little reason to think that the rise of movie budgets would be stemmed. Consider *Toy Story* (1995), Pixar's successful pioneer in CGI technology. The original film was reported to cost $30 million. The sequel, *Toy Story 2* (1999), cost $80 million.[42] It's a safe guess that the main part of that budget increase went right into the pockets of the creators of Woody, Buzz Lightyear, and their friends. The cycle continues.

Appendixes

Notes

Index

Appendix A
Market Shares of Domestic Box Office/Rentals and Video Revenues

Domestic Theater Market Shares (Figure 1.1)

The five-year market share averages in Figure 1.1 are calculated from annual data and include all subsidiary companies of each studio. For studios that entered or exited the industry during one of the five-year intervals shown in Figure 1.1, shares are calculated based only on the years that studio was in business. Thus, the total market shares for the five-year interval periods in Figure 1.1 may total slightly more than 100 percent in some years. For the 1947–1950 period, Paramount shares are based only on 1947 and 1950 revenues; for MGM, only for 1949 and 1950. For the 1951–1955 data points, Columbia, RKO, and Warner shares are based only on the years 1951–1954. Beginning in 1971, "MGM/Loew's" includes all United Artists revenues.

Share estimates for 1947–1955 are calculated from U.S. film rental income reported in annual financial reports of the nine largest studios, as provided by Michael Conant, *Antitrust in the Motion Picture Industry* (Berkeley: University of California Press, 1960), pp. 121, 128. The base is total film rental income from 1947–1955 for the ten national U.S. distributors, submitted in U.S. congressional hearings and reported by Conant, p. 120. The ten national distributors are assumed to account for 100 percent of all film rentals in the United States during those years.

Data for 1956–1995 are compiled from annual reports in *Variety*, which appear to be based throughout on both U.S. and Canadian rentals (Canada generally contributing about 10 percent of the total), although this is not made explicit in all years. Data for 1996–2003 are from annual reports in *Motion Picture Investor* (Kagan Research, formerly Kagan World Media and Paul Kagan Associates). For years before 1970, annual share data are compiled from *Variety* tables of individual top-performing films. From 1971 to 1995, the summary market share tables were regularly reported directly in *Variety,* as were the Kagan data.

From 1956 until 1988, *Variety* data are based only on movies earning at least $1 million in rentals. From 1989 to 2003, both *Variety* and Kagan market shares are based on all movies tracked by the Nielsen EDI Summary Database, which includes virtually all feature films released theatrically in the United States. (Both Kagan and *Variety* may modify the EDI data slightly; see Kathleen O'Steen, "EDI Puts 1993 B.O. in Boffo Big Time," *Variety,* Jan. 10–16, 1994, p. 13 for discussion.) Beginning in 1993, the market shares are based on total box office receipts rather than actual rentals received by the studios. Throughout the 1956–2003 period, the original data source is reports made to the data collectors by the distributors of each film. Note that DreamWorks is included in the residual category throughout.

The annual market share data from 1970 and later have been reproduced, though in somewhat modified form, by Harold L. Vogel, *Entertainment Industry Economics: A Guide for Financial Analysis,* 5th ed. (Cambridge: Cambridge University Press, 2001).

A note on accuracy and possible bias. Data collection methods have greatly improved over time; more recent data are therefore likely to be more accurate. In some earlier years, data were apparently based on year-end summary estimates made by studio executives or *Variety,* and in some cases those estimates were made for anticipated total rentals rather than actual rentals to date. Aggregation of the data over the five-year intervals is intended to average out such year-to-year inaccuracies.

For years between 1956 and 1989, market shares of the smaller studios and the "residual" category in Figure 1.1 tend to be underestimated because smaller companies were disproportionately responsible for lower-revenue films and average revenues from theaters greatly increased over this period.

We were able to estimate the extent of this bias for some earlier years by comparing *Variety* results for movies of $1 million or more with market shares derived using Conant's data for four overlapping years, 1951–1954. Table A.1 indicates these comparisons for those four years.

These comparisons show that although the direction of bias in the *Variety* data tends to be in favor of larger studios as expected, differences are generally minor and the rank order of studios by market shares is nearly the same in both data sets.

Table A.1   Market share comparisons by percentage, *Variety* and Conant, 1951–1954

Studio	*Variety*	Conant
Fox	19.8	18.1
MGM	18.8	18.8
Paramount	16.5	14.9
Warner	15.7	11.4
Universal	11.1	12.6
RKO	6.4	7.6
Columbia	6.3	8.7
UA	4.2	5.7

Video Market Shares (Figure 1.2)

The video market shares shown in Figure 1.2 are based on total wholesale shipments for rental and sale: for 1987–1996, annual reports in *Video Investor* (Paul Kagan Associates); for 1997–1998, *Billboard* (Feb. 6, 1999), p. 55; for 1999–2003, *Hollywood Aftermarket* (Adams Media Research, various issues). The Kagan data include only feature films, while post-1997 data include all video products. Available data suggest no major bias in market share trends due to this change in definitions. A breakdown of 2003 DVD "sell-through" shipments (which accounted for 74.0 percent of all video shipments for that year) indicates that 22.0 percent of revenue volume was non–feature film content, including 13.3 percent TV shows, 3.5 percent "kidvid," and 5.2 percent other content (Hollywood Aftermarket, March 31, 2004, p. 6). (Content breakdowns of DVD rental and VHS rental and sales were unavailable.)

From 1991 to 1996, Warner's share includes MGM/UA; in 1990, MGM/UA and Warner Home Video (WHV) made an agreement to grant WHV certain home video distribution rights with respect to new motion pictures and the motion picture library of MGM/UA. DreamWorks is included in the residual throughout.

Appendix B
Stability of World Theatrical Rentals, 1948–1975

Written with Weiting Lu

Table B.1 presents figures on world film rentals of the major U.S. distributors. Data on total and individual MPAA company world theatrical rentals for 1948–1966 are primarily from Robert W. Crandall, "The Postwar Performance of the Motion Picture Industry," *Antitrust Bulletin* 2 (Spring 1975): 78–80. Individual firm data for 1967–1975, and for a few of the earlier years, were compiled directly by us from annual financial reports. Total world theatrical rentals for all MPAA distributors combined are from Harold L. Vogel, *Entertainment Industry Economics: A Guide for Financial Analysis,* 5th ed. (Cambridge: Cambridge University Press, 2001), pp. 52–53. Crandall's data were originally compiled from annual financial reports, although he makes estimates for some years.

Missing data in a few cases are due to unavailability of annual reports. In most cases, companies did not report data in usable form. (After 1975, only sporadic usable data are available; most firms began aggregating theatrical revenues with revenues from television and other media, or aggregating all entertainment revenues.)

To calculate the stability index shown in Figure 2.2, "average percentage variation around the mean change," the following procedure was used:

1. For each year, we calculated the percentage change from year $t - 1$ to t in total world theatrical rentals for all MPAA distributors, as reported by Crandall or Vogel.

2. We made a comparable calculation for all individual firms for which we had data in both year $t - 1$ and t.
3. The "average percentage variation around the mean annual change" (Table B.1, next to last column) was calculated as the average of the absolute variation of (2) around (1).

The last column of Table B.1 shows the standard deviation of the individual studio variations around the mean annual change, which closely tracks the average percentage variation.

Table B.1 Stability of world film rentals of U.S. theatrical distributors, supporting data, 1948–1975

Year	World theatrical rentals of MPAA companies ($ millions)								Total MPAA companies	Annual % change in total	Average % variation around the mean annual change	Standard deviation of the variation around the mean annual change
	Columbia	MGM	Para-mount	RKO	20th Fox	United Artists	Universal	Warner Bros.				
1948	46.9	101.9	62.8	68.9	84.2	24.0	56.9	63.3	508.9	—	—	—
1949	53.5	98.4	55.3	54.0	94.3	23.9	56.4	63.9	499.7	-1.8%	8.3%	11.6%
1950	57.2	102.8	60.8	48.2	90.8	19.0	55.2	66.0	500.0	0.1%	7.7%	10.1%
1951	55.4	107.0	69.8	58.7	92.5	19.5	64.7	67.0	534.6	6.9%	7.6%	9.0%
1952	59.1	109.0	75.6	60.2	93.2	28.9	63.6	69.1	558.7	4.5%	8.2%	16.3%
1953	60.3	105.7	81.3	56.1	105.7	38.2	69.9	66.4	583.6	4.5%	9.3%	12.6%
1954	80.2	110.1	78.8	46.1	106.4	43.4	77.3	67.0	609.3	4.4%	10.1%	14.7%
1955	81.6	103.7	86.3	54.0	110.5	53.6	76.9	72.6	639.2	4.9%	7.4%	9.6%
1956	79.3	106.0	68.9	64.2	112.8	63.7	77.0	73.4	645.3	0.9%	8.0%	12.4%
1957	83.3	98.4	77.7		117.5	69.7	71.1	75.5	593.2	-8.1%	12.0%	7.7%
1958	87.2	102.6	69.2		104.4	83.6	53.7	65.0	565.7	-4.6%	12.8%	14.9%

1959	83.3	102.2	69.7	96.1	90.0	49.2	68.7	559.2	−1.1%	5.2%	6.3%
1960	79.4	102.6	74.3	91.8	82.5	55.4	60.3	546.3	−2.3%	7.0%	8.6%
1961	81.5	110.0	63.8	79.5	86.2	60.4	53.8	535.2	−2.0%	9.4%	10.2%
1962	77.8	99.7	57.5	71.6	96.6	69.8	47.6	520.6	−2.7%	9.6%	11.4%
1963	74.2	97.8	61.5	74.1	95.3	66.5	54.6	524.0	0.6%	5.6%	7.1%
1964	85.8	117.8	73.4	73.0	138.4	68.4	45.6	602.4	15.0%	16.5%	19.7%
1965	70.5	107.4	65.2	102.5	149.2	66.3	66.8	627.9	4.2%	20.6%	25.7%
1966	86.2	114.5	66.3	132.2	126.8	69.2	87.2	682.4	8.7%	14.5%	16.6%
1967	113.7	139.7		130.6	123.7	68.3		713.7	4.6%	15.4%	16.1%
1968	131.1	134.7		123.9	131.7	63.0	102.0	711.3	−0.3%	7.8%	9.6%
1969	95.6	132.0		84.7	125.2	63.4	95.6	665.4	−6.4%	12.0%	13.8%
1970	138.0	98.5		120.7	118.0	95.4	64.2	741.3	11.4%	37.3%	37.9%
1971	113.0	111.1		155.7	97.2	57.8	86.3	684.7	−7.6%	27.8%	29.6%
1972	110.0	105.1		116.3	153.0	61.9	144.3	827.7	20.9%	39.1%	37.2%
1973	101.5	99.4		144.5	163.8	87.5	152.7	819.3	−1.0%	15.9%	18.8%
1974	111.3	80.2		160.2	142.7	205.1	275.5	1,040.7	27.0%	55.8%	60.7%
1975				212.5	187.4	289.0	202.3	1,232.2	18.4%	42.1%	31.1%

Appendix C
U.S. Distributor Revenue by Source

Methods

Table C.1 shows annual estimates in terms of percentage breakdowns for total U.S. distributor revenues from the distribution of theatrical feature films in the United States and foreign markets. These data underlie Figure 3.1. Merchandise licensing revenues are excluded.

U.S., 1947–1949: Aggregate film rental income of the ten national U.S. film distributors for 1947–1955, reported by Michael Conant, *Antitrust in the Motion Picture Industry* (Berkeley: University of California Press, 1960), p. 120, are assumed to represent 100 percent of U.S. film rental income. Television revenues during this period were mostly from the sale of old theatrical features, and are assumed to be zero in 1947 and 1948 and $2 million in 1949, the latter based on an estimate by Dennis Joseph Dombkowski, "Film and Television: An Analytical History of Economic and Creative Integration," (Ph.D. diss., University of Detroit, 1982), p. 170.

U.S., 1970–1980: Theatrical rentals are estimated by adjusting aggregate MPAA company rentals from U.S. theaters, as reported by Harold Vogel, *Entertainment Industry Economics: A Guide for Financial Analysis,* 5th ed. (Cambridge: Cambridge University Press, 2001), pp. 52–53, upward by the non-MPAA residual in domestic market share data reported annually in *Variety* (Appendix A), to arrive at an estimate of total domestic theater rentals for all distributors. That residual averaged 10.7 percent over the period.

Network television revenues are total amortized expenditures for theatrical feature films by the three commercial networks as reported by Dombkowski, "Film and Television," p. 433 (original data from FCC annual reports). Syndicated television revenue estimates are based on the assumption that the 39.5 percent average ratio of total syndicated to network television sales of theatrical features reported by David Londoner, *Take 2* (Wertheim and Co., 1981), p. 12, for 1978–1981 applied throughout the 1970–1980 period.

For distributor revenues from pay TV and home video, 1981 estimates reported in *Motion Picture Investor* (Paul Kagan Associates), Jan. 28, 1987, p. 1, were extrapolated backward using the percentage household penetration of VCRs and pay TV subscriptions (see Appendix F for sources). For example, if VCR penetration in 1980 was x percent of its level in 1981, we multiplied 1981 video revenues by x percent to obtain 1980 video revenues.

U.S. and foreign markets, 1981–2002: Author's calculations derived from estimates by Kagan Research and its predecessor firms for all media (excluding domestic and international licensing revenues), as reported in *Motion Picture Investor,* Aug. 6, 2004, p. 4; Sept. 12, 2003, p. 4; Jan. 31, 1989, p. 2; Jan. 28, 1987, p. 1; and *The State of Home Video* (Carmel, Calif.: Paul Kagan Associates, 2000), p. 119.

Foreign markets prior to 1981: Although available data were limited, it is evident that the proportion of total U.S. studio theatrical film revenues from foreign markets was substantially higher in the 1960s and 1970s than in the early 1980s. Harold Vogel, *Entertainment Industry Economics,* 5th ed. (Cambridge: Cambridge University Press, 2001), pp. 52–53, reports annual aggregate data for theater rentals from MPAA member companies beginning in 1965. These data show the MPAA companies' foreign share to range from 48.6 percent to 54.5 percent between 1965 and 1969 before it declined to a range of 33.2 percent to 42.3 percent between 1981 and 1985. MPAA company revenues from foreign theaters undoubtedly account for the great majority of all total U.S. distributor revenues during these years. See Will Tusher, "Majors' O'seas Gross 30–35 percent of Total," *Variety,* Mar. 31, 1983, p. 5; and A. D. Murphy, "How U.S. Majors Perform Overseas," *Variety,* May 15, 1974, p. 1.

Reliability Issues

Comparable data for U.S. distributor revenues over time are available from sources other than Kagan, including Veronis and Shuler Associates, *Communication Industry Forecast* (annual), Adams Media Research, *Hollywood Aftermarket;* Vogel, *Entertainment Industry Economics;* David Londoner, *Take 2;* and David J. Londoner, "The Changing Economics of Entertainment," in Tino Balio, ed., *The American Film Industry* (Madison: University of Wisconsin Press,

Table C.1 U.S. distributor revenue from distribution of theatrical feature films by source, 1947–2003

	Domestic (% of total domestic)					Total domestic revenues ($ millions)	Foreign (% of total foreign)				Total foreign revenue ($ millions)	Foreign revenue as % of total revenue	Total revenue ($ millions)
Year	Theaters	Broadcast TV	Basic cable TV	Pay TV[a]	Home video		Theaters	Broadcast TV	Pay TV[a]	Home video			
1947	100%	0%	0%	0%	0%	365							
1948	100%	0%	0%	0%	0%	345							
1949	99%	1%	0%	0%	0%	346							
1970	73%	27%	0%	0%	0%	612							
1971	73%	27%	0%	0%	0%	591							
1972	72%	28%	0%	0%	0%	667							
1973	71%	29%	0%	0%	0%	669							
1974	78%	22%	0%	0%	0%	817							
1975	79%	20%	0%	1%	0%	896							
1976	73%	25%	0%	2%	0%	932							
1977	75%	22%	0%	3%	0%	1,257							
1978	75%	20%	0%	4%	0%	1,581							
1979	68%	20%	0%	7%	5%	1,769							
1980	63%	19%	0%	11%	7%	2,053							
1981	50%	20%	0%	16%	14%	2,416	84%	8%	0%	8%	1,111	31%	3,527
1982	52%	17%	0%	17%	13%	2,743	72%	9%	0%	19%	1,127	29%	3,870

Year													
1983	53%	13%	1%	20%	12%	2,976	65%	8%	0%	27%	1,542	34%	4,518
1984	48%	10%	2%	18%	21%	3,547	50%	12%	0%	38%	1,633	32%	5,180
1985	37%	10%	2%	15%	36%	4,307	43%	14%	1%	42%	2,075	33%	6,382
1986	38%	10%	2%	15%	36%	4,366	38%	15%	2%	44%	2,690	38%	7,056
1987	37%	8%	2%	13%	40%	4,758	37%	15%	3%	45%	3,291	41%	8,049
1988	36%	8%	2%	14%	40%	5,206	35%	18%	4%	42%	4,122	44%	9,328
1989	33%	11%	2%	15%	38%	6,087	35%	22%	4%	38%	5,239	46%	11,326
1990	30%	13%	4%	15%	38%	6,859	35%	20%	6%	39%	6,131	47%	12,990
1991	31%	7%	2%	16%	43%	7,004	32%	18%	9%	41%	6,420	48%	13,424
1992	28%	9%	4%	15%	44%	7,807	28%	19%	9%	44%	6,537	46%	14,344
1993	32%	7%	3%	10%	47%	7,865	34%	17%	8%	41%	7,156	48%	15,021
1994	30%	8%	3%	10%	50%	9,235	32%	15%	9%	44%	7,705	45%	16,940
1995	26%	8%	4%	10%	51%	10,204	28%	17%	9%	45%	9,253	48%	19,457
1996	25%	7%	6%	10%	52%	11,904	29%	17%	11%	43%	10,379	47%	22,284
1997	26%	6%	7%	10%	50%	12,651	30%	19%	12%	40%	11,097	47%	23,748
1998	26%	5%	8%	11%	50%	13,557	32%	17%	13%	38%	11,670	46%	25,227
1999	30%	5%	9%	11%	45%	13,877	30%	21%	14%	36%	12,617	48%	26,494
2000	26%	5%	10%	10%	49%	15,348	26%	21%	15%	38%	13,333	46%	28,681
2001	27%	4%	9%	10%	50%	16,525	25%	18%	16%	41%	13,392	45%	29,916
2002	25%	4%	8%	9%	54%	19,960	25%	16%	14%	45%	16,012	45%	35,972
2003	23%	3%	9%	9%	56%	21,619	25%	14%	12%	49%	18,196	46%	39,815

a. Includes premium networks, hotel and home PPV/VOD, airlines, other direct payment.

1985), pp. 603–632, although for shorter intervals of time, for the U.S. market only, or for MPAA members only. The Kagan and other data are all estimates made by industry analysts based on a variety of trade association and industry resources. The published estimates vary from source to source, but except in very few cases, revenue estimates are within 10 percent and are often identical. All sources to which we had access show the same basic trends in the significance of the various movie media, although Kagan's revenue estimates tend to be somewhat higher. We based our estimates primarily on Kagan because of that source's long continuity and relatively comprehensive breakdowns.

Appendix D
Prices, Distributor Revenue, and Viewing Estimates, 1948, 1975, and 2002

Retail Prices per Transaction (Tables 2.1, 3.1)

Theaters: U.S. box office revenues divided by theater admissions (*International Motion Picture Almanac,* New York: Quigley Publishing Co., annual). Other media: trade association or trade literature reports.

Realized Retail Price per Viewing, 2002 (Table 3.1)

Retail price per transaction divided by estimates of the number of viewers per transaction. Video sales and rentals: based on the median reported number of viewings per sales and per rental transactions, from Video Store Magazine's *2002 Consumer Survey,* (tabulations provided to the author); PPV assumed to be the same as video rental; pay cable and basic cable estimates based on the average number of movie hours actually watched and the average number of viewers per household, both as reported in *TV Dimensions* (New York: Media Dynamics, 2002) and an estimate of the proportion of movies that are theatrical.

Gross Studio Revenue per Viewing (Table 2.1: 1948, 1975)

Theaters: total distributor rental revenue from theaters (Appendix C) divided by the number of theater admissions; broadcast networks, 1975: estimated studio revenue from network television (Appendix D), divided by the total number of exhibition hours of theatrical films (*Variety,* Oct. 6, 1976, p. 46). Independent TV stations: estimate based on viewing data by program type for the mid-1970s as reported in *TV Dimensions* (1996).

Annual Number of Viewings per Capita (Tables 2.1, 3.1)

Theaters: theater admissions divided by the adult population of the United States, multiplied by 1.25–1.5 in 1948 to account for estimated double feature attendance. Television, 1975: based on network ratings data for theatrical films published in *Variety*, viewing hours for independent and affiliate stations and for PBS by type of program for the mid-1970s as reported in *TV Dimensions* (1996), and author's estimates of the proportion of feature films that are theatrical. All media except theaters, 2002: based upon average weekly household viewing estimates by medium and by type of program, and the number of viewers per household, all as reported by *TV Dimensions* (2002), and estimates of the percent of exhibited movies that are theatrical.

Appendix E
Video Windows, 1988–2002

Written with Sung-Choon Lee

The reported statistics in Figures 4.1, 4.2, and 4.3 and the Chapter 4 text are from a database of 2,078 major theatrical feature films released on video in the United States between January 1, 1988, and December 31, 2002 (except for an interval in calendar years 1998 and 1999), supplied to us by *Video Store Magazine* (VSM), now *Home Media Retailing*. The VSM data track video market performance of virtually all significant feature film videos released in the United States. We merged the VSM data, which originally included 2,554 movies, with theatrical performance and related data obtained from the Nielsen EDI Summary Database and *www.variety.com*. Missing or inexact video release dates for some years were obtained from Kagan Research. Those procedures resulted in 2,511 movies. We included in our final dataset only the 2,078 movies that had simultaneous release on at least twenty-four theater screens and had box office revenues of at least $1 million.

Tables E.1 and E.2 show basic descriptive statistics for the 2,078-movie sample. Note that observations in Table E.1 are entered for the year of video release. "Out-of-market days" (Table E.2) is defined to be the number of days between theater closing and video release. Theater closing is the date when the movie is dropped from the Nielsen EDI tracking system, which generally includes the top 120 movies in any given week. Theater close date information was not available for any 2002 movies. The smaller number of observations in Table E.2 reflects missing data for theater close dates.

For both the window and out-of-market days, the mean tends to be some-

Table E.1   The video window: descriptive statistics, 1988–2002

Year	Obs	Mean	Median	Minimum	Maximum	Variance
1988	125	209.2	201.0	70	594	5,711.6
1989	132	202.5	195.0	104	410	2,804.2
1990	130	193.3	187.0	77	388	2,303.5
1991	136	186.8	177.0	62	350	1,909.5
1992	132	191.2	187.5	61	376	2,039.2
1993	140	188.0	184.5	89	446	2,289.9
1994	152	183.4	175.0	110	553	2,334.5
1995	142	180.2	179.0	95	333	1,165.0
1996	165	180.9	179.0	95	368	2,232.3
1997	174	178.1	172.0	60	592	2,685.6
1998	90	173.6	168.0	102	319	1,430.5
1999	89	165.8	165.0	100	711	4,219.8
2000	179	176.6	172.0	97	333	1,758.2
2001	175	166.5	158.0	95	382	1,718.0
2002	117	170.8	165.0	95	277	1,667.5
Total	2,078	183.1	178.0	60	711	2,476.6

what larger than the median because of a few movies with very long video windows. There were eighteen movies in the 1988–2002 sample having video windows over 365 days; those windows ranged from 368 to 711 days.

Table E.3 shows Pearson product-moment correlation coefficients between the theater run length, the video window, and out-of-market days for all movies having a total theater run length of twenty-six weeks or less.

Further details are reported in David Waterman and Sung-Choon Lee, "The Intertemporal Distribution of Media Products: An Empirical Study of the 'Video Window'" (working paper, Department of Telecommunications, Indiana University, Dec. 17, 2002), which covers the 1988–1997 portion of the database.

Table E.2   The out-of-market gap: descriptive statistics, 1988–2002 averages

Weeks in theater release	Obs	Mean	Median	Minimum	Maximum	Variance
1	6	168.5	159.5	125	251	1,896.3
2	38	148.1	145.5	83	216	1,061.0
3	45	156.2	160.0	41	251	1,953.8
4	58	156.9	156.0	82	278	2,122.6
5	91	135.7	137.0	42	223	1,353.0
6	89	141.0	133.0	28	438	3,079.2
7	89	133.9	124.0	69	328	1,983.6
8	81	120.2	119.0	40	285	1,513.2
9	79	114.1	111.0	42	344	2,358.3
10	97	113.8	109.0	41	286	2,111.0
11	80	103.0	100.5	33	202	1,617.9
12	93	107.1	103.0	19	628	4,576.9
13	76	98.8	89.0	33	286	2,028.0
14	91	90.4	80.0	12	312	2,961.1
15	70	67.6	61.5	−44	187	1,465.9
16	76	67.1	61.0	−16	286	2,557.8
17	80	58.7	57.5	−16	140	1,018.6
18	72	64.0	54.0	−20	243	2,082.3
19	65	53.7	47.0	−9	461	4,279.2
20	57	45.8	40.0	−16	149	1,378.4
21	69	30.7	26.0	−44	117	1,101.8
22	56	38.0	26.0	−37	215	2,493.8
23	38	31.0	26.0	−16	139	1,220.3
24	43	17.8	12.0	−37	126	1,046.4
25	35	21.7	12.0	−36	196	1,842.3
26	28	−2.1	−2.0	−44	123	1,107.0
Total	1,702	91.3	89.0	−44	628	3,849.8

Table E.3   Correlation matrix: video windows, 1988–2002

	VTC-TO	VO-VTC	VO-TO
VTC-TO	1.0000		
VO-VTC	−0.6669**	1.0000	
	0.0000		
VO-TO	0.0676**	0.6983**	1.0000
	0.0053	0.0000	

VTC-TO: theater run length
VO-TO: video window (theater open date to video open date)
VO-VTC: out-of-market gap
$N = 1,702$
** $p < .05$

Appendix F
Comparative Analysis of Movie Industries and Trade in the United States and the EUJ5 Countries, Statistical Data, 1950–2003

Written with Sang-Woo Lee and Weiting Lu

Box Office Market Shares (Figures 5.1, 5.2)

For Italy, France, and Germany, historical data were originally collected by national film or quasi-government organizations. Japanese, British, and U.S. data originate from trade associations or press organizations. For some earlier years, as indicated below, data are from compilations using these original sources made by Thomas H. Guback, *The International Film Industry* (Bloomington: Indiana University Press, 1969) and Michael Thiermeyer, *Internationalisierung von Film und Filmwirtschaft* (Cologne: Böhlau, 1994). All data are derived from actual performance records of individual films, although methodologies vary somewhat. In some cases, data are based on box office receipts; in others, on the number of admissions or on the division of distributor receipts. These methodologies track closely, however, and appear to be applied consistently over time for individual countries. Where data were available from multiple sources, differences were generally very minor.

Domestic market-share data for European countries include coproductions, nearly all of those with other European countries. Thus there is some double counting, although these films, especially minority coproductions, tend to earn relatively very small proportions of the total audience; see *Results, 1995* (Paris: Centre National de la Cinematographie), May 1996. Coproduction activity within Europe was relatively high in the 1960s and 1970s, and has increased again to high levels since the 1980s. Although formal coproduction between

U.S. and European producers is much less common, U.S. studios have invested in European film productions over a long period of time. European film organizations in at least France, Italy, and Germany, ascribe relatively strict criteria in terms of production principals and use of language for a movie with U.S. financial involvement to qualify as a "national" film or a formal coproduction, and thus to be included in their domestic market share statistics. Although American production and marketing expertise are undoubtedly applied in many cases with an eye to American release potential, American investments in European films that do qualify as national films or coproductions appear in the great majority of cases to involve products primarily intended for the European market. An exception may be the U.K., which has always maintained a close relationship with U.S. major studios, and which shares a common language with America. The definition of an American versus a British film is murkier, and the market-share data inspire less confidence. Coproductions do not appear to be a significant factor in the Japanese case. Discussion of these issues of market shares and coproductions, including statistical data, is available in Guback, *The International Film Industry, BFI Film and Television Handbook* (London: British Film Institute, 1995), and various reports by the European Audiovisual Observatory (EAO), European national film organizations, *Screen Digest*, and *Variety*.

General government statistics covering international trade in motion pictures and other media products are generally not useful due to measurement problems involving intellectual property products. For methodological discussion, see Stephen Siwek and Harold Furchtgott-Roth, "Copyright Industries in the U.S. Economy" (prepared by Economists Incorporated for the International Intellectual Property Alliance, 1990); U.S. Dept. of Commerce/International Trade Administration, *U.S. Industry and Trade Outlook* (New York: DRI/McGraw-Hill, annual), and National Telecommunications and Information Agency, *Globalization of the Mass Media*, no. 93-290, 1993.

Data Sources: Box Office Market Shares of U.S. Films in the EUJ5 (Figure 5.1)

France

1948–1951: Thiermeyer, Table 44.

1952–1966: Guback, p. 55.

1967–1986: Thiermeyer, Table 44.

1987–2000: EAO, *Statistical Yearbook* (1997, pp. 92–95; 1999, pp. 95–98; 2001, p. 93).

2001–2003: EAO, *Focus* (2002, p. 32; 2003, p. 32; 2004, p. 34).

Germany

1955–1966: Guback, p. 57.

1967–1979: Thiermeyer, Table 16.

1980–1986: *Screen Digest* (April 1992, p. 84).

1987–2002: EAO, *Statistical Yearbook* (1997, pp. 92–95; 1999, pp. 95–98; 2003, vol. 3, pp. 42–46).

Italy

1950–1965: Guback, p. 53.

1966–1979: Thiermeyer, Table 66.

1980–1985: *Screen Digest* (April 1992, p. 84).

1986–2000: EAO, *Statistical Yearbook* (1997, pp. 92–95; 1999, pp. 95–98; 2001, p. 93).

2001–2003: EAO, *Focus* (2002, p. 34; 2003, p. 34; 2004, p. 36).

U.K.

1980–1991: *Screen Digest* (April 1992, p. 84).

1992–2000: EAO, *Statistical Yearbook* (1997, pp. 92–95; 1999, pp. 95–98; 2001, p. 93).

2001–2003: EAO, *Focus* (2002, p. 36; 2003, p. 36; 2004, p. 38).

Japan

1980–1996: EAO, *Statistical Yearbook* (1997, pp. 92–95; 1999, pp. 95–98).

Data Sources: Box Office Market Shares of Domestic Films in the EUJ5 (Figure 5.2)

France

1950–1951: Thiermeyer, Table 44.

1952–1966: Guback, p. 55.

1967–1979: Thiermeyer, Table 44.

1980–1986: *Screen Digest* (April 1992, p. 84).

1987–2000: EAO, *Statistical Yearbook* (1997, pp. 92–95; 1999, pp. 95–98; 2000, pp. 110–113; 2001, p. 93).

2001–2003: EAO, *Focus* (2002, p. 32; 2003, p. 32; 2004, p. 34).

Germany

1955–1966: Guback, p. 57.

1967–1979: Thiermeyer, Table 16.

1980–1986: *Screen Digest* (April 1992, p. 84).

1987–2000: EAO, *Statistical Yearbook* (1997, pp. 92–95; 1999, pp. 95–98; 2000, pp. 110–113; 2001, p. 92).

2001–2003: EAO, *Focus* (2002, p. 28; 2003, p. 28; 2004, p. 30).

Italy

1950–1965: Guback, p. 53.

1966–1979: Thiermeyer, Table 66.

1980–1985: *Screen Digest* (April 1992, p. 84).

1986–2000: EAO, *Statistical Yearbook* (2000, pp. 110–113; 2001, p. 94).

2001–2003: EAO, *Focus* (2002, p. 34; 2003, p. 34; 2004, p. 36).

U.K.

1950–1991: Thiermeyer, Table 55.

1992–1998: EAO, *Statistical Yearbook* (1997, pp. 92–95; 1999, pp. 95–98; 2000, pp. 110–113; 2001, p. 93).

2001–2003: EAO, *Focus* (2002, p. 36; 2003, p. 36; 2004, p. 38).

Japan

1955–1979: Motion Picture Producers Association of Japan *(www.eiren.org)*.

1980–1996: EAO, *Statistical Yearbook* (1997, pp. 92–95; 1999, pp. 95–98).

2001–2003: EAO, *Focus* (2002, p. 46; 2003, p. 46; 2004, p. 50).

Box Office Market Shares of Foreign Movies in the United States

Annual data for percentage market shares of foreign films since 1981 are published in *Screen Digest* (August 1997, p. 117) and EAO *Statistical Yearbooks* (annual). An annual compilation for 1969–1990 also appears in *Variety* (Oct. 21, 1991, p. 12). These reports, which exclude U.S.-financed British films, indicate the following average market shares: 1969–1974: 6.8 percent; 1975–1979: 4.8 percent; 1980–1984: 3.5 percent–4.8 percent; 1985–1989: 2.7 percent–3.1 percent; 1990–1994: 2.7 percent; 1995–1999: 5.9 percent; 2000–2003: 6.1 percent. Detailed data on distributor revenues from foreign film release in the United States by country of origin for the years 1958–1964 are compiled from *Variety* special reports in Guback, *The International Film Industry*, p. 86. Based on U.S. box office statistics and upper and lower bounds for total distributor rentals in these years, a best estimate of the average market share of all foreign films over the 1958–1964 period, including U.S.-financed British productions, is 17.0 percent–22.3 percent. Excluding all British productions, the estimated range is 7.4 percent–9.7 percent. While the large majority of British productions were undoubtedly U.S. studio-financed films intended for the American market, British national films tend to be a large single contributor to revenues of foreign films in the United States, suggesting the latter range to be a significant underestimate of a historically comparable measure of foreign market share excluding only U.S.-financed British movies. As Guback discusses, however, some French, Italian, and other foreign movies produced during this period may have been primarily intended for the U.S. market.

Consumer Spending on Movie Media (Table 5.3, Figures 5.3, 5.4)

In nearly all cases, financial data were obtained in national currencies and, for comparative purposes, were converted to U.S. dollars at current exchange rates. Missing data for some countries in some years that were estimated as indicated below involved relatively insignificant spending levels. GDP and exchange rate data are from the annual *International Financial Statistics* (Washington, D.C.: International Monetary Fund).

Data Sources: Consumer Movie Spending
United States
Theater box office
1950–1998: *International Motion Picture Almanac,* 2000 (New York: Quigley Publishing Co.).
1999–2003: *2003 MPA Market Statistics* (MPAA), p. 4.

Premium pay TV
1974–1984: *Kagan Media Index,* Jan. 31, 1996, p. 3.
1985–1993: Veronis, Suhler, and Associates, *Communications Industry Forecast* (1999), p. 193.
1994–2003: Adams Media Research, *Hollywood Aftermarket* (Sept. 30, 2002, p. 3; June 30, 2004, p. 3).

PPV/VOD television
1987–1993: Kagan Research, *Consumer Entertainment Spending* (2003, p. 65).
1994–2002: Cable television PPV/VOD reported by Kagan Research, *Consumer Entertainment Spending* (2003, p. 65), plus DBS PPV/VOD as reported by *Screen Digest,* April 2003, pp. 121–123 (original source, Carmel Group).

Video rental/sales
1979–1981: interpolated based on VCR penetration.
1982–2002: Kagan Research, *Consumer Entertainment Spending* (2003, p. 65).

France, Germany, Italy, and U.K.
Theater box office
1950–1991: Thiermeyer, Tables 8, 39, 63, 54.
1992–2003: EAO, *Focus* (2003, pp. 28, 32, 34, 36; 2004, pp. 30, 34, 36, 38).

Premium pay TV
1986–1995: EAO, *Statistical Yearbook* (1996, p. 152), except Germany 1991–1995, Italy 1992–1995, and U.K. 1993–1995 are linear interpolations.
1996–2002: Screen Digest, Ltd. (data provided to the author).

PPV/VOD
1995–1998: *Screen Digest,* January 1999, p. 10.
1999–2002: EAO, *Statistical Yearbook* (2003, vol. 4, p. 78). 2003: *Screen Digest* (February 2004, p. 43).

Video rentals/sales
1979–1987: Linear interpolation.
1988–1996: EAO, *Statistical Yearbook* (1988–1990, p. 113; 1991, p. 110; 1992–1996, p. 124).
1997–2001: Screen Digest Ltd., *European Video, Market Assessment and Forecast* (2002, pp. 140, 156, 230); EAO, *Statistical Yearbook* (2003, pp. 69, 72–73).
2002: EAO, *Statistical Yearbook* (2003, vol. 3, pp. 69, 72–73).

Japan
Theater box office
1950–1999: Motion Picture Producers Association of Japan *(www.eiren.org)*.
2000–2003: EAO, *Focus* (2004, p. 50).

Premium pay TV
1991–2003: author calculation based on total revenues of Wowow *(www.wowow.co.jp)* and other premium networks as reported by ZenithOptimedia, *TV in Asia Pacific to 2012,* September 2003.

Video rentals/sales
1980–1985: Linear interpolation.
1986–1996: Jouhou Media Hakusyo *(Information Media White Paper),* annual (Tokyo: Dentsu Institute).
1997–2002: EAO, *Statistical Yearbook* (2003, vol. 3, pp. 69, 72–73).

Movie Media Penetration and Usage (Figures 5.5–5.9)

Household and total adult population data used to calculate penetration and per capita usage data are from *International Financial Statistics* (International Monetary Fund) and EAO, *Statistical Yearbooks*. Japanese household data for 1965–1998 are from Organization of Nihon Shinbun Kyokai; for 1999–2003, estimated by authors.

Data Sources: Movie Media Penetration and Usage
United States
Box office admissions
International Motion Picture Almanac, 2000.
2000–2003: *2003 MPA Market Statistics* (MPAA), p. 8.

Video rentals/sales transactions
1982–1989: *Kagan Media Index* (June 30, 1997, p. 14; June 23, 1993, pp. 12–13).
1990–1994: Paul Kagan Associates, *The State of Home Video* (2000, p. 92).
1995–2002: *Motion Picture Investor,* April 4, 2003.

VCR/DVD households
1976–1998: Paul Kagan Associates, *The State of Home Video* (2000, p. 28).
1999–2003: *2003 MPA Market Statistics* (MPAA), p. 29.

France, Germany, Italy, and U.K.
Box office admissions
1950–1998: *European Cinema Yearbook; Screen Digest* (various issues); EAO, *Statistical Yearbook* (various issues).
1999–2003: EAO, *Focus* (2004, pp. 30, 34, 36, 38).

Video rental/sales transactions
1990–1998: EAO, *Statistical Yearbook* (1995, p. 111; 1996, p. 110; 1997, p. 107; 1999, p. 121).
1999–2001: *European Video, Market Assessment and Forecast* (2002, pp. 144, 160, 234, 372).
1999–2002: EAO, *Statistical Yearbook* (2003, vol. 3, pp. 66, 71).

VCR/DVD households
1980–1998: *Screen Digest* (various issues).
1999–2001: *European Video, Market Assessment and Forecast* (2002, pp. 138, 154, 228, 366).

2002–2003: France, Germany, Italy: Eurodata-TV data provided to authors by EAO; U.K.: International Video Federation in collaboration with Screen Digest Ltd., *The European Video Yearbook* 2004 (Brussels, 2004, p. 94).

Japan

Box office admissions

1955–1989: Motion Picture Producers Association of Japan *(www.eiren.org)*.

1990–1998: EAO, *Statistical Yearbook* (1995, p. 111; 1996, p. 110; 1997, p. 107; 1999, p. 121).

2000–2003: EAO, *Focus* (2004, p. 50).

Video rentals/sales transactions

1990–1998: EAO, *Statistical Yearbook* (1995, p. 111; 1996, p. 110; 1997, p. 107; 1999, p. 121).

Number of VCR households

1980–1998: *Screen Digest* (various issues).

Sources of Revenues to Domestic Theatrical Distributors from Domestic Media, 1994–1995 (Table 5.4)

U.S.: Appendix C. France, Italy, and Germany: Authors' estimates derived from EAO, *Statistical Yearbook,* 1995–1996 and Terry Ilott, "Television and Film" (unpublished manuscript, Madrid Business School, 1995). Theatrical distributor revenues from theaters, pay television, and videocassettes are estimated by applying average distributor markup percentages to published estimates of box office, pay television, and videocassette final market revenues that were attributable to national and coproduced feature films in each country. For broadcast television, ratios of the total programming expenditures to total revenues are multiplied by the percentage of total domestic television programming hours devoted to national and coproduced films, and then applied to the total advertising and license fee revenues of all television.

Appendix G
Determinants of U.S. Box Office Market Shares in the EUJ5, 1950–2003

Written with Sang-Woo Lee

The Models

Our models generally follow the two-country model in Steven S. Wildman and Stephen E. Siwek, *International Trade in Films and Television programs* (Cambridge, Mass.: Ballinger, 1988)—that is:

(1) $\quad S_{iA} = I_i/(\Sigma_i I_i + d\Sigma_j I_j)$

(2) $\quad S_{iB} = dI_i/(d\Sigma_i I_i + \Sigma_j I_j)$,

where i and j represent producers of individual films in countries A and B, respectively; $i = 1....N_A$, and $j = 1....N_B$. That is, Ns thus indicate the number of movies produced in each country. S_{iA} is the market share of producer i in country A. I_i and I_j are the production expenditures of producers i and j, and d is the cultural discount factor, assumed to be the same for both countries, where $0 < d < 1$. Comparable equations are defined for S_{jA} and S_{jB}.

Total consumer spending on movies, R_A and R_B, is assumed to be fixed in each country. Profit functions are then defined as:

(3) $\quad \Pi_i = R_A S_{iA} + R_B S_{iB} - I_i = 0$

(4) $\quad \Pi_j = R_A S_{jA} + R_B S_{jB} - I_j = 0$,

assuming that marginal costs are zero.

Producers are monopolistically competitive with free entry, and there is free trade. Each producer maximizes profits with respect to its investment levels, I_i and I_j. Wildman and Siwek proceed to show by example that with symmetry (that is, all producers within each country invest the same), $R_A > R_B$ implies $I_i > I_j$, $N_A > N_B$, $S_{iA} > S_{jA}$, and $S_{iB} > S_{jB}$, for all i and j. That is, the producers in countries with the larger and wealthier domestic market will produce more expensive movies, and also more movies, and thus will tend to dominate trade. It follows that R_A/R_B should be positively correlated with $\Sigma_i R_A S_{iA}/\Sigma_j R_A S_{jA}$ and $\Sigma_i R_B S_{iB}/\Sigma_j R_B S_{jB}$. See Bjorn Frank, "A Note on the International Dominance of the U.S. in the Trade in Movies and Television Fiction," *Journal of Media Economics* 5 (1992): 31–38, for technical analysis and extensions of the Wildman and Siwek model.

Based on this result, five basic statistical models are specified for testing the effects of changes over time in R_A/R_B on $\Sigma_i R_A S_{iA}/\Sigma_j R_A S_{jA}$ and $\Sigma_i R_B S_{iB}/\Sigma_j R_B S_{jB}$, in the United States and its five major trading partner countries: France, Germany, Italy, the U.K., and Japan (EUJ5):

Model (1): $USBOXSHARE_{i,t} = \alpha_i + \beta \ (BOXSPENDRATIO_{i,t-1}) + \varepsilon_{i,t}$
Model (2): $USBOXSHARE_{i,t} = \alpha_i + \beta \ (TOTALSPENDRATIO_{i,t-1}) + \varepsilon_{i,t}$
Model (3): $USBOXSHARE_{i,t} = \alpha_i + \beta \ (BOXADMISSIONRATIO_{i,t-1}) + \varepsilon_{i,t}$
Model (4): $USBOXSHARE_{i,t} = \alpha_i + \beta \ (BOXPERGDPRATIO_{i,t-1}) + \varepsilon_{i,t}$
Model (5): $USBOXSHARE_{i,t} = \alpha_i + \beta \ (TOTALPERGDPRATIO_{i,t-1}) + \varepsilon_{i,t}$

where variables are defined as follows:

$USBOXSHARE_i$: the box office market share of U.S. movies in country i.
$BOXSPENDRATIO_i$: the ratio of country i's total theater box office spending to that of the United States.
$TOTALSPENDRATIO_i$: the ratio of country i's total theater box office, premium pay TV, pay-per-view, video rentals, and video sales spending to that of the United States.
$BOXADMISSIONRATIO_i$: the ratio of country i's total theater box office admissions to that of the United States.
$BOXPERGDPRATIO_i$: the ratio of country i's total theater box office spending as a percentage of GDP to that of the United States.
$TOTALPERGDPRATIO_i$: the ratio of country i's total theater box office, premium pay TV, pay-per-view, video rentals and video sales spending as a percentage of GDP to that of the United States.

BOXSPENDRATIO and *TOTALSPENDRATIO* are defined in terms of U.S. dollars at prevailing exchange rates.

The use of box office spending data in Model (1) specifies consumer spending on movies less completely than does all primary movie spending in Model (2), but Model (1) avoids the imprecision of adding revenues from sources that return income to the distributor at different points in time and may have divergent wholesale markup rates. Model (3) avoids the problems of cross-country financial comparisons at current exchange rates. The spending-per GDP-variables in Models (4) and (5) rely on financial comparisons, but have the advantage of implicitly avoiding the problems of irrelevant influences on exchange rates over time.

The one-year lag in all of the models reflects an expected time delay from observed consumer spending to release of new movies. In general, it takes about one year from the beginning of production to a movie's release. The appropriate lag could be longer or shorter.

The ratio specification in these models is imprecise in that the influence of trade with other countries is ignored. However, nondomestic, non-U.S. movies have earned by far the lowest market shares in all of these countries.

Methodology

The actual observations combined in the estimations (as described in Appendix F) included only years for which market share data were directly available, as follows: France, Italy, 1950–2003; Japan, 1980–1996; Germany, 1955–2003; U.K., 1980–2003.

Since we have a pooled cross-section/time series data set, OLS, fixed effects, or random effects estimation could be appropriate. Considering the panel structure of the data, the general estimation model is written as:

$$(5) \quad y_{i,t} = \alpha_i + X_{i,t}\beta + \varepsilon_{i,t}$$

where α_i represents the effects specific to different countries, but is constant across time. The error term $\varepsilon_{i,t}$ varies independently across time and across countries.

Depending on the assumption about the individual country effects,

$$(6) \quad y_{i,t} = \alpha_i + \beta'X_{it} + \varepsilon_{it}$$

for the fixed effects model. Alternatively,

$$(7) \quad g_{i,t} = a_i + \beta'X_{it} + \mu_i + e_{it}$$

Table G.1   Random effects model estimates

Dependent variable: *USBOXSHARE*

Independent variable	Model 1	Model 2	Model 3	Model 4	Model 5
Constant	62.9944** (8.33)	62.3925** (7.08)	60.7226** (7.78)	60.1456** (7.12)	59.2899** (6.74)
BOXSPENDRATIO	−0.6191** (−2.81)				
TOTALSPENDRATIO		−0.6245** (−2.85)			
BOXADMISSIONRATIO			−0.4195** (−3.19)		
BOXPERGDPRATIO				−0.0766** (−2.27)	
TOTALPERGDPRATIO					−0.0698** (−2.17)
No. of observations	191	191	191	190	190

Note: t-ratios given in parentheses.

** $p < 0.05$

for the random effects case, where μ_i is an error term representing the extent to which the intercept of the *i*th cross-sectional unit differs from the overall intercept, and ε_{it} is the usual error term unique to each observation. If the country-specific term, α_i, is the same across all units, then OLS provides a consistent and efficient estimator. However, if countries have the same average impact on market share, subject to an additional error term that differs for each individual country, the random effects model is more appropriate; that is, $\alpha_i = \alpha + \mu_i$, where α_i represents independent random variables with the same mean (α) and variance (σ_μ^2).

Results

Table G.1 shows the random effects estimates. All coefficients are statistically significant and in the hypothesized directions at the .05 significance level, sup-

Table G.2   Variance of error terms in random effects models

	Model 1	Model 2	Model 3	Model 4	Model 5
Var [u]	289.35	372.27	317.38	369.71	413.63
Var [e]	168.52	136.83	131.49	171.77	164.02
F-test[a]	4.69**	6.82**	6.50**	3.67**	3.93**
Lagrange multiplier test[b]	0.0000	0.000	0.0000	0.0000	0.0000
Hausman's test[c]	0.4154	0.8032	0.6447	0.8768	0.6793

a. Indicates the F-statistic for testing the joint significance of the country effects.
b. Significance level at which the hypothesis $\sigma_\mu^2 = 0$ [zero] is rejected.
c. Probability of retaining random-effects model over fixed-effects model, using Hausman's test of appropriateness of assumption.
**$p < 0.05$.

porting the hypothesis that market shares of U.S. films in the five countries are negatively related to the ratio of domestic to U.S. spending on movies.

Table G.2 shows test results for the appropriateness of fixed versus random effects models. First, given all of the confidence levels of the F-statistics for testing the joint significance of the individual country effects in Models (1)–(5), the evidence is in favor of a country specific effect in the data. The Lagrange multiplier test gives the confidence level at which the hypothesis $\sigma_\mu^2 = 0$ may be rejected. Since p-values of the Lagrange multiplier test for these models are statistically significant, the random-effects model is indicated to be more appropriate than OLS. Finally, Hausman's test shows that there is no significant correlation between μ_i and the independent variables, implying that the random-effects specification is appropriate.

We also estimated all models using fixed effects; but, because these results were very similar, we report only the random effects estimations. All models reported were corrected for autocorrelation with the Prais–Winsten method.

Overall, then, the statistical results indicate consistent support of the home market model.

Calculation of Cultural Discount Factors (Table 5.2)

Average discount factors are calculated using the formula:

(8) $d_{BA} = I_A \cdot S_{BA}/I_B \cdot S_{AA}$

where d_{BA} indicates the discount factor for films produced in country B and distributed in country A, S is market share, and I is investment. Similarly for d_{AB} and other combinations.

Equation (8) follows directly from solution of equations (1) and (2) above, assuming $\Sigma_i I_i = I_A$, and similarly for country B.

Appendix H
Movie Production Costs and Animated Movie Data

The MPAA has reported average production, or negative cost, information for its membership since 1970, although these statistics have apparently been published by the MPAA only for years since 1980, in annual *Economic Review*s, and more recently as "U.S. Entertainment Industry: MPA Market Statistics" *(www .mpaa.org)*. These data are the basis for Figure 6.1. The MPAA's 1970–1979 unpublished production cost series was obtained from the MPAA and is also published by Harold L. Vogel, *Entertainment Industry Economics: A Guide for Financial Analysis,* 2nd ed. (Cambridge: Cambridge University Press, 1990), p. 86. For years since 1988, the MPAA has also published separate average production cost information for "MPAA subsidiary/affiliate" companies. (The pre-1988 MPAA series did not include any features released by such companies.)

According to the MPAA, published averages include "production cost, studio overhead and capitalized interest" and are based on actual financial data, not estimates. The data do not, however, include all movies released by MPAA companies, only those that are "new features financed in whole or in part by MPAA companies" (according to 1985 *Economic Review*, p. 7). These presumably include the large majority of MPAA member releases, but since the number of movies on which the average estimate is based is not released, it is not possible to use the MPAA cost series to calculate trends in total industry production investment or in the average cost of all MPAA-released features. The trend in the total number of feature films released by MPAA companies, also shown in Figure 6.1, is therefore not strictly comparable to the production cost trend also indicated. However, MPAA members account for the overwhelming proportion of total box office receipts in the United States.

Production cost data for individual features are contained in the Nielsen EDI Summary Database, and these are the basis for the comparison of animated and nonanimated movie production cost trends between 1988 and 2002 shown in Figure 6.4.

The Nielsen EDI Summary Database is the standard statistical resource for the industry and is the basis for weekly box office reports published in *Variety*. The individual production cost data in the Nielsen EDI data are estimates, originating from the film's producers or from analysts, and it is difficult to determine how they compare from film to film with respect to inclusion of overhead, participation payments, and so forth. See Peter Bart, "Pic Budgets: True Lies," *Variety*, June 5, 2000, p. 1, for a discussion of flaws in individual film production cost data.

The segment of the Nielsen EDI Summary Database to which we had access reported information for 6,028 movies released in U.S. theaters between 1988 and 2002 (not including reissues), of which 145 were labeled as "animated" (74 of those released between 1998 and 2002). Figure 6.4 is based only on the 2,666 movies (86 of which were animated) for which both box office and production cost information were reported. For all animated and nonanimated EDI movies released from 1988 to 2002, those with production cost information accounted for 91 percent and 96 percent, respectively, of the total U.S. box office receipts earned by all such movies in the database. Thus, the movies excluded from the animated film cost trend analysis were relatively insignificant in economic terms.

Coding of the animated films by type of production technology was conducted in conjunction with the *imbd.com* Internet movie database. Movies labeled as CGI include four films that combined CGI with at least some significant live action. The 2-D category includes five movies that combined 2-D with significant live action, two "stop motion" features, two movies that combined stop motion with live action, and one movie that combined 2-D with CGI but was predominantly 2-D. With these 11 movies excluded, the 1998–2002 CGI versus 2-D average cost comparisons were almost identical to those reported in the text: $87 million for CGI films and $47 million for 2-D. More detailed statistical comparisons are available in David Waterman, "The Effects of Technological Change on the Quality and Variety of Information Products" (paper presented at the National Bureau of Economic Research Conference on the Economics of the Information Economy, Cambridge, Mass., May 7–8, 2004).

Use of the Nielsen EDI Summary Database to estimate general tends in production costs over time is not advisable because the percentage of all movies with production cost information increased over time, from 37 percent in the 1988–1990 period to 72 percent in 2000–2002. That increase apparently occurred because production-cost information began to be obtained for a larger percentage of low-budget features. These factors are thus likely to bias trends significantly.

Appendix I
Motion Picture Industry Employment

Figure 6.2 shows the total number of persons employed during one week in the month of March each year, as reported by the U.S. Census of Business, which is conducted approximately every five years. The census provides relatively crude indications of trends over time since all employees of a given business are categorized on the basis of whether the firm's primary business activity is "motion picture production (except television)."

The reported trends in Figure 6.2 are generally corroborated by related Census of Business series. Total U.S. employment in "motion picture and television production and distribution services" as a whole rose from 64,600 in 1972 to 249,200 in 1992, the most recent year for which those overall categories were reported in comparable form. "Services allied to motion picture production" rose from 11,975 to 162,217 over the same period. In 1997, the new census category of "tele-production and other post-production services" reported employment of 33,205, a category that has almost certainly boomed since then as a result of special effects technology.

Comparable data from the 2002 Census of Business were not yet available, but employment growth has evidently been slower. In the state of California, which accounts for about 70 percent of total "motion picture industry" revenues and 60 percent of its employment (U.S. Dept. of Commerce, "A Report on Film Industry Employment," Jan. 20, 2001, p. 25), movie production was virtually stagnant from 1997 to 2001 (183,300 to 185,100 employees) after sharp increases before that date, although reported increases in "runaway" production could account for some of this decline. For related information, see data provided by the Entertainment Industry Development Corporation, *Annual Reports* of the Economic Development Corporation of Los Angeles County, and "U.S. Entertainment Industry: MPA Market Statistics" (MPAA, annual).

Appendix J
Credits Analysis, Top Ten Movies, 1971 and 2001

Selection of the top ten movies for 1971 and 2001 was based on *Variety* year-end box office reports. Compilations in Table 6.1 were based on end credits appearing on the actual films wherever possible. For two of the 1971 movies (*Little Big Man* and *The Owl and the Pussycat*) and four of the 2001 movies (*The Lord of the Rings, Monsters, Inc., The Mummy Returns,* and *Pearl Harbor*) we relied on credits listed in the *www.imdb.com* database, either because a video of the actual movie was not available or because the credits on the video were too small to be reliably coded. Analysis of the twelve movies for which we had actual end-credit information showed that *www.imdb.com* listings tend to under-report actual credits. Only credits that *imdb.com* reported to be authenticated as appearing on the original film were counted. Thus, we excluded "uncredited" credits that were listed by *imdb.com* for some movies.

Credits were coded according to the following criteria.

Cast:

    Stunt artists.

    Other cast: all other acting personnel.

Crew:

    Producers: all with "producer" in the title.

    Sound: includes "sound department," "original music," and other people related to sound productions, such as mixer, music production supervisor, sound editor, singer, sound effects, etc.

Special effects: individuals under the category of "special effects" or with a title of "special effects."

Visual effects/special effects related: individuals under the category of "visual effects"; crewmembers, supervisors, consultants, technicians, etc. with titles or within categories of "digital effects," "3D graphics," "animation," and related terms.

Writers: all those credited with the words "story," "writer," "screenplay," "script," "written by," "book," "dialogue," "additional dialogue," or similar terms.

Other crew: all other personnel credited on the movie.

All subcontractor credits in which individual names do not appear are counted as one credit.

Appendix K
Movie Genre Analysis

Written with Weiting Lu

Our genre analysis consisted of two parts. The first was a cross-country study of the United States and the EUJ5 countries for 2001, and the second a time series study of U.S. genres for the years 1967–2001. Both studies made use of genre information for theatrical feature films available from the *imdb.com* database, which covers virtually all significant theatrical feature films released worldwide. The *imdb.com* database makes use of nineteen different genre categories, two or more of which are assigned to a single movie in many cases.

Cross-Country Study, 2001

We assembled lists of the top twenty performing movies in terms of box office receipts for the United States, France, Germany, Italy, the U.K., and Japan, and in the "global" (total worldwide) market from *Focus: World Film Market Trends,* annual reports published by the European Audiovisual Observatory.

Of these films, our analysis included only those movies ranking in the top twenty lists that were domestic national productions; all coproductions were excluded. Table K.1 shows detailed results for the twelve most frequently occurring genres in the global list. Each entry shows the total number and percent of movies that had the indicated genre as at least one of the labels it was given by *imdb.com*. For example, 42 of the 94 top global movies, or 45 percent, had "action" as at least one of its genre labels. See also Table 6.2 and related text discussion.

Table K.1 Distribution of movie genres in the global, U.S., and EUJ5 markets: top twenty box office movies, 1997–2001

IMDB genre	Global		U.S.		France		Germany		Italy		U.K.		Japan		EUJ5	
	N	%	N	%	N	%	N	%	N	%	N	%	N	%	N	%
Action	42	45%	39	41%	5	21%	2	18%	1	5%	0	—	3	15%	11	13%
Adventure	27	29%	27	29%	2	8%	0	—	0	—	0	—	4	20%	6	7%
Comedy	41	44%	45	48%	19	79%	6	55%	17	81%	8	89%	0	—	50	59%
Crime	7	7%	9	10%	4	17%	1	9%	0	—	0	—	0	—	5	6%
Drama	32	34%	25	27%	8	33%	3	27%	6	29%	4	44%	4	20%	25	29%
Family	18	19%	20	21%	2	8%	0	—	0	—	1	11%	3	15%	6	7%
Fantasy	19	20%	15	16%	6	25%	0	—	0	—	0	—	3	15%	9	11%
Horror	11	12%	13	14%	2	8%	1	9%	0	—	0	—	3	15%	6	7%
Musical	2	2%	2	2%	0	—	1	9%	0	—	1	11%	0	—	2	2%
Romance	18	19%	15	16%	3	13%	1	9%	4	19%	1	11%	0	—	9	11%
Sci-fi	17	18%	14	15%	2	8%	0	—	1	5%	0	—	0	—	3	4%
Thriller	23	24%	26	28%	4	17%	2	18%	0	—	0	—	2	10%	8	9%
"Violence-prone" index	63	67%	66	70%	11	46%	3	27%	4	19%	0	—	6	30%	24	28%
Total movies	94		94		24		11		21		9		20		85	

U.S. Genre Trend Study, 1967–2001

We assembled the top twenty performing movies for each year from 1967 to 1987 from annual *Variety* lists of top box office movies, and for years from 1988 to 2001 from the Nielsen EDI Summary Database. Those steps created a total base of 700 movies. We then excluded all international coproductions, yielding a final database of 600 movies.

Comparable to methodology of the 2001 cross-sectional study, Table K.2 shows the percentage of movies that had each of the twelve most frequently occurring genres assigned to it over the thirty-five-year period, grouped by the five-year intervals shown in Figure 6.3. Year-to-year fluctuations were substantial.

For each of the twelve most frequently appearing genres and for the "violence-prone" index, we estimated the following regression model using annual data

$$(1) \quad y_i = a + bt_i + \varepsilon_i$$

where i indicates each of the twelve most frequently appearing genres and the violence-prone index, and t indicates years, $1 \ldots 35$, and ε_i is an error term.

The top two rows of Table K.3 show the resulting coefficients and statistical significance of the thirteen regressions. As the last column of Table K.2 indicates, the average number of genres per movie recorded by *imdb.com* increased substantially over the period. Methodological details about *imdb.com*'s genre coding process were unavailable. We thus could not determine whether increases over time in the percentage of movies to which a particular genre was assigned occurred because of some change in the methodology of assigning genres or because movies in the sample had in fact become more "homogenized," thus requiring a larger number of genre labels. As a conservative measure, we therefore deflated time trends in all the individual genre labels by the average number of genres recorded per movie in each year. The regressions in the bottom half of Table K.3 show time trend regressions using the deflated data.

Only five of the twelve deflated genre labels were statistically significant at the 5 percent level, compared to nine of the undeflated labels. It is unclear how the violence-prone index should be deflated over time, so a price-deflated regression analysis was not conducted. Recall, however, that the violence-prone index is defined to apply to all movies for which any one of several genre labels are applied. Since the probability that a given movie has any particular genre label increased over time, any "genre inflation" effect will thus be magnified for the undeflated violence-prone index.

Table K.2 Percentage of movies to which the twelve most frequently occurring genres and the violence-prone index were assigned, five-year intervals, 1967–2001

Years	Action	Adventure	Comedy	Crime	Drama	Family	Fantasy	Horror	Musical	Romance	Sci-fi	Thriller	V-P index	Average no. of genres per movie
1967–71	16%	14%	35%	11%	50%	12%	2%	3%	9%	12%	6%	10%	42%	2.13
1972–76	19%	15%	26%	18%	53%	16%	3%	6%	11%	6%	6%	19%	53%	2.17
1977–81	24%	18%	51%	7%	26%	10%	13%	9%	8%	16%	15%	17%	51%	2.27
1982–86	33%	25%	47%	12%	33%	14%	11%	5%	7%	15%	14%	14%	59%	2.39
1987–91	36%	16%	54%	22%	36%	18%	15%	10%	4%	18%	13%	29%	65%	2.88
1992–96	40%	20%	41%	9%	44%	15%	12%	5%	6%	18%	10%	37%	62%	2.78
1997–2001	42%	30%	47%	9%	27%	21%	17%	13%	2%	17%	14%	28%	70%	2.95
Overall (1967–2001)	32%	21%	44%	13%	37%	16%	12%	8%	6%	15%	12%	24%	60%	2.57
Total no. of movies with the label	194	124	266	77	219	94	71	48	38	90	72	144	360	

Table K.3 Regression analysis of U.S. genre trends over time, 1967–1971

Dependent variable	Action	Adventure	Comedy	Crime	Drama	Family	Fantasy	Horror	Musical	Romance	Sci-fi	Thriller	Violence-prone index
Undeflated													
Beta	0.1823**	0.0832**	0.0989**	−0.0123	−0.1157**	0.0504**	0.0902**	0.0389*	−0.0555**	0.0552**	−0.0370	0.1390**	0.165***
t-value	6.20	2.71	2.49	−0.45	−2.78	2.36	3.38	1.94	−3.22	2.53	1.68	3.79	5.22
Deflated													
Beta	0.0070**	0.0022	0.0003	−0.0023	−0.0130**	0.001	0.0042**	0.0014	−0.0044**	0.0014	0.0008	0.0054**	NA
t-ratio	3.73	1.2	0.09	−1.38	−5.01	0.75	2.56	1.19	−3.79	1.17	0.62	2.67	NA

N = 35 for each regression.
*** 1% sig. level.
** 5% sig. level.
* 10% sig. level.

Notes

Abbreviations

EAO   European Audiovisual Observatory
MPAA   Motion Picture Association of America
NYT   *New York Times*
VSDA   Video Software Dealers Association
WSJ   *Wall Street Journal*

Introduction

1. Chasman quoted in Aljean Harmetz, *Rolling Breaks and Other Movie Business* (New York: Knopf, 1983), p. 170.
2. Joseph D. Phillips, "Film Conglomerate Blockbusters," in Gorham Kindem, ed., *The American Movie Industry: The Business of Motion Pictures* (Carbondale: Southern Illinois University Press, 1982), pp. 325–335. See also Douglas Gomery, *Shared Pleasures* (Madison: University of Wisconsin Press, 1992), Chapters 10–11, and Christopher Anderson, *Hollywood TV: The Studio System in the Fifties* (Austin: University of Texas Press, 1994) for studies of this period.
3. Annual financial reports; Donald Leroy Perry, "An Analysis of the Financial Plans of the Motion Picture Industry for the Period 1929 to 1962" (Ph.D. diss., University of Illinois, 1967).
4. Thomas T. Vogel, Jr., "There's No Stimulus Like Show Business," *WSJ*, Sept. 22, 1995, p. A2.
5. See Appendix C. Worldwide distributor revenues as a percent of GDP increased from .10 percent in 1970 to .36 percent in 2003. The 1970 estimate assumes 45 percent of total revenue from foreign markets. Merchandise licensing rights (for manufacture of toys based on movie characters and the like) are not included in either year.
6. European Union, *Report by the Think-Tank on the Audiovisual Policy in the European Union* (Luxembourg, 1994), p. 17.
7. EAO, *Focus 2004: World Film Market Trends* (Strasbourg, France, 2003), p. 20.

8. Author's estimate: 95 percent (U.S. share of its domestic theatrical market) of 40 percent (U.S. share of world box office admissions) + 75 percent (U.S. share of foreign theatrical markets) of 60 percent (remaining proportion of world box office admissions) = 83 percent (U.S. share of the world theater market). As discussed in Chapter 5, U.S. share of the world video market is probably higher.

9. EAO, *Focus 2002: World Film Market Trends* (Strasbourg, France, 2002), p. 12.

10. Kristin Thompson, *Exporting Entertainment: America in the World Film Market, 1907–1934* (London: British Film Institute, 1985), p. 123. These claims were made in the 1920s and 1930s.

11. Quoted in Kerry Segrave, *American Films Abroad: Hollywood's Domination of the World's Movie Screens from the 1890s to the Present* (Jefferson, N.C.: McFarland, 1997), p. 270.

12. Well documented histories of these trade battles are recorded in Ian Jarvie, *Hollywood's Overseas Campaign: The North Atlantic Movie Trade, 1920–1950* (Cambridge: Cambridge University Press, 1992); Thomas H. Guback, *The International Film Industry* (Bloomington: Indiana University Press, 1969); Thompson, *Exporting Entertainment;* and Segrave, *American Films Abroad.*

13. See especially Arthur De Vany and W. David Walls, "Bose-Einstein Dynamics and Adaptive Contracting in the Motion Picture Industry," *Economic Journal* 106 (November 1996): 1493–1514; and Arthur De Vany and W. David Walls, "Uncertainty in the Movie Industry: Does Star Power Reduce the Terror of the Box Office?" *Journal of Cultural Economics* 23 (November 1999): 285–318. Arthur DeVany, *Hollywood Economics: How Extreme Uncertainty Shapes the Film Industry* (London: Routledge, 2004), is a collection of the author's previously published and other academic papers, including the above-cited works. See also David Forrest Prindle, *Risky Business: the Political Economy of Hollywood* (Boulder: Westview, 1993); Richard E. Caves, *Creative Industries: Contracts between Art and Commerce* (Cambridge, Mass.: Harvard University Press, 2000). From an industry insider's perspective, see William Goldman, *Adventures in the Screen Trade: A Personal View of Hollywood and Screenwriting* (New York: Warner Books, 1984).

1. The Players

1. The standard resource for information and analysis of motion picture industry market structure, business functions, and financial performance

is Harold L. Vogel, *Entertainment Industry Economics: A Guide for Financial Analysis* (5th ed., Cambridge: Cambridge University Press, 2001; 1st ed., 1986). Other relevant sources include Barry Russell Litman, *The Motion Picture Mega-Industry* (Boston: Allyn and Bacon, 1998); and Janet Wasko, *Hollywood in the Information Age: Beyond the Silver Screen* (Austin: University of Texas Press, 1995).

2. For a concise discussion of film financing methods, see "The Strategy and Sources of Motion Picture Finance" (Harvard Business School, case no. 9-203-007, Nov. 14, 2002).

3. Bruce Orwall, "Handicapping *Seabiscuit*," *WSJ,* July 24, 2003, p. B1.

4. David Germain, "The Emperor's New 'Clones': Jedi Master Lucas Ponders Life after *Star Wars*," *Associated Press Newswire,* May 15, 2002.

5. The Disney studio had existed for a number of years before, but distributed its movies through RKO.

6. Merissa Marr, Dennis K. Berman, and Peter Grant, "Sony Group to Buy MGM for $3 Billion," *WSJ,* Sept. 14, 2004, p. A3.

7. American International Pictures was founded in 1954 and existed until its merger with Filmways in 1979. Allied Artists was founded in 1946 and declared bankruptcy in 1979. Orion was formed in 1978 and existed independently until it was sold to MGM in 1997.

8. Although RKO's average market share was no higher than Universal's in the 1947–1950 period (Figure 1.1), it had started on a steady decline, which continued until the company's bankruptcy in the mid-1950s.

9. *United States v. Paramount Pictures, Inc. et al.,* 334 U.S. 131 (1948); Michael Conant, *Antitrust in the Motion Picture Industry* (Berkeley: University of California Press, 1960).

10. "Major Studio Releases, 1992–2003," *Variety Deal Memo* (Informa Media Group), Dec. 16, 2002. These data do not include reissues or "some pickups." (Releases for 2003 anticipated.)

11. Shares for some individual years are higher. The largest individual market share recorded for a single year was 30.0 percent (largely due to *E.T.*) by Universal Pictures in 1982.

12. Studio-to-studio theater and video market share comparisons in these figures are limited by historical changes in studio ownership or joint ventures in video distribution, the inclusion of non–feature film products in some years for video revenues, and because a studio's theatrical and video divisions do not necessarily release the same menu of theatrical features. See Appendix A.

13. "Hollywood Couples," *The Economist,* Jan. 9, 1999, p. 79; Bernard Weinraub, "Expect Top Studio Heads to Roll If Some of 1997's Many

Blockbusters Fail," *NYT,* Jan 6, 1997, p. D7; Tom King, "Mars Wars," *WSJ,* Feb. 4, 2004, p. W1.

14. Arthur De Vany and W. David Walls, "Bose-Einstein Dynamics and Adaptive Contracting in the Motion Picture Industry," *Economic Journal* 106 (November 1996): 1493–1514.

15. See ibid.; and Liran Einav, "Not All Rivals Look Alike: Estimating an Equilibrium Model of the Release Date Timing Game" (working paper, Department of Economics, Stanford University, 2003).

16. Weinraub, "Expect Top Studio Heads to Roll."

17. Robert W. Crandall, "The Postwar Performance of the Motion Picture Industry," *Antitrust Bulletin* 2 (Spring 1975): 49–88. Crandall presented a descriptive analysis based on individual firm theatrical rentals data and a variety of anecdotal and other evidence.

18. Peter Bart, "Bankers Quake over Hollywood's Soaring Costs," *Daily Variety,* Mar. 14, 1994, p. 19; Elizabeth Guider, "Can Film Biz Curb Squander-Lust?" *Variety,* Mar. 29, 2004, p. 6.

19. Bruce M. Owen, Jack H. Beebe, and Willard G. Manning, Jr., *Television Economics* (Lexington, Mass.: Lexington Books, 1974) made a similar case regarding attempts of the three main television networks to control production costs.

20. Bill Carter, "Suddenly at ABC, the Future Is Now," *NYT,* Aug. 1, 1995, p. D1.

21. "How to Manage a Dream Factory," *The Economist,* Jan. 18, 2003, p. 73. see also Michael Wolf, *The Entertainment Economy: How Mega-Media Forces Are Transforming Our Lives* (New York: Times Books, 1999); Goldman, *Adventures in the Screen Trade;* and William Goldman, *Which Lie Did I Tell? or: More Adventures in the Screen Trade* (New York: Pantheon, 2000) for relevant commentary on entertainment industry management.

22. Martin Arnold, "Making Books: Does Synergy Really Work?" *NYT,* July 16, 1998, p. E3; Geraldine Fabrikant and David D. Kirkpatrick, "AOL's Need: A New Vision," *NYT,* Feb. 2, 2003, p. C1; Bruce Orwall and Kyle Pope, "Disney, ABC Promised 'Synergy' in Merger: So What Happened?" *WSJ,* May 16, 1997, p. A1.

23. See Vogel, *Entertainment Industry Economics,* Chapters 2–3.

24. Some of these percentages have probably declined since 1998, not only in the case of Universal due to its acquisition by GE, but also Paramount, due to the merger of its parent company, Viacom, with CBS in 2000.

25. Bruce Orwall, "Disney's Net Fell by 41% in Period, Hit by Movie Flop," *WSJ,* Jan 31, 2003, p. B8.

26. Marc Graser and Carl DiOrio, "Better Unwed than in the Red," *Variety,* Sept. 29, 2003, p. 11.

27. Jonathan Bing and Cathy Dunkley, "Thinking Big, Spending Big," *Variety,* May 5, 2003, p. 1.

28. Bruce Orwall, "Universal's Anxious Summer," *WSJ,* May 22, 2003, p. B1.

29. For a relevant discussion of media conglomerate management with a focus on Viacom (owner of Paramount Pictures), see Thomas R. Eisenmann and Joseph L. Bower, "The Entrepreneurial M-Form: A Case Study of Strategic Integration in a Global Media Firm" in Joseph L. Bower and Clark G. Gilbert, eds., *From Resource Allocation to Strategy* (New York: Oxford University Press, 2005).

2. Television

1. Fredric Stuart, "The Effects of Television on the Motion Picture Industry: 1948–1960," in Gorham Kindem, ed., *The American Movie Industry: The Business of Motion Pictures* (Carbondale: Southern Illinois University Press, 1982), pp. 257–307 is a detailed statistical study. See also Michael Conant, *Antitrust in the Motion Picture Industry* (Berkeley: University of California Press, 1960).

2. *TV Dimensions 2004* (New York: Media Dynamics), p. 66.

3. Conant, *Antitrust in the Motion Picture Industry.*

4. Related by Douglas Gomery, *Shared Pleasures* (Madison: University of Wisconsin Press, 1992), pp. 77–79.

5. Detailed histories of the studio system era can be found in Joel W. Finler, *The Hollywood Story* (New York: Crown, 1988); Gomery, *Shared Pleasures;* Christopher Anderson, *Hollywood TV: The Studio System in the Fifties* (Austin: University of Texas Press, 1994); and Tino Balio, ed., *The American Film Industry* (Madison: University of Wisconsin Press, 1985), among others.

6. Finler, *The Hollywood Story,* p. 72.

7. Ibid., p. 73.

8. Anderson, *Hollywood TV,* p. 56.

9. See ibid. and Finler, *The Hollywood Story* for related discussion of this period. The trend toward improving the quality of movie products had progressed since the early days of the industry, as audiences became

more sophisticated and impatient with cheaper production values. Although they had declined by the time of television, B pictures continued to be produced at Columbia, Universal, and Warner Brothers until the mid-1950s. Serials, such as Columbia's *Jungle Jim,* also continued until this time (Finler, *The Hollywood Story*).

10. How the transformation of the old Hollywood studio system to the modern era changed the contracting process has been the subject of several economic studies, including Darlene C. Chisholm, "Asset Specificity and Long-Term Contracts: The Case of the Motion Pictures Industry," *Eastern Economic Journal* 19 (Spring 1993): 143–155; Darlene C. Chisholm, "Profit-Sharing versus Fixed-Payment Contracts: Evidence from the Motion Pictures Industry," *Journal of Law, Economics, and Organization* 13 (April 1997): 169–201; Mark Weinstein, "Profit-Sharing Contracts in Hollywood: Evolution and Analysis," *Journal of Legal Studies* 27 (January 1998): 67–112; Richard E. Caves, *Creative Industries: Contracts between Art and Commerce* (Cambridge, Mass.: Harvard University Press, 2000); and John Sedgwick, "Profit Differentiation at the Movies: Hollywood, 1946–1965," *Journal of Economic History* 62 (September 2002): 676–705.

11. Our explanation in this paragraph for the breakdown of the studio system is consistent with commentary by Caves in *Creative Industries* and an explanation by Chisholm in "Asset Specificity and Long-Term Contracts." Chisholm argues that contracting was sustainable in the studio-system era because studios made "asset-specific" investments—that is, sunk cost investments in promoting talent and developing those individuals' careers that would be lost if the talent could then be hired away by another studio. This system was no longer sustainable when the studios could not reliably take repeated advantage of these investments.

12. Anderson, *Hollywood TV.*

13. Calculated from Weinstein, "Profit-Sharing Contracts in Hollywood," pp. 72–73; original data from Finler, *The Hollywood Story,* and the annual publication *International Motion Picture Almanac* (New York: Quigley Publishing Co.). Film counts vary from source to source, but all show the same trend.

14. See Finler, *The Hollywood Story* for extensive discussion of the spectaculars and attempts by the studios to outdo television in this period.

15. Robert W. Crandall, "The Postwar Performance of the Motion Picture Industry," *Antitrust Bulletin* 2 (Spring 1975): 69, reporting data presented in congressional hearings.

16. Anderson, *Hollywood TV,* p. 187.

17. Ibid., p. 162.

18. "Made-for-TV Movies: 1975–76 Network Primetime Season at a Glance," *Variety,* Sept. 3, 1975, p. 61. Theatrical feature negative costs: Harold L. Vogel, *Entertainment Industry Economics: A Guide for Financial Analysis,* 2nd ed. (Cambridge: Cambridge University Press, 1990), p. 86, reporting MPAA data.

19. Scott Collins and Nellie Andreeva, "CBS to Dig Deep for *Raymond,*" *Hollywood Reporter,* Jan. 10, 2003.

20. MPAA, *U.S. Entertainment Industry: 2004 MPA Market Statistics,* (see Appendix H); Mike Schneider and Greg Spring, "The Green behind the Screen," *Electronic Media,* Aug. 2, 1999, p. 19.

21. Author's calculations based on studio revenue data compiled by Crandall, "The Postwar Performance of the Motion Picture Industry," and the author (see Appendix B); and numbers of films released by studio, as reported by Weinstein, "Profit-Sharing Contracts in Hollywood," pp. 72–73.

22. As reported in Appendix C, television accounted for about 25 percent of domestic revenues from theatrical film distribution for the period 1970–1975. Data are not available for foreign television rentals during this period, but on the assumption that the 1981–1983 ratio of foreign television to U.S. TV revenues of .23 applied to the 1970–1975 period, total television would have contributed about 15 to 20 percent of total distributor revenue from all sources.

23. See especially Finler, *The Hollywood Story.*

24. Weinstein, "Profit-Sharing Contracts in Hollywood," and Sedgwick, "Profit Differentiation at the Movies" also argue, with limited data, that movie studio risk rose over this general time frame.

25. An exception was RKO, which went out of business in 1957, evidently due to mismanagement.

26. John Sedgwick and Michael Pokorny, "The Risk Environment of Film Making: Warner Bros. in the Interwar Years," *Explorations in Economic History* 35 (April 1998): 196–220. H. Mark Glancy, "MGM Film Grosses, 1924–1948: The Eddie Mannix Ledger," *Historical Journal of Film, Radio, and Television* 12(2) (1992): 127–144, also reports evidence of greater variation in the profitability of A than B films for all MGM movies released from 1924 to 1948.

27. For histories of this period, see especially Finler, *The Hollywood Story;* a corporate history of Fox is found in Aubrey Solomon, *Twentieth Century–Fox: A Corporate and Financial History* (Metuchen, N.J.: Scarecrow Press, 1988), and of Paramount in Bernard F. Dick, *Engulfed: The Death of*

Paramount Pictures and the Birth of Corporate Hollywood (Lexington: University Press of Kentucky, 2001).

28. Finler, *The Hollywood Story,* p. 241.

29. Solomon, *Twentieth Century–Fox,* pp. 140–145.

30. Sedgwick, "Profit Differentiation at the Movies."

31. Ibid.; "The Strategy and Sources of Motion Picture Finance" (Harvard Business School, case no. 9-203-007, Nov. 14, 2002); Andrew Hindes and Martin Peers, "H'wood Rivals Do the Splits," *Variety,* July 28, 1997, p. 1.

32. Simon Whitney, "The Motion Picture Industry," in *Antitrust Policies: American Experience in Twenty Industries* (New York: Twentieth Century Fund, 1958), and especially Conant, *Antitrust in the Motion Picture Industry,* present extensive economic analysis of the *Paramount* case and focus mostly on market entry issues. Among other authors claiming the various alleged effects of *Paramount* are Paul Kerr, ed., *The Hollywood Film Industry: A Reader* (New York: Routledge and Kegan Paul, 1986); Anderson, *Hollywood TV;* Gomery, *Shared Pleasures;* and John Izod, *Hollywood and the Box Office, 1895–1986* (New York: Columbia University Press, 1988).

33. Conant, *Antitrust in the Motion Picture Industry;* Whitney, *The Motion Picture Industry.* Crandall, in "The Postwar Performance of the Motion Picture Industry," argues that the *Paramount* decrees had no lasting effects on market entry or industry coordination of production decisions (Chapter 2). See also Arthur De Vany and Ross D. Eckert, "Motion Picture Antitrust: The Paramount Case Revisited," *Research in Law and Economics* 14 (1991): 51–112.

34. Jose Carbajo, David De Meza, and Daniel J. Seidmann, "A Strategic Motivation for Commodity Bundling," *Journal of Industrial Economics* 38 (1990): 283–298; and Michael D. Whinston, "Tying, Foreclosure, and Exclusion," *American Economic Review* 80 (1990): 837–859. The gist of these models is that if there is a monopolized market and a competitive market, but competition in the latter is imperfect, then independent suppliers can be forced out of the competitive market because a reduced output would prevent them from realizing economies of scale.

35. See, for example, Anderson, *Hollywood TV;* Gomery, *Shared Pleasures;* Tino Balio, ed., *Hollywood in the Age of Television* (Boston: Unwin Hyman, 1990); Balio, *The American Film Industry;* and William Boddy, *Fifties Television* (Urbana: University of Illinois Press, 1990).

36. Data in this paragraph are based on Appendix C and U.S. Department of Commerce general economic statistics.

37. *Chicago Tribune* (various); Conant's *Antitrust in the Motion Picture Industry* describes the general pattern based on court documents.

38. Conant, in *Antitrust in the Motion Picture Industry,* identified and discussed the price discrimination motive for the multitheater movie release sequence. David Waterman, "Prerecorded Home Video and the Distribution of Theatrical Feature Films," in Eli M. Noam, ed., *Video Media Competition: Regulation, Economics, and Technology* (New York: Columbia University Press, 1985), pp. 221–243; and Bruce M. Owen and Steven S. Wildman, *Video Economics* (Cambridge, Mass.: Harvard University Press, 1992) develop the intertemporal price discrimination model descriptively for the modern multimedia release system.

   Dropping the price of a product over time is not necessarily evidence of price discrimination. Falling prices may reflect a decline in the value of a product over time, or falling costs. The general conditions under which intertemporal price discrimination can be profitable, however, seem easily fulfilled in the movie case. As demonstrated in general by Nancy L. Stokey, "Intertemporal Price Discrimination," *Quarterly Journal of Economics* 93 (August 1979): 355–371, these conditions are basically just that the time discount rates of enough consumers must be greater than those of sellers (that is, the studio is willing to wait at least as long as those consumers are), and that there is significant dispersion in consumer price demand. See also Louis Phlips, *The Economics of Price Discrimination* (New York: Cambridge University Press, 1983); and Hal R. Varian, "Price Discrimination," in Richard Schmalensee and Robert D. Willig, eds., *Handbook of Industrial Organization* (New York: Elsevier Science, 1989), pp. 597–654.

   Some authors dispute the intertemporal price discrimination interpretation of movie release. De Vany and Eckert, "Motion Picture Antitrust," primarily interpret the release sequence to be an information collection device by which studios learn about and adapt to the true audience demand for a movie. Suchan Chae, "Can Time Preference Be an Instrument for Price Discrimination?" *Economics Letters* 81 (November 2003): 173–177 challenges the price discrimination interpretation on theoretical grounds.

39. For the general case, see Eric Maskin and John Riley, "Monopoly with Incomplete Information," *Rand Journal of Economics* 15 (Summer 1984): 171–196; Michael Mussa and Sherwin Rosen, "Monopoly and Product Quality," *Journal of Economic Theory* 18 (August 1978): 301–317; and Varian, "Price Discrimination." Some particular, but intuitively reason-

able, assumptions about valuation of quality by high- versus low-price-demand consumers are necessary for quality segmentation to work. See Chapter 3 for further discussion of quality segmentation in movie release.

40. David Waterman, "Economic Essays on the Theatrical Motion Picture Industry" (Ph.D. diss., Stanford University, 1979).

41. U.S. Department of Commerce, Census of Business, *Census of Selected Service Industries: Motion Picture Industry* (subject series, various). These data are in terms of "screens," not theater buildings per se, and differ somewhat by source. Before the mid-1960s, multiscreen theaters were of negligible significance.

42. The major studios did not begin releasing movies to the broadcast networks until about 1956, but by the mid-1960s most of them had licensed their main film libraries to television. Anderson, *Hollywood TV;* Balio, *The American Film Industry;* Balio, *Hollywood in the Age of Television.*

43. S. Susan Yang, "The Strategy of Durable Goods Monopolists: An Example of the Movie Industry" (working paper, Department of Telecommunications, Indiana University, 1999). Yang's sample consisted of the 293 movies exhibited during the 1970–1972, 1974–1976, and 1978–1980 periods, as reported in annual *Variety* tabulations.

44. Author's calculation based on Federal Communications Commission, *Annual Report* (1976).

45. Author's estimate based on annual theatrical movie ratings compilations published in *Variety.*

46. These data also understate the feature-films-on-TV habit, since made-for-TV movies, which the broadcast networks had started producing and exhibiting in the mid-1960s and later were shown by independent broadcast stations, are not included. In 1975, made-for-TV films accounted for about half the networks' movie showings; but they were a smaller fraction, probably under 15 percent, of the movies that appeared on independent television stations. See Appendix D.

47. Since 1975, real admission prices have declined somewhat and stabilized, fluctuating between $6.85 in 1975 and $5.06 in 1996, and reaching $5.81 in 2002, the latter average approximately 76 percent above its 1948 level.

48. Robert D. Lamson, in "Measured Productivity and Price Change: Some Empirical Evidence on Service Bias, Motion Picture Theaters," *Journal of Political Economy* 78 (March–April 1970): 291–305, assumes that both the quality of movies and the quality of theaters remained constant over the period. He interprets the price change as an example of how (contrary to prevailing wisdom of the time) productivity in service indus-

tries can increase. Crandall, in "The Postwar Performance of the Motion Picture Industry," finds the price increase to be supporting evidence of his thesis that the *Paramount* decision failed to curb the collusion among movie distributors that the Court found to have existed.

49. Gomery, *Shared Pleasures.*

50. Elaine Hatfield, John R. Cacioppo, and Richard L. Rapson, "Primitive Emotional Contagion," in Margaret S. Clark, ed., *Emotion and Social Behavior* (Newbury Park, Calif.: Sage, 1992), pp. 151–178, reviews this literature. See also Gary Becker, "A Note on Restaurant Pricing and Other Examples of Social Influences on Price," *Journal of Political Economy* 99 (October 1991): 1109–1116, for an argument that consumers enhance the benefits of other people at restaurants and other events, in part by reassuring them that they are doing the right thing.

51. A U.S. government report, *The Motion Picture Industry Study* (Washington, D.C.: prepared for the Office of National Recovery Administration, Division of Review, 1936), p. 81, stated that in the 100 largest U.S. cities, U.S. distributors earned approximately 40 percent of their total U.S. rentals from first-run theaters. Although these larger cities accounted for the overwhelming proportion of total U.S. rentals, the relative contribution of first-run theaters in smaller towns and cities was generally higher. A sample of major features released during 1943–1944 earned between 35.1 percent and 50.5 percent of their total rentals in the 100 largest cities from first-run exhibition (Conant, *Antitrust in the Motion Picture Industry,* p. 69). Waterman, in "Economic Essays on the Theatrical Motion Picture Industry," estimated the proportion of studio revenues from first-run exhibition to be at least 80 percent in 1975.

52. Gilbert Vivian Seldes, *The Great Audience* (New York: Viking Press, 1950), p. 38.

53. G. W. Stonier, "The Film: I," in Frederick Laws, ed., *Made for Millions* (London: Contact Publishers, 1947), p. 11.

54. Ibid., p. 8.

55. Arthur Knight, *The Liveliest Art: A Panoramic History of the Movies* (New York: Macmillan, 1957), p. 257.

56. Whitney, *The Motion Picture Industry;* Crandall, "The Postwar Performance of the Motion Picture Industry." Estimates of the rental rate and its changes over time vary, but all available sources either indicate or suggest a rise over the period. Our 1948 and 1975 calculations in Table 2.1 are based on estimated total theater rental revenues of all distributors and total box office receipts, including admission taxes, which declined over the interval. As reported by Whitney, *The Motion Picture Industry,*

p. 169, the rental rate increase was less pronounced in the 1947–1955 period if admission taxes are netted out of total box office receipts. Based on Census of Business data, Crandall, in "The Postwar Performance of the Motion Picture Industry," reports a larger increase in the rental rate, from 30 percent in 1948 to 46 percent in 1963.

57. Whitney, *The Motion Picture Industry,* pp. 170–171.

58. Whitney, in ibid., advanced these among other reasons.

59. Conant, *Antitrust in the Motion Picture Industry,* p. 151. The practice of competitive bidding was mandated by the lower court's 1946 decision in *Paramount,* but that requirement was abandoned by the Supreme Court in 1948.

60. The drop in capacity utilization is reported by Lamson, "Measured Productivity and Price Change," based on Census of Business data.

61. Crandall, in "The Postwar Performance of the Motion Picture Industry," finds the rise of rental rates until the late 1960s to be supporting evidence that the *Paramount* decision failed to quell tacit collusion among the major distributors.

62. Conant, *Antitrust in the Motion Picture Industry,* p. 170.

3. The Pay Media

1. *Cable Program Investor* (Kagan Research, LLC), July 16, 2004, p. 2, reports 34.8 million cable and 12.5 million noncable premium households for 2003, or 43.6 percent of all U.S. TV households.

2. Regarding premium channels, *TV Dimensions 2002* (New York: Media Dynamics, 2003), p. 186, estimates that 85 percent of all premium channel viewing is accounted for by "feature films." *Cable Program Investor* (July 16, 2004, p. 3) reports that 64.9 percent of all 2003 programming expenses of premium networks was for theatrical features. See Ray Richmond, "Home Movies: Theatricals Remain HBO's Programming Backbone," *Hollywood Reporter,* Nov. 2, 2002, p. 14, for discussion of the significance of theatrical films to pay TV networks. Regarding video, *TV Dimensions 2002,* p. 186 reports that 77 percent of all prerecorded video use is for feature films. Adams Media Research (*Hollywood Aftermarket,* Mar. 31, 2004, p. 6) reported that 78 percent of 2003 supplier revenue from video sales was for feature films. VSDA, *2002 Annual Report on the Home Entertainment Industry,* p. 18, states that 89 percent of all retail video rental volume is for theatrical features. Regarding à la carte pay television, *Cable Program Investor,* Sept. 29, 2004, p. 8, estimates that 39

percent of PPV/VOD spending is for theatrical features, the remainder being for events and adult programming.

3. Based on data supplied to the author by Adams Media Research. These statistics exclude "adult" subscription channels, and PPV and video purchases other than movies.

4. Movie media spending as a percentage of U.S. recreation expenditures rose from 3.1 percent in 1975 to 6.2 percent in 2002.

5. Deflation by the CPI is not necessarily the most meaningful index and is intended for illustration. Note that these data do not include revenues from television program production or other media activities that the studios developed over this period. They also exclude income from merchandise licensing rights. Domestic and international merchandise licensing collected by the studios was $2.9 billion in 2003 and has remained at about 6 percent of total distributor revenues from theatrical feature films since 1989. *Motion Picture Investor* (Kagan Research, LLC), Aug. 6, 2004, p. 4; Paul Kagan Associates, *The State of Home Video* (Carmel, Calif.: Paul Kagan Associates, 2000), p. 119.

6. The first major exception was *The Matrix Revolutions* (2003), which was released "day and date" (simultaneously) with standard theaters in November 2003. Gregory J. Wilcox, "Warner Bros. Pictures to Air *Matrix* Film in IMAX Format," *Daily News,* Apr. 24, 2003.

7. Michele Hilmes, *Hollywood and Broadcasting: From Radio to Cable* (Urbana: University of Illinois Press, 1990).

8. For discussion of these experiments, see Roger Noll, Merton Peck, and John McGowan, *Economic Aspects of Television Regulation* (Washington, D.C.: Brookings Institution, 1973).

9. Senate Committee on Interstate and Foreign Commerce, *Television Inquiry, Hearings,* 84th Cong., 2nd sess., 1956, Pt. 3. See especially the testimony of Richard Salant, CBS Vice president, pp. 1285–1307. Subcommittee on Communications and Power of the House Committee on Interstate and Foreign Commerce, *Subscription Television—1969, Hearings,* 90th Cong., 1st sess., 1969.

10. Until court rulings overturned them in the late 1970s, for example, FCC rules mandated that pay TV systems could not show theatrical movies that had been in theatrical release more than two years prior to cablecast. Stanley Besen and Robert Crandall, "The Deregulation of Cable Television," *Law and Contemporary Problems* 44 (1981): 77–124.

11. Author's calculation based on pay cable network ratings reported in Television Bureau of Advertising, *Cable Facts* (August 1984), p. 10, and

revenue/subscription data reported by Paul Kagan and by Christopher H. Sterling, *Electronic Media: A Guide to Trends in Broadcasting and Newer Technologies, 1920–1983* (New York: Praeger, 1984). Calculations assume two hours per movie and 2.0 pay networks per household.

12. The Hartford and other early experiments were all PPV, and speculation at the 1956 and 1969 congressional hearings on pay TV seemed to presume that model. Noll, Peck, and McGowan's detailed economic analysis of the prospects for pay TV, published in 1973 (two years before HBO's national satellite launch), was the first to demonstrate the basic revenue potential of pay TV (and was remarkably prescient on the future of home video), but these authors do not appear to have even mentioned the monthly subscription model.

13. *Hollywood Aftermarket,* June 30, 2004, p. 3: $8.4 billion for premium networks versus $0.8 billion for PPV movies. SVOD is a service for premium network subscribers and is included in that category.

14. *Cable Program Investor,* July 16, 2004, p. 3.

15. *Motion Picture Investor,* Aug. 6, 2004, reported studio revenues of $422 million from all PPV/VOD and $1.398 billion from subscription TV in 2003, which implies a 23.2 percent share of total pay TV studio revenues from PPV/VOD.

16. In 1999, premium cable households subscribed to an average of 2.3 networks (*www.ncta.com,* accessed April 25, 2004).

17. This statement relies on the reasonable assumption that the rate of subscription movie viewership in multipay households rises more slowly than does that number of available movies as additional channels are subscribed.

18. Peter C. Fishburn, Andrew Odlyzko, and Ryan Siders, "Fixed Fee versus Unit Pricing for Information Goods: Competition, Equilibria, and Price Wars," in Brian Kahin and Hal Varian, eds., *Internet Publishing and Beyond* (Cambridge, Mass.: MIT Press, 2000), pp. 167–189.

19. A sparse economic literature on option demand has debated the notion of whether consumers receive a distinct value from having the option of consuming a product or service (e.g., hospital service, telephone calls) whenever desired, but these authors generally assume that a positive marginal price will be paid at the time of consumption. See especially Richard Schmalensee, "Output and Welfare Implications of Monopolistic Third Degree Price Discrimination," *American Economic Review* 71 (1981): 242–247; and Bridger M. Mitchell, "Optimal Pricing of Local Telephone Service," *American Economic Review* 68 (September 1978): 517–537.

20. Stefano DellaVigna and Ulrike Malmendier, "Overestimating Self-Control: Evidence from the Health Club Industry" (NBER working paper, W10819, October 2004).

21. George Stigler first developed a version of this familiar model. See George J. Stigler, "A Note on Block Bundling," in Philip B. Kurland, ed., *The Supreme Court Review* (Chicago: University of Chicago Press, 1963). Gregory S. Crawford, "The Discriminatory Incentives to Bundle in the Cable Television Industry" (working paper, Department of Economics, University of Arizona, 2004) empirically demonstrates its validity in the case of bundling basic cable television channels into tiers.

22. An exception is the theater double feature. In nearly all cases, however, double features combined A with B movies, implying a positive, rather than negative, correlation between patron tastes for the same movies, which is a necessary condition for value averaging to work.

23. An early analytical treatment of "mixed bundling" is William James Adams and Janet L. Yellen, "Commodity Bundling and the Burden of Monopoly," *Quarterly Journal of Economics* 90 (August 1976): 475–498. These authors do not, however, consider the trade-offs between intertemporal and simultaneous mixed bundling. The principles demonstrated in the text example to follow were developed theoretically by Nancy L. Stokey, "Intertemporal Price Discrimination," *Quarterly Journal of Economics* 93 (August 1979): 355–371, and to our knowledge have not previously been interpreted in terms of a numerical application. See also Nancy L. Stokey, "Rational Expectations and Durable Goods Pricing," *Bell Journal of Economics* 12 (Spring 1981): 112–128.

24. For example, if the original "value averaging" in the first North–West example were modified so that the North family would pay $9 for *Daredevil* but had zero demand for *Chicago*, while the Wests' demands were unchanged, the seller could collect a maximum of $12 with à la carte pricing (at a price of either $4 or $6) and a maximum of $18 with bundling only (at a price of $9). By offering the bundle at $10 or an à la carte purchase of either movie at $9 simultaneously, however, the seller could earn $19 ($10 from the Wests and $9 from the Norths).

25. A. Michael Noll, *Television Technology: Fundamentals and Future Prospects* (Norwood, Mass.: Artech House, 1988).

26. Jeffrey A. Hart, *Television, Technology, and Competition: HDTV and Digital TV in the United States, Western Europe, and Japan* (New York: Cambridge University Press, 2004).

27. Erik Gruenwedel, "Does Wall Street Hate Video Rental?" *Video Store Magazine,* May 2, 2004, p. 1.

28. Hal R. Varian, "Buying, Sharing, and Renting Information Goods," *Journal of Industrial Economics* 48 (December 2000): 473–488, shows theoretical conditions under which renting and consumer sharing of information products, such as videos or books, may be more or less profitable to producers and may serve as market segmentation devices.

29. Row (4) ÷ (1); that is, net supplier revenues as a fraction of consumer spending for combined DVD and VHS rentals and for combined DVD and VHS sales respectively. Average turns per video estimated by the author based on retail transactions and rental units sold in 2002, as reported by Adams Media Research.

30. Most video stores charge the same rental prices for DVD and for VHS, but a greater proportion of less expensive catalog titles are on VHS, leading to a higher realized average price for DVDs.

31. Judith McCourt, "Buying Habits Change with March of DVDs," *Video Store Magazine*, Sept. 8, 2002, p. 8.

32. Marie-Louise Mares, "Children's Use of VCRs," *Annals of the American Academy of Political and Social Science* 557 (May 1998): 120–131; see also Emily Yoffe, "Play It Again, Mom (Again and Again . . .)," *NYT*, July 13, 2003, Section 2, p. 9.

33. Video Store Magazine, *2002 Consumer Entertainment Study*, question 45 ("How many times would you say that you or someone in your household watched a video that you purchased?").

34. In three years for which we had separate data for sales and rentals, 1992–1994, Disney averaged a 27.9 percent market share of sales revenue; the next highest was a 11.9 percent share for Warner Brothers (Paul Kagan Associates, *Video Investor*, Oct. 3, 1995, p. 8; Feb. 28, 1993, p. 2). Sales rankings are from "Everything You Always Wanted to Know about "A" Titles but Didn't Know Who to Ask," *Video Store Magazine*, 5th ed. (1997), p. SU-1.

35. In the 2002 *Video Store Magazine* survey, 19 percent replied that their usual intention in buying DVDs was for children under twelve, versus 38 percent for VHS. See McCourt, "Buying Habits Change with March of DVDs."

36. Disney's share of VHS sales has been consistently higher than its share of DVD sales. For example, Disney had a 37.1 percent share of the VHS sales market in 2003, though only a 24.4 percent share of the overall video market (*Hollywood Aftermarket*, Mar. 31, 2004, p. 5). Disney's share of VHS sales has also been far highter than VHS rentals: for 2003, Disney earned only a 4.4 percent market share of the latter market. Available data indicate that in 2004 Disney relinquished its overall lead of the

video market, earning a 17.3 percent share of revenues versus 20.2 percent for Warner (*Home Media Retailing,* Jan. 16–22, 2005, p. 22).

37. The lowest category on the MPAA's annual audience survey, *www.mpaa.org* (accessed Oct. 10, 2004), is ages twelve to fifteen; examination of a selection of theater audience surveys dating back to the 1940s indicates twelve years to be the earliest reported age.

38. Laura M. Holson and Geraldine Fabrikant, "Disney Chief to Leave, Setting Off Race for Job," *NYT,* Sept. 11, 2004, p. A1.

39. Timothy M. Gray, "At One with the Cult of the DVD," *Variety,* Jan. 6, 2003, p. 52.

40. Wilson Rothman, "I Don't Rent. I Own," *NYT,* Feb. 26, 2004, p. G1.

41. McCourt, "Buying Habits Change with March of DVDs."

42. Video Store Magazine, *2002 Consumer Entertainment Study,* question 35.

43. The 2002 survey results in this paragraph are reported by McCourt, "Buying Habits Change with March of DVDs."

44. Judith McCourt, "Consumers Continue to Buy DVD, with Men Leading the Way," *Video Store Magazine,* June 13–19, 2004, p. 28.

45. Jennifer Netherby, "4Q Packed and Ready to Go; Blockbusters Will Drive Spending for the Holidays," *Video Business,* Aug. 4, 2003, p. 7.

46. Joel Waldfogel, "The Deadweight Loss of Christmas," *American Economic Review* 83 (December 1993): 1328–1336.

47. P. J. Huffstutter, "Coming to a DVD Player Near You," *Los Angeles Times,* Apr. 19, 2003, p. C1.

48. Thomas K. Arnold, "Many Say Market Demise of VHS Is Imminent," *Video Store Magazine,* Dec. 21, 2003; "VHS Prepares to Exit the Industry It Built," *Hollywood Aftermarket,* Jan. 30, 2004, p. 2.

49. Seth Goldstein, "Image Acquires Crane Web Unit," *Billboard,* Sept. 5, 1998, p. 10; Eileen Fitzpatrick, "Laserdisc Wholesaler Closes, a Victim of DVD," *Billboard,* May 23, 1998, p. 75.

50. The economics of quality segmentation is developed theoretically by Michael Mussa and Sherwin Rosen, "Monopoly and Product Quality," *Journal of Economic Theory* 18 (August 1978): 301–317. For an exposition of this article and later contributions, see Hal Varian, "Price Discrimination," in Richard Schmalensee and Robert D. Willig, eds., *Handbook of Industrial Organization* (New York: Elsevier Science, 1989), pp. 597–654. For recent extensions and application, see Sherwin Rosen and Andrew M. Rosenfield, "Ticket Pricing," *Journal of Law and Economics* 40 (October 1997): 351–376. The model we present employs basic assumptions that are consistent with the established theory.

51. A fundamental assumption of this model, consistent with the original

theoretical development by Mussa and Rosen in "Monopoly and Product Quality" is that the high-value consumer must not only have a higher absolute demand for the high-quality product, but a higher marginal demand for quality as well.

52. It is evident that the infamous Beta versus VHS format war of the 1970s and 1980s was a drain on industry resources because the quality differences were noticeable to few consumers, permitting no profitable segmentation. James Lardner, *Fast Forward: Hollywood, the Japanese, and the Onslaught of the VCR* (New York: Norton, 1987). It seems clear that quality differences in the brewing Blu-ray versus HD-DVD high-definition DVD contest of the early 2000s are also insufficient to justify the costs of maintaining both.

53. For a detailed history of the period, see Lardner, *Fast Forward*). See also congressional testimony on the first-sale doctrine: *Audio and Video Rental: Hearing before the Subcommittee on Patents, Copyrights, and Trademarks of the Committee on the Judiciary,* Senate Hearing 98-412, 98th Cong., 1st sess. (1983), S. 32 and S. 33, 9–59; and *Record Rental Amendment of 1984,* Report 98-987, 98th Cong., 2nd sess. (1984), 1–10.

54. Martin Peers and John Lippman, "AOL Time Warner Video Chief Quits," *WSJ,* Dec. 23, 2002, p. A3.

55. *Hollywood Aftermarket* (Dec. 31, 2004, p. 4) reports 2004 rental transactions to be 3.2 billion, compared to 1.2 billion video sales, or a rentals-to-sales ratio of approximately 2.75 (preliminary data).

56. Children aged two to eleven were reported to make up 19 percent of all rental-tape viewership in 1995, while they accounted for 14 percent of the general television population. *VCR Diary Study,* October–December 1995, Table 9.

57. According to the VSDA, *2003 Annual Report on the Home Entertainment Industry,* p. 19, 61 percent of VHS and 15 percent of DVD rental volume involved revenue sharing plans. Lardner, *Fast Forward,* also discusses the early history of revenue sharing.

58. Julie Holland Mortimer, "The Effects of Revenue-Sharing Contracts on Welfare in Vertically-Separated Markets: Evidence from the Video Rental Industry," (working paper, Department of Economics, University of California, Los Angeles, 2002). For statistical analysis of video revenue sharing contracts, see also James D. Dana, Jr., and Kathryn E. Spier, "Revenue Sharing and Vertical Control in the Video Rental Industry," *Journal of Industrial Economics* 49 (September 2001): 223–245.

59. The example to follow shows how profits and video availability to con-

sumers are improved by the elimination of double marginalization. Dana and Spier, "Revenue Sharing," and Mortimer, "The Effects of Revenue-Sharing Contracts," discuss this factor, but their papers focus on efficiencies from reduction of uncertainty, retail inventory decisions, and other parameters in revenue sharing contracts.

60. VSDA, *2003 Annual Report on the Home Entertainment Industry* reported average new release prices of $3.05 and catalog prices of $1.99 in 2001, based on a retailer survey.

61. Ibid., p. 17; Geraldine Fabrikant, "Blockbuster Settles Suits on Late Fees," *NYT,* June 6, 2001, p. C1.

62. Fabrikant, "Blockbuster Settles Suits on Late Fees."

63. Holly J. Wagner, "Blockbuster Nixes Late Fees," *Video Store Magazine,* Dec. 19–25, 2004, p. 1.

64. *Hollywood Aftermarket,* Sept. 30, 2004, p. 2 reported mail-order video to account for approximately 5 percent of the video rental market.

65. Stephanie Prange, "What Happens If Retailers Subscribe? Trend toward Subscription Rental Model Could Threaten Revenue from Late Fees," *Video Store Magazine,* July 6, 2003, p. 1.

66. Owen McDonald, "Buy-Backs Gain Favor with Industry," *Video Store Magazine,* Apr. 4, 1999, p. 1.

67. For general analysis of used-goods markets and how they affect profits and strategies of the sellers of new products, see Michael Waldman, "Eliminating the Market for Secondhand Goods: An Alternative Explanation for Leasing," *Journal of Law and Economics* 40 (April 1997): 61–92; and Igal Hendel and Alessandro Lizzeri, "Interfering with Secondary Markets," *RAND Journal of Economics* 30 (Spring 1999): 1–21; and Stanley J. Liebowitz, "Durability, Market Structure, and New-Used Goods Models," *American Economic Review* 72 (September 1982): 816–824.

68. Adams Media Research reports $1.1 billion in used video sales versus $12.7 billion total sales in the United States for 2003 (*Hollywood Aftermarket,* Feb. 27, 2004, p. 3).

69. Holly J. Wagner, "Blockbuster Testing Used Video Trading," *Video Store Magazine,* Feb. 23, 2003, p. 1; Enrique Rivero, "Blockbuster to Dive into Used-DVD Trades," *Video Store Magazine,* Jan. 11, 2004, p. 3.

70. Stephanie Prange, "Many Consumers Engage in Free DVD Trading," *Video Store Magazine,* May 9, 2004, p. 6.

71. Seth Goldstein, "Where Do Used Tapes Go?" *Video Store Magazine,* July 15, 2001, p. 1.

72. Kurt Indvik, "Rev-Share Offers Must Deal with Previewed Selloff Real-

ity," *Video Store Magazine,* Mar. 30, 2003, p. 3. Retailers report that buy-back programs had greatly diminished by 2004 as the used video retail market expanded.

73. For a statistical analysis of First Sale's welfare effects in the video market, see Julie Holland Mortimer, "Price Discrimination and Copyright Law: Evidence from the Introduction of DVDs" (working paper, Department of Economics, Harvard University, 2003). The argument in this section is developed from David Waterman, "Electronic Media and the Economics of the First Sale Doctrine," in Robert Thorne, and John David Viera, eds., *Entertainment, Publishing, and the Arts Handbook* (New York: Clark Boardman and Co., 1987), pp. 3–13.

74. Statement of Nina W. Cornell before the Senate Judiciary Committee on Repeal of the First Sale Doctrine, Apr. 29, 1983, Senate, *Audio and Video First Sale Doctrine: Hearings on S.32,* 98th Cong., 1st sess., 1983, pp. 233–265. For relevant legal perspectives on First Sale, see I. Neel Chatterjee, "Imperishable Intellectual Creations: The Limits of the First Sale Doctrine," *Fordham Intellectual Property, Media and Entertainment Law Journal* 5 (1995): 383; and Richard Colby, "The First Sale Doctrine—the Defense That Never Was?" *Journal of the Copyright Society of the U.S.A.* (1985): 77–107.

75. *Audio and Video Rental: Hearing before the Subcommittee on Patents, Copyrights, and Trademarks of the Committee on the Judiciary,* U.S. Senate; "Record Rental Amendment of 1984: Report 98–987."

76. During the very early days of VCR penetration in the 1970s, the studios apparently did not at first expect there would be a rental market and expressed some interest in eliminating it, but they soon realized that the overwhelming consumer demand was for rentals; Lardner, *Fast Forward.*

77. Statement of Nina W. Cornell before the Senate Judiciary Committee on Repeal of the First Sale Doctrine, Apr. 29, 1983; "A No-Win War in Videocassettes," *Business Week,* May 24, 1982, p. 152; Peter M. Nichols, "Home Video," *NYT,* Mar. 24, 1995, p. B17.

78. Testimony of Alan Hirschfield before the Senate Judiciary Committee on Repeal of the First Sale Doctrine, 1983, pp. 171–211.

79. For example, Paramount Pictures tried to provide rental tapes to certain "authorized dealers" and differently priced sales tapes to certain other dealers. The result was that the rental dealers bought the cheaper tapes from the other dealers (a practice known in the trade as "sideways selling"). Note that leasing rental tapes does not solve the distributor's pricing problem. The result of leasing is that the rental tapes cannot be sold by the stores without the distributor's consent, but if only leasing is

done, there can be no sales market. If the distributor also tries to release low-priced videos to the stores for the sale market, the stores can then rent those tapes.

80. Available data indicate that in 2001, net VHS shipments to sell-through were 539 million, 27 million of which were shipped to rental stores. *Hollywood Aftermarket,* July 26, 2002, p. 3.

81. This predicted result of effective rental and sales market segmentation is complicated by other factors. For example, rising rental prices would increase demand for sales, encouraging sales prices also to rise. The availability of fewer sell-through DVDs for rental would tend to increase their used sale prices, in turn affecting both rental and new sales prices.

82. See Screen Digest Ltd., *European Video: Market Assessment and Forecast, 2002* (London: Screen Digest Ltd., 2002); Jessica Wolf, "Fox's Two-Tiered Pricing Plan Worries U.K. Retailers," *Video Store Magazine,* Jan. 26, 2003, p. 18; and Paul Sweeting, "Code Red?" *Video Business,* Apr. 21, 2003, p. 10.

83. Liran Einav and Barak Y. Orbach, "Uniform Prices for Differentiated Goods: The Case of the Movie-Theater Industry" (working paper, Stanford University, 2005), speculates on the reasons for this phenomenon. For an industry perspective, see Bruce Orwall, "Mr. Bronfman Finds Running a Film Studio Isn't Business as Usual," *WSJ,* Apr. 3, 1998, p. 1.

84. For a discussion, see Louis Phlips, *The Economics of Price Discrimination* (New York: Cambridge University Press, 1983), pp. 215–216.

85. Tom King, "Would You Really See *X-Men* Twice?" *WSJ,* July 21, 2000, p. W1, reported an informal survey in which 10 percent of respondents volunteered that they had seen a film twice since the beginning of the year.

86. "Network Prime Time Movies," *TV Program Stats* (Carmel, Calif.: Paul Kagan Associates), Feb. 28, 1990, p. 1. John Dempsey, "Theatricals Rate Second Look," *Variety,* Sept. 20–26, 1999, p. 33.

87. Catering to theater patrons of the same film has become a component of video release strategies. See Peter M. Nichols, "Land of the Cineplex, Home of the Cassette," *NYT,* July 13, 1997, section 2, p. 1; Joan Villa, "Blockbuster Tests Rent-before-Buy Program," *Video Store Magazine,* Mar. 31, 2002, p. 8.

88. Mike Pearson, "Second *Rings* a Real Treat, Offers Many Extras," *Bloomington Herald-Times,* Nov. 14, 2003, p. C1.

89. Anthony Breznican, "*Beauty and the Beast* Bulks Up for Re-Release on Giant Screens," *Associated Press Worldstream,* Jan. 3, 2002.

4. Controlling the Release Sequence

1. Nielsen EDI Summary Database; see Appendix E.

2. An econometric study of the video window by David Waterman and Sung-Choon Lee, "The Intertemporal Distribution of Media Products: An Empirical Study of the 'Video Window'" (working paper, Department of Telecommunications, Indiana University, Dec. 17, 2002), used an earlier dataset for 1988–1997 to show a median out-of-market period of 83 days, but the average time between the date by which 95 percent of theatrical revenues had been received and the video release date was 123 days, indicating a relatively long period during which residual revenues from theaters trickle in to distributors.

3. Jill Kipnis, "Hollywood Speeds Films to Home DVD Market," *Billboard,* May 3, 2003, p. 1; Marcy Magiera, "Longer Theatrical, Video Windows Sought," *Video Business,* Nov. 8, 1996, p. 6; Seth Goldstein, "Home Video Finds a Lower Spot on Media Food Chain," *Billboard,* Oct. 25, 1997, p. 72.

4. Ronald H. Coase, "Durability and Monopoly," *Journal of Law and Economics* 15 (April 1972): 143–149.

5. A large theoretical literature on time consistency and devices that firms can use to cope with it has developed. Jeremy Bulow, "Durable-Goods Monopolists," *Journal of Political Economy* 90 (April 1982): 314–332 formalized the Coase conjecture to establish conditions under which the time-consistency problem would occur and, building on ideas in Coase, showed how it could be avoided through leasing and other devices. Notable among other theoretical papers are Lawrence M. Ausubel and Raymond J. Deneckere, "One Is Almost Enough for Monopoly," *RAND Journal of Economics* 18 (Summer 1987): 255–274; David A. Butz, "Durable-Goods Monopoly and Best-Price Provisions," *American Economic Review* 80 (December 1990): 1062–1076; Lisa N. Takeyama, "Strategic Vertical Differentiation and Durable Goods Monopoly," *Journal of Industrial Economics* 50 (March 2002): 43–56; and Nancy L. Stokey, "Rational Expectations and Durable Goods Pricing," *Bell Journal of Economics* 12 (Spring 1981): 112–128. See Waterman and Lee, "The Intertemporal Distribution of Media Products" for a more thorough literature review.

6. See especially Michael Waldman, "Durable Goods Theory for Real World Markets," *Journal of Economic Perspectives* 17 (Winter 2003): 131–154.

7. Michael Conant, *Antitrust in the Motion Picture Industry* (Berkeley: University of California Press, 1960); *The Motion Picture Industry Study*

(Washington, D.C.: prepared for the Office of National Recovery Administration, Division of Review, 1936).

8. Conant, *Antitrust in the Motion Picture Industry.*

9. This paragraph is based on a compilation from the *Chicago Tribune* by the author for the eleven movies that opened in Chicago Loop theaters during the week of February 17–25, 1939. In all eleven cases, the three-week initial clearance was adhered to. However, while all movies opened in only one theater, many more downstream theaters played the most popular films. Although no exceptions to the three-week post-Loop-run clearance were observed, the Chicago Film Board could presumably make such exceptions.

10. Conant, *Antitrust in the Motion Picture Industry; The Motion Picture Industry Study.* The boards were ruled illegal by the courts in 1932 under antitrust law, but were then reconstituted to be (or at least to appear to be) less exclusionary of independent exhibitors. The boards were finally outlawed when the Supreme Court ruled in the 1948 *Paramount* decision that they were in violation of the Sherman Act.

11. See especially Conant, *Antitrust in the Motion Picture Industry;* and Simon Whitney, "The Motion Picture Industry," in *Antitrust Policies: American Experience in Twenty Industries* (New York: Twentieth Century Fund, 1958).

12. Although Conant, in *Antitrust in the Motion Picture Industry,* identified the movie release system as intertemporal price discrimination, the issues of time consistency and of maintaining consumer expectations were not discussed.

13. R. Thomas Umstead, "Paramount Windows Will Average 60 Days," *Multichannel News,* Dec. 6, 1993, p. 56.

14. Calculation by the author from Jill Goldsmith, "H'w'd Vexed by Plex Success," *Variety,* May 17, 2004, p. 1.

15. Bjorn Frank, "Optimal Timing of Movie Releases in Ancillary Markets: The Case of Video Releases," *Journal of Cultural Economics* 18 (1994): 125–133; Kagan World Media, *Kagan's European Home Video* (London: Kagan World Media, 1994); Screen Digest Ltd., *European Video: Market Assessment and Forecast* (London: Screen Digest, 2002).

16. Kagan World Media, *Kagan's European Home Video.* Among reports of the general relaxation of European video windows, the legally mandated theater-to-video interval in France was reported to be 6 months as of 2001, down from 9 months in 1996 (Henry Samuel, "DVD Propels France

Vid Figs to Record '01," *Hollywood Reporter,* Feb. 8, 2002). *Screen Digest* (monthly) periodically reports window trends.

17. Kagan World Media, *Kagan's European Home Video.*

18. Joseph Steuer, "NATO to Studios: Pause a Bit before Playing Vids," *Hollywood Reporter,* Oct. 24, 1996, p. 1.

19. Ibid.

20. A series of articles around this time described the NATO initiatives. See especially Monica Roman, "NATO Prexy at Issue with Vid Window: NATO Hears Warning at Confab," *Daily Variety,* Oct. 24, 1996, p. 1; and Jeffrey Daniels, "Kartozian Urges Exhibs to Build with 'Prudence'" *Hollywood Reporter,* Mar. 5, 1997.

21. Magiera, "Longer Theatrical, Video Windows Sought."

22. Note that windows over 365 days are excluded from Figure 4.2. During this period, there was only one such movie (*Wonder Boys,* at 382 days). The windows for 40.8 percent (119 movies) of the 292 movies released in 2001–2002 fell within plus or minus 10 percent (16.5 days) of the 165-day median. The windows for 66.4 percent (194 movies) of the movies fell within 20 percent of the median.

23. As mentioned in Chapter 3, airlines, hotels, and a few other outlets exhibit the movie during this interval, but together these accounted for only 0.4 percent of total distributor domestic revenues from theatrical film release in 2002 (*Motion Picture Investor,* Kagan World Media, Sept. 12, 2003, p. 4).

24. Kipnis, "Hollywood Speeds Films to Home DVD Market."

25. As shown in Appendix E, there was a .70 inverse correlation between length of the video window and the out-of-market gap, but only a .07 correlation between theater run length and the video window. Multivariate regression results reported in Waterman and Lee, "The Intertemporal Distribution of Media Products," for movies released during the period 1988–1997 and having run lengths of twelve weeks or less indicate a strongly negative relationship between window length and the out-of-market gap, but a statistically insignificant relationship between window length and theater run length.

26. For a discussion, see Thomas K. Arnold, "Date Dance Begins for Q4," *Video Store Magazine,* Aug. 15, 2004, p. 3.

27. Liran Einav, "Not All Rivals Look Alike: Estimating an Equilibrium Model of the Release Date Timing Game" (working paper, Department of Economics, Stanford University, Aug. 12, 2003).

28. Waterman and Lee, "The Intertemporal Distribution of Media Products."

29. "Coppola Plans *Apocalypse* as TV Long-Form," *Variety,* Nov. 21, 1980, p. 1.

30. For example, Coppola ordered that there be no bragging about the film's three Golden Globe awards in its consumer marketing campaign. Will Tusher, "Coppola Orders No Golden Globe Boasting in Ads for *Apocalypse*," *Variety,* Feb. 1, 1980, p. 6.

31. Joan Villa, "Theatrical-to-Video Windows Shrinking," *Video Store Magazine,* Mar. 16, 2003, p. 1; Kipnis, "Hollywood Speeds Films to Home DVD Market"; Jessica Wolf, "Columbia Has Had Shortest Theatrical-to-Video Windows," *Video Store Magazine,* May 16, 2004, p. 8; *www.imdb.com* (accessed October 4, 2004).

32. Melinda Saccone, "The Incredible Shrinking Theatrical-to-DVD Window," *Video Store Magazine,* Jan. 2–8, 2005, pp. 1, 29.

33. "McDowall Films Siezed in Piracy Investigation," *NYT,* Jan. 18, 1975, p. 31.

34. "McDowall Cleared by U.S. of Film Piracy Connection," *NYT,* June 3, 1975, p. 25.

35. The MPAA Web site *(www.mpaa.org)* describes a wide variety of specific piracy methods.

36. David Pauly and Lucy Howard, "Crime: The Film Pirates," *Newsweek,* Oct. 17, 1977, p. 90.

37. MPAA, "Film and Video Piracy: It's a Crime," Apr. 29, 1996.

38. See Goeffrey A. Fowler, "Hollywood's Burning Issue: Film Pirates Now Make Copies on Cheap, Mobile Burners; Like a 'Thousand Cockroaches,'" *WSJ,* Sept. 18, 2003, p. B1.

39. "Razors without Blades," *Forbes,* Aug. 20, 1979, p. 40. The going rate to "rent" a 35 mm film print from a theater projectionist was reported to be $300–$500 (Alexander L. Taylor III, "Hollywood's War on Video Pirates; Real-Life Swashbucklers Are Trying to Rip Off This Summer's Hits," *Time,* June 6, 1983, p. 44).

40. Lisa Belkin, "On the Trail of Pirated Video Cassettes," *NYT,* May 18, 1987, p. C13. Jack Valenti, then president of the MPAA, was also quoted in the article as saying that the MPAA estimated that 5 to 10 percent of videocassettes in U.S. video stores were counterfeit copies. The studios earned $1.9 billion from video distribution of theatrical features in 1987 (Appendix C), which results in a proportional loss estimate of 10.5 percent to 15.8 percent.

41. In general, piracy loss estimates should be interpreted with caution. See Stanley M. Besen, "New Technologies and Intellectual Property: An Economic Analysis" (Rand Note N-2601-NSF, May 1986), for a discussion

of common flaws in copyright loss estimates. Loss estimates published by the National Cable Television Association are discussed later in this chapter.

42. "Almost 18,000 Pirate Videos Seized Nationwide; 49 Stores Raided in 4-Day Period," press release, Dec. 8, 1995, *www.mpaa.org* (accessed May 21, 2002); "Film Studios Settle Legal Action against Internet Pirate," press release, June 13, 2001, *www.mpaa.org* (accessed Dec. 12, 2002). From 1995 to 2001, distributor revenue from domestic distribution of theatrical features on videocassettes rose from $6.2 billion to $8.3 billion (Appendix C).

43. For a reader-friendly discussion of DRM technology and its implications for consumers, see Mike Godwin, *What Every Citizen Should Know about DRM, a.k.a. "Digital Rights Management"* (Washington, D.C.: Public Knowledge; New American Foundation, 2004).

44. Matt Lake, "How It Works: Tweaking Technology to Stay Ahead of Film Pirates," *NYT*, Aug. 2, 2001, p. G9. See also "Preserving an Effective DVD Copy Protection System," March 2003, *www.macrovision.com* (accessed Oct. 6, 2004).

45. Diane Mermigas, "Television Feeling Heat of Illegal Copying," *Electronic Media*, Apr. 9, 2001, p. 15; Curtis Lee Fulton, "Intel and AOL Back Mandated Watermark Detection System," *Online Reporter*, June 3, 2002.

46. Fowler, "Hollywood's Burning Issue."

47. MPAA, "First Ever DVD Burner Lab Raided in New York," press release, Mar. 22, 2002, *www.mpaa.org* (accessed May 21, 2002).

48. Fowler, "Hollywood's Burning Issue."

49. Felix Oberholzer and Koleman Strumpf, "The Effects of File Sharing on Record Sales: An Empirical Analysis" (Harvard Business School working paper, 2004) reach the same conclusion for the music industry case.

50. "Cable Theft," *www.ncta.com* (accessed Apr. 25, 2004).

51. The Carmel Group, according to *Screen Digest*, April 2003, p. 124, estimated losses of 4.6 percent ($543 million) for 2002, and growing. Christopher Keough, "DirecTV Gets Aggressive on Signals Theft," *Los Angeles Business Journal*, Dec. 17, 2001, p. 14, reported a piracy loss estimate of $300 million in 2001, or approximately 5 percent of industry revenues. David Lieberman, "Millions of Pirates Are Plundering Satellite TV," *USA Today*, Dec. 2, 2002, p. 1A, stated that there were one to three million illegal DBS subscribers in the United States, which translates to between about 5 percent and 16 percent of total legal DBS subscribers.

52. Among a number of case studies, two available from the Broadband and

Internet Security Task Force (BISTF) reported that a Time Warner Memphis tap audit in 1998 resulted in a 29.6 percent conversion rate; a series of audits by Time Warner Syracuse over the 1995–2001 period resulted in a 26.7 percent conversion of illegal to legal basic service subscribers: *www.broadbandsecurity.bigstep.com* (accessed Oct. 28, 2003). The NCTA's *Ninth Annual Signal Security Ideas Competition, 1996* and *Signal Security Handbook, 1996* report comparable conversion rates, as do press reports of other case studies. See Mark Ribbing, "Comcast Lets Cable Pirates off the Hook," *Baltimore Sun,* Mar. 9, 1998, p. 9C; and "Cable Gets Serious about Theft," *Television Digest,* July 9, 2001.

53. More recently, as permitted by the DMCA, some cable operators have reverted to a strategy of demanding large restitution payments from premium cable thieves in lieu of prosecution. One press report indicated that in 2000 a major operator, Cablevision, identified 5,000 households that it alleged were illegally receiving premium cable service. Of these, 2,000 households were reported to have paid between $1,500 and $3,000 each in response to a letter demanding such payments as an alternative to court prosecution. In one of the cases studies reported on the BISTF Web site, Time Warner of South Carolina claimed that it collected $377,000 in settlements from 357 illegal pay cable receivers that it confronted with the alternative of prosecution (*www.broadbandsecurity* *.bigstep.com,* accessed Oct. 28, 2003).

54. Jennifer Lee, "In Satellite Piracy War, Battles on Many Fronts," *NYT,* May 9, 2002, p. G1.

55. "Cable Industry Pushing for New Anti-Piracy Laws," *Communications Daily,* Jan. 24, 2000. For discussion of similar evidence, see David Waterman, "The Political Economy of Audio-Visual Copyright Enforcement" (working paper, Department of Telecommunications, Indiana University, Mar. 22, 2005).

56. Ronald A. Taylor and Gordon M. Bock, "War against Pay-TV Pirates Heats Up," *U.S. News and World Report,* Dec. 12, 1983, p. 80.

57. Ibid.

58. Gardner F. Gillespie, James J. Moore, and David L. Littleton, "Cable Decoder Piracy White Paper Update: A Summary of Federal Law in the Cable Industry's Anti-Piracy Arsenal" (paper prepared for Hogan and Hartson LLP, 1995); *Intellectual Property and Fast Track Authority: Hearing before the Senate Judiciary Committee Subcommittee on Patents, Copyrights and Trademarks,* 102nd Cong., 1st sess., 1991.

59. See Title I, 17 U.S.C. §1201–1204 (1998).

60. Edmund Mander and Matt Buckler, "Cable TV Amnesty Offer Brings in

80 Violators," *Enfield (Connecticut) Journal Enquirer,* Mar. 8, 1993, Business, p. 1.

61. See Linda Haugsted, "Operators Join Together to Fight Piracy," *Multichannel News,* July 25, 1994, p. 80.

62. See, for example, "Cable Gets Serious about Theft."

63. Charles Haddad, "Upgrade in Thievery Accompanies Digital Cable," *Atlanta Journal and Constitution,* Jan. 6, 2000, p. 1A.

64. See especially Lawrence Lessig, *Free Culture: How Big Media Uses Technology and the Law to Lock Down Culture and Control Creativity* (New York: Penguin Press, 2004); Lawrence Lessig, *The Future of Ideas: The Fate of the Commons in a Connected World* (New York: Random House, 2001); and *Assessing Consumer Access to Digital Entertainment on the Internet and Other Media: Hearing before House Commerce Committee Subcommittee on Telecommunications, Trade and Consumer Protection,* 106th Cong., 1st sess., Oct. 28, 1999 (testimony of Gary Klein).

65. James Lardner, *Fast Forward: Hollywood, the Japanese, and the Onslaught of the VCR* (New York: Norton, 1987); Wendy Gordon, "Fair Use as Market Failure: A Structural and Economic Analysis of the Betamax Case and Its Predecessors," *Columbia Law Review* 82 (December 1982): 1600–1657.

66. "New DVD-VCR Combo, *Video Store Magazine,* Aug. 6, 2000, p. 10.

67. Macrovision Corp., *Home Taping in America—How High Is the Risk of Consumer Copying?* (presentation to the VSDA, April 2000). Data cited later in the text are from several Macrovision surveys conducted from 1993 to 2000, some of them funded by the VSDA. Macrovision and VSDA generally have an economic incentive to present pay TV and PPV piracy and copying problems as severe, and Macrovision has an incentive to indicate that back-to-back video copying of unprotected videos and DVDs is high. In our judgment, the methodological integrity of the Macrovision studies, which were primarily conducted to influence movie studio decision making rather than to lobby legislators, is exceptionally high for privately conducted surveys.

68. This account of the Go-Video story is based on press reports. See especially "Motion Picture Association of America Drops Its Opposition to Go-Video's Dual-Deck Videocassette Recorder," *Business Wire,* Sept. 29, 1988; and "The Future of the VCR: The Record," *The Record,* Mar. 12, 1989, p. 75.

69. DMCA, Section 1201(k).

70. Macrovision Corp., "Pay-Per-View Movie Piracy and Taping in the Home Video Market" (Chilton Research Services, prepared for the VSDA, July 8, 1996), p. 5.

71. Macrovision Corp., "Home Taping in America: The Second National Survey of VCR Owners, Summary Report" (prepared by Schulman, Ronca, and Bucuvalas, 1993), p. 2, reported 6.5 percent in 1990 and 6.6 percent consumer copying rates in 1993. U.S. Office of Technology Assessment (OTA), "Copyright and Home Copying: Technology Challenges the Law," 1989," Tables 12-14, 12-16 indicate that 3.9 percent of VCR owners had copied a prerecorded tape in the past year.

72. Macrovision Corp., "Home Taping in America: The Third National Survey of VCR Owners, Summary of Findings" (prepared by Schulman, Ronca, and Bucuvalas, October 1996), p. 3.

73. OTA, "Copyright and Home Copying," p. 162.

74. Macrovision, "Home Taping in America: The Second National Survey," p. 18.

75. As a general rule, survey respondents tend to overestimate the likelihood that they will buy a product. At the same time, the surveys do not consider the likelihood that low-value consumers would otherwise watch a movie at a later point in the sequence. Also, as we discuss later, those who copy may be more willing to pay to rent or buy the videos because of the value they get from being able to copy them.

76. Macrovision, "Home Taping in America: The Third National Survey," p. 3. The exact responses were that 66 percent would have rented and 35 percent would have purchased.

77. Author's estimates based on copying incidence reports by Macrovision and OTA. Macrovision estimates losses at the retail level by multiplying an estimated number of back-to-back copying incidents based on the survey, by published average retail rental and sales price data, and then adjusts those results by the percentages of respondents who declare that they would have otherwise rented or bought the video. In the 2000 Macrovision survey ("Home Taping in America"), the latter percentages for rentals and sales were 35 percent and 36 percent respectively. The 1989 OTA survey found that copying of prerecorded videos accounted for approximately 2 percent of all "recently acquired" videotapes, compared with 23 percent that were purchased and 54 percent copied from television.

78. Macrovision, "Pay-Per-View Movie Piracy," p. 1.

79. Macrovision, "Home Taping in America," 2000, reported that 30 percent of those who had ordered PPV movies during the past year admitted to having attempted to copy at least one of them. The 15 percent is an extrapolation.

80. Amy Harmon, "Hollywood Goes Digital to Combat High-Tech Piracy," *San Diego Union Tribune,* Jan. 5, 2003, p. A1.

81. Ibid.

82. Although there has never been a groundswell of optimism, the industry has remained divided on the economic prospects for PPV or more sophisticated VOD systems. Warren Lieberfarb, for example, the former Warner Home Video executive who adamantly pushed for DVD sales with little apparent attention to rentals, was reported to favor replacing the video rental window with a copy-protected PPV/VOD window simultaneous with DVD/VHS release. Martin Peers and John Lippman, "AOL–Time Warner Chief Quits," *WSJ,* Dec. 23, 2002, p. A3.

83. The 1989 OTA study indicated that movies were by far the most common type of programming copied from television (38 percent versus 16 percent for sports: Table 12-9).

84. Beginning mainly with Lisa N. Takeyama, "The Welfare Implications of Unauthorized Reproduction of Intellectual Property in the Presence of Demand Network Externalities," *Journal of Industrial Economics* 42 (June 1994): 155–166, a number of authors have indirectly studied piracy enforcement issues in computer software by demonstrating that illegal software usage can in the long run be beneficial to software suppliers because of network effects. That is, illegal users increase the customer base, which may provide the critical mass necessary for successful diffusion of the product, and they also become potential customers of product upgrades issued by the same supplier at a later time. Among other contributors have been Kathleen Reavis Conner and Richard P. Rumelt, "Software Piracy: An Analysis of Protection Strategies," *Management Science* 37 (February 1991): 125–139; Oz Shy and Jacques-Francois Thisse, "A Strategic Approach to Software Protection," *Journal of Economics and Management Strategy* 8 (Summer 1999): 163–190; and Dyuti S. Banerjee, "Software Piracy: A Strategic Analysis and Policy Instruments," *International Journal of Industrial Organization* 21 (January 2003): 97–127. While these papers are primarily theoretical, they offer an economic rationale for an apparent tolerance of copyright infringement by software suppliers. In a related stream of the economic literature, Stan J. Liebowitz, "Copying and Indirect Appropriability: Photocopying of Journals," *Journal of Political Economy* 93 (October 1985): 945–957, Stanley M. Besen, "Private Copying, Reproduction Costs, and the Supply of Intellectual Property," *Information Economics and Policy* 2 (1986): 5–22, and others have shown theoretically that under certain circumstances, consumer copying can be beneficial to suppliers of intellectual property,

generally when two conditions hold: (1) the copiers have lower costs of duplication and distribution than suppliers of the originals; (2) the suppliers are able to appropriate some or all of the value that copiers receive from using the copies. Implicitly, these results offer possible explanations for tolerance by intellectual suppliers of copying activity. See also Stanley M. Besen and Sheila Nataraj Kirby, "Private Copying, Appropriability, and Optimal Copyright Royalties," *Journal of Law and Economics* 32 (October 1989): 255–280.

85. Morgan Gendel, "Pay-Cable Services Try a 'VCR-Friendly' Tack," *Los Angeles Times,* Mar. 12, 1986, p. 1.

86. Prepared testimony of Michael Moradzadeh, Intel Corporation, before the House Commerce Committee, Telecommunications, Trade and Consumer Protection Committee, October 28, 1999. The DVRA was developed by the MPAA in collaboration with equipment manufacturers and home recording rights advocates, but the MPAA later withdrew its support, apparently due to concerns about unrestricted copying or retransmission of digital broadcast signals as the Internet developed; Jon Healey, "Digital Technologies Could Limit Recording, TV: Studios and Broadcasters Hope for Protection, Narrowing the Scope of Personal Use Taping," *Los Angeles Times,* Jan. 5, 2001, p. C5.

87. Federal Communications Commission, "Commercial Availability of Navigation Devices and Compatibility between Cable Systems and Consumer Electronics Equipment," *Federal Register* 68, no. 229 (Nov. 28, 2003). The rules establish upper limits but require mutual consent of copyright holders and multichannel video operators.

88. John Motavalli, "Pay Cables Fear DVD Burn: HBO, Showtime Seek Limits on Digital Copying, but Starz! Has Different View," *Television Week,* May 31, 2004, p. 1.

89. A Federal Appeals Court overturned the FCC's Broadcast Flag Rules in 2005, which required television equipment manufactured in the United States after July 1, 2005, to recognize digital software codes that prevent copying or retransmission of encrypted digital broadcast transmissions. The studios will thus be unable to control digital broadcasts via DRM in the absence of congressional legislation or other means to induce cooperation of equipment manufacturers.

90. "Hollywood Threatens Personal Freedom?" *Digital Music Newsletter,* Jan. 2, 2001, *mp3.about.com* (accessed Sept. 15, 2004).

91. Gary Shapiro, president of the Consumer Electronics Association, quoted in Mike Snider, "No Copying, No Trading, No Kidding: Copyright Fight Might Narrow Our Options," *USA Today,* Mar. 6, 2001, p. D1.

5. Rising American Dominance

1. Hy Hollinger, "Majors Bill a Record $5.97 Billion," *Hollywood Reporter,* July 11, 2000, pp. 3–4; measured in terms of theatrical film rentals, Canada, Spain, and Australia were fifth, sixth, and seventh, respectively. U.K. includes Ireland.

2. *Variety Deal Memo* (London: Informa Media Group), Sept. 23, 2002, p. 7.

3. EAO, *Focus 2004: World Film Market Trends* (Strasbourg, France, 2004).

4. Nondomestic, non-U.S. movies averaged 39 percent and 20 percent box office market shares, respectively, in Germany and France during the decade of the 1970s, but only 8 percent and 10 percent during the 1990s. Michael Thiermeyer, *Internationalisierung von Film und Filmwirtschaft* (Cologne: Böhlau, 1994); EAO, *Statistical Yearbooks* (Strasbourg, France: Council of Europe, 2000). Italy's regional trade has remained roughly steady, at 14 percent during the 1970s and 15 percent during the 1990s.

5. Over the 1980–2003 period for which U.S. shares in the U.K. could be separated, U.S. movies accounted for an average of 83.5 percent of all imported film box office revenues. For Japan, the comparable fraction was 44.5 percent for the 1980–1996 period.

6. Based on Anthony D'Alessandro, "The Top 125 Worldwide," *Variety,* Jan. 24, 2000, p. 22. The other film among the top 25 in 1999, *Notting Hill,* was a U.S.-British coproduction. Similar lists are published annually in *Variety* and in EAO publications.

7. Joseph Garncarz, "Hollywood in Germany," in David W. Ellwood and Rob Kroes, eds., *Hollywood in Europe: Experiences of a Cultural Hegemony* (Amsterdam: VU University Press, 1994), pp. 94–135.

8. Data cited in this paragraph are from EAO, *Statistical Yearbook,* 2003, and various issues of *Screen Digest* (London: Screen Digest Ltd.).

9. Australia's domestic share fell from about 8 percent in 1990 to 3.5 percent in 2003, while as noted in the following text, Korea's domestic share has substantially risen since the mid-1990s. In Latin America, American movies steadily gained ground from 1990 until at least 1998, although domestic box office shares tend to be very low throughout South America and Mexico historically. The highest domestic share reported in 1998 for the Latin American region, including Mexico, was Argentina's 13 percent (*Screen Digest,* July 1999, p. 173); Brazil's domestic box office share was reported to be 21 percent in 2003 (EAO, *Focus 2004,* p. 16).

10. *Variety Deal Memo,* Jan. 15, 2001, pp. 5–6; *Screen Digest,* July 1999, p. 173. See also Manjunath Pendakur, "India's National Film Policy:

Shifting Currents in the 1990s," in Albert Moran, ed., *Film Policy: International, National and Regional Perspectives* (London: Routledge, 1996), pp. 148–171.

11. *Screen Digest,* June 2004: 169. Korea's domestic share fell from about 36 percent in 1981 to 16 percent in 1993, according to *Korean Cinema Yearbook* (Seoul: Korean Film Council, 2000).

12. Ying Zhu, "Chinese Cinema's Economic Reform from the Mid-1980s to the Mid-1990s," *Journal of Communication* 52 (December 2002): 905–921.

13. *CNC Info—Results 1995* (Paris: Centre National de la Cinématographie, May 1996), p. 44. See also European Union, *Report by the Think-Tank on the Audiovisual Policy in the European Union* (Luxembourg, 1994), p. 4; *Variety Deal Memo,* Aug. 18, 2000, pp. 5–8.

14. Screen Digest, Ltd., *European Best Sellers* (London, 1997); from January 1996 to June 1997, 17 of the top 20 French rental videos and 17 of the top sales videos were American movies; the other 3 were French (including one U.S./French coproduction among the top sellers). In Germany, 19 of the top 20 rentals and 19 of the top 20 sales videos were U.S. movies; the other on both lists was a German film. In Italy, U.S. films numbered 19 of both the top 20 rental and sales videos; no Italian films at all were on either of these lists.

15. John Urquhart, Masayoshi Kanabayashi, Thomas Kamm, and Matt Moffett, "Staying Home—Tales of the Tape," *WSJ,* Mar. 26, 1993, p. R15; *Screen Digest,* Oct. 4, 2004: 294.

16. See especially BLM Partners, *BLM Study 90,* 9 vols. (Paris: BLM Partners, 1991); EAO, *European Films on European Televisions* (Strasbourg, France: European Audiovisual Observatory, 2000); and annual reports on European film content reported in EAO *Statistical Yearbooks.* Anthony Pragnell, *Television in Europe* (Manchester, England: European Institute for the Media, 1985); André Lange and Jean-Luc Renaud, *The Future of the European Audiovisual Industry* (Manchester, England: European Institute for the Media, 1989); and Michel Dupagne, "Factors Affecting the International Syndication Marketplace in the 1990s," *Journal of Media Economics* 5 (1992): 3–29 have compiled statistical data on television imports.

17. Shigeru Hagiwara, "Rise and Fall of Foreign Programs in Japanese Television," *Keio Communication Review* 17 (1995): 3–26.

18. Several *Variety* articles are cited in Kerry Segrave, *American Films Abroad: Hollywood's Domination of the World's Movie Screens from the 1890s to the Present* (Jefferson, N.C.: McFarland, 1997). Statistical compi-

lations in Thiermeyer, *Internationalisierung von Film und Filmwirtschaft* indicate the proportion of American theatrical movies shown in these years to be in the 50 percent range.

19. EAO, *European Films on European Televisions,* pp. 16, 27; EAO, *Statistical Yearbooks* (annual). See also Segrave, *American Films Abroad.*

20. Among these are European Union, *Report by the Think-Tank;* Council of Europe, "European Cinema, a Common Future" (paper presented at the Eighth Conference of European Ministers Responsible for Cultural Affairs, Budapest, Oct. 28–29, 1996); Jean-Paul Cluzel and Guillaume Cerruti, "Mission de Reflexion et de Propositions sur le Cinema Francais I, II," (Inspection Generale des Finances, December 1992); and House of Commons, National Heritage Committee, "The British Film Industry, Second Report" (London, 1995).

21. Commission of the European Communities, "Strategy Options to Strengthen the European Programme Industry in the Context of the Audiovisual Policy of the European Union," Green Paper 6 (1996), p. 6, reported that only 20 percent of European films go beyond national frontiers.

22. The 1993–1994 data are reported in Terry Ilott, *Budgets and Markets: A Study of the Budgeting of European Film* (London: Routledge, 1996), p. 33. In the 1990s, the European subsidy systems moved to EU-wide efforts; Media I and its successor, Media II, were designed as EU-wide subsidy programs designed to boost coproduction and joint marketing activities among European nations to improve international competitiveness; Nils Klevjer Aas, "Challenges in European Cinema and Film Policy," October–November 2001, *www.obs.coe.int* (accessed Oct. 5, 2004).

23. Martin Dale, *The Movie Game: The Film Business in Britain, Europe, and America* (London: Cassell, 1997). The origins of Dale's data are unclear, and aggregate compilations in Aas, "Challenges in European Cinema and Film Policy," do not appear to support the view that European film production is dominated by subsidy funds. Aas reports subsidies to the entire EU audiovisual sector to be EUR .953 billion in 2000 and the total size of the A-V sector in 1999 to be EUR 58.3 billion, including EUR 10.3 billion total revenues for theaters and video movies (pp. 4–5). See also Ilott, *Budgets and Markets;* Angus Finney, *The State of European Cinema* (London: Cassell, 1996); and the Web site of the EAO *(www.obs.coe.int)* for related data about the economics of European film subsidy systems.

24. EAO, *Statistical Yearbook* (2000), pp. 23–30; EAO, *Statistical Yearbook* (2002), p. 12.

25. This estimate is based on the assumption that non-European countries

accounted for 58 percent of the total foreign market for U.S. audiovisual program exports, as reported for 1998. Although some regions outside of Europe, notably Asia, tend to be more resistant to American movie imports, most of the world's strongest film production industries outside the United States are in Europe. A tabulation of worldwide motion picture production for 1999 indicates that about 62 percent of all film production investment outside the United States was accounted for by Europe, suggesting relatively weak resistance to American exports in non-European countries as a whole (*Screen Digest,* June 2000, p. 184).

26. Among the 118 manufacturing industries or industry groups disaggregated by the U.S. International Trade Administration for 1997, only aerospace, aircraft, chemical and allied products, and petrochemicals involved larger net trade surpluses in dollar terms than audiovisual products, as reported by the EAO for that year. Four other industries had a higher ratio of exports to imports, but these all involved much smaller volumes of trade activity (*www.ita.doc.gov/td/industry/otea/usito98/tables.htm,* accessed July 1, 2001). Probably the largest contributor to the U.S. balance of payments in the intellectual property group is computer software. Available data indicate large surpluses for the United States, though much smaller export-import ratios than in the movie case. See U.S. Department of Commerce, International Trade Administration, Office of Trade and Economic Analysis, Manufacturing, and Services, *U.S. Exports and Imports to Twenty-Five Major Countries by Products,* August 2004; and Gale Mosteller and Stephen E. Siwek, "Copyright Industries in the U.S. Economy" (prepared by Economists Incorporated for the International Intellectual Property Alliance, 2002).

27. EAO, *Statistical Yearbooks* (various).

28. International Federation of Phonographic Industries (IFPI), *The Recording Industry in Numbers 2003,* pp. 166–167 (London: IFPI). The IFPI data probably understate the actual contribution of domestic music production industries to total music industry volume because of the frequency with which music groups outside the United States perform or record music originally created by American artists.

29. N. Riel, "Les Caracteristiques des Best-sellers au Quebec et en France de 1989 à 1994," *Communication* 17 (1996): 249–271 reported that 86 percent of authors listed on best-seller lists in France from 1989 to 1994 were French. A study of the annual twenty-five top-ranking fiction titles in the United States from 1968 to 1992 found that 86 percent of authors were American: Jacques Lemieux and Denis Saint-Jacques, "U.S. Best-Sellers in French Quebec and English Canada," in Emile McAnany and

Kenton Wilkinson, eds., *Mass Media and Free Trade: NAFTA and the Cultural Industries* (Austin: University of Texas Press, 1996), pp. 279–305. A survey of top ten fiction lists published by *The Economist* between 1997 and 2000 showed the national origins of authors to be 76 percent French and 16 percent American in France and 55 percent British and 37 percent American in the U.K.; but in Germany, only 10 percent of authors were Germans, while 46 percent were American. Sarah Bennett, "Best Selling Books: Who Is Writing Them and What Topics Sell?" (working paper, Department of Telecommunications, Indiana University, 2000).

30. U.S. Department of Commerce/International Trade Administration, *U.S. Industry and Trade Outlook* (New York: DRI/McGraw-Hill, 2000).

31. In addition to the sources below, excellent commentaries in *Screen Digest, Variety,* and EAO publications have made valuable contributions.

32. See, for example, Ithiel de Sola Pool, "The Changing Flow of Television," *Journal of Communication* 27 (1977): 139–149; David Waterman, "World Television Trade: The Economic Effects of Privatization and New Technology," *Telecommunications Policy* 12 (June 1988): 141–151; Steven S. Wildman and Stephen E. Siwek, "The Privatization of European Television: Effects on International Markets for Programs," *Columbia Journal of World Business* 22 (Fall 1987): 71–76; Steven S. Wildman and Stephen E. Siwek, *International Trade in Films and Television Programs* (Cambridge, Mass.: Ballinger, 1988); Colin Hoskins and Rolf Mirus, "Reasons for the U.S. Dominance of the International Trade in Television Programmes," *Media, Culture, and Society* 10 (October 1988): 499–515; Colin Hoskins, Stuart McFadyen, and Adam Finn, *Global Television and Film* (Oxford: Oxford University Press, 1997).

33. Thomas H. Guback, *The International Film Industry* (Bloomington: Indiana University Press, 1969), and especially Jeremy Tunstall, *The Media Are American* (London: Constable, 1977) advanced these and related ideas. See also Michael Tracey, "The Poisoned Chalice? International Television and the Idea of Dominance," *Daedalus* 114 (Fall 1985): 17–56; Pierre Sorlin, *European Cinemas, European Societies, 1939–1990* (New York: Routledge, 1991); Pierre Sorlin, *Italian National Cinema, 1896–1996* (New York: Routledge, 1996); and Richard H. Pells, *Not Like Us: How Europeans Loved, Hated, and Transformed American Culture since World War II* (New York: Basic Books, 1997).

34. See especially Wildman and Siwek, "The Privatization of European Television," and Steven S. Wildman, "Trade Liberalization and Policy for

Media Industries: A Theoretical Examination of Media Flows," *Canadian Journal of Communication* 20 (1995): 367–388.

35. Joseph D. Straubhaar, "Beyond Media Imperialism: Asymmetrical Interdependence and Cultural Proximity," *Critical Studies in Mass Communication* 8 (March 1991): 39–59.

36. Scott Robert Olson, *Hollywood Planet: Global Media and the Competitive Advantage of Narrative Transparency* (Mahwah, N.J.: Lawrence Erlbaum Associates, 1999).

37. Tamar Liebes and Elihu Katz, *The Export of Meaning: Cross-Cultural Readings of "Dallas"* (New York: Oxford University Press, 1990), showed how the TV series *Dallas* became highly popular around the world by allowing viewers in different countries to read their own cultural values into it. See also David Puttnam, *Movies and Money* (New York: Knopf, 1998).

38. See especially London Economics, *The Competitive Position of the European and U.S. Film Industries* (Madrid: Media Business School, 1995), and Puttnam, *Movies and Money*.

39. London Economics, *The Competitive Position,* and several other reports published by the Media Business School in Madrid discuss related topics. For an early analysis from a business perspective, see Lange and Renaud, *The Future of the European Audiovisual Industry*.

40. In his well-known general analysis, Michael E. Porter, *The Competitive Advantage of Nations* (New York: Free Press, 1990), sets out a general menu of different possible reasons for why certain countries end up dominating trade in certain products and what factors contribute to sustainability of the advantage over time. Porter emphasizes the role of happenstance, such as the presence of a particular entrepreneur, as a tipping point that can lead to a sustainable trade advantage. Olson, *Hollywood Planet,* applies Porter's model in the context of his study of American dominance in movies and television. See also Eli Noam, "Media Americanization, National Culture, and Forces of Integration," in Eli Noam and Joel C. Millonzi, eds., *The International Market in Film and Television Programs: An Economic Analysis* (New York: Ablex, 1993).

41. Armand Mattelart, *Multinational Corporations and the Control of Culture* (Sussex: Harvester, 1979), and especially Herbert Schiller, *Mass Communications and American Empire* (Boulder: Westview Press, 1969), were early proponents of this model. See also Jorge Schement, Ibarra Gonzalez, Patricia Lum, and Rosita Valencia, "The International Flow of Television Programs," *Communications Research* 11 (April 1984): 163–182 for discussion of these approaches and American hegemony more generally.

42. Schiller, *Mass Communications and American Empire,* claimed an outright conspiracy by government and industry interests to promote the American way of life. Industry and government aggression is a major theme of many works, including Guback, *The International Film Industry;* Kristin Thompson, *Exporting Entertainment: America in the World Film Market, 1907–1934* (London: British Film Institute, 1985); Ian Jarvie, *Hollywood's Overseas Campaign: The North Atlantic Movie Trade, 1920–1950* (Cambridge: Cambridge University Press, 1992); and Segrave, *American Films Abroad.* These authors extensively document, and generally denounce, that aggressive behavior.

43. A notable failure was the 1993 Uruguay round of the General Agreement on Tariffs and Trade (GATT) negotiations, which left Hollywood's products out of the treaty, allowing European quotas on TV program importation to stand. In the end, though, these quotas have remained voluntary and weak in effect. See Segrave, *American Films Abroad.*

44. See especially Guback, *The International Film Industry;* Thompson, *Exporting Entertainment;* and Segrave, *American Films Abroad.* Wildman, "Trade Liberalization and Policy for Media Industries," criticizes this theory.

45. Regarding the U.K., for example, see John Hill, "British Television and Film: The Making of a Relationship," in John Hill and Martin McLoone, eds., *Big Picture, Small Screen: The Relations between Film and Television,* Acamedia Research Monograph no. 16 (Luton, Eng.: University of Luton Press, 1996).

46. Dale, *The Movie Game,* makes an especially vigorous case. See also Ilott, *Budgets and Markets;* Angus Finney, *The State of European Cinema: A New Does of Reality* (London: Cassell, 1996); Puttnam, *Movies and Money;* and Tyler Cowen, *Creative Destruction: How Globalization Is Changing the World's Cultures* (Princeton, N.J.: Princeton University Press, 2002).

47. "English Is Still on the March," *The Economist,* Feb. 24, 2001, p. 50; *Screen Digest,* February 1990, pp. 33–35.

48. Sorlin, *European Cinemas,* and Sorlin, *Italian National Cinema* analyze sociological and cultural changes in the European moviegoing population since the turn of the century.

49. A body of economic literature regards subsidies and other trade protectionist policies as predictable reactions to natural political and economic forces. See Wolfgang Mayer, "Endogenous Tariff Formation," *American Economic Review* 74 (December 1984): 970–985; Gene M. Grossman and Elhanan Helpman, *Interest Groups and Trade Policy* (Princeton, N.J.:

Princeton University Press, 2002); and Pinelopi Koujianou Goldberg and Giovanni Maggi, "Protection for Sale: An Empirical Investigation," *American Economic Review* 89 (December 1999): 1135–1155.

50. An apparent home market advantage has long been observed for many products and services traded on the world market; see Staffan Burenstam Linder, *An Essay on Trade and Transformation* (New York: John Wiley and Sons, 1961). The home market effect was given a rigorous theoretical basis in the form of "new economic geography" models. Paul Krugman, "Scale Economies, Product Differentiation, and the Pattern of Trade," *American Economic Review* 70 (December 1980): 950–959; and Elhanan Helpman and Paul Krugman, *Market Structure and Foreign Trade: Increasing Returns, Imperfect Competition and the International Economy* (Cambridge, Mass.: MIT Press, 1985) showed that imperfect competition in differentiated product industries exhibiting economies of scale would lead to a home market effect if transport costs are significant. Later authors have extended these models to show circumstances under which country-to-country demand differences or different assumptions about costs and competition can lead to similar results: see Robert C. Feenstra, James R. Markusen, and Andrew K. Rose, "Using the Gravity Model Equation to Differentiate among Alternative Theories of Trade," *Canadian Journal of Economics* 34 (May 2001): 430–447; Keith Head, Thierry Mayer, and John Ries, "On the Pervasiveness of Home Market Effects," *Economica* 69 (August 2000): 371–390; and Donald R. Davis and David E. Weinstein, "Market Access, Economic Geography, and Comparative Advantage: An Empirical Test," *Journal of International Economics* 59 (January 2003): 1–23. Rolf Weder, "How Domestic Demand Shapes the Pattern of International Trade," *World Economy* 19 (May 1996): 273–286, is a taxonomy of demand conditions, including variations in income, tastes, and climate, that can generate home market effects.

51. This prediction follows from the large economies of scale in distributing films to additional audiences. Once the first copy of a movie is created, the additional cost of distributing it to consumers in theaters, on television, or via other media throughout the world is relatively low. From the producer's perspective, the marginal benefit of investing another dollar into a given movie's production rises more or less in proportion to the size of that producer's total potential market. Since a producer's domestic market is a disproportionately important part of that total market, producers in countries that have large domestic markets have an incentive to make high-budget movies and more of them. It follows in turn that domestic producers in such countries will tend to have relatively large do-

mestic market shares of consumer spending on movies and will thus account for a disproportionate volume of total world movie export trade.

52. Nielsen EDI Summary Database, *www.boxofficemojo.com/movies* (accessed Oct. 6, 2004).

53. Among numerous studies are Barry R. Litman and Linda S. Kohl, "Predicting Financial Success of Motion Pictures: The 80s' Experience," *Journal of Media Economics* 2 (Fall 1989): 35–50; Jay Prag and James Casavant, "An Empirical Study of the Determinants of Revenues and Marketing Expenditures in the Motion Picture Industry," *Journal of Cultural Economics* 18 (1994): 217–235; and Arthur De Vany and W. David Walls, "Uncertainty in the Movie Industry: Does Star Power Reduce the Terror of the Box Office?" *Journal of Cultural Economics* 23 (November 1999): 285–318.

54. The Nielsen EDI Summary Database indicates a .65 correlation, significant at the 1 percent level, for all movies released in theaters in the United States between 1994 and 1999.

55. D'Alessandro, "The Top 125 Worldwide."

56. Silvio Waisbord, "McTelevision: Understanding the Global Popularity of Television Formats" (paper presented at the Conference of the International Communications Association, Washington, D.C., May 2001). For similar anecdotal evidence, see Albert Moran, *Copycat Television: Globalisation, Program Formats, and Cultural Identity* (Luton, Eng.: University of Luton Press, 1998); Tracey, "The Poisoned Chalice?"; and Wildman, "Trade Liberalization and Policy for Media Industries."

57. The reported estimates implicitly take film content decisions of producers in the United States and France as given. Discounts are undoubtedly less severe for major American productions crafted for the export market. Content of European films is also affected by government subsidies and other media policies that probably turn these films' content inward. Finally, minimum costs of distribution inhibit many movies from being released in foreign markets at all.

58. *CNC Info—Results 1995* (May 1996), pp. 7–8. There were 115 French productions in all, including 28 minority coproductions. French minority coproductions, which often are not produced in French, tend to do poorly at the French box office, accounting for a disproportionately small percentage of total receipts.

59. Nielsen EDI Summary Database; *Variety* data.

60. MPAA, *U.S. Entertainment Industry: 2002 MPA Market Statistics.*

61. EAO, *Statistical Yearbook* (2000).

62. Analysis generally parallel to that of this section for the case of Italy appears in David Waterman and Krishna P. Jayakar, "Da Che Parte Pende la Bilancia Della Competizione Fra L'industria Cinematografica Italiana e Quella Statunitense?" (How will the Competitive Balance between the Italian and American Film Industries Evolve?) *L'Industria* 20 (September 1999): 393–415; David Waterman and Krishna P. Jayakar, "The Competitive Balance of the Italian and American Film Industries," *European Journal of Communication* 15 (December 2000): 501–528; and, for the case of Japan, Sang-Woo Lee, "An Economic Analysis of the Movie Industry in Japan," *Journal of Media Economics* 15 (2002): 125–139.

63. Exchange-rate comparisons over time are problematical because they reflect changing expectations, productivity differences in particular industries, and a variety of other country-specific factors that are not necessarily related to the purchasing power of movie producers. See, for example, Richard C. Marston, "Real Exchange Rates and Productivity Growth in the United States and Japan," in Sven W. Arndt and J. David Richardson, eds., *Real-Financial Linkages among Open Economies* (Cambridge, Mass.: MIT Press, 1987): 71–76.

64. During World War II, American movie production was very active, while most commercial activity in Europe was virtually shut down in connection with war efforts. Cinemas were also damaged in some countries. See Guback, *The International Film Industry.*

65. For history and analysis of multichannel and pay TV development in Europe, see Martin Cave, "Regulating Digital Television in a Convergent World," *Telecommunications Policy* 21 (August 1997): 575–596; Peter Humphreys, *Mass Media and Media Policy in Western Europe* (Manchester, Eng.: Manchester University Press, 1996); Alessandro Silj, ed., *The New Television in Europe* (London: Libbey, 1992); Richard Collins, *From Satellite to Single Market: New Communication Technology and European Public Servcie Television* (London: Routledge, 1998); and EAO *Statistical Yearbooks* and *Screen Digest* reports. For Japanese pay TV development, see *TV in Asia Pacific to 2012* (London: ZenithOptimedia), September 2003.

66. Screen Digest, Ltd., *European Digital Pay Television Platforms* (London, 2003); periodic reports in *Screen Digest;* and *TV in Asia Pacific to 2012.* See also Christopher H. Sterling, *Electronic Media: A Guide to Trends in Broadcasting and Newer Technologies, 1920–1983* (New York: Praeger, 1984); and the National Cable Television Association's Web site *(www.ncta.com).*

67. *Kagan Media Index* (Paul Kagan Associates), Nov. 30, 1993. In 2003, overall PPV penetration in the United States was 48 percent of TV households, compared to France, 27 percent; Germany, 2 percent; Italy, 15 percent; and UK, 32 percent. *Hollywood Aftermarket* (Adams Media Research), July 30, 2004, p. 4; *Screen Digest,* February 2004, p. 41.

68. *Screen Digest,* October 2003, p. 294; for U.S. data, see Appendix F. These estimates include all content, which is mainly sports and "adult" in addition to theatrical features. Japanese PPV spending data were unavailable, and presumably very low.

69. EAO, *Statistical Yearbook,* 1994–1995, Table 2.14. Cable penetration in the smaller countries of Europe was generally higher, but for western European countries overall, only 10–12 percent in 1985; Jurgen Muller, "Cable Policy in Europe: The Role of Transborder Broadcasting and Its Effects on Cable TV," *Telecommunications Policy* 11 (1987): 259–268; Waterman, "World Television Trade."

70. U.S. and European data calculated from *www.ncta.com* and Screen Digest Ltd., *European Digital Pay TV Platforms;* for Japan: Jouhou Media Hakusyo, Information Media White Paper, Dentsu Institute for Human Studies (Tokyo, annual).

71. Sterling, *Electronic Media.*

72. Screen Digest Ltd., *European Digital Pay TV Platforms;* "Statistics and Resources" (*www.ncta.com*, accessed Feb. 2, 2005).

73. Regarding Europe, see *Variety Deal Memo,* Jan. 19, 2001. For the United States, see Appendix C.

74. See Sorlin, *European Cinemas* and Sorlin, *Italian National Cinema* for the effects of generational changes on European movie going habits.

75. The ratio of aggregate EUJ5 to aggregate U.S. consumer spending rose from .49 to 1.01 between 1955 and 1998, evaluated at current exchange rates, and at least increased for each of the individual EUJ5 countries. Relative trends in GDP were comparable.

76. As indicated briefly in Chapter 1, ABC and CBS both had short-lived theatrical film production enterprises. The last to go out of business was CBS Films, in 1973. The ABC television network and Paramount Pictures were jointly owned in the 1950s, but these companies disintegrated in the 1960s. More recently, start-up of the Fox Network in 1986 by Twentieth Century Fox and the mergers of ABC and Disney in 1994, and of CBS and Viacom (current owner of Paramount Pictures), have reunited television networking and film production under the same corporate umbrellas.

77. Hill, "British Television and Film," p. 153; Ilott, *Budgets and Markets,* pp. 33–36; Dale, *The Movie Game.*

78. Ilott, *Budgets and Markets,* pp. 33–34.

79. Ibid., p. 34; Hill, "British Television and Film," p. 153.

80. Hill, "British Television and Film," p. 164.

81. Chun-Gil Lee, *Improving the Film Distribution Structure: Policy Proposal* (Seoul: Korean Cultural Policy Institute, 1998). According to the Japanese Motion Picture Producers Association, Japanese theatrical movie distributors received 45 percent of their domestic income from theaters, 50 percent from video, and 15 percent from television in 1998. Since pay TV still earned very minor revenues in Japan by that date, the 15 percent is probably almost entirely from free broadcast sources.

82. Ilott, *Budgets and Markets;* and Hill, "British Television and Film."

83. The actual number of movies shown on TV was very low compared to the current market, reflecting very limited broadcast channel capacity at the time. In 1970, German TV showed 637 movies, compared to 15,475 in 1993. In France, the growth was from 378 to 918 movies over the same time period. In the U.K., 960 movies were shown in 1975, and 2,123 in 1993. In Italy, the trend from 1975 to 1992 was 115 to 10,996 (Thiermeyer, *Internationalisierung von Film und Filmwirtschaft*).

84. Eli Noam, *Television in Europe* (New York: Oxford University Press, 1991); Humphreys, *Mass Media and Media Policy;* EAO, *Statistical Yearbooks.*

85. Hill, "British Television and Film" articulates this case. See also Ilott, *Budgets and Markets.*

86. Dale, *The Movie Game;* Terry Ilott, "Television and Film" (manuscript, Madrid Business School, 1995); and Ilott, *Budgets and Markets* generally take this view, while Hill, "British Television and Film" attributes minor significance to the involvement of broadcast TV organizations on film content.

87. Commission of the European Communities, "Report on the Implementation of the EU Electronic Communications Regulatory Package," Nov. 19, 2003, Brussels; Grischa Perino and Gunther G. Schulze, "Competition, Cultural Autonomy, and Global Governance: The Audio-visual Sector in Germany," Hamburg Institute of International Economics, Report no. 232, 2003; Campbell Gray, "Late Starter? Japan's Pay TV Market," *Multichannel News International,* February 2002: 34.

88. Cave, "Regulating Digital Television in a Convergent World"; Noam, *Television in Europe;* and Silj, *The New Television in Europe;* W. Hoffman-Riem, "New Media in West Germany: The Politics of Legitimization," in

Kenneth Dyson and Peter Humphreys, eds., *The Political Economy of Communications: International and European Dimensions* (London: Routledge, 1996); Raymond Kuhn, *The Media in France* (London: Routledge, 1995).

89. Stanley Besen and Robert Crandall, "The Deregulation of Cable Television," *Law and Contemporary Problems* 44 (1981): 77–124; Robert W. Crandall, "Competition and Regulation in the U.S. Video Market," *Telecommunication Policy* 21 (August 1997): 649–660. Following court decisions in the 1970s freeing cable TV networks from content regulation, cable system rates were deregulated in 1984, but then reregulated in 1992.

90. Manuel Alvarado, ed., *Video World-Wide: An International Study* (London: J. Libbey, 1988); Douglas A. Boyd, Joseph D. Straubhaar, and John A. Lent, *Videocassette Recorders and the Third World* (White Plains, N.Y.: Longman, 1988); John Tydeman and Ellen Jakes Kelm, *New Media in Europe: Satellites, Cable, VCRs, Videotex* (New York: McGraw-Hill, 1986).

91. *Screen Digest,* November 2004, p. 332.

92. The theory that improved piracy enforcement helps domestic producers relatively more than foreign (i.e., American) producers, as implied by the home market model, depends on the assumption that enforcement equally affects domestically produced and imported products. Governments, however, may have an incentive to enforce against piracy of domestically produced products but not imported products, in which case the theory may not hold.

93. Other than to encourage consistent consumer expectation of video window lengths, legislated video windows in Europe may have been intended to protect theater owners from video competition. The legally mandated video window in France of one year, later reduced to nine and then to six months, has earned repeated complaints from the MPAA as excessively long; see MPAA, *Trade Barriers to Export of Film Entertainment,* 1999 Report to the U.S. Trade Representative, p. 53.

94. MPAA, *Trade Barriers to Export of Film Entertainment,* 2003 Report to the U.S. Trade Representative.

95. *Screen Digest,* September 2000, p. 280.

96. *Screen Digest,* September 1999, p. 233.

6. What Has Hollywood Done with the Money?

1. Pauline Kael, "The Current Cinema: Why Are Movies So Bad? or, The Numbers," *New Yorker,* June 23, 1980, pp. 84–93.

2. Michiko Kakutani, "Taking Out the Trash," *New York Times Sunday Magazine,* June 8, 1997, p. 30; for similar commentary, see Lynn Hirschberg, "Is the Face of America That of a Green Ogre?" *New York Times Magazine,* Nov. 14, 2004, p. 91.

3. David Thomson, "The Dark Excitements of 1971," *NYT,* Dec. 30, 2001, p. AR7.

4. Rick Lyman, "Moviegoers Are Flocking to Forget Their Troubles," *NYT,* June 21, 2002, pp. C1, C6.

5. Neal Gabler, "Just Like a Movie, but It's Not," *NYT,* Aug. 4, 2002, sec. 4, p. 1. Gabler cites television producer Paul Rosenthal as originator of the "illusion of entertainment" phrase.

6. Among many examples, see Dan Cox, "Soaring Star Salaries Induce Labor Pains," *Variety,* Sept. 11–17, 1995, p. 1; Robert W. Welkos, "How to Spend $78 Million," *Newsday,* Apr. 11, 1999, p. D06; Lorenza Munoz, "Movie Production Costs Soared in 2002; At ShoWest, MPAA Head Jack Valenti Laments the Price Impact of Special Effects and Technology," *Los Angeles Times,* Mar. 5, 2003, p. E2.

7. Michael Ruby, Martin Kasindorf, and Pamela Lynn Abraham, "Inside Hollywood," *Newsweek,* Feb. 13, 1978, pp. 70–76.

8. Cobbett Steinberg, *Reel Facts: The Movie Book of Records* (New York: Vintage Books, 1978), pp. 66–69.

9. Jonathan Bing, David Bloom, Claude Brodesser, and Cathy Dunkley, "Actors Savor Star Bucks," *Variety,* Apr. 1, 2002, p. 1.

10. Welkos, "How to Spend $78 Million."

11. Anne Thompson, "Lord of the Paycheck: Film Directors Move Up," *NYT,* Oct. 28, 2003, p. B1; Welkos, "How to Spend $78 Million"; Jeffrey Daniels, "High Price of Talent Gets Blame for TV Budget Woes," *Hollywood Reporter,* Apr. 21, 1995.

12. John Horn, "Studios' Latest Special Effect: Budgets out the Window," *Los Angeles Times,* May 13, 2003, p. A1.

13. Daniels, "High Price of Talent." There are large differences in this proportion from film to film, though higher-budget movies usually have higher proportions of above-the-line expenses. For sample movie budgets, see Art Linson, "The $75 Million Difference," *New York Times Sunday Magazine,* Nov. 16, 1997, p. 87.

14. Peter Bart, "H'Wood's Slow Shooters," *Variety,* Feb. 13, 1995, p. 9. For other examples, see *Variety,* Sept. 11–17, 1995, p. 1.

15. Bart, "H'Wood's Slow Shooters."

16. Patrick Goldstein, "The Big Picture: A Nod to the Blockbuster Boys of Summer," *Los Angeles Times,* May 20, 2003, p. E1.

17. Gillian Lord, "Eyeing Kubrick," *Daily Telegraph,* June 26, 1999, p. 122.
18. John-Michael Howson, "Crediting a Cast of Thousands," *Illawarra Mercury,* May 2, 1998, p. 19.
19. As of 1996, producers used a forty-two-page manual that shows the negotiated, contractual obligations they have to list production personnel ("Notice to Producers," Alliance of Motion Picture and Television Producers, May 21, 1996).
20. Kathleen A. Hughes, "Enough Already: The Plethora of Producers Is a Hollywood Joke," *WSJ,* Dec. 7, 1989. pp. A1, A8; See also Peter Bart, "In This Biz, Everyone Takes Credit, Due or Otherwise," *Daily Variety,* Sept. 19, 1994, p. 19; Robert W. Welkos, "Such a Production," *Los Angeles Times,* Dec. 8, 1991, p. CAL4.
21. Robert W. Welkos, "Some Producers Must Stand Aside at Academy Award Ceremony," *Los Angeles Times,* Feb. 23, 2002, p. 3D.
22. Special and visual effects are usually distinguished in movie end credits: the former includes computer-generated explosions, alien aircraft, and the like; the latter generally include miniature model construction and photography, matte paintings, and the like.
23. Alice Rawsthorn, "Effects Facility Set to Boost Film Industry," *Financial Times,* Dec. 18, 1998, p. 4.
24. The principal effects contractor on *Titanic,* Digital Domain, was reported to have billings of $40 million out of a total budget estimated at about $200 million. Kris Goodfellow, "Mayday! Mayday! We're Leaking Visuals! A Shakeout of the Special Effects Houses," *NYT,* Sept. 29, 1997, p. D1.
25. Horn, "Studios' Latest Special Effect."
26. Screen Credits Manual, *www.wga.org* (accessed Oct. 6, 2004).
27. Peter Bart and Peter Guber, *Shoot Out: Surviving Fame and (Mis)Fortune in Hollywood* (New York: G. P. Putnam's Sons, 2002), p. 68.
28. Bart, "In This Biz."
29. Bart and Guber, *Shoot Out,* p. 71.
30. Ibid., p. 63.
31. Robert W. Welkos, "Movies: It Can Set You Reeling; How Did the Average Cost of a Studio Film Reach $75 Million?" *Los Angeles Times,* Dec. 20, 1998, p. CAL5.
32. Derek Elley, "Film Reviews: DVD—*Lawrence of Arabia,*" *Variety,* Apr. 2, 2001, p. 18.
33. Sharon Waxman and Paul Farhi, "Going Down with the Ship? *Titanic* Typifies the Huge Risks, Rewards of Hollywood's Epic Ambitions,"

Washington Post, May 25, 1997, p. H01; Trip Gabriel, "Roll Film! Action! Cut! Edit, Edit, Edit," *NYT,* May 5, 1997, p. D1.

34. John Horn, "The Road to 'Pearl Harbor'" *Newsweek,* May 14, 2001, p. 43.

35. The French Connection, directed by William Friedkin (1971), DVD, Widescreen ed., Twentieth Century Fox Home Entertainment, 2001, disc 2.

36. Horn, "Studio's Latest Special Effect."

37. Bart and Guber, *Shoot Out;* Kael, "The Current Cinema." For similar commentary, see Rex Weiner, "Titanic Pix Daunt Studio Crunchers, Triggering . . . Budgetary Bedlam," *Variety,* Mar. 10, 1997, p. 1; Richard Schickel, "When Hollywood Was Managed," *Fortune,* Feb. 17, 1986, p. 143.

38. Bart, "H'Wood's Slow Shooters."

39. Welkos, "How to Spend $78 million."

40. Peter Bart, "*Pluto*'s Retreat: What Planet Were They On?" *Daily Variety,* Aug. 26, 2002, p. 20; Danny Craydon, "Pluto Nash (2002)", *www.bbc.co.uk* (accessed Feb. 2, 2005).

41. Aljean Harmetz, "Hollywood Battles Killer Budgets," *NYT,* May 31, 1987, p. C1; Claudia Eller, "In Denial, Studios Continue Lavish Ways," *Los Angeles Times,* May 14, 1996, p. D6; Michael Medved, "Is Hollywood Losing Its Touch?" *USA Today,* Mar. 20, 2001, p. 13A; "Hollywood's Fading Charms," *The Economist,* Mar. 22, 1997, p. 73.

42. Elizabeth Guider, "Can Film Biz Curb Squander-lust?" *Variety,* Mar. 29, 2004, p. 6; Elizabeth Guider, "Pic Biz Thinks Big and Sinks Big," *Variety,* May 3, 2004, p. 6.

43. See, for example, *Los Angeles Herald-Examiner,* Mar. 12, 1963, p. 6.

44. Bart and Guber, *Shoot Out,* p. 259. Some similar ideas are in William Goldman, *Adventures in the Screen Trade: A Personal View of Hollywood and Screenwriting* (New York: Warner Books, 1984); William Goldman, *Which Lie Did I Tell? or: More Adventures in the Screen Trade* (New York: Pantheon, 2000).

45. Kael, "The Current Cinema."

46. An analogy can be made to reliability theory in operations research. In effect, spending money to strengthen some links in a chain is only cost effective if other links are strengthened as well. Michael Kremer, "The O-Ring Theory of Economic Development," *Quarterly Journal of Economics* 108 (August 1993): 551–575.

47. West quoted in Welkos, "How to Spend $78 million."

48. Gabriel, "Roll Film! Action!"

49. Lyman, "Moveigoers are Flocking to Forget their Troubles."

50. Ibid.; Carl DiOrio, "Promo Blitz Fuels Booming Biz," *Variety*, June 10, 2002, p. 9.

51. Lyman, "Moveigoers Are Flocking to Forget Their Troubles."

52. "Video Cartridges: A Promise of Future Shock," *Time*, Aug. 10, 1970, pp. 40–41.

53. Ruby, Kasindorf, and Abraham, "Inside Hollywood."

54. Bruce M. Owen and Steven S. Wildman, *Video Economics* (Cambridge, Mass.: Harvard University Press, 1992) review this "program choice" literature, which originated with Peter O. Steiner, "Program Patterns and Preferences, and the Workability of Competition in Radio Broadcasting," *Quarterly Journal of Economics* 66 (May 1952): 194–223.

55. The trade-off between endogenous set-up costs and product variety was recognized for the newspaper market by James N. Rosse, "Daily Newspapers, Monopolistic Competition and Economies of Scale," *American Economic Review* 57 (May 1967): 522–533, but was not theoretically developed until Avner Shaked and John Sutton, "Product Differentiation and Industrial Structure," *Journal of Industrial Economics* 36 (December 1987): 131–146. They show that if marginal costs are constant or increase slowly enough under plausible demand conditions, high-quality firms can undercut low-quality firms as market size increases, resulting in a lower bound on (minimum level of) industry concentration. That is, larger markets do not necessarily produce greater product variety. John Sutton, *Technology and Market Structure: Theory and History* (Cambridge, Mass.: MIT Press, 2001) builds upon both that model and Sutton's own *Sunk Costs and Market Structure: Price Competition, Advertising and the Evolution of Concentration* (Cambridge, Mass.: MIT Press, 1991) to empirically investigate the effects of R&D intensity on industry concentration. Steven Berry and Joel Waldfogel, in "Product Quality and Market Size" (National Bureau of Economic Research, NBER working paper 9675, Cambridge, Mass., May 2003), apply a similar model to demonstrate empirically that the average quality of daily newspapers increases with local market size, but that market fragmentation does not occur. These works, involving endogenous set-up costs, build upon theoretical analysis of the trade-offs between fixed set-up costs and product variety developed by Kelvin Lancaster, "Socially Optimal Product Differentiation," *American Economic Review* 65 (September 1975): 567–585; Michael Spence, "Product Selection, Fixed Costs, and Monopolistic Competition," *Review of Economic Studies* 43 (June 1976): 217–235; Michael

Spence and Bruce Owen, "Television Programming, Monopolistic Competition, and Welfare," *Quarterly Journal of Economics* 91 (February 1977): 103–126; and Avinash K. Dixit and Joseph E. Stiglitz, "Monopolistic Competition and Optimum Product Diversity," *American Economic Review* 67 (June 1977): 297–308.

56. David Waterman, "'Narrowcasting' and 'Broadcasting' on Nonbroadcast Media: A Program Choice Model," *Communication Research* 19, no. 1 (February 1992): 3–28. Owen and Wildman, in *Video Economics,* also show how the proliferation of media outlets can increase program budgets, but they do not give explicit attention to programming content.

57. Author's calculation based on the Nielsen EDI Summary Database.

58. The data to follow are the initial stage of a statistical study of the historical causes of movie genre shifts conducted by Weiting Lu, Michael Zhaoxu Yan, and this author.

59. The annual proportion of total U.S. box office receipts accounted for by the top twenty films from 1988 (the earliest year for which useful data were available) to 2002 was 46.6 percent, with no evident trend.

60. See Richard E. Caves, *Creative Industries: Contracts between Art and Commerce* (Cambridge, Mass.: Harvard University Press, 2000) for discussion of demand and supply forces leading to this phenomenon.

61. Although he did not use this term specifically, the seminal development of this idea is due to Sherwin Rosen, "The Economics of Superstars," *American Economic Review* 71 (December 1981): 845–858. The numerical example to follow is our interpretation of Rosen's model.

62. William J. Baumol and William G. Bowen, *Performing Arts, The Economic Dilemma* (Cambridge, Mass.: MIT Press, 1968). With the development of computer software, some recent indications suggest that productivity is becoming more widespread than many thought would be possible. Jon E. Hilsenrath, "Behind Surging Productivity: Immune Sectors Catch the Bug," *WSJ,* Nov. 7, 2003, p. A1.

63. Cast and crew, which account for virtually all above-the-line and the majority of below-the-line costs, typically make up the great proportion of most movie budgets overall. Wages for below-the-line craft personnel have risen over time, but those increases have apparently been far below those of top talent (Cox, "Soaring Star Salaries Induce Labor Pains"; Waterman, "'Narrowcasting' and 'Broadcasting,'" p. 25).

64. Gary Levin, "Pixar Offers Peek at *Toy Story* Technology," *Daily Variety,* Apr. 13, 1996, p. 13; Bruce Kirkland, "Toying with Technology: Disney Launches Another Animation Revolution with *Toy Story,*" *Toronto Sun,* Nov. 19, 1995, p. S14.

65. Levin, "Pixar Offers Peek"; Lisa Gubernick, "The Animation Revolution," *WSJ,* June 27, 2003, p. W5.

66. Claudia Eller, "Sony to Launch Feature Animation Unit," *Los Angeles Times,* May 9, 2002, p. C1.

67. Glenn Whipp, "Drawing to a Close: *Home on the Range* May Be Disney's Last Stand at Hand Animation," *Los Angeles Daily News,* Apr. 1, 2004, p. U4; Ellen Wolff, "*Life Aquatic* for 2-D," *Daily Variety,* Dec. 9, 2004, p. A4.

68. David Waterman, "The Effects of Technological Change on the Quality and Variety of Information Products" (paper presented at the NBER All Universities Conference on the Economics of the Information Economy, Cambridge, Mass., May 7–8, 2004) offers a theoretical analysis that underlies the narrative and the numerical example to follow. A variety of more general demand functions generate results comparable to those of the example.

69. Eller, "Sony to Launch Feature Animation Unit"; "Report: Disney Plans Major Cutbacks in Feature Animation Unit," *Associated Press Newswires,* Apr. 24, 2001.

70. Goldman, *Adventures in the Screen Trade,* p. 40; Tom King, "The *Gosford Park* Goof," *WSJ,* Mar. 1, 2002, p. W4.

71. "Arundel Partners: The Sequel Project," (Harvard Business School, Case no. 9-292-140, June 12, 1992). A more recent trade article reported a similar pattern; see Dan Cox and Benedict Carver, "Low Scores for Encores," *Variety,* Oct. 26–Nov. 1, 1998, p. 1.

72. Claudia Eller, "Films in Black: Why Studios Love Sequels," *Los Angeles Times,* Jan. 27, 2002, p. E2; see also Carl DiOrio, "H'w'd: A Sequel Opportunity Town," *Variety,* June 16, 2003, p. l; and John Lippman, "Studio's Summer Schooling," *WSJ,* Sept. 3, 2004, p. W8.

73. See, for example, Bernard Weinraub, "From the Folks Who Brought You *Ishtar,*" *NYT,* May 4, 1997, sec. 4, p. 2; Anita Gates, "Well, At Least the Popcorn Is Good," *NYT,* Nov. 27, 1998, p. B25.

74. Caves, *Creative Industries,* suggests the latter reason for blockbuster failures.

75. The basic idea that executive or other labor performance is generally difficult to evaluate when profit outcomes depend on the overall performance of a team was recognized by Armen A. Alchian and Harold Demsetz, "Production, Information Costs, and Economic Organization," *American Economic Review* 62 (December 1972): 777–795. A large subsequent literature has mostly focused on how to preserve optimal incentives in teamwork and how to properly compensate executive perfor-

mance, but the works do not address the issues of product quality we discuss. Notable papers on the subject include Bengt Holmstrom, "Moral Hazard in Teams," *Bell Journal of Economics* 13 (Autumn 1982): 324–340; Jean Tirole, "A Theory of Collective Reputations (with Applications to the Persistence of Corruption and to Firm Quality)," *Review of Economic Studies* 63 (January 1996): 1–22; Marianne Bertrand and Sendhil Mullainathan, "Are CEOs Rewarded for Luck? The Ones without Principals Are," *Quarterly Journal of Economics* 116 (August 2001): 901–932; and, for sports team management specifically, Gerald W. Scully, *The Market Structure of Sports* (Chicago: University of Chicago Press, 1995).

76. Goldman, *Adventures in the Screen Trade.*

77. The Treasury Deptartment identified Louis B. Mayer, production executive of the Loew's Corporation, as the nation's highest-paid corporate executive in 1937 (at $1.2 million), and a number of other industry leaders made the top list in that and subsequent years into the 1940s. "Reveal Salaries of Film Greats and U.S. Business Executives," *Los Angeles Herald-Examiner,* Apr. 7, 1939, p. A1; "Skouras' Name Leads High Pay List in 1947," *Los Angeles Herald-Examiner,* n.d., pp. 1, 4 (Margaret Herrick Library, Academy of Motion Picture Arts and Sciences, Beverly Hills, Calif.); Gary Strauss and Barbara Hansen, "Special Report: Bubble Hasn't Burst Yet on CEO Salaries Despite the Times," *USA Today,* Mar. 31, 2003, sec. Money, p. 1B.

78. Bruce Orwall, "Universal Chief Quits in Wake of Movie Flops," *WSJ,* Dec. 1, 1998, p. B1.

79. Peter Bart, "Canton's Karma," *Variety,* Sept. 23–29, 1996, pp. 5, 145.

80. Bernard Weinraub, "Films Vault to the Top with Tricks, Not Stars," *NYT,* July 9, 1996, p. C11.

81. Marc Graser, "They've Learned Their Lessons," *Variety,* Sept. 1, 2003, p. 9.

82. Dade Hayes, "Bombs Away: Biz Disavows Duds," *Variety,* Mar. 20, 2000, p. 7.

83. The importance of track records for movie production personnel themselves is studied by Wayne E. Baker and Robert R. Faulkner, "Role as Resource in the Hollywood Film Industry," *American Journal of Sociology* 97 (September 1991): 279–309; and Robert T. Faulkner and Andy B. Anderson, "Short-Term Projects and Emergent Careers: Evidence from Hollywood," *American Journal of Sociology* 92 (January 1987): 879–909. See also David Forrest Prindle, *Risky Business: The Political Economy of Hollywood* (Boulder: Westview, 1993).

84. Joe Russo and Larry Landsman, *Planet of the Apes Revisited: The Behind-*

the-Scenes Story of the Classic Science Fiction Saga (New York: St. Martin's Press, 2001); Harold L. Vogel, *Entertainment Industry Economics: A Guide for Financial Analysis* (Cambridge: Cambridge University Press, 1998), p. 86.

85. Russo and Landsman, *Planet of the Apes Revisited,* p. 261; "Big Rental Films of 1968," *Variety,* Jan. 8, 1969, p. 15.

86. Nielsen EDI Summary Database.

87. Roger Ebert, "*Planet of the Apes* off Target," *Chicago Sun-Times,* July 27, 2001, p. 29.

88. The *imdb.com* database lists 164 "external reviews," a perusal of which indicates this to be the majority view.

89. Desson Howe, "Apes Not Ready for Primate Time," *Washington Post,* July 27, 2001, p. WE32.

90. See, for example, *http://www.lowcomdom.com/film/p/planet_of_the_apes .html* (accessed Oct. 22, 2004).

91. Nielsen EDI Summary Database.

92. "125 Top Grossing Films Worldwide in 2001," *www.variety.com* (accessed Oct. 5, 2004).

93. In general, price discrimination is socially beneficial in terms of economic welfare if total output increases as a result; see Richard Schmalensee, "Output and Welfare Implications of Monopolistic Third Degree Price Discrimination," *American Economic Review* 71 (March 1981): 242–247; and Hal R. Varian, "Price Discrimination and Social Welfare," *American Economic Review* 75 (September 1985): 870–875. For a media-specific analysis, see Spence and Owen, "Television Programming, Monopolistic Competition, and Welfare."

7. Hollywood's Digital Future

1. Sarah McBride, "Studios Set Deals in Bid to Get PCs to Show Movies," *WSJ,* July 14, 2004, p. D4.

2. Eric A. Taub, "DVDs Meant for Buying but Not for Keeping," *NYT,* July 21, 2003. p. C1.

3. Gary Gentile, "Self-Destructing DVDs About to Reach a Wider Audience," *Associated Press Newsires,* Nov. 16, 2004.

4. A. Michael Noll, "Internet Pricing vs. Reality," *Communications of the ACM* 40 (August 1997): 118–121; Eli Noam, "Will Internet TV Be American," in Eli Noam, Jo Groebel, and Darcy Gerbarg, eds., *Internet Television* (Mahwah, N.J.: Lawrence Erlbaum Associates, 2004), pp. 235–242;

Andrew Odlyzko, "Implications for the Long Distance Network," in Noam et al., *Internet Television*, pp. 9–18.

5. See Yannis Bakos and Erik Brynjolfsson, "Bundling Information Goods: Pricing, Profits, and Efficiency." *Management Science* 45 (December 1999): 1613–1630 and Yannis Bakos and Erik Brynjolfsson, "Bundling and Competition on the Internet," *Marketing Science* 19 (Winter 2000): 63–82 for economic analysis of bundling on the Internet.

6. According to www.riaa.com (accessed Oct. 11, 2004), based on the value of retail shipments. Most economic studies of the effect of file sharing on music sales have indicated that sales have suffered some harm. See especially Stan J. Liebowitz, "Will MP3s Annihilate the Record Industry? The Evidence So Far," *Advances in the Study of Entrepreneurship, Innovation, and Economic Growth* 15 (2004): 229–260. An exception is Felix Oberholzer and Koleman Strumpf, "The Effects of File Sharing on Record Sales: An Empirical Analysis" (Harvard Business School working paper, 2004), which generally does not find statistically significant effects of file sharing on CD sales. See also "Music's Brighter Future," *The Economist*, Oct. 30, 2004, p. 71, for discussion.

7. See, for example, Erik Gruenwedel, "MPAA Ban Battle Latest in Copy-Thwarting War," *Video Store Magazine*, Oct. 26, 2003, p. 1. The summary of an MPAA-funded, survey-based study of Internet movie file sharing in eight countries, including the United States (Worldwide Internet Piracy Study, MPAA Press Release, July 8, 2004) claims a finding that file sharing negatively affects legitimate sales in the subject countries, including the United States (*www.mpaa.org*, accessed Nov. 8, 2004).

8. For related discussion of bandwidth issues and movie file sharing prevalence, see Scott Morrison and Peter Thal Larsen, "Hollywood's Piracy Epic—the Film Industry Tries to Repel the Threat from the Internet Raiders," *Financial Times*, Sept. 12, 2003, p. 23; Simon Byers, Lorrie Cranor, Eric Cronin, Dave Kormann, and Patrick McDaniel, "Analysis of Security Vulnerabilities in the Movie Production and Distribution Process," *Telecommunications Policy* 28 (August–September 2004): 619–644 (a selection of papers from the Thirty-first Annual TPRC Conference on Communication, Information, and Internet Policy, Arlington, Va., Sept. 19–21, 2003); Mike Godwin, *What Every Citizen Should Know about DRM, aka "Digital Rights Management"* (Washington, D.C.: Public Knowledge; New American Foundation, 2004); and papers presented at the CITI conference "Peer-to-Peer Video as a Mass Medium: Business, Technology, Community, and Law," Columbia University, New York,

Sept. 10, 2004, especially Viktor Mayer-Schonberger, "Crouching Tiger, Hidden Dragon: Proxy Battles over P2P Movie Sharing," (Kennedy School of Government, Harvard University) and Michael A. Einhorn and Bill Rosenblatt, "Peer-to-Peer Networking and Digital Rights Management: How Market Tools Can Solve Copyright Problems," Policy Analysis no. 534, Feb. 17, 2005 (Washington, D.C.: Cato Institute).

9. OECD, *Information Technology Outlook 2004: Information and Communication Technologies* (Paris: Organisation for Economic Co-operation and Development, 2004).

10. Encryption (scrambling) of DVD content allows the copyright owner to control what hardware the software can be played on, by means of the decryption keys that those machines are equipped with. The hacker who broke the CSS code, Shawn Fanning, was prosecuted by the MPAA for posting the decryption code (DeCSS, or Decrypted Content Scrambling System) on the Internet. A practical effect of Fanning's actions is that DVD content can be put "in the clear" for compression and Internet transmission. Godwin, *What Every Citizen Should Know,* argues that the practical effects of DeCSS on the industry have been minor.

11. For discussion of recent legal and political studio activities, see Lorraine Woellert, "Why the Grokster Case Matters: the High Court Faces a Hard Choice between Innovation and Copyright Protection," *Business Week,* Dec. 27, 2004, p. 50; Laura M. Holson, "Studios Moving to Block Piracy of Films Online," *NYT,* Sept. 25, 2003, p. 1; Geoffrey A. Fowler, "Hollywood's Burning Issue," *WSJ,* Sept. 18, 2003, p. B1; and "Digital Rights Issue Alive, Despite Leahy," *Television Digest,* Mar. 18, 2002.

12. Gary Gentile, "Studios to Educate Consumers on the Harm of Movie Piracy," *Associated Press Newswires,* July 22, 2003.

13. Michael McCarty, "Hollywood Hunts for Pirates: Movie Industry Gets Creative to End Illegal Downloading," *USA Today,* July 31, 2003, p. B3; Marc Graser, "New Gizmos May Outsmart the Pirates," *Variety,* Oct. 6, 2003, p. 106.

14. Kim Peterson, "RealNetworks, Starz Join to Offer Movie Downloads," *Seattle Times Technology Reporter,* June 14, 2004, p. C1.

15. One empirical study (Byers et al., "Analysis of Security Vulnerabilities") found that a majority of feature films obtained through file sharing were "DVD quality." For discussion of video compression formats, see Marc Saltzman, "Future of Movie Downloading Needs a Good Squeeze: Compression Is Key to Success," *USA Today,* Nov. 17, 2003, p. E14; and Ben Waggoner, "Codecs for Shiny Discs—What's the Best Codec Choice

When You Need to Deliver Video on a CD and DVD Shiny Disc?" *Digital Video Magazine,* Jan. 1, 2005, p. 56.

16. Wilson Rothman, "For DVD's, a New Definition," *NYT,* Dec. 2, 2004, p. E1.

17. In the real market, studio competition would presumably bid down prices so that consumers net part of the cost savings, but studios would benefit to some extent. In music, the legitimate Internet market for individual song files could probably not even exist without the extremely low download costs.

18. "I Want My P2P," *The Economist,* Nov. 20, 2004, p. 65. IBM beta-tested a similar system in the mid-1990s. Its Cryptolopes software involved the collection of secondary payments via a centralized "license clearinghouse." The project was dropped in 1997. Tim Clark, "IBM Closes Cryptolopes Unit," Cnet News.com, Dec. 17, 1997, *www.news.com* (accessed Oct. 10, 2004).

19. Alessandro Acquisti, "DRM, Darknets, and Economic Incentives for Platform Providers" (paper presented at the Thirty-Second Annual TPRC Conference on Communication, Information, and Internet Policy, Arlington, Va., Oct 1–3, 2004).

20. Lawrence Lessig, *Free Culture: How Big Media Uses Technology and the Law to Lock Down Culture and Control Creativity* (New York: Penguin Press, 2004).

21. Neil Weinstock Netanel, "Impose a Noncommercial Use Levy to Allow Free Peer-to-Peer File Sharing," *Harvard Journal of Law and Technology* 17 (Fall 2003): 1–84; see also Willam Fisher, *Promises to Keep: Technology, Law, and the Future of Entertainment* (Stanford, Calif.: Stanford University Press, 2004).

22. Barry Layne, "PPV Detour for Marley Biopic," *Hollywood Reporter,* June 25, 1992, pp. 1, 6.

23. Catherine Hinman, "Films May Premiere on Pay TV in Future," *Orlando Sentinel,* May 11, 1993, p. E1.

24. Gentile, "Self-Destructing DVDs About to Reach a Wider Audience."

25. Roger Ebert, "Sites, Camera, Action," *Yahoo! Internet Life,* Apr. 2002, pp. 99–100, 159.

26. "Studios Reject PPV before Theatrical Plans," *Screen Digest,* July 1, 1993.

27. Marc Graser, "H'wood's Direct Hits," *Variety,* Sept. 13, 2004, pp. 1, 60.

28. John Dempsey, "Theatricals Rate Second Look," *Variety,* Sept. 20, 1999, pp. 1–3.

29. Joan Villa, "Suppliers Look to Box Office to Add Luster to Cable Movies," *Video Business,* Apr. 14, 1997, pp. 4, 8.

30. Scott Moore, "Disney Wishes upon a Proven Star: Robin Williams Encore Goes Direct to Video," *Washington Post,* Aug. 11, 1996, p. Y7; "Genies of the Small Screen," *The Guardian,* Jan. 2, 1998.

31. Marc Graser, "H'wood's Direct Hits."

32. John Tagliabue, "Film Redux in Europe: Action!" *NYT,* Feb. 24, 1996, p. 17. Adam Dawtrey, "H'wood Battles Local Heroes," *Variety,* July 15, 2002, p. 1. Mary Sutter, "H'wood Buries Overseas Pix," *Variety,* Jan. 25, 1999, p. 1. Adam Dawtrey, Alison James, Liza Foreman, Ed Meza, David Rooney, and John Hopewell, "Yanks Rank but Locals Tank," *Variety,* Dec. 18, 1999, p. 1.

33. Michael E. Porter, *The Competitive Advantage of Nations* (New York: Free Press, 1990) lists a number of general factors that tend to sustain trade dominance of particular countries over time. Specific analyses of the industry's agglomeration into the geographic area of southern California are in Asu Aksoy and Kevin Robins, "Hollywood for the Twenty-First Century: Global Competition for Critical Mass in Image Markets," *Cambridge Journal of Economics* 16 (1992): 1–22; Michael Storper and Susan Christopherson, "Flexible Specialization and Regional Industrial Agglomerations," *Annals of the Association of American Geographers* 77 (March 1987): 104–117; Michael Stroper, "The Transition to Flexible Specialization in the U.S. Film Industry: External Economies, the Division of Labour, and the Crossing of Industrial Divides," *Cambridge Journal of Economics* 13 (June 1989): 273–305; Allen J. Scott, "A New Map of Hollywood: The Production and Distribution of American Motion Pictures," *Regional Studies* 36 (December 2002): 957–975; and Keith Acheson and Christopher J. Maule, "Understanding Hollywood's Organization and Continuing Success," *Journal of Cultural Economics* 18 (1994): 271–300.

34. Alan Riding, "French Fume at One Another over U.S. Films' Popularity," *NYT,* Dec. 14, 1999, p. B1.

35. Josh Chetwynd, "Hollywood Experiments Online with 'Quantum' Leap to Features," *USA Today,* May 4, 2000, p. 1D.

36. For example, *www.bmwfilms.com* and *www.skyy.com* (accessed Dec. 5, 2003).

37. "AtomFilms" (Harvard Business School, case no. 9-701-063, 2001).

38. Peter Broderick, "Moviemaking in Transition," *Scientific American,* November 2000, pp. 61–69.

39. "HD Interviews: Interview with Brian LaBelle," *www.panasonic.com* (accessed Sept. 22, 2004).

40. Rick Lyman, "Movie Stars Fear Inroads by Upstart Digital Actors," *NYT,* July 8, 2001, p. 1.

41. Transcript, *Nightline,* "Movie Magic: You Can't Believe Your Eyes," July 19, 2001, ABC News.

42. Nielsen EDI Summary Database.

Index